BARRON'S

SAT* 2400

Aiming for the Perfect Score

4th Edition

Linda Carnevale, M.A.
Former English Teacher
Cold Spring Harbor High School
Cold Spring Harbor, New York

Roselyn Teukolsky, M.S.
Former Math Teacher
Ithaca High School
Ithaca, New York

BARRON'S

Authors' Credentials and Qualifications

Linda Carnevale holds a Masters of Arts from Columbia University's Teachers College. Before leaving full-time teaching to raise her three sons, Ms. Carnevale was a tenured teacher of English at Cold Spring Harbor Schools in Cold Spring Harbor, Long Island, New York. She is the author of Barron's *Hot Words for the SAT* and Barron's *ACT English, Reading, and Writing Workbook* and has published in a variety of local and national publications, including *Long Island Parents & Children, Long Island Quarterly, Modern Bride,* and Conde Nast's *BRIDE'S* magazines. Her poems were selected for publication in the 2009 and 2012 anthologies of poems about Long Island titled *Paumanok: Poems and Pictures of Long Island.* Ms. Carnevale, a sought-after SAT and ACT verbal coach, has repeatedly scored a perfect 800 on the SAT verbal section. Presently, she is a professional development trainer specializing in English language arts, critical reading, and literacy. Ms. Carnevale conducts workshops through the CIT (Curriculum, Instruction, & Technology) and the SETRC (Special Education & Training Resource Centers) of Nassau BOCES, which serves 57 public school districts throughout Nassau County, New York.

Roselyn Teukolsky has an M.S. degree from Cornell University and is a math teacher at Ithaca High School in Ithaca, New York. She has published articles in *The Mathematics Teacher* and in the National Council of Teachers of Mathematics Yearbook, and is the author of Barron's *AP Computer Science Exam* review book and Barron's *ACT Math and Science Workbook.* She has received the Edyth May Sliffe Award for Distinguished Mathematics Teaching and the Alfred Kalfus Distinguished Coach Award from the New York State Math League (NYSML). Mrs. Teukolsky has been teaching, and helping students with their SAT preparation, for 34 years.

All inquiries should be addressed to:
Barron's Educational Series, Inc.
250 Wireless Boulevard
Hauppauge, New York 11788
www.barronseduc.com

ISSN (Print only): 2166-6547
ISSN (Print with CD-ROM): 2166-6555

ISBN (Book only): 978-1-4380-0020-6
ISBN (Book with CD-ROM): 1-4380-7189-3

PRINTED IN THE UNITED STATES OF AMERICA
9 8 7 6 5

10%
POST-CONSUMER
WASTE
Paper contains a minimum
of 10% post-consumer
waste (PCW). Paper used
in this book was derived
from certified, sustainable
forestlands.

CONTENTS

Welcome to the 2400 Club   **1**

Who Is This Book For?   1

What Sets This Book Apart from the Rest?   1

What Exactly Is on the SAT?   2

2400 Club Icons   3

Get in the Game   3

    2400 Club Test-Day Checklist   3

PART 1: THE CRITICAL READING SECTIONS   **5**

Chapter 1: Sentence-Level Reading   **7**

2400 Club Strategies: 7

Bring Your Word to the Blank   8

Locate a Context Clue   9

Assign a Positive (+) or Negative (–) Value to the Blank   9

Never Do's!   11

Keep Level-Headed   12

Say the Sentence to Yourself to Ensure That It Makes Sense   16

High Scorer's Strategy Acronym   16

Practice Test Questions   17

    Answers and Explanations   19

Chapter 2: Paragraph-Level Reading   **23**

2400 Club Strategies (the 4Ps of Paragraph Reading):   23

Paraphrase as You Read   23

Predict the Answer   24

Pare Down the Answer Choices   24

Pick the Best Answer   24

Practice Test Questions on Paragraphs   24

    Answers and Explanations   26

Practice Test Questions on Paired Paragraphs   29

    Answers and Explanations   30

Chapter 3: Long-Passage Reading   **33**

2400 Club Global Strategies: 33

Hunting and Gathering   33

Passage Evidence   33

Listening   34

Critical Reading Secret Formula   34

    Read   35

React, Using ABS 35

Interact 36

Visualize 36

2400 Club Strategies: 37

Read Longer Passages Piece by Piece 37

Divide and Conquer 41

Sip, Don't Slurp 42

Skim, Don't Skip 42

Be Savvy About Sidebars 42

The Italicized Blurb—Know the Author/Know the Topic 42

Outline Reading Approach 43

Extract the Main Idea from the Passage 46

Answer Line-Reference and Sidebar Questions First 47

Words-in-Context Questions 48

Delve into Higher-Order Thinking Questions 50

Skipping Hard Questions Responsibly 51

Identify the Author's Mood and Tone as You Read 51

The Vocabulary of Tone 52

The Vocabulary of Mood 52

Narrow In on the *Best* Answer Choice 52

Reading Technique: The Rule of Thirds 54

Global Questions Should Be Answered at the Very End 56

Remember Those Globals!! 57

Paired-Passage and Global Questions 58

Additional Strategies for Reading Long Passages 58

To Read or Not to Read the Questions First—
That Is the Perennial Decision 58

Read and Heed Key Words in the Question and
Answer Choices 59

No Line References, So Not a Global Question! What Now? 60

Critical Reading No-No's 60

Debunking the Myth: Vocabulary Just Doesn't Matter That Much
Anymore to Rank on the SAT 61

High Scorer's Strategy Acronym 62

Practice Test Questions 63

Answers and Explanations 68

Very Hard Long Passages 72

Practice Test Questions 72

Answers and Explanations 74

Practice Test Questions/Paired Long Passages 76

Answers and Explanations 82

Chapter 4: 2400 Club Grand Mixture **87**

Practice Test Questions 87

Answers and Explanations 98

PART 2: THE WRITING SECTIONS   107

Chapter 5: Writing the 25-Minute Essay   109
2400 Club Comprehensive Strategies: 109
Take a Side   109
Have a Timing Plan   110
Engage Your Reader   114
Edit, Using the 2400 Club Checklist   115
Support Your Thesis with Examples   116
Sentence and Vocabulary Variety   117
Assess What You Have Written   118
Your Voice   119
More 2400 Club Strategies: 119
Eliminate SMOG   119
High Scorer's Strategy Acronym   123
Practice Assignments   124
Essay Scoring Guide   125
Sample Essays: 11–12 Range, 10–11 Range, and 8–9 Range   127

Chapter 6: English Grammar and Usage   133
Timing Practice When You're Crushed for Time   133
New Writing Strategy! Grammar Counting: 1, 2, 3   134
2400 Club Grammar-Savvy TIPS: 136
Take Care to Read the Original Versions of Sentences or
    Paragraphs Very Carefully   136
Identify, First, All Verbs and Pronouns That Are Underlined 136
Pay Close Attention to the Nonunderlined Portions of
    Sentences and Paragraphs   137
Select "No Error" Approximately 15–20 Percent of the Time 137
Hierarchy of Grammar Glitches   138
    Verb Errors   138
    Pronoun Errors   141
    Faulty Idioms   143
    Lack of Parallelism   146
    Diction Errors   147
    Misplaced Modifiers   149
    Adjective Versus Adverb Errors   150
    Plural–Singular Inconsistency   151
    Redundancy and Wordiness (Relatives of Flabby Phrasing) 151
    Faulty Comparisons   152
    Run-ons (Comma Splices) and Fragments 155

Chapter 7: Improving Sentences   159
2400 Club Strategies: The 4Cs of Improving Sentences   159
Correctness   160
Clarity   160
Conciseness   160
Colloquialisms   161
    Be Alert to Introductory Phrases   161

Be a Grammar Guru—Know Your Mantras   162
Follow Through   162
Practice Test Questions   162
Answers and Explanations   167

Chapter 8: Identifying Sentence Errors   169

The Overpreparation Method: Find the Error, Name the Error,
Fix the Error   169
Warm-Up Exercises   170
Answers and Explanations   172
Practice Test Questions   173
Answers and Explanations   177

Chapter 9: Improving Paragraphs   181

You Become the Editor   181
Peer Editing   181
Your Job in a Nutshell   182
2400 Club Strategy: Read, Read, Reread   182
Practice Test Questions   183
Answers and Explanations   185

Chapter 10: 2400 Club Grand Mixture   187

Practice Test Questions   187
Answers and Explanations   194

PART 3: THE MATH SECTIONS   199

Chapter 11: Getting Started   201

Math on the SAT   201
Easy Versus Hard Questions   201
Grid-Ins   206
What Are They?   206
What the Answers Cannot Be   207
Gridding-in Rules   207
Question Difficulty   207
Scoring   207
Final Tip   208
Tips for the SAT Math Sections   210
Question Difficulty   210
Guessing   210
The Test Booklet   211
Your Answer Sheet   211
Calculators   211
How to Use the Graphing Calculator   212
Some Final Tips   213

Chapter 12: Strategies for Solving SAT Math Problems   215

Pick a Number   215
Plug-In   219

The Graphing Calculator 223
   Identifying a Graph 223
   Intersection of Two Graphs 224
   Transformations 225
   Inequalities 226
Some Additional Tips 227
   Geometry 227
   Simultaneous Equations 228
   Shaded Areas 229
   Sets 230

Chapter 13: Topics in Arithmetic   231
Sets 231
   Sets of Numbers 231
   Consecutive Integers 231
   Factors and Multiples 232
   Prime Numbers 232
   Rational Numbers 232
   Sets and Elements 232
   Union and Intersection 233
   Squares and Square Roots 233
   Ratio, Proportion, Percents 234
   Percent Increase and Decrease 235
Counting and Probability 236
   Counting 236
   Permutations and Combinations 236
   Probability 237
     Events 237
     Probability of an Event 237
     Mutually Exclusive Events 238
     Independent Events 238
Sequences and Series 242
   Arithmetic and Geometric Sequences and Series 242
   Sequences Involving Exponential Growth 242
Practice Test Questions 244
   Answers and Explanations 246

Chapter 14: Topics in Algebra   251
Exponents 251
   Scientific Notation 252
   Monomials 253
Polynomials 253
   Factoring 253
Rational Expressions 254
Absolute Value 254
Direct and Indirect Variation 254
   Rate Problems 254

Solving Equations and Inequalities 256
   Linear Equations and Inequalities 256
   Quadratic Equations and Inequalities 256
   Equations with Radicals 257
   Equations with x^2 257
   Exponential Equations 257
   Equations with Rational Expressions 257
   Inequalities with Rational Expressions 257
   Equations and Inequalities with Absolute Value 257
Systems of Linear Equations and Inequalities 260
Functions 262
   Definition 262
   Function Notation 263
   Domain and Range 264
   The Linear Function 265
   The Quadratic Function 267
   Transformations 271
   Functions as Models 275
   Unfamiliar Definitions of Functions 276
Practice Test Questions 277
   Answers and Explanations 281

Chapter 15: Topics in Geometry **289**
Points, Lines, Angles 289
   Parallel Lines 290
Triangles 292
   Types of Triangles 292
   Some Triangle Facts 293
   Special Right Triangles 293
   Trigonometric Ratios 293
   Similar Triangles 294
Quadrilaterals and Polygons 296
   Quadrilaterals 296
   Angles in a Quadrilateral 296
   Polygons 297
Areas and Perimeters 298
   Area 298
   Perimeter 299
Circles 300
   Circumference and Area 300
   Arc and Sector 300
   Tangents 301
   Inscribed Circles and Polygons 301
Solid Geometry 302
   Prisms and Cylinders 302
   Cones and Pyramids 303

Coordinate Geometry 305

    Distance 305

    Slope 306

    Geometric Transformations 306

    Symmetry 307

Geometric Probability 309

Practice Test Questions 310

    Answers and Explanations 313

Chapter 16: Topics in Statistics   **321**

Averages 321

    Arithmetic Mean 321

    Median 321

    Mode 322

    Weighted Average 322

Data Interpretation 323

    Tables (Matrices) 323

Graphs 323

    Circle Graphs 323

    Line Graphs 324

    Bar Graphs 325

    Pictographs 325

    Scatterplots 326

        Line of Best Fit 327

    Tips for Solving Problems That Involve Statistical Graphs ... 328

Practice Test Questions 328

    Answers and Explanations 332

Chapter 17: Word Problems   **335**

Why the Fuss? 335

How to Approach a Word Problem 335

    Problem Types 336

    Translating English into Math 337

    Some Additional Tips 337

Practice Test Questions 341

    Answers and Explanations 344

Chapter 18: 2400 Club Grand Mixture   **349**

Practice Test Questions 350

    Answers and Explanations 360

Appendix: Upper-Level Vocabulary Building   **373**

2400 Club Vocabulary Immersion 373

Four-Letter-Word List for Club Members 374

Upper-Level Word Lists for Club Members 375

Exercise: Choose the Correct Synonym 379

Useful Math Formulas   **384**

ACKNOWLEDGMENTS

We owe thanks to many people who helped in the creation of this book.

We are grateful to our editor, Linda Turner, for her unflagging patience and advice. We would also like to thank Wayne Barr for his guidance and the production staff at Barron's for their work in making the book happen. Special thanks to our production manager, Debby Becak, and exceptional copyeditors, Ruth Flohn and Nina Hnatov. Thanks also to the evaluators of the manuscript, who came up with some excellent suggestions for improvement.

We had some invaluable help from our students. Garrett Tate and Ali Mehravari painstakingly combed through the math section of the book looking for errors. They were unstinting in offering advice and suggestions. A special thank-you to Andrea B. Goetz, Dana Jean, Brian Tashman, and Jean Benz, skillful writers who generously took the time to write under deadline pressure and who allowed their exemplary essays to be featured in this book. We extend much appreciation to all of our students who helped us to understand the intricacies and challenges of this test from their points of view.

Thank you to Andrea Kochie at Ithaca High School for sharing the latest SAT materials. Thank you to Steven Levy for his enthusiastic contribution to the vocabulary exercise that debuted in the second edition. Warm regards to our former colleagues at Cold Spring Harbor High School and Ithaca High School.

This book could not have happened without the understanding and support of family members and the kind words of encouragement from friends. With much appreciation to Laura Halperin, whose support and guidance from the inception of this project have been invaluable. And a special thank-you to Brenda Cooper for her daily messages of encouragement. Much gratitude to our husbands, who were devoted partners in this project from the beginning, Sandro Carnevale and Saul Teukolsky. Hugs to our children, Phillip, Andrew, and Luca Carnevale, and Rachel and Lauren Teukolsky. We dedicate this book to them.

Linda Carnevale
Old Brookville, NY
Roselyn Teukolsky
Ithaca, NY
August 2012

WELCOME TO THE 2400 CLUB

If the words SAT 2400 CLUB are calling your name, then you are a top student, a strong reader, and a motivated, serious test taker. You are ready for the big leagues, and you don't have time for piddling advice such as "Focus on what you're reading," "Use your calculator for long division," or "Clear your mind before you start the grammar section." You want select, inspired strategies that can make a difference to your score.

As you work through this book, focus on the strategies given for each question type. We want you to have it all: the basics *and* beyond. We leave no stone unturned as we share with you a multitude of tips and techniques that have enabled us to achieve perfect scores in our respective areas of expertise. You *can* realize your personal best score!

The math and verbal coaching in this book is thorough, multifaceted, and effective. Wherever possible, we offer alternative approaches to answering questions. We let you in on the do's and don'ts of smart test taking. If you score 700 or above on each of the three sections of the new SAT, you will enter the ranks of the top 5 percent of students, the 2400 Club.

WHO IS THIS BOOK FOR?

This book is for *you* since you aspire to achieve a perfect score on the SAT. With consistent use of this book as part of your plan of study, you could achieve more than you think you're capable of! Week after week, read through the strategies and work hard on the practice exercises. Visualize yourself approaching the ranks of the top 5 percent of test takers. We have every confidence in you. You can do it!

WHAT SETS THIS BOOK APART FROM THE REST?

The majority of test takers can get the easier questions right—the level 1 and 2 questions. A good many can do well also on the level 3's, which are of medium difficulty. However, to achieve a score that stands out to the Ivy Leagues and the scholarship committees, you have to crack a good number of the harder, level 4 and 5, questions. Analysis of the math part of the SAT shows that, on average, 25 percent of all questions are ranked as hard—the level 4 and level 5 questions. More interestingly, a test taker who gets every level 1, 2, and 3 question correct, but misses every level 4 and 5, can max out only at a 650 score. For where you want to go and for what you want to achieve, a 650 split may not cut it.

Think of this book as a push to the finish line. Let's strive to get you as close to an 800 as possible on each of the three sections. For the verbal parts, original strategy acronyms help you to answer questions on the critical reading section and to write a high-scoring essay. For the tricky math questions, some "nonclassroom" strategies show you how to achieve surprisingly fast and successful results. With practice you will start to recognize which strategies apply to particular questions.

WHAT EXACTLY IS ON THE SAT?

There are three sections on the SAT: Critical Reading, Mathematics, and Writing. Each is scored on a scale of 200–800, meaning that the maximum possible total score is 2400.

The test lasts for 3 hours and 25 minutes. Here is what you can expect:

Mathematics Section—worth 800 points

- 70 minutes of math: two 25-minute sections and one 20-minute section
- Multiple-choice questions where you select the answer from five choices
- Grid-in questions where you provide the answer in a small grid

Critical Reading Section—worth 800 points

- Sentence completions (critical reading at the sentence level)
- Paragraph-length critical reading
- Paired-paragraph critical reading
- Long-passage critical reading
- Paired-long-passage critical reading

Writing Section—worth 800 points

- Contents very similar to that of the (now obsolete) SAT II Writing Test
- A 25-minute essay
- 49 multiple-choice questions on standard English grammar and usage that include identifying sentence errors, improving sentences, and improving paragraphs

You should know that one of the 25-minute multiple-choice sections will not count toward your score. This could be a math, reading, or writing section. The Educational Testing Service uses this "experimental section" to calibrate new questions for future tests. Since you won't know which section is experimental, you will need to give every section your all.

2400 CLUB ICONS

As you work through this book, you will spot several icons, each of which provides you with a helpful test-taking tip.

Active Pencil

Whenever you see the **Active Pencil** icon, expect a recommendation showing you how to use your sharpened pencil as a test-taking tool. Smart test takers stay on top of their tasks by writing as they think. This gives them an edge and helps them to keep focused.

Time Saver

Look for the **Time Saver** icon to get tips on how to enhance your test-taking speed, without losing accuracy. High scorers know that time is of the essence on the SAT.

Calculator

Look for the **Calculator** icon for alternative solutions to some of the math problems. Judicious use of your calculator can save you time and effort on several questions.

> The 2400 Club knows all the tricks and applies them accordingly.

GET IN THE GAME

Acing the SAT has much to do with getting in the game. Think of it this way: When a goal-keeper shows up at a 5-hour soccer tournament, she is equipped and ready, with a mind-set toward winning. She has with her cleats, shin guards, goalie gloves, padded goalie shorts, and a goalkeeper's jersey. She is also equipped with at least two water bottles, a sports drink, and energy-sustaining snacks. She is ready for the task.

When you show up on the SAT test day, will you be geared up and ready? The night before, pack each of the following items in a small tote bag, and bring them to the test. Use this checklist to make sure you're good to go:

2400 Club Test-Day Checklist

- ❏ Your admission ticket
- ❏ Proper ID, such as a driver's license or student ID card
- ❏ At least two sharpened #2 pencils
- ❏ A hand-held pencil sharpener, in case the one available to you is defunct

❏ A graphing calculator (preferable) or scientific calculator
❏ An extra set of fresh batteries; we've heard too many sad stories about batteries that go dead
❏ A water bottle
❏ A couple of energy-sustaining snacks
❏ A small package of tissues
❏ Cough drops, in case you start to cough or your throat becomes dry

Make sure that you're bright-eyed and alert on the day of the test. Get a good night's sleep, and save the late-night partying for another weekend.

The 2400 Club is always prepared and leaves nothing to chance.

PART 1

THE CRITICAL READING SECTIONS

SENTENCE-LEVEL READING

PARAGRAPH-LEVEL READING

Paired Paragraphs

LONG-PASSAGE READING

Paired Long Passages

Chapter 1

SENTENCE-LEVEL READING

Okay, obviously the College Board is really into critical reading since it devotes an entire 800-point section to this skill on the SAT. Here's an overview of the format of the critical reading section, which is worth 800 points:

Critical Reading (multiple-choice)

Sentence completions	19 questions
Passage-based reading	48 questions
Total	67 questions
Time allotted	70 minutes (two 25-minute sections; one 20-minute section)

Breathe easily; as you can see, this section does not consist of long, paired-passage readings alone. Did you know that this section contains sentence completions (good old fill-in-the-blanks)? The College Board thinks of sentence completions as "reading at the sentence level." *Drum roll, please: . . .* introducing paragraph reading and paired paragraphs, relatively new additions that debuted on the SAT in March 2005. Thank goodness, though, the critical reading section does not deal entirely with ultralong and unspeakably obscure paired-passage readings!

When you work on sentence completions, no guesswork is allowed when it comes to filling in the blanks. Sure—more often than not, more than one answer choice may seem to work. Still, as a 2400 Club member, your task is to read the sentence, absorb its overall sense, and fill in the blank with the answer choice *that fits best*. The six step-by-step strategies that follow coach you through a process that is methodical and comprehensive so that you can correctly answer even the hardest sentence completions.

2400 Club Strategies

Strategy 1: **B**ring your word to the blank.

Strategy 2: **L**ocate a context clue.

Strategy 3: **A**ssign a positive or negative value to the blank.

Strategy 4: **N**ever do's!

Strategy 5: **K**eep level-headed.

Strategy 6: **S**ay the sentence to yourself to ensure that it makes sense.

STRATEGY 1: BRING YOUR WORD TO THE BLANK

Let your own word roll off your tongue as you carefully read through the entire sentence. When you practice at home, read each sentence aloud to absorb its sense. Go with your hunch and supply your own word for every blank. Your own word can be basic: *good, bad, more, less, generous, cheap, big, small.* The important thing is that you make an educated guess or a *prediction* for the blank.

*Read through the sentence, and **predict** a word that you think would fit in the blank.*

To avoid getting sidetracked by "decoys" or "false positives" (traps in the answer choices), it is imperative that you bring your own word to the blank *before* you look at the answer choices. Sometimes the answer choices may confuse you, distracting you from your initial *feel* for the blank. Once you've brought your own word to the blank, look for the answer choice that most closely matches your word.

As you read the sentence, instead of simply saying "blank" for the empty line, say one of the following:

"blanked"   "blanking"   "blanks"   "blankly"

How do you know which version of "blank" to say? Simply scan the answer choices to see the *endings* of the words. If the answer choices end in *-ly*, then say "blankly"; *-ing*, say "blanking." Saying "blanking" or "blanked," for example, can help you to get a clearer understanding of the sentence's overall sense. Try this novel technique and see whether it makes a difference for you. Though simple and straightforward, this strategy can be very effective.

Examples

1. Nina has never been one who likes <u>"blanking"</u> when it comes to long-term projects, for she prefers to work alone and at her own pace.

    (A) procrastina*ting* (B) collud*ing* (C) collabora*ting* (D) speculat*ing* (E) diversify*ing*

2. Once the play date kicked off, the bedlam stirred up by the Tanner twins and the Garvey triplets could not be <u>"blanked"</u>, despite the mothers' soothing voices and earnest pleading.

    (A) quell*ed* (B) persuad*ed* (C) incit*ed* (D) expurgat*ed*
    (E) exasperat*ed*

When working on sentence completions, cross off answers that you know don't work. Some test takers simply cross off the letter of the answer choice; others take a more decisive stance and cross off the *entire* answer choice. The latter approach eliminates verbal clutter.

*Don't underestimate the process of elimination techniques (herein, called **PET**); PET is a powerful strategy that moves you closer to the right answer and simplifies your task. Crossing off bogus or weak answer choices prevents you from being distracted by unlikely answers and keeps you focused on finding the best choice.*

Sentence Completion Answers

1. **C**: although *procrastinating* works, *collaborating* works best.

2. **A**: *quelled* means soothed or calmed.

STRATEGY 2: LOCATE A CONTEXT CLUE

When you work on hard sentence completions, filling in the blanks has nothing to do with guessing or with what *sounds* right! You must have a method to find the best answer choice. If you have no *clue* as to what type of word the blank requires, then get a clue! A context clue! Search for context clues within the sentence to help you understand what is needed in the blank. Within almost every sentence, there is a context clue (or clues). The test designers shudder at the possibility of two answer choices that work equally well. That scenario would present them with a serious debacle. Can you imagine the deluge of E-mail from disgruntled test takers who want to argue for *their* answers?

2400 Club test takers distinguish between an answer choice that is a sort-of fit and an answer that is the *perfect* fit. The perfect fit is the answer choice that is supported by one or more context clues. Let's hypothetically take some sentence completions. If the context clue is "sparing of words," the likely answer is *taciturn*. If the clue is "always sitting around," the likely answer is *sedentary*. If the clue is "very, very tiny," the feasible answer is *infinitesimal*. If the clue is "very conscientious about manners and behavior," the supported answer is *punctilious*. Likewise, if the clue is "a magical object," the likely answer is *talisman*. Context clues leave no room for guesswork or ambiguity. In fact, sometimes they appear more like straightforward definitions, as in the examples just given. Don't be clueless when it comes to sentence completions—get a clue, a context clue!

The context clue is underlined in the following sentence:

Despite his <u>stubborn demeanor and insistence on training *his* way</u>, Hector is not the most _____ soccer coach the young athletes have known.

(A) strenuous (B) philistine (C) befuddled (D) obdurate (E) effusive

The context clue supports *obdurate*, which means stubborn.

 Underline key words and phrases within the sentences. These key parts are context clues that indicate to you what the blank requires.

STRATEGY 3: ASSIGN A POSITIVE (+) OR NEGATIVE (–) VALUE TO THE BLANK

Is there a word on the tip of your tongue that just won't make its way out?

Do you kind of know what "blanked" or "blanking" means, but you just can't put the meaning into words?

Is "Bringing your word to the blank" hard to do? When working on a sentence-completion question, sometimes it's difficult to come up with your own word that fits the blank. At the same time, are you having a hard time locating a context clue within the sentence?

Word values move you closer to the right answer.

If you feel tongue-tied when it comes to expressing your own word for the blank or if you can't seem to find a context clue, then simply jot down a positive (+) or negative (−) sign in the blank to indicate *your feel* for the needed word. Even if it's hard for you to come up with a denotation (dictionary definition or literal meaning), you can very often come up with the blank's connotation—its *feel or undertone*.

Context clues are actually the parts of the sentence that subtly tune you into the value, either positive or negative, of the blank. If putting your finger on the context clue isn't easy, then trust your gut sense (visceral feel) for the blank's positive or negative value.

Sharpening Skills—Word Values

Read each sentence carefully, keeping your ears and eyes peeled for context clues. Then circle Positive word, Negative word, or Unknown value to indicate your "word value" for the blank.

1. **Regretfully, team captain Marc started to _____ the young players as soon as basketball practice ended.**

    Positive word   Negative word   Unknown value

Additional strategy, using Active Pencil: With your pencil, jot a positive (+) or negative (−) sign next to each answer choice as shown below. If the word value is unknown, leave the word as is.

    (A) laugh +   (B) study +   (C) race   (D) belittle −   (E) praise +

2. **To the author's delight, the controversial book received praise and _____ from most major critics.**

    Positive word   Negative word   Unknown value

3. **Regardless of his _____ nature, Pedro decided not to extend a helping hand to his avaricious neighbors this time.**

    Positive word   Negative word   Unknown value

4. **Though gossip has painted an unpleasant and downright _____ picture of the new member of the community, I have learned first hand that Ms. Appleton is actually forthright and well mannered,**

    Positive word   Negative word   Unknown value

5. **Contrary to his pleasant and convivial nature, Jack decided not to attend several holiday parties; he was becoming uncharacteristically _____ and _____.**

    Positive word   Negative word   Unknown value

Coaching:
You can usually figure out whether a blank is + or − by paying attention to the nuances and undertones in the sentence. For instance, did you notice "To the author's delight"? This phrase certainly puts the sentence into the positive realm.

Word Values—Answers

1. This sentence lacks a context clue that keys us into the precise meaning of the blank. However, you can assign a negative (–) value to the blank, since the sentence begins with a negative term, *regretfully*.

2. The blank is linked to *praise* with the conjunction *and*; this tells us that the needed word is on a par with or similar to *praise*. Therefore, you would assign a + to the blank.

3. A subtle but key context clue is the word *not*. Downsize this sentence to something like: *Regardless of* his "helpful" nature, Pedro chose NOT to help . . . . Considering this simplified form of the sentence, you see that the blank requires a positive word, such as *obliging* or *accommodating*.

4. The context clues are *unpleasant and downright*. Since the blank is linked to *unpleasant* with the conjunction *and*, these adjectives must be similar. Also, the word *actually* in the second clause of the sentence shows that Ms. Appleton's being *forthright and well mannered* is the opposite of the picture painted by the gossip. The blank gets a negative value.

5. The context clues are *Contrary to his pleasant and convivial nature . . .* and *uncharacteristically*, so you need two negative values for the blanks. Likely answer choices would be *sullen* and *reclusive*.

Penciling a positive (+) or negative (–) sign in the blank is a good way to narrow down the answer choices. If you know you need a positive term, then you can use PET (Process of Elimination Technique) to eliminate all of the negative terms in the answer choices. By doing this, you will be getting closer to the right answer.

STRATEGY 4: NEVER DO'S!

You shouldn't eat at a potluck dinner unless you first bring something to the table. Likewise, never sniff around the answer choices until you *first* bring something to the blank. For hard sentence completions, a cursory reading of the sentence followed by a look at the answer choices won't cut it. In fact, that's the formula for falling into answer-choice *traps* and picking wrong answers that are just *decoys* or *false-positives*.

2400 Club Coaching: *High scorers bring something of their own to the blank first, before pondering the answer choices.*

Answering hard sentence completions takes active participation. 2400 Club test takers are mentally prepared to fill in the blanks on sentence completions. Don't come empty-headed or empty-handed. Remember this: *You need to bring something to dinner.*

What can you bring to the blank? It's worthwhile to review Sentence Completion Strategies 1–3 in their simplified form:

Strategy 1: Your word
Strategy 2: Context clue
Strategy 3: Positive (+) or negative (–)

Depending on how hard the sentence completion is, and also on what's going on in your head, you can bring to the blank one of these strategies, or a medley of them, like a tossed salad. You can bring them mentally or jot them down as follows:

Mentally! Keep info in your head.	Jot down the info.
Strategy 1: Your word	Write your word in the blank.
Strategy 2: Context clue	Underline the context clue.
Strategy 3: Positive (+) or negative (−)	Jot down a + or − in the blank.

Whether you jot something down in the blank is up to you. It's really a matter of test-taking style. For some, an active pencil keeps them focused and in control. For other test takers, especially those who don't write quickly, jotting things down takes up too much precious time. Experiment with both ways and—once again—discover what works for you.

The Bottom Line

When you're filling in the blank, you're not looking for any word that can fly! You're looking for the *best* choice, that is, a choice firmly supported by a context clue and/or your word prediction.

Never Settle

Never settle for the first answer choice that *seems* to fit. If choice B sounds good, for example, don't stop there. Continue on: plug-in and try choices A, C, D, and E. Search thoroughly, leaving no stone unturned. Considering all choices takes discipline, and that's what this test takes.

STRATEGY 5: KEEP LEVEL-HEADED

Did you know that the test makers rank sentence completion questions (and math questions) on the SAT according to their levels of difficulty? This is helpful to know as you work through the sentence completion section since these questions start off easy (levels 1 and 2) and then become medium in difficulty (level 3); at the end of the section are the hardest questions (levels 4 and 5).

High-Scorers Are Level-Headed as They Work on Sentence Completions

Level 1	Level 2	Level 3	Level 4	Level 5
Easiest	Easier	Medium	Harder	Hardest
Level of	Level of	Level of	Level of	Level of
Difficult	Difficulty	Difficulty	Difficulty	Difficulty

In the other verbal section, questions appear in random order of difficulty. The first question may be a level 4; the next, a level 1; and so forth.

As you work on a page of sentence completions, the first column typically has the easier questions. However, if the first column seems like a walk in the park, the second column is certainly no picnic! The second column (the last three or four questions especially) contains the heavy-hitters, the hardest of the sentence completion questions.

Part of what makes sentence completions hard (in addition to their more complex sentence structure) is the level of vocabulary in the answer choices. On hard (level 4 or 5) sentence completions, it's not uncommon to find words such as *vitriolic*, *didactic*, and *occlusion*. Unless you spend your free time reading Jane Austen or Charles Dickens, to join the 2400 Club you have to get serious about learning some hard words.

A bit of advice:
Study the top-tier vocabulary lists at the end of this book. Start with the four-letter words, and work your way up to the heavy hitters.

Back to keeping "level-headed": If you are on question 2 in a sentence completion section and you are spending lots of time "reading into" the subtleties of the sentence and its grammatical syntax, you're probably missing the point. There is probably a simple, straightforward solution you haven't seen. Chances are that this question is only a level 1 or level 2 (easy).

The Vocabulary of Hard Sentence Completion Questions

The following words were the correct answers or among the answer choices for hard (difficulty levels 4 and 5) sentence completion questions from the College Board's *Official SAT Study Guide*, 2nd edition. No wonder some test takers call this the *vocabulary* section.

As this list shows, it is imperative to learn a broad, upper-level vocabulary in order to confidently gain a level of facility with hard sentence completion questions. If you know the majority of the words in the list, then you are happily on your way to getting a host (a large number, myriad, legion) of level 4 and level 5 sentence completion questions correct. Kudos!

Good News: Memorize the definitions of a plethora (abundance) of hard words, and you can take them with you on test day. Take them with you by committing them to your memory by using mnemonic devices. Barron's *HOT WORDS for the SAT, 4th edition* gives numerous examples of mnemonic (memory) devices at the end of each lesson.

TEST 1: jingoism, ossified, venerable, viable, cryptic, judicious, jubilant, pugnacious, supercilious, belligerence, indigence, perfidy, aspersion, tenacity

TEST 2: flotsam, reconnaissance, decimation, raiment, sustenance, churlish, laconic, stature, cantankerous, mercurial, corrosive, disingenuous, implacable, phlegmatic, retrenchment, preeminence, unequivocal, effusive, incorrigible, tenuous, ineffable, bucolic, prolific, lugubrious, sundry, remonstrance, erudition, plausible, lassitude, painstaking, fabrication, chicanery

TEST 3: obscure, deferential, sanctimonious, clairvoyant, discriminating, conducive, bereft, miscreants, anomalies, tacit, fervent, impetuous, antipodes, bifurcations, dichotomies, filial, avuncular, convivial, funerary, cacophonous, syncopated, mellifluous

TEST 4: fastidious, sedulous, vindictive, rhetoric, petulant, mercenary, treacly, cursory, prosaic, meticulous, consecrated, ineffable, consummate, presumptive, deleterious, vacillated, fidelity, wavered, vindication, discernment, holistic, censure, equitable, eulogy, smugness, legitimate

TEST 5: byzantine, adroit, nefarious, devious, lackadaisical, onerous, slipshod, partisanship, intemperance, acumen, irreverence, ingenuous, arcane, abstruse, didactic, lucid, concise, esoteric, insolence, magnanimity, pettiness, solicitousness, consecration, autonomy, effacement, apolitical, seditious, insurrectionists, subversive, nonpartisan, corollary, precursor

TEST 6: perquisites, tribulations, irreproachable, reprehensible, afflictions, undermines, censured, confounds, repertory, barrage, libelous, rehash, paucity, cacophony

TEST 7: dubious, contemptible, disparaging, sporadic, gratuitous, amalgamation, conflagration, concordance, entourage, aberration, debacle, faction, dearth, affluence, affability, equanimity, truculence, abstruse, unequivocal, impenetrable, esoteric, arcane, hackneyed, lucid, grating, denounced, supplant, winnow, finagle

TEST 8: phlegmatic, apathetic, conciliatory, vigilant, penurious, frugal, flabbergasted, miffed, jaded, wary, censures, exacerbates, delineates, amiable, glacial, taunting, nondescript, tremulous, lithe, fickle, reprieve

TEST 9: obstinacy, hubris, impetuosity, valor, callousness, extravagant, circumscribed, scrupulous, impulsive, irreverent, corroborated, extant, belied, debilitated, tempered, irresolute, officious, rancorous, myopic, punctilious, despoiled, shrewd, imprudent, denuded, dispatch, presumption, reverence, induction, amalgam, occlusion

TEST 10: obsequious, lackadaisical, dispersion, exploitation, husbandry, extirpation, altruism, exemplars, eccentric, erudition, enigmas, invocation, prospectus, manifesto, arbitration, mandate

Conversely, if you are on the *last* question in a sentence completion section and you think the answer is obvious, you're missing the point. Most likely, this is a level 4 or 5 question, and the answer choice is a difficult vocabulary word with a subtle context clue or clues to support it. Most of the time, the correct answer to a hard sentence completion is a very hard vocabulary word. For example, on the October 2004 PSAT, correct answer choices to hard sentence completions included *execrable, unctuous, vitriolic,* and *obfuscation.* Hard questions typically have hard answer choices. The correct answers are, most often, off-the-bell-curve words such as *leviathan, sybarite, anathema,* and *untenable.*

> **Coaching:**
> *The "level-headed" 2400 Club member knows, when in doubt, to pick off-the-bell-curve words on the hardest sentence-completion questions.*

Top scorers are not easily daunted. They don't sit around obsessing about all the hard words they don't know. Top scorers don't take a self-defeating attitude such as, "There's an infinite number of words that could possibly appear on the SAT. I can't learn *all* of them, so I'll never get those level 4 and level 5 sentence completions." Instead, 2400 Club members build confidence and bolster their verbal scores by amassing an upper-level vocabulary. When it comes to hard sentence completions, top scorers understand that, even if they don't happen to know *myopic, amalgam,* or *hubris,** they can eliminate the other answer choices whose definitions they do know and whose definitions they know don't fit the blank. 2400 Club test takers focus on what they know and maximize that knowledge, letting it work for them as they reach their maximum potentials. To give yourself the best shot at a 2400, know your *Hot Words for the SAT* (Barron's), and learn the words listed in Appendix A at the end of this book.

Sharpening Skills—Being Level-Headed

Let's say you are working on a two-blank sentence-completion question. Let's also say that this question is the second-to-last one in its group. Being level-leaded, you know that this question is most likely a level 4 or a level 5. Suppose these are the answer choices:

(A) delighted...fly
(B) deprecatory...goad
(C) ascetic...veer
(D) colorful...speak
(E) reticent...elicit

> **Coaching**
> *High-scorers maintain an awareness of the **difficulty levels** of questions as they work.*

First, use PET and eliminate choices that you feel don't work. If you cannot predict a word for the blank, find a context clue, or even get a sense of the blank's value (Strategies 1–3), which two choices would you eliminate? Eliminate (A) and (D) because the vocabulary in these choices is too basic for an upper-level question.

(A) delighted...fly
(B) deprecatory...goad
(C) ascetic...veer
(D) colorful...speak
(E) reticent...elicit

> *Always use your **Active Pencil** to decisively eliminate answer choices. (See example to left.)*

Be level-headed in another sense as well. Be calm, breathe evenly, work methodically, pace yourself, and look at the testing session as *your* chance to show *them* (the test makers) what you know.

---

* *These three words actually appeared on the PSAT in October 2004. Not surprisingly, they were the correct answers to hard sentence-completion questions.*

STRATEGY 6: SAY THE SENTENCE TO YOURSELF TO ENSURE THAT IT MAKES SENSE

The acid test: Read the sentence as you have completed it. Does it make sense? A final reading of the sentence is recommended before you move on to the next question. Make sure, of course, that you have prudently considered all five answer choices. For the vast majority of questions, there should be one or two specific context clues to support your choice.

 Habitually cross off answers that you know don't work. Don't underestimate PET— Process of Elimination Technique. PET moves you closer to the right answer and simplifies your task. Crossing off prevents you from being distracted by unlikely answer choices and keeps you focused on finding the *best* choice.

HIGH SCORER'S STRATEGY ACRONYM

- Do you consider yourself a visual learner?
- Do you have a strong memory?
- Do you "get it" once you see it?
- Have mnemonic devices helped you with learning in the past?

If so, then consider the six strategies for critical reading at the sentence level as spelling the word "BLANKS." After all, questions on critical reading at the sentence level are also known as sentence completions, or filling in the BLANKS. Consider this acronym:

B	**ring** your word to the blank.
L	**ocate** a context clue.
A	**ssign** a positive or negative value to the blank.
N	**ever** do's!
K	**eep** level-headed.
S	**ay** the sentence to yourself to ensure that it makes sense.

File a "mental picture" of this acronym in your mind's eye. Then, on test day, call up this picture as a test-taking tool to remind you of important strategies for sentence completion questions.

PRACTICE TEST QUESTIONS

Directions: Each of the following sentences contains one or two blanks; each blank indicates that a word or set of words has been left out. Below the sentence are five words or phrases, lettered (A) through (E). Select the word or set of words that <u>best</u> completes the sentence.

Note: *The answer explanations that follow these questions are very thorough. Sometimes a sentence completion is hard because of the vocabulary it contains. Because everyone's vocabulary is different, some "challenging" words may be a breeze for you. Tough words are listed in the answer explanations to illustrate that vocabulary strength is a great asset to you when answering hard sentence completions. Use an Active Pencil (see explanation on page 2) as you work through these exercises.*

1. Equipped with a large air hockey table, billiards, foosball, and table tennis, the recreation room provides myriad ways for the children to _____ themselves.

    (A) divulge
    (B) retract
    (C) divert
    (D) disavow
    (E) bemuse

2. Located on the lower level, the guest quarters were not only _____ but also _____; they were spacious and roomy enough to feel comfortable while being small and intimate enough to feel snug.

    (A) capacious..lavish
    (B) slipshod..ornate
    (C) renovated..razed
    (D) commodious..cozy
    (E) isolated..complacent

3. Since the entire family has a(an) _____ for watching a broad spectrum of movies, a home theater was _____ welcomed by all family members.

    (A) predilection..meagerly
    (B) aversion..vehemently
    (C) fallacy..hardly
    (D) conundrum..fervidly
    (E) affinity..fervently

4. Despite _____ technological innovations, including cell-phone cameras, pagers, hand-held computers, and a multitude of other devices intended to streamline and ease our hectic lives, life does not seem to be getting simpler.

    (A) myriad
    (B) meager
    (C) jocular
    (D) jaded
    (E) enigmatic

5. Far from exciting and novel, _____ household tasks include taking out the garbage, washing the dinner dishes, and folding the laundry.

    (A) energizing
    (B) motivating
    (C) quotidian
    (D) enervating
    (E) grubby

6. Instead of elucidating the complex process of wiring an eleven-room home for ceiling speakers and the Internet, Jack paints an incomprehensible picture of a "smart home" and further _____ the intricacies of home-networking.

   (A) obfuscates
   (B) inspires
   (C) cites
   (D) regenerates
   (E) rebuffs

7. The second-grader uses a copious supply of sculpting gel on his hair each and every morning before school, leaving an _____ residue of green goop in the restroom sink.

   (A) effacing
   (B) onerous
   (C) inane
   (D) ingratiating
   (E) unctuous

8. Often late to the workplace or downright absent, Hal found his job as widget-maker neither diverting nor enlightening; in fact, he perceived it as an anathema, and he transparently _____ his job.

   (A) rekindled
   (B) execrated
   (C) defiled
   (D) exasperated
   (E) finagled

9. It takes an incisive sense of direction and a clarity of mind to navigate the tortuous, mazelike corridors of the medieval palace, whose floor plan is nothing short of _____.

   (A) byzantine
   (B) archaic
   (C) quixotic
   (D) enveloping
   (E) gruesome

10. So that you don't get stuck in the mud and get your trousers wet, I suggest that you _____ the small boggy area and try to avoid the larger quagmire up ahead.

    (A) circumscribe
    (B) circumvent
    (C) circumlocute
    (D) circulate
    (E) encircle

11. To foster enriching experiences for her children during the summer, Mrs. Aidan avoided conflicts that would _____ her from scheduling _____ summer activities that included golf lessons, swim lessons, and a multisports camp.

    (A) resign..vilifying
    (B) beseem..unyielding
    (C) bolster..sundry
    (D) hinder..enervating
    (E) preclude..edifying

12. Overwhelming desk clutter and towering piles of paper make it difficult to find relatively _____ items such as earring backs and electronic discs the size of dimes.

    (A) indeterminate
    (B) inestimable
    (C) infinitesimal
    (D) infinite
    (E) indiscriminate

ANSWERS AND EXPLANATIONS

1. C	**4.** A	**7.** E	**10.** B
2. D	**5.** C	**8.** B	**11.** E
3. E	**6.** A	**9.** A	**12.** C

These answer explanations serve a trifold purpose. First, they point out grammatical components of the sentence that can make it tricky. Second, they coach you through suggested strategy steps, such as "Bring your word to the blank" and "Locate a context clue." Third, challenging words, which often characterize the hardest questions, are noted.

1. Why it's tough: cumbersome sentence with long introductory phrase modifying *room*; lots of commas
Your word (possibilities): *entertain? enjoy?*
Context clue: *recreation*
Challenging vocabulary: *myriad, retract, divert, disavow, bemuse*
Best answer: **C**; *divert*, in this context, means to entertain.

2. Why it's tough: lengthy compound sentence; the blanks are connected with the correlative conjunction pair *not only/but also*; hard vocabulary
Your word (possibilities): *big?/comfy?*
Context clues: The two context clues follow the colon: *spacious and roomy; small and intimate/snug.*
Challenging vocabulary: *capacious, lavish, slipshod, ornate, razed, commodious, complacent*
Best answer: **D**; *commodious* means spacious; *cozy* means snug, as mentioned in the context clue.

3. Why it's tough: complex sentence that starts off with a subordinate adverbial clause; heavy vocabulary
Your word (possibilities): *liking?/enthusiastically?* or *enjoyment?/happily?*
Context clue: *welcomed by all*
Challenging vocabulary: *spectrum, predilection, aversion, vehemently, fallacy, conundrum, fervidly, affinity, fervently*
Best answer: **E**; an *affinity* is a strong liking for something; *fervently* means passionately or ardently.

4. Why it's tough: ponderous sentence; need to pick up on context clues and key words
Your word (possibilities): *handy? many?*
Context clue: *multitude*   Other key word: the opposite indicator, *Despite*
Challenging vocabulary: *myriad, meager, jocular, jaded, enigmatic*
Best answer: **A**; *myriad* means a large number.

5. Why it's tough: challenging vocabulary; need to pick up on opposite-indicating phrase *far from*, at the beginning of the sentence
   Your word (possibilities): *boring? dull?*
   Context clue: *far from exciting and novel*
   Challenging vocabulary: *novel, quotidian, enervating, grubby*
   Best answer: **C**; *quotidian* means ordinary, daily, commonplace.

6. Why it's tough: You need to notice the opposite-indicating context clue *instead of*
   Your strategies: Use the opposite-indicator *instead of* to select a word that means the antithesis of *elucidating* (making clear)
   Your word (possibilities): *complicates? confuses?*
   Challenging vocabulary: *elucidating, intricacies, obfuscates, cites, rebuffs*
   Best answer: **A**; *obfuscates* means obscures. **Scary fact:** *Obfuscation* appeared on the October 2004 PSAT.

7. Why it's tough: a vocabulary-laden sentence; hard answer choices
   Your strategies: Look for something relating to a quality of gel, since the context clue is *residue of green goop . . .* ; use your knowledge to define and discredit as many answer choices as you can; continue this process of elimination to arrive at *unctuous*. **Scarier fact:** *Unctuous* also appeared on the October 2004 PSAT.
   Your word (possibilities): *sticky? oily?*
   Challenging vocabulary: *copious, effacing, onerous, inane, ingratiating, unctuous*
   Best answer: **E**; *unctuous* means oily or greasy.

8. Why it's tough: long compound sentence; hard vocabulary in sentence and answer choices; you may be faced with "close contenders" in the answer choices because B, C, and D can all be considered strong negative words.
   Your strategies: Read the sentence saying, "Hal transparently *blanked* his job" to get a better flow; using context clues *often late . . . or absent, neither diverting nor enlightening, anathema,* you can assign a negative (–) value to the blank.
   Your word (possibilities): *hated? really disliked?*
   Challenging vocabulary: *diverting, anathema, transparently, execrated, defiled, finagled.*
   Best answer: **B**; *execrated* means loathed or detested.

9. Why it's tough: tough vocabulary; need to understand that the answer choice must be an adjective to describe *floor plan,* and not the age of the palace (B, *archaic*) or its hallways (corridors). These hallways may or may not be D (*enveloping*); nor should the blank be related to *tortuous* (could be misinterpreted as involving torture, misleading test takers into selecting E (*gruesome*).
   Your strategies: Sniff out context clues such as *takes an incisive* (penetrating) *sense of direction* and *mazelike*
   Your word (possibilities): *complicated? winding?*
   Challenging vocabulary: *incisive, tortuous, byzantine, quixotic*
   Best answer: **A**; *byzantine* means very complex, labyrinthine.

10. Why it's tough: long, introductory adverbial clause (*So that you . . . mud);* tricky
answer choices that can easily be confused, especially since four of them share the
same prefix, *circ-.*
Your strategies: Focus carefully on the distinct meaning of each word; the key context clue is *avoid,* and since you don't want to get stuck in the mud, you should not
only stay clear of the *quagmire* (swamp) but also, logically, (circumvent) the small
boggy area (a bog is a marsh or wetland).
Your word (possibilities): *avoid? bypass? go around?*
Challenging vocabulary: answer choices, because all contain *circ-;*
boggy, quagmire
Best answer: **B**; *circumvent* means to bypass or go around.

11. Why it's tough: double blanks; complex sentence with a long, introductory clause
and a host of commas; heavy vocabulary.
Your strategies: Understand the purpose behind Mrs. Aidan's efforts; context clue is
to cultivate enriching experiences for her children.
Your word (possibilities): *interesting?* (a positive word)
Challenging vocabulary: *vilifying, sundry, enervating, foster*
Best answer: **E**; *preclude* (prevent)..*edifying* (instructive).

12. Why it's tough: a mouthful of a sentence; tricky answer choices, all containing the
prefix *in-*
Your strategies: Detect size contrast between *overwhelming . . . towering piles* and *relatively* (small) *items* that would be hard to find; yes, the items seem random, so *indiscriminate* could work, but the context clues more definitively point to items that are
small and hard to find.
Your word (possibilities): *very small? tiny?*
Challenging vocabulary: *indeterminate, infinitesimal, indiscriminate*
Best answer: **C**; *infinitesimal* means very, very small or minuscule.

Chapter 2

PARAGRAPH-LEVEL READING

Good news: Since March 2005, a sizable portion of the critical reading section has been "downsized" to include paragraph reading and paired paragraphs! Did you know that paragraphs used to appear on the SAT back in the seventies and eighties? This is a retro-move in test design. When it comes to critical reading at the paragraph level—no sweat. Here's your step-by-step method, the 4Ps of paragraph reading that empower you to sail through this section of the test.

2400 Club Strategies

Strategy 1: **P**araphrase as you read.

Strategy 2: **P**redict the answer.

Strategy 3: **P**are down the answer choices.

Strategy 4: **P**ick the best answer.

STRATEGY 1: PARAPHRASE

As you read, translate the author's language into your own words. "A pastoral vista" becomes "a country scene," and "putting on airs of pretense" could be "acting stuck up." An individual who "utilizes his intellectual faculties" becomes a guy who "uses his brain." Paraphrasing cuts the passage down to size.

Start by paraphrasing phrases, then go on to full sentences. Soon you'll work up the stamina to paraphrase several sentences at a time. Paraphrasing is a valuable skill that helps you build meaning, layer by layer, as you read. With practice, you will have the skill needed to read a full paragraph in one gulp and paraphrase the entire thing faultlessly. The test makers do sprinkle a few tough words in these paragraphs, and a strong vocabulary will help you comprehend accurately.

Cutting the author's language down to size can simplify the passage so that you're more comfortable with it. With comfort, you'll find it easier to absorb the ideas expressed in the paragraph.

STRATEGY 2: PREDICT

As you read each question, predict what the answer will be. Predict *before* you read the answer choices and you will put yourself in the driver's seat. Predict *before* considering the answer choices and you will prevent the befuddlement that sometimes comes with reading several answer choices that sound convincing. With *your* ideas foremost in mind, you'll be able to sift through the second-rate answers and focus in on the very best one. Base your prediction exclusively on textual evidence. Avoid adding year personal biases and expectations. Good predictors know that the proof is in the passage.

STRATEGY 3: PARE DOWN

In other words, narrow in on the best answer by using PET, the process of elimination technique. Cross off choices that you can rule out for one reason or another. If even a *small part* of an alluring answer is not supported by the passage, then that choice should be scrapped.

A *word of caution:* Don't become overzealous with crossing off! Never scrap an answer choice simply because it contains one or more words that are unfamiliar. This choice should be retained; it could be the right answer! When doing practice questions, look up words you don't know. Write them in a notebook or make flash cards for these words.

"Fear of the unknown" is the reason for crossing off answers that contain unknown terms. This is not smart test-taking. The 2400 Club has no such fear—you are *intrepid*!

STRATEGY 4: PICK

Choose the very best answer, never settling for second best. On easy and medium-level-of-difficulty questions, most test takers can reduce the answer choices to two. What remains? The best answer and the "runner-up." Selecting the second-best answer (the runner-up) may deserve a pat on the back, but you **will *lose* one-fourth point for the wrong answer**. There's no half credit on the SAT. Though runner-ups are tempting, you will learn to see that each one has some aspect that discredits it. It can look like and feel like a duck, but if it has a fin, it ain't no duck! (Pardon the *ain't* and the double negative; they're for rhetorical effect.)

PRACTICE TEST QUESTIONS ON PARAGRAPHS

Note: *Typically, on the SAT two questions are given for each paragraph. For extra practice, 2400 Club members, you are given <u>four</u> questions to answer on the first paragraph. All test directions are approximations of directions on the SAT; they tell you what you need to do.*

> **Directions:** Read each passage below, and then answer the questions that follow. The correct response may be stated outright or merely suggested in the passage.

Questions 1–4 are based on the following passage. *This paragraph is taken from* Personal Experience of a Physician, *written by John Ellis.*

Homoeopathy is strictly a scientific system of medicine. It is based upon
a law of nature—"Similia similibus curantur," or the law that remedies
will cure symptoms and diseases similar to those which they will cause

Line
5

when taken by healthy persons. It is wonderful with what care, skill, and perseverance the new *Materia Medica* has been developed, mostly by intelligent physicians, commencing with Hahnemann, taking the different remedies in varying doses, and carefully and patiently watching the symptoms that follow, and writing them down day after day; and then, when similar symptoms occur in case of disease, giving the remedies and

10

carefully watching and writing down the results. Allopathic physicians, as a rule, have not the slightest conception of the vast amount of patient and persevering labor in this direction which has been done by physicians as well educated as they are, and most of whom have graduated in the same schools, who have devoted their lives to this work. Are not these facts

15

worthy of the consideration of every physician in the world who desires the highest good of his fellow men?

1. Based on the information presented in this passage, you can infer that *Materia Medica* (line 5) most likely refers to

   (A) a maternal approach to medicine
   (B) a medical tome that outlines therapeutic procedures for open-minded physicians
   (C) an international panel of well-reputed researchers in the field of homeopathy
   (D) the system and science of the novel homeopathic medicine
   (E) a collection of tangible, medical materials such as stethoscopes, vials, and dispensers

2. In lines 6–10 and on the basis of the entire passage, "taking the different remedies...and writing down the results" conveys the idea that

   (A) homeopathy is a painstaking and prudent process
   (B) Hahnemann was not simply diligent; he was obsessive-compulsive
   (C) the practice of allopathic physicians is much more laid back and inaccurate than that of homeopathic physicians
   (D) the skills required of an investigative journalist are similar to those required of a physician
   (E) to avoid misconceptions, patients must persevere no matter how laborious the path

3. John Ellis implies that mankind can receive "the highest good" (lines 15 and 16) under which of the following conditions?

   (A) Doctors begin "carefully watching and writing down the results" (line 10).
   (B) Physicians, worldwide, make being "well educated" (line 13) their overarching goal.
   (C) Doctors exercise "patient and persevering labor in this direction" (lines 11 and 12).
   (D) Doctors inexorably dedicate themselves to "allopathic" (line 10) modes of medicine.
   (E) There is global commitment to homeopathy.

4. Author Ellis does all of the following in this scientific passage EXCEPT

(A) define a scientific term
(B) name a pioneer in the field of homeopathy
(C) include a specimen of Latin terminology
(D) pose a rhetorical question
(E) harshly condemn the practices of allopathic physicians

Questions 5 and 6 are based on the following passage.

In this paragraph, taken from Mary W. Shelley's science fiction classic, Frankenstein, *the narrator describes a being to whom she is growing increasingly attached.*

> Even broken in spirit as he is, no one can feel more
> deeply than he does the beauties of nature. The
> starry sky, the sea, and every sight afforded by these
> wonderful regions seem still to have the power of
> Line
> 5 elevating his soul from earth. Such a man has a double
> existence: he may suffer misery and be overwhelmed by
> disappointments, yet when he has retired into himself,
> he will be like a celestial spirit that has a halo
> around him, within whose circle no grief or folly ventures.

5. In line 7, "retired" most closely means

(A) fallen asleep
(B) abandoned his profession
(C) calmed down
(D) withdrawn
(E) passed away

6. It can be inferred from the description of the man in lines 6–9 that the author regards him as

(A) a duplicitous person whose evil side and good side coexist
(B) an indomitable, godlike character who practices artifice
(C) a peaceful, protected being
(D) an enigma with a false exterior
(E) a supernatural visitant with a mission of misery

ANSWERS AND EXPLANATIONS

1. D	**3.** C	**5.** D
2. A	**4.** E	**6.** C

1. OBSCURE (LATIN) TERM-IN-CONTEXT QUESTION. **As a disciplined critical reader, reread up, at, and around this term in order to glean its meaning in context.** Pertinent part:

> It is wonderful with what care, skill, and perseverance the new *Materia Medica* has been developed, mostly by intelligent physicians, commencing with Hahnemann, taking the different remedies in varying doses, and carefully and patiently watching the symptoms that follow, and writing them down day after day; and then, when similar symptoms occur in case of disease, giving the remedies and
> 10 carefully watching and writing down . . . .

Choice (A) is bogus since *maternal* cannot be substantiated; nowhere is there mention of mothers, grandmothers, or the female touch. (B) is out since a "tome" (a big book or volume) is not "developed" (line 5) by a process, but is written by an author. (C) *Materia Medica* sounds lofty enough and appears very important with its two capital letters, but there's no evidence that this is a name of a group of international researchers. This answer choice would require a great deal of creativity on your part. (E) is tempting since *Materia* could relate to tangible objects, but no specific medical materials are ever mentioned. **(D)** is the answer.

2. QUESTION THAT REQUIRES UNDERSTANDING THE SUBTLETIES OF PART OF THE PASSAGE AS IT RELATES TO THE PASSAGE AS A WHOLE. **Skim over the lines within the sizable sidebar, focusing on the purpose of this part of the passage in terms of the whole.** Avoid (B) since it is an unsubstantiated, borderline-extreme answer. Perhaps allopathic practice is "more laid back," but no evidence is presented to support its being "inaccurate"; (C) is out. Active pencil! (D) is out since it's a jump (based on your conjecture)! (E) is tempting. First, "misconceptions" might ring true since "slightest conception" follows in line 11. Second, "patient" appears in line 11, which hasty test takers could mistake for "patients," a word that appears in choice (E). Lines 6–10 delineate the work required of physicians, not patients, so (E) is not the answer. The answer is **(A)** since the process, as described, is certainly meticulous ("painstaking") and careful ("prudent").

3. TOUGH INFERENCE QUESTION THAT ALLUDES TO SEVERAL TERMS AND PHRASES USED THROUGHOUT THE PASSAGE. **Using line references where given, refer to the passage to see what answer choice would confirm mankind's receiving "the highest good."** (A) "Carefully watching and writing down the results" is not all that's needed for doctors to bestow the "highest good" upon man. (B) Being "well educated" is not enough to enable physicians, whether allopathic or homeopathic, to transfer the "highest good" to men, especially since "well educated" (in context) refers to two types of medical education. (A) and (B) are out. You're using PET! (D) is out since "allopathic" medicine is presented as antithetical to homeopathic medicine. Active pencil! (E) is a tempting, decoy answer. Yes, this author advocates homeopathy, yet he never says that commitment must be

worldwide. (In line 15, the phrase "in the world" might seem to validate this answer, but rereading the last line of the paragraph clarifies that the phrase does not support choice (E). The answer is **(C)** since "in this direction" (line 12) refers to the direction of homeopathy, which is the system of medicine the author advocates.

4.   TIME-CONSUMING "ALL/EXCEPT" QUESTION **Use your memory of what you've read and skim the passage, when you need to, to confirm four of the five answer choices.** (A) Ellis defines a scientific term in lines 1 and 2. (B) Ellis names a homeopathy pioneer in line 6. (C) "Similia similibus curantur" (line 2) is a sampling of Latin terminology. Ellis concludes with a rhetorical question, so (D) is out. The answer is **(E)**.

5.   WORD-IN-CONTEXT QUESTION. **2400 Club members are open-minded when it comes to what a word may actually mean *in* a particular context.** What's hard is that, in this paragraph, the *in-context* definition is a world apart from the more common literal definition, (B). Neither (B) nor (A) fits the context. Choice (C) cannot be supported because there is no prior evidence that the man was upset or hyper. Using PET, you are left with (D) and (E). The man does not die (E), since the sentence describes his "double *existence*" (lines 5 and 6). The answer is **(D)**; even though he may suffer openly, he has "retired *into himself*" (big context clue!) and has a different inner spirit that envelops him: "like a celestial spirit that has a halo around him, within whose circle no grief or folly ventures."

6.   TRICKY INFERENCE QUESTION COUPLED WITH SOME CHALLENGING VOCABU-LARY WORDS: *celestial, folly*. **Consider carefully the description of the man.** Pertinent part:

> he may suffer misery and be overwhelmed by
> disappointments, yet when he has retired into himself,
> he will be like a celestial spirit that has a halo
> around him, within whose circle no grief or folly ventures.

The answer choices are chock-full of awesome vocabulary, too: *duplicitous* (deceitful, dishonest); *indomitable* (unconquerable); *artifice* (trickery); and *enigma* (a mystery or riddle). The passage offers no evidence that the man is duplicitous (A), practices artifice (B), or is a puzzling man (D). Also, there's no context clue that the man is supernatural or is on a mission of misery (E). The answer is **(C)** since the passage says that he is "like a celestial (heavenly) spirit that has a halo around him." The halo encircles him like a protective shield.

PRACTICE TEST QUESTIONS ON PAIRED PARAGRAPHS

> **Directions:** The questions that follow the two passages in this section relate to the content of both and to their relationship. The correct response may be stated outright in the passages or merely suggested.

The first passage is excerpted from Out of Doors—California and Oregon, *by J. A. Graves;* the *second, from* At the Earth's Core, *a work of fiction by Edgar Rice Burroughs.*

Passage 1

In the pasture were swales of damp land, literally
overgrown with wild blackberry bushes. They bore prolific
crops of long, black, juicy berries, far superior to the
tame berries, and they were almost entirely free from
seeds. Many a time have I temporarily bankrupted my
stomach on hot blackberry roll, with good, rich sauce.
The country fairly teemed with game. Quail and rabbit
were with us all the time. Doves came by the thousands
in the early summer and departed in the fall. In winter
the wild ducks and geese were more than abundant. In the
spring wild pigeons visited us in great numbers. There was
one old oak tree which was a favorite resting-place with
them. Sheltered by some live oak bushes, I was always
enabled to sneak up and kill many of them out of this tree.

Passage 2

We must have traveled several miles through the
dark and dismal wood when we came suddenly upon a
dense village built high among the branches of the trees.
As we approached it my escort broke into wild shouting
which was immediately answered from within, and a moment
later a swarm of creatures of the same strange race
as those who had captured me poured out to meet us.
Again I was the center of a wildly chattering horde.
I was pulled this way and that. Pinched, pounded,
and thumped until I was black and blue, yet I do not
think that their treatment was dictated by either cruelty
or malice—I was a curiosity, a freak, a new plaything,
and their childish minds required the added evidence of all
their senses to back up the testimony of their eyes.

1. In context, "tame" (line 4) most likely refers to blackberries that are

    (A) orderly and cultivated
    (B) docile and untainted
    (C) easier to pick and tastier to eat
    (D) domesticated and demure
    (E) tart and acerbic

2. Which most accurately describes the sentiments that the Passage 1 author has toward the "old oak tree" and "oak bushes" (lines 12 and 13) with respect to the sentiments that the Passage 2 author has toward the "wood" (line 16)?

    (A) Passage 1 author feels a sense of ownership and affectation; Passage 2 author, of self-protection.
    (B) Passage 1 author feels a sense of nostalgia and whimsy; Passage 2 author, of scathing hostility.
    (C) Passage 1 author feels a sense of comfort and cover; Passage 2 author, of foreboding and gloom.
    (D) Neither author feels a personal connection to these natural elements.
    (E) Both authors have a curious sense of detachment from most natural settings and the objects within them.

3. According to Passage 2 as a whole, the author uses the phrase "poured out" (line 21) to convey which of the following regarding the "creatures" in line 20?

    (A) They are an unruly and belligerent bunch intent on doing the narrator serious harm.
    (B) They pile around the narrator because of their enthusiastic curiosity about him.
    (C) They are primitive, yet intelligent.
    (D) Their effusive emotions cause them to be disorderly and impulsive.
    (E) Their bodily movements mirror their inner spirits, which are abundantly generous.

4. In line 25, "dictated" most nearly means

    (A) ordained
    (B) tyrannized
    (C) prescribed
    (D) determined
    (E) ordered

ANSWERS AND EXPLANATIONS

1. A   **3.** B

2. C   **4.** D

1. SUBTLE WORD-IN-CONTEXT QUESTION **Carefully read up, down, and around line 4 to get a sense of this word in its context.** " Tame" most closely refers to blackberries that are, according to the narrator, inferior to the ones described in the lines 1–3 as "overgrown," "wild," and "prolific." The best antithetical description of the tame berries is **(A)**, *orderly and cultivated.* There is no evidence to validate the other choices. Since the narrator prefers the "overgrown" berries, perhaps the tame ones are less tasty **(E)**, *tart and acerbic,* but there is no *proof* in the paragraph to support this conjecture.

2. QUESTION COMPARING/CONTRASTING SIMILAR ELEMENTS THAT APPEAR IN BOTH PASSAGES **In each passage, read closely around the three line references to glean a sense of the authors' feelings toward these elements of nature.** Pertinent parts:

   (Passage 1)

   There was
   one old oak tree which was a <u>favorite resting-place</u> with
   them. <u>Sheltered</u> by some live oak bushes, I was always
   enabled to sneak up and kill many of them out of this tree.

   (Passage 2)

   <u>dark and dismal</u> wood

   With these significant parts in focus, you can readily see from the underlined context clues that the best answer is **(C)**: *Passage 1 author feels a sense of comfort and cover; Passage 2 author, of foreboding and gloom.* For (A), *ownership* could work, but *affectation* could not (unless, of course, you misread this word as *affection*). For (B), *nostalgia* could work, but not *whimsy.* You should make it a habit to avoid an extreme answer such as *scathing hostility.* (D) and (E) are out since the woods are significant to both authors.

3. MEANING OF A VERB PHRASE IN CONTEXT **Read at, up, down, and around this line reference to get a sense of the subtler implications of the phrase "poured out."** Who are the "creatures"? Focus on the pertinent part to recall who the creatures are and why they "poured out." Pertinent part:

   20   later a swarm of *creatures* of the same strange race
       as those who had captured me *poured out* to meet us.
       Again I was the center of a wildly chattering horde.
       I was pulled this way and that. Pinched, pounded,
       and thumped until I was black and blue, yet I do not
   25   think that their treatment was dictated by either cruelty
       or malice—I was a curiosity, a freak, a new plaything,
       and their childish minds required the added evidence of all
       their senses to back up the testimony of their eyes.

To paraphrase these lines, a bunch of creatures came running out to meet the narrator and his friend. The creatures surrounded the narrator, talking loudly and grabbing at him because of their curiosity, which stemmed from their childish and inquisitive minds. The answer cannot be (A) since the passage states "their treatment was not dictated by cruelty or malice" (lines 25 and 26) (C) is out since no statement implies that the creatures are *intelligent*. (D) is also out; yes, their emotions are effusively displayed, but the creatures are not portrayed as *impulsive*. There's not a shred of proof for (E): who can tell whether the creatures' spirits are *abundantly generous*? The answer is **(B)**.

4. WORD-IN-CONTEXT QUESTION **Consider this verb in the larger context in which it is used:** "I do not think that their treatment was <u>dictated</u> by either cruelty or malice." (A) is out, since *ordained* connotes an appointment to a religious order. (B), *tyrannized*, is too strong to fit this context. (C), *prescribed*, relates to a written order, as one for medicine. (E), *ordered*, could be the second-best answer, but, as you know—*sniffle, sniffle*—no partial credit is given on the SAT. Second best doesn't cut it; the *best* answer is **(D)**.

Chapter 3

LONG-PASSAGE READING

Hunting and gathering, listening . . . these are skills that humankind has been practicing since the dawn of time. To some extent, they're built into our genetic code—innate, inherent, intrinsic—you get the idea. How hard can they be? Ask a caveman. No, really, here's how these skills apply to critical reading at the long-passage level.

Here are two analogies to mull over that pertain to critical reading:

1. *Critical reading is like hunting and gathering—hunting, that is, for context clues.*
2. *Critical reading is like listening very carefully—listening (in your mind) to what the author is saying.*

2400 Club Global Strategies

HUNTING AND GATHERING

Context clues come in several forms: groupings of words that are scattered through the text, a phrase, or, simply, a significant word. Each word an author uses means something. The author's choice of words offers clues as to his or her meaning, point of view, mood, and attitude. To answer critical reading questions accurately, you have to sniff out and scope out the context clues in the passage.

PASSAGE EVIDENCE

Just as there is no guesswork in sentence completions, so there is no guesswork in critical reading and no "maybe this answer works." There is no place for personal conjecture or creativity. Do not "read into" anything. You're probably a cerebral type, so you may be prone to do just that, but resist. Do the work required to get the right answers: gather the evidence! In addition to collecting specific words that function as context clues, gather phrases and sentences that support a particular answer choice. These items are called passage evidence.

> *"Passage evidence"* refers to words, phrases, and sentences that support the best answer choice.

LISTENING

Listen (in your mind) so carefully that you get a full sense of the author's viewpoints and attitudes. Listen so carefully that you can, in a sense, paraphrase what he or she is saying without injecting your opinions or any other outside information. Listen clearly, resisting the impulse to call upon what you've learned from your textbooks or from educational television programming. Even the Discovery and History channels will not help you here.

Think of it this way. The author, lying on the couch, is telling a story, and you are sitting in a leather swivel chair, note-book in hand, listening carefully to everything he or she is say-ing. You are even taking mental notes in addition to written ones. This patient-therapist model represents the kind of careful listening you need to succeed when working on critical reading at the long-passage level.

Be such a good listener that you can paraphrase just what the author has said. Immerse yourself in the author's perspective, and—above all—do not think for yourself. Independent thinking, or thinking too deeply, can get you in trouble on the SAT.

2400 Club Coaching: *High scorers "listen" very carefully as they read.*

More Coaching: *High scorers are loyal to what is expressed in the passage. They never select answers that distort or stray from what is said by the author.*

CRITICAL READING SECRET FORMULA

The critical reading secret formula is a global strategy that you can use as you read para-graphs, long passages, or paired passages.

> ✳ Critical Reading Secret Formula = Read + React + Interact *plus* Visualize ✳

When you read, you're in charge. You should put yourself into an active reading mode. Don't let the author's words run over your head like rainwater. You must absorb what is said; in other words, you need to become an *active reader*. The formula above is your recipe for active reading. If you employ these steps as you read, you will be in a strong posi-tion to absorb and recall all the points that the author puts forth.

Critical reading on the SAT is a far cry from reading for pleasure. On this test, have you ever seen an action-packed passage on basketball? The latest fashions? The greatest gaming systems? Snowboarding a black diamond? No! In case you haven't noticed, the Educational Testing Service does not go out of its way to make the reading passages inter-esting. Rarely or never will you find a reading passage on snowboarding, mountain biking, baseball, or the raddest strip malls.

Former critical reading topics have included: black American fiction and the romance novel, nuclear reactors and particle accelerators, emigrating from Poland to Canada, ancient Athens as a model of democracy, the mating habits of red-winged blackbirds, and a Chinese-American grapples with her cultural identity. Reading rather dry, often convoluted passages on such topics requires discipline. Psyche yourself up to get into the pas-sages and to follow the active reading formula as a way to disci-pline yourself as you read. Here's the high scorer's reading credo: *I'll get the passage; it won't get me.*

2400 Club Coaching: *High scorers abandon their personal theories of the world and get into the author's head instead.*

Read

As you read, get into the author's head. See the world through the author's eyes, no matter how strange his or her "world view" may seem to you. Abandon any feelings, biases, and reasoning that you associate with the topic; read the passage with your mind as a clean slate. As you read, etch the author's point of view and vision onto your mental slate so that passage evidence is available for you to call upon later.

React, Using ABS

Reading is not about having words, like raindrops, run over your head. It's about absorbing the words and letting them impact you. As you read, react to what you're reading! Obviously you cannot talk aloud; the proctor might think you're losing it! But a dialogue should be going on *in your head*—a dialogue between you and what the author is saying in the passage. Using your active pencil, you may even want to jot down marginal notes or symbols next to paragraphs that indicate your reactions. For example: *Great idea!* or **Unreal!** or *??* or *!!* or *Very sad* or *Brave!* or ☹ or ☺ or ✱, as the passage moves you. See the Gallery of Symbols on page 36.

Let ABS (**A**bbreviations, **B**rief Notations, **S**ymbols) remind you of a few pencil-to-paper ways in which you may react to a passage as you read. To put ABS into practice, start off by requiring yourself to write one or more ABS notations, as explained below, for every paragraph that you read. Try jotting down ABS notations in the margins as you work through practice passages, and see if ABS helps you to connect with greater clarity to the contents of the passages.

With practice, you may find that you only need to write ABS notations for every second or third paragraph that you read. Experiment with ABS and see what works most effectively for you.

"A" Stands for Abbreviations

You can write, in abbreviated form, your reactions to what you are reading. Instead of writing "role reversal between mother and daughter," simply write *mthr-dghtr RR*. Instead of writing "nostalgic for his younger days," write *nstgc-youth*. Instead of "very bitter relationship break-up," *bttr bk-up*. You get the idea. The key is to write your reactions in an abbreviated form so that it is quick and won't clutter up the margins and obscure the passage that you will—no doubt—need to refer back to. Practice reacting in abbreviated form as you work through the practice exercises in this book and/or CD-ROM.

"B" Stands for Brief Notations

Brief notations are basically the same as abbreviations, yet they serve as an additional reminder to keep your written reactions *brief* and simple. Brief notations may or may not be abbreviated, but they should be brief: one or two words at most! If you must write more than that, then abbreviations should kick in!

Examples of brief notations that might appear in the margins of critical reading passages: *conflict, truce, money, intrigue, fallacy, harmful rumor, equal rights, adaptation, cultural value,* and so on. These one- or two-word marginal memos will come in handy as you navigate the passage, for the second time, as you look for details and evidence to support the best answer choice. Your marginal notes will serve as reminder "messages" for you, helping you to keep track of all that you have read and how the information is laid out in the passage.

"S" Stands for Symbols

If you like doodling and drawing, using symbols to respond to the reading will suit you well. We've touched upon symbols, but the potential for symbols is virtually limitless. Develop your own repertory of symbols that you can use to express your feedback and response to the various reading passages on the SAT. Consider the "Critical Reading Gallery of Symbols" below:

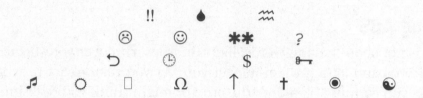

Be creative. Think outside the box! Which symbols might you use in addition to the ones presented in the Symbol Gallery above?

To get a six-pack, you must work your abs. To get as close to an 800 as possible, add ABS to your critical reading strategy repertoire.

Talk to yourself: "That's an odd way of looking at tree bark" or "I wonder what it would be like to have broad, colorful shoulder patches like the black raven."

Ask yourself: "Why would this dude want to study extraterrestrial radio static? How could he take such a risk and contradict all the current data?"

Silently ponder: "Who knew that certain cultures communicate through the fruit they serve?" or "Is this author gently poking fun, or is he being downright sarcastic?"

Reacting while reading will make you a more effective reader. You will absorb more and remember more.

Interact

Try to connect with the passage on some level. Interacting while reading will help you to retain what is being discussed. Relate the passage to yourself. Again, get an internal dialogue going. For example:

"I wouldn't want to leave my hometown either."

"I know what it's like to feel as though my identity has many aspects."

"I never realized that deserts could be cold."

"I never thought of a bat as a flying mouse!"

"If I were an investigative journalist, I'd also be skeptical about my information sources."

Again, don't let the words run over your head like rainwater.

Visualize

Your mind's eye is very powerful. Put it to work for you as you read the critical reading passages. For many of us, vision is our predominant learning modality. If the passage is about a midwestern prairie, visualize the countryside as delineated by the author. In your mind's eye, paint pictures of the rustic bridges, the serene landscape, and the tall yellow daffodils that the author describes.

If the passage is about a New England town meeting, visualize the details that the author mentions. Can you see the assembled townspeople? Can you imagine what they're talking about? Can you picture the inside of the quaint church where the New Englanders have convened?

If the passage is about a futuristic museum design, imagine the building's interior and exterior just as the author depicts them. Use your imagination to bring the cold steel to life. See the sharp angles of the futuristic building. Imagine the ebony and scarlet color combination the author describes.

Leisure reading can occur while you're at the beach watching the surf. Leisure reading can occur while you're eating pizza. You can even read a good book while catching the sports highlights on TV. Pleasure reading and critical reading on the SAT, however, are a world apart. When the passages are long, esoteric, and sometimes downright boring, reading comprehension requires focused attention and smart strategies.

2400 Club Strategies:

Strategy 1: **R**ead longer passages piece by piece.

Strategy 2: **E**xtract the main idea from the passage.

Strategy 3: **A**nswer line-reference and sidebar questions first.

Strategy 4: **D**elve into higher-order thinking questions.

Strategy 5: **I**dentify the author's mood and tone as you read.

Strategy 6: **N**arrow in on the *best* answer choice.

Strategy 7: **G**lobal questions should be answered at the very end.

STRATEGY 1: READ LONGER PASSAGES PIECE BY PIECE

How to read the passage, that is the question. Should I read the entire passage? Should I read just the first third? Should I read just the beginning and the end? Should I read the questions and then go back to the passage to hunt for answers? Most students are in a quandary about how to approach the critical reading sections.

You're smart, a high achiever, so it's unlikely that you'll have any trouble reading the entire passage—piece by piece. What does a "piece" of the passage look like? That's up to you. For some, a "piece" is a paragraph or two. For others, a "piece" is a half or a third of the passage. Experiment with reading "pieces" at a time, and you'll discover what works for you. Read so that you can maintain your concentration. After you read each piece, turn to the questions and answer the ones based on that piece. Working in this way keeps you focused and prevents you from getting befuddled by taking in too much information at a time.

Breaking a long passage into "pieces" is one way to downsize a potentially daunting task. You are probably a strong and avid reader; nevertheless, breaking a long passage into pieces gives you an edge by helping you to stay focused as you read and to answer the questions that correspond to each piece. High scorers know there is no real advantage to reading a passage in one spurt. In fact, if you read the entire thing in one gulp (all 80 lines, let's say), then, when you have to deal with questions based on the first couple of paragraphs, you will end up wasting time rereading those early parts of the passage. The early paragraphs will no longer be fresh in your mind after you've slogged through 80 lines or more.

As illustrated below, a "piece" is usually a paragraph or two. (Your first piece should always include the introductory, italicized "blurb" that precedes the passage.) You are self-directed and motivated, so decide what works best for you. The dotted lines show where this passage might be downsized into manageable pieces.

Reading Long Passages
Do not read the entire long passage at once.

Likewise, don't answer all the questions in one spurt.

Instead, follow a strategic and pragmatic process or "modus operandi."

Version 1—Illustrates reading the passage in five pieces
(for the prudent reader who wants to stay *very* focused)

This passage is taken from Charles Darwin's writings, The Expression of the Emotions in Man and Animals.

No doubt as long as man and all other animals are viewed
as independent creations, an effectual stop is put to our
natural desire to investigate as far as possible the causes
of Expression. By this doctrine, anything and everything can
Line
5   be equally well explained; and it has proved as pernicious with
respect to Expression as to every other branch of natural history.
With mankind some expressions, such as the bristling of the hair under
the influence of extreme terror, or the uncovering of the teeth under
that of furious rage, can hardly be understood, except on the belief
10 that man once existed in a much lower and animal-like condition.
The community of certain expressions in distinct though allied species,
as in the movements of the same facial muscles during laughter by man
and by various monkeys, is rendered somewhat more intelligible,
if we believe in their descent from a common progenitor.
15 He who admits on general grounds that the structure and habits
of all animals have been gradually evolved, will look at the whole
subject of Expression in a new and interesting light.

Dotted lines show where passage can be cut into pieces.

....

The study of Expression is difficult, owing to the movements
being often extremely slight, and of a fleeting nature.
20 A difference may be clearly perceived, and yet it may be impossible,
at least I have found it so, to state in what the difference consists.
When we witness any deep emotion, our sympathy is so strongly
excited, that close observation is forgotten or rendered
almost impossible; of which fact I have had many curious proofs.
25 Our imagination is another and still more serious source of error;
for if from the nature of the circumstances we expect
to see any expression, we readily imagine its presence.

Dotted lines show how you may read this long passage in manageable chunks.

Notwithstanding Dr. Duchenne's great experience, he for a long
time fancied, as he states, that several muscles contracted
30 under certain emotions, whereas he ultimately convinced himself
that the movement was confined to a single muscle.

In order to acquire as good a foundation as possible, and to ascertain,
independently of common opinion, how far particular movements
of the features and gestures are really expressive of certain states
35 of the mind, I have found the following means the most serviceable.
In the first place, to observe infants; for they exhibit many emotions,
as Sir C. Bell remarks, "with extraordinary force"; whereas, in after life,
some of our expressions "cease to have the pure and simple source
from which they spring in infancy."[18]

40 In the second place, it occurred to me that the insane ought to
be studied, as they are liable to the strongest passions, and give
uncontrolled vent to them. I had, myself, no opportunity of doing this,
so I applied to Dr. Maudsley and received from him an introduction
to Dr. J. Crichton Browne, who has charge of an immense asylum
45 near Wakefield, and who, as I found, had already attended to the subject.
This excellent observer has with unwearied kindness sent me copious
notes and descriptions, with valuable suggestions on many points;
and I can hardly over-estimate the value of his assistance. I owe also,
to the kindness of Mr. Patrick Nicol, of the Sussex Lunatic Asylum,
50 interesting statements on two or three points.

Thirdly Dr. Duchenne galvanized, as we have already seen, certain muscles
in the face of an old man, whose skin was little sensitive, and thus
produced various expressions which were photographed on a large scale.
It fortunately occurred to me to show several of the best plates,
55 without a word of explanation, to above twenty educated persons
of various ages and both sexes, asking them, in each case,
by what emotion or feeling the old man was supposed to be agitated;
and I recorded their answers in the words which they used.
Several of the expressions were instantly recognized by almost everyone,
60 though described in not exactly the same terms; and these may,
I think, be relied on as truthful, and will hereafter be specified.
On the other hand, the most widely different judgments were pronounced
in regard to some of them. This exhibition was of use in another way,
by convincing me how easily we may be misguided by our imagination;
65 for when I first looked through Dr. Duchenne's photographs,
reading at the same time the text, and thus learning what was intended,
I was struck with admiration at the truthfulness of all, with only
a few exceptions. Nevertheless, if I had examined them without
any explanation, no doubt I should have been as much perplexed,
70 in some cases, as other persons have been.

Version 2—Illustrates reading the passage in three pieces
(for the more voracious reader who can sustain concentration with longer pieces)

This passage is taken from Charles Darwin's writings The Expression of the Emotions in Man and Animals.

No doubt as long as man and all other animals are viewed as independent creations, an effectual stop is put to our natural desire to investigate as far as possible the causes of Expression. By this doctrine, anything and everything can
5 be equally well explained; and it has proved as pernicious with respect to Expression as to every other branch of natural history. With mankind some expressions, such as the bristling of the hair under the influence of extreme terror, or the uncovering of the teeth under that of furious rage, can hardly be understood, except on the belief
10 that man once existed in a much lower and animal-like condition. The community of certain expressions in distinct though allied species, as in the movements of the same facial muscles during laughter by man and by various monkeys, is rendered somewhat more intelligible, if we believe in their descent from a common progenitor.
15 He who admits on general grounds that the structure and habits of all animals have been gradually evolved, will look at the whole subject of Expression in a new and interesting light.

The study of Expression is difficult, owing to the movements being often extremely slight, and of a fleeting nature.
20 A difference may be clearly perceived, and yet it may be impossible, at least I have found it so, to state in what the difference consists. When we witness any deep emotion, our sympathy is so strongly excited, that close observation is forgotten or rendered almost impossible; of which fact I have had many curious proofs.
25 Our imagination is another and still more serious source of error; for if from the nature of the circumstances we expect to see any expression, we readily imagine its presence. Notwithstanding Dr. Duchenne's great experience, he for a long time fancied, as he states, that several muscles contracted
30 under certain emotions, whereas he ultimately convinced himself that the movement was confined to a single muscle.
In order to acquire as good a foundation as possible, and to ascertain, independently of common opinion, how far particular movements of the features and gestures are really expressive of certain states
35 of the mind, I have found the following means the most serviceable. In the first place, to observe infants; for they exhibit many emotions, as Sir C. Bell remarks, "with extraordinary force"; whereas, in after life, some of our expressions "cease to have the pure and simple source from which they spring in infancy."[18]

---

*Reading in pieces keeps you **focused**. Reading with **concentration** keeps you aware of what is stated or implied in the passage.*

40   In the second place, it occurred to me that the insane ought to
be studied, as they are liable to the strongest passions, and give
uncontrolled vent to them. I had, myself, no opportunity of doing this,
so I applied to Dr. Maudsley and received from him an introduction
to Dr. J. Crichton Browne, who has charge of an immense asylum

45 near Wakefield, and who, as I found, had already attended to the subject.
This excellent observer has with unwearied kindness sent me copious
notes and descriptions, with valuable suggestions on many points;
and I can hardly over-estimate the value of his assistance. I owe also,
to the kindness of Mr. Patrick Nicol, of the Sussex Lunatic Asylum,

50 interesting statements on two or three points.
    Thirdly Dr. Duchenne galvanized, as we have already seen, certain muscles
in the face of an old man, whose skin was little sensitive, and thus
produced various expressions which were photographed on a large scale.
It fortunately occurred to me to show several of the best plates,

55 without a word of explanation, to above twenty educated persons
of various ages and both sexes, asking them, in each case,
by what emotion or feeling the old man was supposed to be agitated;
and I recorded their answers in the words which they used.
Several of the expressions were instantly recognized by almost everyone,

60 though described in not exactly the same terms; and these may,
I think, be relied on as truthful, and will hereafter be specified.
On the other hand, the most widely different judgments were pronounced
in regard to some of them. This exhibition was of use in another way,
by convincing me how easily we may be misguided by our imagination;

65 for when I first looked through Dr. Duchenne's photographs,
reading at the same time the text, and thus learning what was intended,
I was struck with admiration at the truthfulness of all, with only
a few exceptions. Nevertheless, if I had examined them without
any explanation, no doubt I should have been as much perplexed,

70 in some cases, as other persons have been.

Divide and Conquer

"Divide and conquer" is another name for long-passage reading strategy 1: reading in pieces. *Ask.com* defines divide and conquer as a political-military strategy of "gaining and maintaining power by breaking up larger concentrations of power into chunks that individually have less power than the one implementing the strategy. The concept refers to a strategy that breaks up existing power structures and prevents smaller power groups from linking up."

Apply the divide and conquer premise to long critical reading passages and paired long passages by "chopping up" the reading passages into paragraphs. Read one paragraph at a time; then "jump out" of the passage to answer questions that correspond to that paragraph. Unlike the ACT, whose reading comprehension questions tend to come from random parts of the passage, the SAT usually presents questions in the order of the material presented, making the divide and conquer technique particularly effective.

Sip, Don't Slurp

Now you have seen two ways of reading a long passage *in pieces*. Do you see how the "pieces" method can help you to feel in better control of a lengthy passage? The 2400 Club knows the value of "sip, don't slurp" when it comes to digesting the passage. There's really no advantage to reading a long passage in one big, gurgling gulp.

"Sip, don't slurp" brings to mind another point. Sip carefully the parts of the passage that you mark with sidebars or line references (see page 47), for you are guaranteed to have questions that pertain to these parts. Just because a portion of the passage has no sidebars or line references, however, doesn't mean you should skip over it.

Skim, Don't Skip

As mentioned above, there will always be portions of the passage that do not contain either sidebars or line references. These "unmarked" portions can be as small as a few lines or as large as a few paragraphs. No matter the case, skim, don't skip. The fact that these parts are not referenced doesn't mean you shouldn't read them. You don't need to scrutinize them painstakingly, but you should skim them, or "speed read" through these unmarked portions. Remember: you need to understand overarching aspects of the passage such as main idea, author's tone, and author's purpose in order to answer global questions (see Strategy 7).

 Skimming parts of the passage is a time saver, but you have to be wise about when to skim and when to really focus.

Be Savvy About Sidebars (Refer to page 47)

- <u>When sidebars are short</u> (3 lines or fewer) You should scrutinize the lines; the passage evidence is likely to be subtle.
- <u>When sidebars are long</u> (4 lines or more) You should skim the lines to find the validating information that you need in order to select the right answer.
- <u>When sidebars are nonexistent</u> You should skim these parts; don't skip them altogether!

The Italicized Blurb—Know the Author/Know the Topic

Make sure the first "piece" that you read either is the italicized blurb or contains the blurb that introduces the passage. As Strategy 2 tells you (page 46), the blurb is one place that is likely to contain the main idea of the passage. There's another reason, though, why the blurb is important and should not be overlooked: more often than not, it names the author of the passage. This tidbit of information can be helpful when answering certain questions. Also, knowing the author helps to develop a point of view as you read. Therefore, as you read the italicized blurb, ask yourself, "Who is the author?" For authors who have written passages in the College Board practice book, you might ask: Is this author

- a physicist or a botanist?
- a German composer or a Korean-American poet?
- a Colonial American dramatist or a Columbian novelist?
- a doctor specializing in neurological disorders?
- a scholar of African-American culture?
- a critic of modern architecture or a historian?

Knowing the author establishes a mind-set and focus, and gives you a valuable edge as you embark on the passage reading.

> **2400 Club Coaching:**
> *Extract important information from the italicized blurb that precedes each long reading passage. Pertinent information includes "Who's the author?" and "What's the topic?"*

Outline Reading Approach

If you work sluggishly through the sentence completions and the paragraph-based reading, you may find yourself short of time for the long-passage reading. Fortunately, as you learn more high-frequency and high-end vocabulary words, and as you become more savvy with test-taking strategies, you will undoubtedly increase your speed on the sentence completions and paragraphs, freeing up time for the long passages.

If, however, timing is a persistent concern, try Outline Reading. If you have self-tested and timed yourself several times, and still can't get through the long passages (even if taken piece by piece), try this middle-ground approach.

Checklist: Outline Reading in Greater Detail

(Remember: The Outline Reading approach applies to long-passage reading and paired long-passage reading.)

- Before reading the passage, refrain from doing the following:
  Do not read the questions first. Time sapper.
  Do not attempt to memorize the questions before reading the passage. Time sapper.
  Do not read or skim the sets of five answer choices first. Also a time sapper.
  Do not attempt to remember a series of seven to twelve reading questions. *Big time sapper.*
- Skim the questions for numbers (numbers pop!) and quickly mark the passage with line references and sidebars accordingly.
- Skim the introductory, italicized material. Underline the main focus of the passage(s).
- Carefully and actively (*read + react + interact + visualize*) read the introductory paragraph. If this paragraph is unusually short, read the next paragraph as well for good measure. It is particularly important to absorb the ideas expressed in opening paragraphs.
- Read the first two sentences (topic sentence and one more for good measure) of each body paragraph. Skim or skip (depending on your pacing as a test taker) the rest of each body paragraph. If you have not marked a particular body paragraph with line references and sidebars, you may be able to skip it. Give it a try!

- Trust your judgment. Read short body paragraphs ("bite-size" paragraphs) in their entirety. Read long paragraphs with this time-saving approach: read the first two sentences, skim the middle, read the last sentence.
- Carefully and actively read the concluding paragraph.
- It is prudent to revisit the passage for most questions: reread generously around line references, reread sidebars, and skim pertinent parts of the passage . . . as you hunt for context clues and textual evidence.

Try Outline Reading to see if it works for you.

Outline Reading is effective because this method provides you with an overall sense of the passage and a framework for how the information is laid out. Below is an example of how outline reading works. The bold parts are the parts that you should read with focus and concentration. The nonbold parts you can read in a more hasty, superficial fashion, *slowing down wherever there are sidebars or line references.* Remember: you should *still* be reading piece by piece (a paragraph or two at a time, for example) and answering related questions after reading each piece.

This passage is taken from Charles Darwin's writings
The Expression of the Emotions in Man and Animals.

*Carefully read the **italic blurb** that appears at the top of the passage, and attentively read the **introductory paragraph**.*

No doubt as long as man and all other animals are viewed as independent creations, an effectual stop is put to our natural desire to investigate as far as possible the causes of Expression. By this doctrine, anything and everything can

Line
5 **be equally well explained; and it has proved as pernicious with respect to Expression as to every other branch of natural history. With mankind some expressions, such as the bristling of the hair under the influence of extreme terror, or the uncovering of the teeth under that of furious rage, can hardly be understood, except on the belief**

10 **that man once existed in a much lower and animal-like condition. The community of certain expressions in distinct though allied species, as in the movements of the same facial muscles during laughter by man and by various monkeys, is rendered somewhat more intelligible, if we believe in their descent from a common progenitor.**

15 **He who admits on general grounds that the structure and habits of all animals have been gradually evolved, will look at the whole subject of Expression in a new and interesting light.**

The study of Expression is difficult, owing to the movements being often extremely slight, and of a fleeting nature.
20 A difference may be clearly perceived, and yet it may be impossible, at least I have found it so, to state in what the difference consists. When we witness any deep emotion, our sympathy is so strongly excited, that close observation is forgotten or rendered almost impossible; of which fact I have had many curious proofs.
25 Our imagination is another and still more serious source of error; for if from the nature of the circumstances we expect to see any expression, we readily imagine its presence. **Notwithstanding Dr. Duchenne's great experience, he for a long time fancied, as he states, that several muscles contracted**
30 **under certain emotions, whereas he ultimately convinced himself that the movement was confined to a single muscle.**

Peruse the topic sentence of every body paragraph.

Read the last sentence of particularly long body paragraphs.

In order to acquire as good a foundation as possible, and to ascertain, independently of common opinion, how far particular movements of the features and gestures are really expressive of certain states
35 **of the mind, I have found the following means the most serviceable.** In the first place, to observe infants; for they exhibit many emotions, as Sir C. Bell remarks, "with extraordinary force"; whereas, in after life, some of our expressions "cease to have the pure and simple source from which they spring in infancy."[18]

Read the topic sentence of every body paragraph.

40 **In the second place, it occurred to me that the insane ought to be studied, as they are liable to the strongest passions, and give uncontrolled vent to them.** I had, myself, no opportunity of doing this, so I applied to Dr. Maudsley and received from him an introduction to Dr. J. Crichton Browne, who has charge of an immense asylum
45 near Wakefield, and who, as I found, had already attended to the subject. This excellent observer has with unwearied kindness sent me copious notes and descriptions, with valuable suggestions on many points; and I can hardly over-estimate the value of his assistance. I owe also, to the kindness of Mr. Patrick Nicol, of the Sussex Lunatic Asylum,
50 interesting statements on two or three points.

Read the topic sentence of every body paragraph.

Thirdly Dr. Duchenne galvanized, as we have already seen, certain muscles in the face of an old man, whose skin was little sensitive, and thus produced various expressions which were photographed on a large scale. It fortunately occurred to me to show several of the
55 **best plates, without a word of explanation, to above twenty educated persons of various ages and both sexes, asking them, in each case, by what emotion or feeling the old man was supposed to be agitated; and I recorded their answers in the words which they used. Several of the expressions were instantly recognized by almost everyone,**

Attentively read the concluding paragraph in full.

60 though described in not exactly the same terms; and these may,
I think, be relied on as truthful, and will hereafter be specified.
On the other hand, the most widely different judgments were pronounced
in regard to some of them. This exhibition was of use in another way,
by convincing me how easily we may be misguided by our imagination;
65 for when I first looked through Dr. Duchenne's photographs,
reading at the same time the text, and thus learning what was intended,
I was struck with admiration at the truthfulness of all, with only
a few exceptions. Nevertheless, if I had examined them without
any explanation, no doubt I should have been as much perplexed,
70 in some cases, as other persons have been.

Long and dry critical reading passages can be daunting and confusing, even for AP English or AP European History students. If you are a voracious and avid reader, you may be inclined to read the passage in halves or thirds—or even to read the entire thing in a single gulp. Determining what a "piece" of the passage means is a matter of personal style and preference. Experiment to discover what works best for you as you navigate the reading passage.

STRATEGY 2: EXTRACT THE MAIN IDEA FROM THE PASSAGE

Read with your eye peeled for the main idea. Cultivate this habit as you practice reading long passages. Knowing the main idea is very helpful in answering questions involving the author's main purpose, the best title for the passage, and the author's point of view. Having a handle on the main idea is also helpful when it comes to answering a "mouthful" of a question such as this: "With which of the following statements would the author most likely agree/disagree?"

2400 Club Coaching: *Maintain a focused rhythm of concentration as you work through the SAT. Train yourself to block out distractions.*

 Know where to find the main idea.

More often than not, you can find the main idea in one *or more* of these three places:

1. The italicized blurb (introductory material that precedes the passage)
2. The thesis (usually the last line of the first paragraph)
3. Somewhere in the concluding paragraph (usually at the end)

Outline reading should have familiarized you with these three imperative areas of the passage.

Once you feel you have hit on the main idea of the passage, use your pencil to underline it or jot a bold asterisk (*) nearby in the margin. Your pencil markings will help you later when you must answer a main idea, primary purpose, or any type of "global" question (question that pertains to the whole passage) later on.

STRATEGY 3: ANSWER LINE-REFERENCE AND SIDEBAR QUESTIONS FIRST

Let's review our critical reading process so far:

Strategy 1 told you that you're not going to read the entire, long passage in one big chunk. You read in "pieces." Thank goodness!

Strategy 2 told you the three places where you are most likely to find the main idea.

Now, **Strategy 3** is very important: *Before you begin reading the passage piece by piece*, you should skim the questions for *line numbers* and mark the text accordingly. Numbers within questions signal that you are going to be asked about a specific area of the text. According to the line numbers given in the questions, you should mark the passage with "sidebars" and "line references." When you do practice tests, mark the passage in this manner. Once you get the hang of this strategy, it takes only a small amount of time and will save you time later as you refer to the passage to find the evidence that supports the best answer.

2400 Club Coaching: *Contrary to popular opinion, while there's little value to **reading** the questions beforehand, there's great value to **skimming** the questions ahead of time to locate line references and **marking** the passage accordingly.*

The passage below illustrates two ***line references*** (lines 4 and 13), and a ***sidebar*** that spans lines 10–14. These line references and sidebars correlate with questions that are asked, based on the Darwin reading passage (reproduced below), such as the following: In line 4, "this doctrine" most closely refers to. As a general rule, line references are rather brief: a word, a phrase, or just a line or two of text. Sidebars are longer, usually spanning three lines or more. Keep sidebars simple; a roughly drawn vertical line is all that is required. This is how text marked with sidebars and line references might look:

No doubt as long as man and all other animals are viewed
as independent creations, an effectual stop is put to our
natural desire to investigate as far as possible the causes
of Expression. By <u>this doctrine</u>, anything and everything can
line reference
Line
5   be equally well explained; and it has proved as pernicious with
respect to Expression as to every other branch of natural history.
With mankind some expressions, such as the bristling of the hair under
the influence of extreme terror, or the uncovering of the teeth under
that of furious rage, can hardly be understood, except on the belief
10   that man once existed in a much lower and animal-like condition.
The community of certain expressions in distinct though allied species,
sidebar   as in the movements of the same facial muscles during laughter by man
and by various monkeys, is rendered somewhat more <u>intelligible</u>,
line reference
if we believe in their descent from a common progenitor.
15   He who admits on general grounds that the structure and habits
of all animals have been gradually evolved, will look at the whole
subject of Expression in a new and interesting light.

2400 Club Coaching: *The correct answer to a hard **words-in-context** question is often the word's lesser known secondary or tertiary meaning.*

Do you ever wonder how carefully you should read the passages?

This isn't driver's education, but think of your text markings as "road signs" and let them guide you as you read. You can read the parts of the passage *without* sidebars and line references in a more cursory or superficial fashion. (See Outline Reading, pages 43–46.)

The sidebars and line references with which you have marked the passage are road signs that tell you precisely where to slow down and pay close attention because you know there will be questions relating to those areas of the text. Your text markings (sidebars and line references) will guide you in creating a rhythm as you read through the passage.

In the example above, lines 10–14 are particularly important; there will be not only a question pertinent to those five lines as a unit, but also a question about the word *intelligible,* which appears in line 13. Remember: you must consider the line references within their context: "5 lines up and 5 lines down" is a good rule of thumb to follow. If no context clue can be found and no light is shed on the question by using "5 lines up and 5 lines down," consider a broader context, "6 lines up and 6 lines down" or "7 lines up and 7 lines down," until you find passage evidence that validates an answer choice.

Words-in-Context Questions

Hard words-in-context questions can be very challenging. They may appear straightforward, but analysis of model tests shows that words-in-context questions are often ranked as *hard.* On hard questions, the "regular meaning" of the word that comes most readily to mind is most likely *not* the correct answer. More often, the meaning of the word *in context* is its lesser used meaning, even its secondary or tertiary meaning (for example, "pretender" for one who claims a throne; "charged" for inspired; "classic" for well known; "halting" for limping; "credit" for believe; and "crush" for a crowd of people). The preceding examples were all taken from practice SATs published by the College Board.

Word meanings rely heavily on context; it's worthless to answer a word-in-context question without going back to the passage to read at *and around* that line.

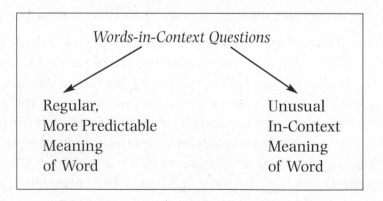

Words-in-Context Questions

Regular,
More Predictable
Meaning
of Word

Unusual
In-Context
Meaning
of Word

Sharpening Skills—Words in Context

Picture some hypothetical passage (bet you've never been asked to do that before). Suppose that you are asked the meaning of "happy" as used in line 52. You should read the word within a sizable context. (Remember: "5 lines up, 5 lines down" is a good rule of thumb.) At the very least, you should start by reading lines 50–54. You see how the word is used: "a *happy* circumstance." Now look at the answer choices:

(A) spontaneous (B) joyful (C) unexpected (D) lucky
(E) celebrated

If you hadn't read the word in the context of the passage, you would probably pick one of the "regular" meanings, such as *joyful* or even *celebrated*. But if the context of the passage reveals that the circumstances arose from sheer good fortune, then the answer is (D), *lucky*.

Answer the more straightforward, line-reference questions first. Then answer the higher-order inference questions that typically take more time.

No matter its difficulty level, each correctly answered question earns you a point.

Sharpening Skills—Secondary and Tertiary Meanings of Words

The College Board sometimes features unlikely or lesser-known definitions of words. This can make sentence completion and critical reading questions particularly tricky and hard. For example, "consequences" may be positive (+) or negative (–) in connotation, depending on context. Although many of us have a negative association for the term "consequences," in the following answer choice, the context of the paragraph reveals that these "consequences" were *positive* in nature and effect: (E) Harriet's bold redesign had far-reaching *consequences*.

Correct Answer	What Test Takers Might Think the Word Means	What the Word Means Within Context of the Passage*	Question Difficulty
conviction	being charged with a crime; jail sentence	strongly held personal belief	hard
crush	pulverize; orange soda; boy-girl affection	crowd of people Context Clue: "mob"	hard
discriminating	prejudice	selective	hard
halt	stop	to stop and start Context Clue: "limping gait" Note: gait is a manner of walking.	hard
hail	rain down balls of ice; praise	welcome	hard
treacherous	dangerous	disloyal	hard

*Examples in this chart are from questions appearing on actual SATs.

Sharpening Skills—Pay Attention to Prefixes

Noticing and underlining prefixes is important, no matter what type of question you are answering. Whether you are working on a line-reference question, a sidebar question, or a words-in-context question, avoid careless errors by underlining prefixes within the reading comprehension questions *and* answer choices. This simple pen-to-paper strategy will clarify meaning so you can answer questions more accurately by avoiding careless errors.

If an answer choice contains the word *inflexible*, students, in haste, often misread it as *flexible* and therefore erroneously (wrongly, inaccurately) pick that choice. Consider the question and answer choice that follow.

In both passages, the author suggests that the mannerisms of "those at war" (line 59) were greatly influenced by

(C) the agency's <u>in</u>adequate control over the radio media

In answer choice C, the prefix *in-* is the two-letter disqualifier! The prefix makes the entire answer choice incorrect. Now that's tricky!

To avoid careless comprehension errors, use your Active Pencil to underline prefixes as in the words below.

<u>dis</u>agree
<u>im</u>material
<u>in</u>accuracy
<u>in</u>consequential
<u>in</u>flexible
<u>mis</u>interpret
<u>un</u>orthodox

STRATEGY 4: DELVE INTO HIGHER-ORDER THINKING QUESTIONS

Pace yourself by answering higher-order thinking questions (time-sapping doozies) *after* you have answered the "directed" questions for which you have marked sidebars and line references. Higher-order questions can be recognized by their use of words and phrases such as *infer, suggests, implies, it can be concluded that, it seems that, most closely means*.

Once you've done your outline reading and have answered the more straightforward line-reference questions, you are ready to tackle these harder questions. Always embed these questions in a broad context so that you get a fuller sense of the author's message and point of view. For example, if a test question asks what you can infer from the phrase "loftier yet understated" in line 34, you should read broadly around this phrase. On a harder question like this one, you should read *at least* from about line 29 to line 39 to get a solid sense of the phrase in its context.

Inference questions require higher-order thinking skills, a sort of synthesis between what is stated and what you can glean as insight. Inference demands a sort of reading between the lines, a mining for something that's beneath surface-level information. Challenge yourself to go below the words and into the "subtext." Inference questions require you to draw conclusions by reasoning beyond given facts.

Skipping Hard Questions Responsibly

If you find that you're spending too much time grappling with an inference question, skip it for the time being. Try the global questions first, and return to the tough ones later.

 The 2400 Club knows not to spend too much time grappling with any one question. It also knows how to temporarily skip and later return to questions responsibly.

Skipping questions sounds carefree, like skipping rope when you were a child. Feeling nostalgic? In fact, skipping questions comes with two responsibilities:

1. Remember to return to the question. Boldly circle the entire question in your test booklet, providing yourself with a conspicuous reminder that this question is being saved for later.

2. Remember to pay attention to how you grid in the bubble sheet. This may sound like a petty caveat, but many unfortunate students have skipped a question here or there, forgotten to skip the corresponding line of "bubbles" on the answer sheet, filled in the wrong ovals, and ended up with a bubbling-in debacle that had them erasing furiously and wasting precious time!

> **Skipping Questions:** *The 2400 Club knows how to skip questions responsibly, without ending up in a quagmire.*

Yes, skipping this or that question and saving it for later sounds innocuous, but beware! The 2400 Club takes skipping seriously and knows how to handle it without incurring a bubble-sheet nightmare.

STRATEGY 5: IDENTIFY THE AUTHOR'S MOOD AND TONE AS YOU READ

- You're a sensitive reader, and you get that the author wishes he were a kid again, but do you get that he is creating a mood that is *nostalgic* or *reminiscent?*
- You're a sharp reader, and you get that the author, a competitive scientist, is belittling his contemporaries, but do you get that his tone is *deprecatory* or *disparaging?*
- You're an insightful reader, and you get that the author regrets his hurtful actions, but do you get that the mood conveyed is *contrite* or *penitent?*
- You easily pick up on subtle context clues, and you get that the author is angry, but do you get that he is expressing a mood that is *indignant* or *belligerent?*

More often than not, the problem is not that you don't get the author's tone or mood—it's that you may not know the word that describes what you are sensing. Challenge yourself to learn this additional tier of vocabulary. As you read the passages, be aware of expressions of tone and mood so that you'll be prepared to answer related questions. The vocabulary lists given below are rich and varied but by no means exhaustive.

> **Vocabulary Coaching:** *The 2400 Club gets an edge on critical reading questions by becoming familiar with the meanings and subtle distinctions of the vocabularies of tone and mood.*

The Vocabulary of Tone

Admonishing—*warning*

Aloof—*detached*

Apologetic—*being sorry; admitting fault*

Assertive—*strongly stating*

Cautious—*hesitant*

Confrontational—*argumentative*

Contrite—*remorseful*

Cynical—*seeing worst in people*

Defensive—*protecting one's point of view*

Derisive—*ridiculing*

Empathetic—*having feeling for others*

Emphatic—*stressing one's points*

Entreating—*begging, pleading*

Explanatory—*explaining*

Inquisitive—*asking questions*

Nostalgic—*remembering the past*

Penitent—*remorseful*

Reflective—*remembering the past*

Sardonic—*sarcastic*

Scathing—*harsh*

Scholarly—*intellectual, cerebral*

Sensationalistic—*exaggerating emotions*

Skeptical—*doubtful*

Tentative—*hesitant*

Understated—*mildly suggested; unstressed*

Why—*bitter or ironic*

The Vocabulary of Mood

Amusement—*humor*

Bemusement—*puzzlement*

Detachment—*lack of concern*

Disdain—*scorn*

Disparagement—*belittlement*

Indignation—*anger*

Irony—*incongruity*

Mockery—*derision; insincere imitation*

Objectivity—*realism; factualism; having no opinion*

Optimism—*positive thinking*

Pessimism—*negative thinking*

Smugness—*self-satisfaction; complacency*

Top scorers avoid extreme answer choices for tone and mood. In general, authors want to come across as level-headed and reasonable, not as off their rockers. It is highly unlikely for the mood or tone of a passage to be:

☒ scathingly critical   ☒ impenetrably scholarly   ☒ feverishly indignant

☒ downright outraged   ☒ painfully distrustful   ☒ unbearably arrogant

Use your pencil and PET to cross off answer choices that are extreme. By so doing, you will narrow in on the correct answer.

STRATEGY 6: NARROW IN ON THE *BEST* ANSWER CHOICE

Narrow in on the best answer choice by using the good old, tried-and-true process of elimination. First, cross off answer choices that are not supported in any way, shape, or form by the passage. These are "bogus" or "fluff" answer choices that are not confirmed by something, somewhere, that the author says. Also, avoid picking answers just because they *appear* fair, reasonable, true, or intelligent.

Narrowing in on the best answer choice has everything to do with *first* knowing precisely what the question is asking. Use your Active Pencil to underline key words in the question itself. This discipline will keep you focused on what you are supposed to answer.

Once you're clear on what the question is asking, you can see more clearly which answer choices are bogus and which could work.

Sharpening Skills—Key Words

Underline the key word or words in the following questions. The key words should signal precisely what you are supposed to answer.

1. With which of the following statements would the Passage 2 author most likely disagree?
2. The example in the final paragraph serves to illustrate which of the following sentiments?
3. Which of the following personal endeavors most closely contradicts the author's public statements?
4. The form of the author's argument is best described as . . .
5. Which of the following detracts least from the author's perspective on telecommuting?

Key Words—Answers

Some subjectivity and subtlety are involved in underscoring key words. This answer key illustrates possible ways of underlining key words in each question.

1. With which of the following statements would the <u>Passage 2 author</u> most likely <u>disagree</u>?
2. The example in the <u>final paragraph</u> serves to <u>illustrate</u> which of the following <u>sentiments</u>?
3. Which of the following <u>personal</u> endeavors most closely <u>contradicts</u> the author's public statements?
4. The <u>form</u> of the author's argument is best described as . . .
5. Which of the following <u>detracts</u> <u>least</u> from the author's perspective on <u>telecommuting</u>?

High scorers use this acid test: Has the author written something that confirms all aspects of the answer I have chosen? If you can't find the evidence in the passage, then cross off that answer choice—it's bogus.

When reading a critical reading question, high scorers take very seriously the words "According to the author," "The author suggests," and "The author mentions."

They know that they must select an answer that is substantiated, somewhere in the text, by what the author has written. "According to the author," for instance, does not mean any of the following:

2400 Club Coaching: *Take "According to the author" very seriously.*

- According to your personal opinion or perspective
- According to your conjecture
- According to your gut feeling or common sense
- According to your parents, teachers, relatives, coaches, or advisors
- According to your assumptions
- According to your creativity or imagination
- According to your speculation or conjecture (opinion or guess)

> High scorers never accept or select *partially correct* answer choices. Even one word that is not validated somewhere in the passage can discredit an entire answer choice.

If an answer choice is the best, it's *all* right, each and every word of it. Don't settle for partially correct answers. Remember: second-best or partially correct answers do not receive partial credit on the SAT.

As mentioned previously, be sure to winnow out extreme answer choices, which are melodramatic or excessive. For example, it's unlikely that an author's mood would be "downright disgusted" or "superbly elated."

Cross off answers that you know don't work. Don't underestimate PET—the process of elimination, it moves you closer to the right answer and simplifies your task.

Decisive crossing off prevents you from being distracted by unlikely answer choices and keeps you focused on finding the *best* answer choice.

(A) ~~Bogus or fluff answer~~
(B) ~~Bogus or fluff answer~~
(C) Runner-up or second-best answer *
(D) ~~Bogus or fluff answer~~
(E) Best answer!

Remember: no partial credit is given on the SAT. If your answer is incorrect, you lose one fourth of a point.

Once you're down to two answer choices, your cerebral wheels really have to start turning. What do you do now? First, go back to the pertinent part of the passage and seek out context clues that validate one answer over the other. Second, scrutinize the answer choices. If a mere one word is "off" or inaccurate, that answer choice is invalid.

The more you practice finding validating proof in the passage, the more adept you will become at distinguishing the second-best from the best answer. When they're down to two answer choices, 2400 Clubbers never resort to *eeny, meeny, miny, mo.* Neither should you.

Reading Technique: The Rule of Thirds

A unique reading strategy, the Reading Rule of Thirds helps you narrow in on the *best* answer choices instead of picking "false positives," "traps," and "decoys" that diminish your critical reading score. It helps you decide which answers to pick when you are down to two choices. Typically, the majority of test takers can cross off two choices with relative ease, finding themselves down to two or three answer choices. With more skimming and rereading of the pertinent parts of the passage, many test takers are able to then eliminate an additional answer choice.

Now they find themselves "down-to-two," pencil hovering over choice B and choice D . . . vacillating between choice A and choice E . . . debating whether choice D or choice E is best. We all know that uncomfortable position, making us feel uneasy, even a little queasy.

We've done a lot of hard work: we've read the question carefully, we've reread a broad context around the references line(s), and we feel confident about the three choices we have eliminated. Yet, two answer choices remain! Now our wheels start grinding. We're feeling indecisive. They both look good. Which to choose? Rule of Thirds to the rescue!

The Rule of Thirds Is an Active Pencil Technique

Use your Active Pencil to divide your remaining answer choices into *thirds* by making two quick and simple horizontal lines. Next, scrutinize each third to make sure it is completely valid and substantiated (confirmed, verified) by what is stated or implied in the passage.

The College Board test makers are tricky. More often than not, a "decoy" answer choice seems to work quite well. However, this choice is the runner-up and will cost you a fourth of a point on your raw score. The runner-up choice is incorrect, a "false positive," usually because of *one* disqualifying word or phrase. In fact, there are decoy answer choices that are $\frac{4}{5}$ths correct, $\frac{8}{9}$ths correct, $\frac{10}{11}$ths correct, and so on. That's how tricky test questions can be. Reading Rule of Thirds to the rescue!

Consider this question and corresponding answer choice:

The author enumerates (lists) "marketing, product banning, and measures taken against disingenuous (dishonest, deceitful) businesses" in lines 38–40 in order to

(C) Unequivocally verify that recent college graduates altered the procedures of the corporate business world through their actions

Rule of Thirds:

      ✘   ✔
(C) *unequivocally verify* that recent college graduates / altered the procedures of the

                          ✔
corporate business world / through their actions

"Unequivocally verify" is the disqualifying phrase. It is too strong and definitive of a verbal phrase, based on passage evidence. The passage does not *unequivocally (undoubtedly, absolutely) verify (prove, confirm)* that the graduates changed corporate America.

Rule of Thirds Backward:

            ✔   ✔
(A) through their actions . . . altered the procedures of the corporate business world . . .

    ✘
unequivocally verify that recent college graduates

Time Saver: When critical reading questions start with *Which of the following, if true,* or *Which of the following, if available,* you can assume that the choices are "given" as true or available. Knowing this obliterates (eliminates) the time that you might otherwise take trying to determine which choices are true or available.

Consider this sample hard question in which key words and potentially hard words are italicized:

Which of the following, if *true*, would *debunk* (contradict) the *legitimacy* (soundness, authority) of the author's assumption about the effect of technological innovations *enumerated* (listed, itemized) in lines 73–82?

Rule of Thirds:

(E) The townspeople had always / regarded new technology as threatening / and potentially damaging to human relationships.

In this case, the Rule of Thirds helps us to focus on and validate each and every third of the answer choice. Use your Active Pencil to put a check mark (✔) above each third for which you find support in the passage.

Rule of Thirds Backward:

(E) and potentially damaging to human relationships . . . regarded new technology as threatening . . . The townspeople had always

READ ANSWER CHOICES BACKWARD To help you focus on each and every word within the answer choice, read the answer choices backward. Read backward in segments or in groups of phrases like this:

Reading backward, choice (A) *was annoyed that she permitted Willa to infuriate him in public*, becomes:

(A) *in public . . . to infuriate him . . . she permitted Willa . . . was annoyed that*

Reading backward forces you to closely consider and scrutinize all the parts of the answer choice. With close examination, "public" is revealed as the single disqualifying word that makes this choice incorrect. That's tricky! When we revisit the passage's introductory material, we find that it says, "During a family barbeque . . .," which may likely be held at home and, therefore, not necessarily in *public*.

Though this technique might at first seem odd, it works. This technique forces you to read and consider each and every word. Try reading the answer choices backward to see if this unique strategy works for you. Of course, reading backward is always followed by reading the answer choice forward.

STRATEGY 7: GLOBAL QUESTIONS SHOULD BE ANSWERED AT THE VERY END

Global questions are those that focus on the overarching ideas of the passage. In other words, they are based on the whole passage. You should save these questions until the end, after you have digested the passage as a whole. Be aware that global questions may appear anywhere in the lineup of critical reading questions. Even if the very first question is global—and often it is—you should save it until the end.

Global questions are predictable, so you should always keep them in mind when you read a passage. There's no need to peruse the critical reading questions ahead of time. Usually, the questions fall into two categories: line reference/sidebar and global.

Examples of Global Questions

■ Based on what is stated in the passage, the author's main purpose is . . .

■ Which of the following provides the best title?

■ The author's attitude toward the individual discussed is primarily one of . . .

■ The author's overall tone is best described as . . .

■ Based on what is expressed in the passage, the author would most likely agree/disagree with which of the following statements?

■ The mood conveyed by the author is primarily one of . . .

■ Which of the following statements, if true, would most strongly undermine the author's point of view?

Remember Those Globals!!

Even the brightest students sometimes *forget* to answer the global, overarching questions on the SAT. Here's why: the test taker encounters a global question in the very first question on the passage. She then sees another global shortly after the first one. She knows that she should save them until the end, so she skips them, planning to return to them at a later time. But after answering all of the remaining questions, she simply forgets about those two globals! (Of course, since our test taker is very bright, she most likely would have answered the questions correctly.)

As the adage says, out of sight, out of mind.

How can you remember those global questions? Suppose you discover that questions 1 and 4 are global. Here's how to remember to return to them: at the very end of the series of questions, write 1 and 4 to remind yourself. This basic strategy can preclude your sacrificing points because of overlooking a few questions.

Also, boldly circle the global questions right on your test booklet. Do not simply circle the question *number*; boldly and broadly circle the entire question, including the five answer choices. This sweeping circle will provide you with a conspicuous reminder to return to those questions when you're ready.

Use your pencil to boldly circle questions to which you want to return later. In the critical reading sections, for example, circle global questions, which are based on the reading passage as a *whole*. In math sections, circle hard questions on which you need more thought. Your circles should be bold, dark, and sweeping. Bold circles are conspicuous (in your face!); you are unlikely to miss them and to forget to go back to those questions!

Paired-Passage and Global Questions

On paired-passage reading, two passages are juxtaposed for the sake of comparison and contrast. Your task is to read each one and get a sense of their differences and similarities. To answer global questions about double passages, you should ask yourself these questions as you read through the second passage:

- Are the passages more similar to, or more different from, each other?
- Do the authors see eye to eye on the issue at hand?
- Are the authors supporting or undermining each other?
- Do the authors have similar tones or moods, or are they quite different?

You're an insightful reader. Often you can begin to answer these questions after reading the first paragraph or two of Passage 2.

ADDITIONAL STRATEGIES FOR READING LONG PASSAGES

To Read or Not to Read the Questions First—That Is the Perennial Decision

When it comes to critical reading, whether or not to read the questions first is truly a matter of preference. Try both ways to see which works best for you. For many test takers, reading the questions before the passage is a waste of time. You will have to read the questions carefully later anyway.

As step 3 of the READING acronym indicates, you should skim the questions for line-number references. Numerals stand out, so they are easy to spot without actually reading the question. Skimming for numbers and marking the text can be done very quickly and really helps you as you read, since you have a "road map" of the parts on which questions are based. Marking the text for ten questions usually takes only 25–35 seconds. Try it and see for yourself.

As for the rest of the questions, test designers do not typically reinvent the wheel when it comes to the types of questions they ask. For this reason, beyond skimming for line numbers, scrutinizing the remaining questions is not practical. Instead, acquaint yourself with and anticipate frequently asked question types as you read. In this way, you'll be more prepared and better able to answer them quickly and easily. Frequently asked questions include:

- Author's mood, tone, or attitude?
- Primary purpose of passage?
- Best title?
- Form and structure of passage?
- Words–in–context questions?
- Statement with which the author would be most likely to agree or disagree?

Read and Heed Key Words in the Questions and Answer Choices

Traditional key words include: *all, except, least, most, not, never, often, rarely, usually*. Both traditional and more subtle key words are underlined in the examples that follow. Some examples illustrate pivotal words in the question only; others illustrate key words in the question *as well as* in the correct answer. Medium and hard refer to the question's level of difficulty. Revealingly, none of the questions below are easy in difficulty. Keep your eyes peeled for and underline key words in questions and answer choices. Examples illustrate hard question formats.

HARD QUESTION STRUCTURE: The author of Passage 2 would probably agree with which of the following assertions about the explanation of *The Lost Horizon* offered in Passage 1 ?

ANSWER: It is not representative of the way *The Lost Horizon* is typically discussed in English classrooms.

HARD QUESTION STRUCTURE: Which of the following, if true, would most directly disprove what "Astronomers initially conjectured" (line 22)?

ANSWER: People do not tend to speculate about extraterrestrial life when they look up into the skies at night, marveling at the constellations and shifting light. (The negating adjective *not* makes all the difference. Underline key words.)

HARD QUESTION FORMAT: Which of the following, if available, would most effectively undermine the "underlying premise" (line 69)?

HARD QUESTION FORMAT: The example in lines 14–17 primarily suggests that . . .

ANSWER: Palmer's insights into natural disposition were not apparent in his daily life. (Once again, the correct answer contains the key word *not*.)

HARD QUESTION STRUCTURE: Which of the following, if true, would undermine the veracity of the author's assumption about the consequences of urbanization discussed in lines 45–57? (*Undermine* often appears within reading comprehension questions and answer choices. It means to weaken, sap the energy of; also, to contradict, belie.)

ANSWER: Residents have always considered industry and urbanization as desirable. (Use your Active Pencil to underline the key word in the correct answer choice: *always*.)

HARD QUESTION FORMAT: In line 62, the phrase "distressing pleasure" suggests that Yolanda's enjoyment is tempered by . . . (Key word, *tempered*, means lessened, alleviated the severity of.)

HARD QUESTION STRUCTURE: Which of the following situations, if true, would be most analogous to the dilemma presented in the passage?

No Line References, So Not a Global Question! What Now?

If you are asked about something specific in the passage and no line reference is given, skim the question for a key term that centers in on what information the question is seeking. Whenever possible, let the key term be a proper noun since proper nouns are capitalized and therefore easier to find in the passage. Skimming the passage for dates, whenever relevant, is a good idea too since numbers also stand out. Once you've found your key term, read around it to find the context clue that points to the best answer choice.

 When a question does not provide line references, astute students skim the question for key terms, underline them, and then hunt them down in the passage.

To illustrate this time saver, key terms are underscored in the following questions:

1. Which of the following was the most significant aspect of <u>Mendel's</u> research on peas and inherited traits? (Skim passage for <u>Mendel</u>.)

2. In which two ways are <u>minerals</u> different from the other elements that are mentioned? (Skim passage for <u>minerals</u>.)

3. When the family emigrated from <u>Poland</u> in <u>1732</u>, which emotion was predominant among the three siblings? (Skim for both <u>Poland</u> and <u>1732</u>.)

You now have a disciplined, step-by-step, and thorough method to follow for critical reading at the passage level. Now that you know what to do, let's iron out what you *should not* do in terms of "smart" answering on the critical reading sections.

Critical Reading No-No's

- **No** guesswork*
- **No** answering based on your outside reading or knowledge
- **No** answering based on your opinions or beliefs
- **No** "reading into" the passage, or reading beyond what the author is actually saying
- **No** selecting answers just because you think they're probably true
- **No** selecting answers just because they appear reasonable
- **No** random guessing, without first trying hard to eliminate as many answer choices as you can (applies to all sections)

*A note about guesswork: Even when you've narrowed down the answer choices to two—(B) or (D), let's say—you still should not guess. Instead, the high scorer returns to the pertinent part(s) of the passage and rereads for context clues and other evidence that validate one answer, (B) or (D), over the other.

The bottom line for 2400 Club critical reading: Select only answers that are substantiated by words, phrases, or sentences in the italicized blurb or the passage. In other words, an answer choice must be based on passage evidence only! As previously pointed out, sometimes context clues are several lines away (either up ↑ or down ↓) from the line referenced by a question. Likewise, sometimes passage evidence and clues are outside the sidebar indicated by the question. For example, if the sidebar indicates lines 34–37, the context clue that confirms the correct answer could appear in lines 30 and 31 or lines 39 and 40.

Debunking the Myth: Vocabulary Just Doesn't Matter That Much Anymore to Rank on the SAT

"PHEW!! NOW THAT ANALOGIES ARE OUT OF THE PICTURE, SO IS VOCABULARY!" an uninformed, high school sophomore cries out in delight.

"YES!! LET'S TOSS THESE DOG-EARED FLASH CARDS. THERE'S NO NEED FOR THEM NOW THAT ANALOGIES ARE HISTORY!" exclaims another deluded, future SAT taker.

Though very happy, these students just don't understand the role of vocabulary on the SAT. Do you?

Try out the self-tests that follow. Ready for an eye-opener?

Self-Test 1

How many of the following words can you readily and accurately define?

vituperative	pernicious	ubiquitous	erudition
impetuosity	portent	respite	laudatory
obsequious	vilified	censorious	prose
dilatory	duplicitous	sallow	verdant
doggerel	exculpated	variegated	sonorous

How did you do? If you struggle with these words but say to yourself consolingly, "No biggie—don't have to worry about vocabulary since analogies will no longer be on the SAT," you're making a big mistake.

The scoop on the sampling above: *All of these words appeared in sentence-completion questions on the actual May 2004 SAT I.* The elimination of analogies on the SAT does not mean you're out of the woods when it comes to amassing an upper-level, college-bound vocabulary.

Self-Test 2

Ready for another group of zingers? How many of the words in the sampling below do you know? Also, how many of them can you confidently and correctly use in sentences?

plume	calibrated	olfactory	fanfare
despondent	efficaciously	occluded	balm
conjuror	heed	coherent	scant

Again, how did you do? If you struggled with these words but cling to your mantra, "No biggie—don't have to worry about vocabulary since analogies will no longer be on the SAT," you're just kidding yourself.

The scoop on the sampling above: *All of these words appeared in critical reading passages on the May 2004 SAT I.* Remember: just because analogies have been scrapped, you are *not* in the clear when it comes to acquiring a challenging vocabulary. Even the strongest readers find obstacles in the form of unknown words as they work through critical reading passages.

Self-Test 3

For how many of the words below can you easily and accurately rattle off definitions or familiar phrases?

insinuate	conform	pathological	unorthodox
indifference	elicit	nostalgia	objectivity
elusive	underscore	alludes	giddy
subsequent	anecdote	entails	ambivalence
rigor	complement	amateur	diverting
flux	compartmentalize	illusory	provincial
notion	mystical	skepticism	bemusement

The words above appeared in a long critical reading passage on an actual SAT.

SUMMARY: HIGH SCORER'S STRATEGY ACRONYM

■ Has anyone ever told you that your "learning style" is predominantly visual?

■ Do you have a photographic memory?

■ Have acrostics or acronyms helped you to remember processes or information in the past?

■ When you learn, do you find yourself drawn to diagrams, charts, and other visual cues?

If so, then consider the seven strategies listed below for critical reading as spelling the word "READING." Here is the high scorer's acronym:

R	**ead** longer passages piece by piece.
E	**xtract** the main idea from the passage.
A	**nswer** line-reference questions first.
D	**elve** into higher-order-thinking questions last.
I	**dentify** the author's mood, tone, and point of view as you read.
N	**arrow** in on the *best* answer choice.
G	**lobal** questions should be answered at the very end.

If you're a visual learner, on test day one or more of the boldfaced words listed will pop into your mind, prompting you to remember a strategy approach for reading and answering questions on long passages.

PRACTICE TEST QUESTIONS

Note: The directions in this book are not verbatim repetitions of directions on actual College Board tests, but these directions tell you what you need to know.

Passage 1

> **Directions:** Read the passage below, and then answer the questions that follow. The correct response may be stated outright or merely suggested in the passage.

The following is an excerpt from American author F. Scott Fitzgerald's 1922 novel The Beautiful and Damned.

At eleven he had a horror of death. Within six impressionable years his parents had died and his grandmother had faded off almost imperceptibly, until, for the first time since her marriage, her person held for one day an unquestioned supremacy over her own drawing room. So to Anthony life
Line
5   was a struggle against death that waited at every corner. It was as a concession to his hypochondriac imagination that he formed the habit of reading in bed—it soothed him. He read until he was tired and often fell asleep with the lights still on.

His favorite diversion until he was fourteen was his stamp collection;
10 enormous, as nearly exhaustive as a boy's could be—his grandfather considered fatuously that it was teaching him geography. So Anthony kept up a correspondence with a half dozen "Stamp and Coin" companies and it was rare that the mail failed to bring him new stamp-books or packages of glittering approval sheets—there was a mysterious fascination in transfer-
15 ring his acquisitions interminably from one book to another. His stamps were his greatest happiness and he bestowed impatient frowns on any one who interrupted him at play with them; they devoured his allowance every month, and he lay awake at night musing untiringly on their variety and many-colored splendor.

20 At sixteen he had lived almost entirely within himself, an inarticulate boy, thoroughly un-American, and politely bewildered by his contemporaries. The two preceding years had been spent in Europe with a private tutor, who persuaded him that Harvard was the thing; it would "open doors," it would be a tremendous tonic, it would give him innumerable
25 self-sacrificing and devoted friends. So he went to Harvard—there was no other logical thing to be done with him.

1. It can be inferred from lines 2–4 that Anthony's grandmother

   (A) was not much into housekeeping
   (B) haunted her grandson unmercifully
   (C) was directly responsible for her grandson's hypochondria
   (D) became a mother figure to Anthony
   (E) played a submissive role during her married life

2. The form and structure of this passage are best described as

   (A) scattered flashbacks
   (B) present to past chronology
   (C) chronological biography
   (D) concrete examples followed by general statements
   (E) simultaneously reflective and visionary

3. In line 10, "exhaustive" most nearly means

   (A) tiring
   (B) irritating
   (C) fatiguing
   (D) extensive
   (E) comprehending

4. Which best describes Anthony's attitude toward those who disrupt him while he is engaged in activities related to his stamp collecting (lines 16 and 17)?

   (A) solicitous
   (B) contemptuous
   (C) nonchalant
   (D) aloof
   (E) sullen

Passage 2

> **Directions:** Read the passage below, and then answer the questions that follow. The correct response may be stated outright or merely suggested in the passage.

This passage is taken from Charles Darwin's natural science writings, The Expression of the Emotions in Man and Animals.

No doubt as long as man and all other animals are viewed
as independent creations, an effectual stop is put to our
natural desire to investigate as far as possible the causes
of Expression. By this doctrine, anything and everything can
be equally well explained; and it has proved as pernicious with
respect to Expression as to every other branch of natural history.
With mankind some expressions, such as the bristling of the hair under
the influence of extreme terror, or the uncovering of the teeth under
that of furious rage, can hardly be understood, except on the belief
that man once existed in a much lower and animal-like condition.
The community of certain expressions in distinct though allied species,
as in the movements of the same facial muscles during laughter by man
and by various monkeys, is rendered somewhat more intelligible,
if we believe in their descent from a common progenitor.
He who admits on general grounds that the structure and habits
of all animals have been gradually evolved, will look at the whole
subject of Expression in a new and interesting light.
　　The study of Expression is difficult, owing to the movements
being often extremely slight, and of a fleeting nature.
A difference may be clearly perceived, and yet it may be impossible,
at least I have found it so, to state in what the difference consists.
When we witness any deep emotion, our sympathy is so strongly
excited, that close observation is forgotten or rendered
almost impossible; of which fact I have had many curious proofs.
Our imagination is another and still more serious source of error;
for if from the nature of the circumstances we expect
to see any expression, we readily imagine its presence.
Notwithstanding Dr. Duchenne's great experience, he for a long
time fancied, as he states, that several muscles contracted
under certain emotions, whereas he ultimately convinced himself
that the movement was confined to a single muscle.
　　In order to acquire as good a foundation as possible, and to ascertain,
independently of common opinion, how far particular movements
of the features and gestures are really expressive of certain states
of the mind, I have found the following means the most serviceable.
In the first place, to observe infants; for they exhibit many emotions,
as Sir C. Bell remarks, "with extraordinary force"; whereas, in after life,
some of our expressions "cease to have the pure and simple source
from which they spring in infancy."

40   In the second place, it occurred to me that the insane ought to
be studied, as they are liable to the strongest passions, and give
uncontrolled vent to them. I had, myself, no opportunity of doing this,
so I applied to Dr. Maudsley and received from him an introduction
to Dr. J. Crichton Browne, who has charge of an immense asylum

45   near Wakefield, and who, as I found, had already attended to the subject.
This excellent observer has with unwearied kindness sent me copious
notes and descriptions, with valuable suggestions on many points;
and I can hardly over-estimate the value of his assistance. I owe also,
to the kindness of Mr. Patrick Nicol, of the Sussex Lunatic Asylum,

50   interesting statements on two or three points.
         Thirdly Dr. Duchenne galvanized, as we have already seen, certain muscles
in the face of an old man, whose skin was little sensitive, and thus
produced various expressions which were photographed on a large scale.
It fortunately occurred to me to show several of the best plates,

55   without a word of explanation, to above twenty educated persons
of various ages and both sexes, asking them, in each case,
by what emotion or feeling the old man was supposed to be agitated;
and I recorded their answers in the words which they used.
Several of the expressions were instantly recognized by almost everyone,

60   though described in not exactly the same terms; and these may,
I think, be relied on as truthful, and will hereafter be specified.
On the other hand, the most widely different judgments were pronounced
in regard to some of them. This exhibition was of use in another way,
by convincing me how easily we may be misguided by our imagination;

65   for when I first looked through Dr. Duchenne's photographs,
reading at the same time the text, and thus learning what was intended,
I was struck with admiration at the truthfulness of all, with only
a few exceptions. Nevertheless, if I had examined them without
any explanation, no doubt I should have been as much perplexed,

70   in some cases, as other persons have been.

1. It can be inferred from the beginning of
the opening paragraph that with regard
to "this doctrine" (line 4) the author feels

(A) inherently drawn
(B) curiously engaged
(C) belligerently vexed
(D) emphatically opposed
(E) rigidly aligned

2. In line 13, "intelligible" most nearly
means

(A) vociferous
(B) insightful
(C) understandable
(D) intelligent
(E) intellectual

3. Lines 18–24 suggest that Darwin would most likely disagree with which of the following statements?

(A) The subtle distinctions between an expression of discouragement and one of disappointment are easily noted.

(B) Humans can become absorbed in the emotions of others.

(C) Changes in facial expressions are faint rather than pronounced.

(D) Sometimes it's hard to notice whether another was feeling anxious or was simply eager.

(E) People's faces are dynamic and compelling.

4. In line 37, "after life" most nearly means

(A) spiritual life

(B) life after death

(C) a more conscientious life

(D) a time late in life

(E) a time later in life

5. Darwin portrays D. Chrichton Browne primarily as

(A) a lurid and egocentric individual

(B) a debunker of widespread misconceptions

(C) an intellectual inferior

(D) a rival of Dr. Maudsley

(E) an invaluable and supportive colleague

6. The structure of the second half of the passage is best described as

(A) a listing of random vignettes

(B) a series of three suggestions for case studies

(C) assessments of statistical values

(D) haphazard, romanticized musings

(E) causes followed by their tangible effects

7. In the final paragraph, the author suggests that various people's interpretations of the photographs taken of "the face of an old man" (line 52) are

(A) ludicrous

(B) unpredictable

(C) subjective

(D) inconsequential

(E) objective

8. In context, "galvanized" (line 51) most closely means

(A) surged

(B) electrified

(C) solidified

(D) embalmed

(E) incited

ANSWERS AND EXPLANATIONS

Passage 1

1. E	**3.** D
2. C	**4.** B

1. HARD INTERPRETATION QUESTION **Reread lines 2–4 carefully, trying to "downsize" them by paraphrasing them in your own words.**
The significant lines are "his grandmother had faded off almost imperceptibly, until, for the first time since her marriage, her person held for one day an unquestioned supremacy over her own drawing room." To paraphrase: Almost without notice his grandma had become lifeless; then one day—for the first time since she became a married woman—she became the dominant person in her bedroom" (or something similar; paraphrasing is a subjective process). This passage is not about housekeeping or haunting her grandson, so (A) and (B) are bogus. Neither is it suggested that grandma has caused Anthony's hypochondria; (C) is out. Sure, grandmothers sometimes play "mother figures" to grandchildren, but this passage provides no evidence to support (D). The best answer is **(E)**.

2. QUESTION ON STRUCTURE AND FORM OF PASSAGE **Skim the passage, paying close attention to transitional language between paragraphs.** This exercise can help you get a sense of the passage's overall organization. (B), *present to past chronology*, is tempting since time order is significant; this passage, however, goes in the reverse, past to present. **(C)**, *chronological biography*, is the best choice since ¶ 1 is about Anthony at age eleven; ¶ 2, at age fourteen, and ¶ 3, at age sixteen. Time order is chronological; this passage is biography because it tells about the boy's life.

3. WORD-IN-CONTEXT QUESTION **Consider the word within its context, looking for clues to its precise meaning:** "his stamp collection; enormous, as nearly exhaustive as a boy's could be." *Exhaustive* is an adjective that modifies *stamp collection*. The context clue for the meaning of *exhaustive* is *enormous*, the word that precedes it. The best answer is **(D)**, *extensive*.

4. GLOBAL QUESTION ON AUTHOR'S ATTITUDE, WITH TRICKY KEY WORD *NOT*
Use sidebars, looking for clues about the author's attitude: "His stamps were his greatest happiness and <u>he bestowed impatient frowns on any one who interrupted him at play with them</u>." The context clue that illustrates the boy's attitude is underlined. The best answer is **(B)**, *contemptuous*, which means scornful. This boy, a stamps aficionado, had *impatient frowns* for any philistine who disrupted him while engaged in his leisure pursuit. To answer correctly, you need to have a handle on the words in the answer choices. Here's a quick rundown: *solicitous* (A) means showing concern for others; *nonchalant* (C) means casual; *aloof* (D) means distant or uninterested; and *sullen* (E) means sad and gloomy.

Passage 2

1. D	**4.** E	**7.** C
2. C	**5.** E	**8.** E
3. A	**6.** B	

1. HARD INFERENCE QUESTION SIGNALED BY "INFERRED" **Embed "this doctrine" in context by rereading lines 1–6**, then seek out context clues that indicate how the author feels about the doctrine explained in the opening lines. Lines 5 and 6 indicate that the author finds the doctrine to be "pernicious" (very harmful): "By this doctrine, anything and everything can be equally well explained; and it has proved as pernicious with respect to Expression as to every other branch of natural history." Therefore, the answer is **(D)**, *emphatically opposed*. (C), *belligerently vexed*, can be eliminated as an extreme choice. Also eliminate (A), (B), and (E) since they indicate that the author is in agreement with the doctrine.

2. WORD-IN-CONTEXT QUESTION **Embed "intelligible," an adjective, in its broader context**, lines 11–17: "The community of certain expressions in distinct though allied species, as in the movements of the same facial muscles during laughter by man and by various monkeys, is rendered somewhat more intelligible, if we believe in their descent from a common progenitor. He who admits on general grounds that the structure and habits of all animals have been gradually evolved, will look at the whole subject of Expression in a new and interesting light." Try to paraphrase the tricky parts, expressing them in your own words, something like this: The group of different expressions in separate but related species...becomes more intelligible if we believe that the species come from a common ancestor. As you can see, a strong vocabulary greatly assists with paraphrasing. (A), *Vociferous*, means loud and therefore does not work in this sentence. (B), *insightful*, is not the answer even though you might pick this if you carelessly misread "intelligible" in line 13 as "intelligent." (D), *intelligent*, and (E), *intellectual*, are tricky decoys since they start with the same six letters as "intelligible." The correct answer is **(C)**, *understandable*.

3. INFERENCE QUESTION BASED ON A SEVEN-LINE SIDEBAR (LINES 18–24) **Be sure to notice a key word in the question, "disagree."** In the question, the word "suggest" indicates that this is a hard, inference-level question. Read over the lengthy sidebar, lines 18–24:

> The study of Expression is difficult, owing to the movements
> being often extremely slight, and of a fleeting nature.
> A difference may be clearly perceived, and yet it may be impossible,
> at least I have found it so, to state in what the difference consists.
> When we witness any deep emotion, our sympathy is so strongly
> excited, that close observation is forgotten or rendered
> almost impossible; of which fact I have had many curious proofs.

Determine four statements with which Darwin agrees; the odd man out is your answer! Consider (A), *The subtle distinctions between an expression of discouragement and one of disappointment are easily noted.* Since Darwin says, "The study of Expression is difficult and it may be impossible to ...state in what the difference consists," this must be the statement he would disagree with. **(A)** is the answer. With this same passage evidence in mind, Darwin must agree with (D), *Sometimes it's hard to notice whether another was feeling anxious or was simply eager.* Let's be certain we can eliminate the remaining answers. (B), *Humans can become absorbed in the emotions of others*: Darwin agrees, since he writes "When we witness any deep emotion, our sympathy is so strongly excited. . . ." (C), *Changes in facial expressions are faint rather than pronounced*, is a statement Darwin would support since he writes "the movement being often extremely slight, and of a fleeting nature." Can we invalidate (E)? Yes: Darwin mentions the "movements" (line 18) of the face and states that witnessing the emotions displayed by the face evokes our strong sympathy; certainly, *people's faces are dynamic and compelling.*

4. PHRASE-IN-CONTEXT QUESTION **Embed the given expression in a wide enough context (lines 32–39) so that you can ascertain its meaning within the passage:** "In order to acquire as good a foundation as possible, and to ascertain, independently of common opinion, how far particular movements of the features and gestures are really expressive of certain states of the mind, I have found the following means the most serviceable. In the first place, to observe infants; for they exhibit many emotions, as Sir C. Bell remarks, "with extraordinary force"; whereas, in <u>after life</u>, some of our expressions "cease to have the pure and simple source from which they spring in infancy."

    Since the life in line 37 refers to that of infants, the "after life" would offer contrast. (D) and (E) present a challenge since they are so alike. The correct answer is **(E)**, *a time later in life*, since (D), *a time late in life*, would refer to old age. The idea is that infants are more expressive, through their features and gestures, than older individuals. Notice that line 38 says that we are not as "pure and simple" as we were during our infancy. We can surmise that *later in life*, as things become more complicated, we become less naïve. This change doesn't necessarily occur in old age, *late in life*, but would take place as we mature. (C), *a more conscientious life*, would not necessarily be in contrast to the life of an infant, who may or may not have a "conscience," depending upon one's definition. There is no clear evidence that "after life" refers to either (A), *spiritual life*, or (B), *life after death*.

5. CHARACTERIZATION QUESTION **Spot the key term, "D. Chrichton Browne," and skim around it for details that illustrate this character.** The passage says, "This excellent observer has with unwearied kindness sent me copious notes and descriptions, with valuable suggestions on many points; and I can hardly overestimate the value of his assistance." This is a positive appraisal of D. Browne, so let's cross off the negatives—goodbye to (A), (B), and (C). Did you know that a "debunker" proves false or contradicts established beliefs and/or customs? (D) is not validated by passage evidence. The answer is **(E)**.

6. QUESTION ON PASSAGE STRUCTURE **If you didn't pick up on the organizational structure while you were reading, go back to the second half of the passage and skim to get a sense of how it's "built."** Notice "In the *first place*...observe infants" (line 36), followed by "In the *second place*, it occurred to me that the insane ought to be studied" (lines 40 and 41), and finally, "*Thirdly* Dr. Duchenne galvanized, as we have already seen, certain muscles in the face of an old man" (line 51). Therefore, answer is **(B)**, a series of three suggestions for case studies. The passage evidence just laid out is not (A), *a listing of random vignettes*, since the concepts presented are not random, but rather are related ideas about whom to study. Also, the word *vignettes* is highly visual and descriptive, which this listing is not. (C) is out since statistics are nowhere to be found. Also, there are no *romanticized musings* in the latter half of this passage, so eliminate (D). (E), *causes followed by their tangible effects*, is so vague that it's tempting, but closer consideration reveals that the cause-effect dynamic is not quite here.

7. INFERENCE QUESTION BASED ON SUBTLE DESCRIPTIONS **Skim through the final paragraph, looking for clues about how the author describes** "various people's interpretations" of the enlarged photos of the old man's face. The last paragraph is chunky; you shouldn't simply rely on your memory or take a guess. As always, your answer should be based on the acid test: *according to the author.* The onus is on you to find something in the last paragraph that validates one of the answer choices. Have you found the pertinent part of the paragraph? Here it is, with context clues underlined:

   Several of the expressions were instantly recognized by almost everyone,
   Line
   60   though <u>described in not exactly the same terms</u>; . . .
   the most <u>widely different judgments were pronounced</u>
   in regard to some of them. ...
   <u>how easily we may be misguided by our imagination</u>.

   It sounds as though the participants had diverse ways of describing the photos and "widely different judgments," and their imaginations influenced their interpretations. Now that you have found the evidence, which is the best answer? (A), *ludicrous*, is out since the author is not mocking or downright dismissing the interpretations of the observers. (B) and (D) are not validated; here nothing says that the interpretations were *unpredictable* or *inconsequential* (trivial). Did you notice that (C) and (E) are opposites? Which is right? Are the interpretations based on opinion (subjective) or fact (objective)? The answer is **(C)**, *subjective*.

8. WORD-IN-CONTEXT QUESTION **Be open to the multifarious meanings of "galvanized," an action verb.** To illustrate the importance of open-mindedness when it comes to words-in-context questions, let's consider three possible meanings for galvanize: (1) to apply an electric current, (2) to excite someone into doing something, and (3) to coat metal with a topping of zinc. Now contemplate the word in its context: "Thirdly Dr. Duchenne <u>galvanized</u>, as we have already seen, certain muscles in the face of an old man, whose skin was little sensitive, and thus

produced various expressions which were photographed on a large scale." Choices (A) and (B), *surged* and *electrified*, relate to the first meaning of galvanize but do not fit this context. If the old man's face were (C) *solidified*, no expressions could be detected; cross off this choice with your active pencil. (D), *embalmed*, relates, in an eerie way, to "old" (line 57) but to nothing else. The correct answer is **(E)**, *incited* (roused, stirred up).

VERY HARD LONG PASSAGES

A recipe for making peanut butter s'mores or the ultimate chocolate chip cookie would be more fun, but let's talk about the recipe for a very hard critical reading passage.

> **Recipe for a very hard critical-reading passage** = stuffy + convoluted + cryptic + theoretical + abstruse = the passage you are about to read.

Read in digestible pieces, and hold on tight (stay focused).

PRACTICE TEST QUESTIONS

> **Directions:** Read the passage below, and then answer the questions that follow. The correct response may be stated outright or merely suggested in the passage.

The following passage is excerpted from philosopher Immanuel Kant's The Metaphysical Elements of Ethics, *first published in 1780.*

If there exists on any subject a philosophy (that is,
a system of rational knowledge based on concepts), then
there must also be for this philosophy a system of pure
Line
5   rational concepts, independent of any condition of intuition,
in other words, a metaphysic. It may be asked whether
metaphysical elements are required also for every practical
philosophy, which is the doctrine of duties, and therefore
also for Ethics, in order to be able to present it as
10   a true science (systematically), not merely as an aggregate
of separate doctrines (fragmentarily). As regards pure
jurisprudence, no one will question this requirement; for
it concerns only what is formal in the elective will, which
has to be limited in its external relations according to
15   laws of freedom; without regarding any end which is the
matter of this will. Here, therefore, deontology is a mere
scientific doctrine (*doctrina scientiae*).
      Now in this philosophy (of ethics) it seems contrary
to the idea of it that we should go back to metaphysical
20   elements in order to make the notion of duty purified
from everything empirical (from every feeling) a motive
of action. For what sort of notion can we form of the
mighty power and Herculean strength which would be sufficient
to overcome the vice-breeding inclinations, if Virtue is
25   to borrow her "arms from the armory of metaphysics,"
which is a matter of speculation that only few men can handle?

Hence all ethical teaching in lecture rooms, pulpits, and popular books, when it is decked out with fragments of metaphysics, becomes ridiculous. But it is not, therefore, useless, much less ridiculous, to trace in metaphysics the
30 first principles of ethics; for it is only as a philosopher that anyone can reach the first principles of this conception of duty, otherwise we could not look for either certainty or purity in the ethical teaching. To rely for this reason on a certain feeling which, on account of the effect
35 expected from it, is called moral, may, perhaps, even satisfy the popular teacher, provided he desires as the criterion of a moral duty to consider the problem: "If everyone in every case made your maxim the universal law, how could this law be consistent with itself?" But if
40 it were merely feeling that made it our duty to take this principle as a criterion, then this would not be dictated by reason, but only adopted instinctively and therefore blindly.

But in fact, whatever men imagine, no moral principle
45 is based on any feeling, but such a principle is really nothing else than an obscurely conceived metaphysic which inheres in every man's reasoning faculty; as the teacher will easily find who tries to catechize his pupils in the Socratic method about the imperative of duty and its
50 application to the moral judgment of his actions. The mode of stating it need not be always metaphysical, and the language need not necessarily be scholastic, unless the pupil is to be trained to be a philosopher. But the thought must go back to the elements of metaphysics,
55 without which we cannot expect any certainty or purity, or even motive power in ethics.

1. According to the author, all of the following would be antithetical to "a metaphysic" (line 6) EXCEPT

(A) an individual's visceral sense
(B) a pure certitude
(C) man's free will
(D) an intended outcome
(E) a personal reminiscence

2. In the first paragraph of the passage, the author does which of the following?

  I. Defines a term
 II. Cites an expert
III. Gives the Latin name for a term
IV. Explains the distinction between two terms
 V. All of the above

(A) I only
(B) II only
(C) I and II only
(D) I, III, and IV only
(E) V

3. Lines 22–26, "For what sort of notion . . . few men can handle?" can be described as

(A) a hyperbole that accents the disparity between male and female inner strengths
(B) an alliterative description of philosophical ideas
(C) an extended metaphor that contrasts good and evil
(D) a simile that contains powerful imagery
(E) a rhetorical question that contains both a mythological allusion and a personification of a human attribute

4. In context, the expression "decked out" in line 27 most closely means

(A) detailed and described
(B) bedecked with ornaments
(C) dressed up and bejeweled
(D) combated vehemently
(E) adorned with filigree

5. In line 41, "dictated" most nearly means

(A) divulged
(B) ordained
(C) avowed
(D) determined
(E) mandated

6. What can you infer about the assumption the author is making in lines 51–53, "The mode of stating it need not be always . . . be trained to be a philosopher"?

(A) The majority of students will become befuddled by a high level of pedagogic, philosophical instruction.
(B) Only for the student who plans to become a practicing philosopher is an erudite and intellectual level of training required.
(C) Today's philosophical teaching is, regrettably, over the heads of most average students.
(D) A pupil's inner state of morality greatly affects the way he conducts himself during a Socratic seminar.
(E) Contemporary, philosophical instruction is wasted on students who have very little sincere interest in the discipline.

ANSWERS AND EXPLANATIONS

1. B	**3.** E	**5.** D
2. D	**4.** A	**6.** A

1. HARD ALL/EXCEPT QUESTION, requiring you to know that *antithetical* means opposite to **Scope out context clues up/down/around line 5 that indicate what a metaphysic is.** The context clue is "a system of pure rational concepts, independent of (excluding) any condition of intuition," so (A), (C), (D), and (E) are all out since they involve an aspect of intuition, which you can think of as perception or insight. Active Pencil! These choices involve something other than "pure rational concepts." The only exception is **(B)**, which is the correct answer. Like roman-numeral-list questions, ALL/EXCEPT questions tend to be time-consuming.

2. HARD TIME-CONSUMING ROMAN-NUMERAL-LIST QUESTION **Peruse paragraph 1 to find examples of each of the items in the Roman numeral list.** Place a check mark next to each item you find so that you can keep track of what you have located in paragraph 1. You don't want to waste precious time finding more than one example!
   I. The author defines "philosophy" in line 1 and "metaphysic" in line 5.
   II. No expert or authority is quoted.
   III. The Latin term *doctrina scientiae* appears in line 16.
   IV. The author explains the difference between "a true science" and "an aggregate of separate doctrines" in lines 9 and 10.
   The correct answer is **(D)**.

3. HARD INTERPRETATION QUESTION **Reread the lines quoted in the question carefully, and try to "downsize" them by paraphrasing in your own words.** Choice (A) might appear true, but it is actually a false-positive, an only-partly-true decoy answer. The idea of *hyperbole* (great exaggeration) is touched upon (*mighty power and Herculean strength*), but this answer choice should be tossed out since nowhere in the lines quoted is the difference stressed between the inner strengths of male and female. Alliteration requires the repetition of an initial consonant sound, as in "**r**edolent **r**ed **r**oses." No alliteration occurs, so cross off (B). A metaphor is a direct comparison without *like* or *as*, for example, "Love is a red rose." No metaphor appears in lines 21–25; eliminate (C). A simile is a figure of speech in which a comparison is made using either *like* or *as*, as in "She had lips like cherries." There's no simile in the lines indicated, so (D) is out. The correct answer is **(E)**. A *rhetorical question* is asked simply for effect. The mythological allusion (reference) is to Hercules, and Virtue is personified in the passage, for she is "to borrow her arms."

4. HARD EXPRESSION-IN-CONTEXT QUESTION **Reread the sentence in which "decked out" appears. Seek out clues to elucidate its meaning.** This question is particularly hard because of the vocabulary in the answer choices: *bedecked, bejeweled,* and *filigree.* These words may present obstacles or, at the least, cause some hesitation. The author is saying that, when Ethics is taught in classrooms, teachers tend to "deck it out" or dress it up with items of information that relate to metaphysics. But he does not mean dressed up literally, so (B), (C), and (E) are out. (D) does not make sense since teachers in their right minds do not simultaneously include something in their teaching and oppose it passionately. The answer is **(A)**.

5. HARD VOCABULARY WORD-IN-CONTEXT QUESTION **Reread carefully the sentence in which "dictated" appears to get a sense of the word's context.** Predict a substitute for the word. Carefully select the closest answer choice. (A) is out since *divulged* usually means revealed secret information. (B) is out also, since the connotation of *ordained* has to do with an individual being formally assigned priestly or holy orders. *Avowed* and *mandated* don't quite fit, so cross out (C) and (E). The answer is **(D)**.

6. HARD INFERENCE AND ASSUMPTION QUESTION **The answer choices are long and heavy-weight, making this question even more challenging. Reread the sidebar: "The mode of stating it need not be always metaphysical, and the language need not necessarily be scholastic, unless the pupil is to be trained to be a philosopher," trying to pick up an underlying message put forth by the author.** (B) is close, but the author is not directly stating that only students who want to become philosophers require *erudite* (scholarly) training. (C) is out since no statement is made about *most average students*. (D), according to common sense, is probably true, yet no evidence in the passage speaks to pupils' morality. Again, (E) makes sense, but no textual evidence supports this choice. The answer is **(A)** since lines 51–54 imply that without training (in philosophy), the pupil would not comprehend explanations coached in metaphysical/scholastic terms. *Befuddled* means confused.

PRACTICE TEST QUESTIONS/PAIRED LONG PASSAGES

Directions: The questions that follow the two passages in this section relate to the contents of both and to their relationship. The correct response may be stated outright or merely suggested.

The following two passages, which are excerpted from the works of two well-known social thinkers, are about slavery in America. Passage 1 is taken from Henry David Thoreau's Slavery in Massachusetts. *Passage 2 is excerpted from Booker T. Washington's autobiography,* Up From Slavery.

Passage 1

Much has been said about American slavery, but
I think that we do not even yet realize what slavery is.
If I were seriously to propose to Congress to make mankind
into sausages, I have no doubt that most of the members
Line
5 would smile at my proposition, and if any believed me
to be in earnest, they would think that I proposed
something much worse than Congress had ever done.
But if any of them will tell me that to make a man
into a sausage would be much worse—would be any
10 worse—than to make him into a slave—than it was
to enact the Fugitive Slave Law—I will accuse him
of foolishness, of intellectual incapacity, of making

a distinction without a difference. The one is just as
sensible a proposition as the other.

15   I hear a good deal said about trampling this law
under foot. Why, one need not go out of his way to
do that. This law rises not to the level of the head
or the reason; its natural habitat is in the dirt.
It was born and bred, and has its life, only in the
20   dust and mire, on a level with the feet; and he who
walks with freedom, and does not with Hindoo mercy
avoid treading on every venomous reptile, will
inevitably tread on it, and so trample it under foot—
and Webster, its maker, with it, like the dirt-
25   bug and its ball.

**Divide and Conquer
the Passage**
*The dotted lines indicate
how you might go about
reading this passage
piece by piece.
At each break, consider
which questions (if any)
you can answer while
that piece is fresh in
your mind.*

Recent events will be valuable as a criticism on
the administration of justice in our midst, or, rather,
as showing what are the true resources of justice in
any community. It has come to this, that the friends
30   of liberty, the friends of the slave, have shuddered
when they have understood that his fate was left to the
legal tribunals of the country to be decided. Free men
have no faith that justice will be awarded in such a
case. The judge may decide this way or that; it is a
35   kind of accident, at best. It is evident that he is
not a competent authority in so important a case.
It is no time, then, to be judging according to his
precedents, but to establish a precedent for the future.
I would much rather trust to the sentiment of the people.
40   In their vote you would get something of some value, at
least, however small; but in the other case, only the
trammeled judgment of an individual, of no significance,
be it which way it might.

It is to some extent fatal to the courts, when the
45   people are compelled to go behind them. I do not wish
to believe that the courts were made for fair weather,
and for very civil cases merely; but think of leaving
it to any court in the land to decide whether more than
three millions of people, in this case a sixth part of a
50   nation, have a right to be freemen or not! But it has
been left to the courts of justice, so called—to the
Supreme Court of the land—and, as you all know,
recognizing no authority but the Constitution, it has
decided that the three millions are and shall continue
55   to be slaves.

Passage 2

I was born a slave on a plantation in Franklin County, Virginia. I am not quite sure of the exact place or exact date of my birth, but at any rate I suspect I must have been born somewhere and at some time. As nearly as I have
60 been able to learn, I was born near a cross-roads post-office called Hale's Ford, and the year was 1858 or 1859. I do not know the month or the day. The earliest impress-sions I can now recall are of the plantation and the slave quarters—the latter being the part of the plantation
65 where the slaves had their cabins.

Of my ancestry I know almost nothing. In the slave quarters, and even later, I heard whispered conversations among the colored people of the tortures which the slaves, including, no doubt, my ancestors on my mother's side,
70 suffered in the middle passage of the slave ship while being conveyed from Africa to America. I have been unsuccessful in securing any information that would throw any accurate light upon the history of my family beyond my mother. She, I remember, had a half-brother and a half-sister. In
75 the days of slavery not very much attention was given to family history and family records—that is, black family records. My mother, I suppose, attracted the attention of a purchaser who was afterward my owner and hers. Her addition to the slave family attracted about as much attention as
80 the purchase of a new horse or cow. Of my father I know even less than of my mother. I do not even know his name. I have heard reports to the effect that he was a white man who lived on one of the near-by plantations. Whoever he was, I never heard of his taking the least interest in
85 me or providing in any way for my rearing. But I do not find especial fault with him. He was simply another unfortunate victim of the institution which the Nation unhappily had engrafted upon it at that time.

So far as I can now recall, the first knowledge that I got of the
90 fact that we were slaves, and that freedom of the slaves was being discussed, was early one morning before day, when I was awakened by my mother kneeling over her children and fervently praying that Lincoln and his armies might be successful, and that one day she and her children might be free. In this connection I
95 have never been able to understand how the slaves throughout the South, completely ignorant as were the masses so far as books or newspapers were concerned, were able to keep themselves so accurately and completely informed about the great National

questions that were agitating the country. From the time that
100 Garrison, Lovejoy, and others began to agitate for freedom, the
slaves throughout the South kept in close touch with the progress
of the movement. Though I was a mere child during the preparation
for the Civil War and during the war itself, I now recall the
many late-at-night whispered discussions that I heard my mother
105 and the other slaves on the plantation indulge in. These
discussions showed that they understood the situation, and that
they kept themselves informed of events by what was termed the
"grape-vine" telegraph.

During the campaign when Lincoln was first a candidate for the
110 Presidency, the slaves on our far-off plantation, miles from any
railroad or large city or daily newspaper, knew what the issues
involved were. When war was begun between the North and the
South, every slave on our plantation felt and knew that, though
other issues were discussed, the primal one was that of slavery.
115 Even the most ignorant members of my race on the remote
plantations felt in their hearts, with a certainty that admitted
of no doubt, that the freedom of the slaves would be the one
great result of the war, if the northern armies conquered. Every
success of the Federal armies and every defeat of the Confederate
120 forces was watched with the keenest and most intense interest.
Often the slaves got knowledge of the results of great battles
before the white people received it. This news was usually gotten
from the colored man who was sent to the post-office for the
mail. In our case the post-office was about three miles from the
125 plantation, and the mail came once or twice a week. The man who
was sent to the office would linger about the place long enough
to get the drift of the conversation from the group of white
people who naturally congregated there, after receiving their
mail, to discuss the latest news. The mail-carrier on his way
130 back to our master's house would as naturally retail the news
that he had secured among the slaves, and in this way they often
heard of important events before the white people at the "big
house," as the master's house was called.

1. In Passage 1 it can be inferred that the Congressional members "would smile" (line 5) for which of the following reasons?

   (A) They believe that the author's proposed intention is ludicrous.
   (B) They are making an effort to conceal their inner scorn toward the author.
   (C) They are sealing the author's proposition with a smile as a way of demonstrating their consent.
   (D) They are mocking the author's demeanor and his point of view.
   (E) They are smiling to mask their inner belief that the author is somewhat deranged.

2. According to the Passage 1 author, "making a distinction without a difference" (lines 12 and 13) can be characterized as all of the following EXCEPT

   (A) an admirable and judicious trait
   (B) a line of argument that Thoreau finds offensive and nearly absurd
   (C) a reasoning process that results from mental obtuseness
   (D) a way of thinking that reflects mental ineptness
   (E) an insensible process of the incompetent mind

Coaching—Paired Long Passages
Read the passages piece by piece, answering pertinent questions as you go.
Answer Passage 1 only questions first.
Then answer Passage 2 only questions. Lastly, answer questions that involve both passages.

---

3. Thoreau does which of the following in paragraph 2 of Passage 1?

   I. Personifies that which is inanimate and intangible
   II. Relates a bit of hearsay
   III. Explains nature's connection to lawmaking
   IV. Contradicts an established fallacy

   (A) I only
   (B) I and II only
   (C) I and IV only
   (D) III only
   (E) III and IV only

4. In Passage 1, which of the following most accurately explains why the friends of the slaves "shuddered" (line 30)?

   (A) The slaves' friends were fearful that they too might become indentured servants one day.
   (B) The slaves' friends internalized the cold and stern emotions of slaveholders and slavery advocates.
   (C) The slaves' friends visibly trembled under the crushing leadership of crooked judges and juries.
   (D) The slaves' friends quivered with uncertainty about the future of the slave institution as they knew it at the time.
   (E) The slaves' friends realized that the future of slavery was in the hands of a legal body.

5. In line 38, "precedents" most nearly means

   (A) retired judges
   (B) predecessors
   (C) legal rivals
   (D) previous colleagues
   (E) prior legal decisions

6. In lines 49 and 50, the author's inclusion of the phrase "a sixth part of a nation" serves mainly to

(A) demonstrate his mathematical prowess

(B) heighten people's understanding of the staggering ratio of slave owners to slaves

(C) underscore the considerable number of slaves as a sizable segment of the population

(D) show his ability to manipulate ratios and statistics

(E) demystify the ambiguities involving the slave population and its general characteristics

7. The first paragraph of Passage 2 reveals which of the following about Booker T. Washington's impressions of his early life?

(A) The situation of his birth and early upbringing are perceived as both distasteful and disdainful.

(B) The circumstances surrounding his birth and early upbringing are opaque and ambiguous.

(C) Despite his efforts, he has learned only very disturbing tidbits about his birth and early youth.

(D) He knows little about his birth because his interest level on this topic was surprisingly very low.

(E) His natal history and beginnings were more like those of a free-spirited vagabond than those of an ill-fated slave child.

8. According to Passage 2, how is the slaves' knowledge of Lincoln's campaign as discussed in lines 109–112 most accurately explained?

I. The mother "fervently praying" (lines 92 and 93)

II. The middle passage of the slave ship (line 70)

III. The grapevine telegraph (line 108)

IV. The mail carrier (line 129)

V. All of the above

(A) I only

(B) II only

(C) II and III

(D) III and IV only

(E) V

9. In view of their contextual meanings in both passages, the term "sausages" (line 4, Passage 1) and the term "horse or cow" (line 80, Passage 2) serve mainly to

(A) accentuate the difference between the value of processed foods and that of natural livestock

(B) create a ludicrous set of images in order to diminish the graveness of the topic of slavery

(C) reference popular examples of food and property that were traded during the 1800s

(D) illustrate the dehumanizing and demeaning aspects of the institution of slavery

(E) trivialize the importance of women during this period in American history

10. The attitude toward slavery held by the passage authors and the attitude toward slavery held by Congress (Passage 1, paragraph 1) are, respectively, best described as

(A) the former attitude is apathetic; the latter is pedantic

(B) the former attitude is resigned; the latter is skeptical

(C) the former attitude is regretful; the latter is matter of fact

(D) the former attitude is mocking; the latter is irreverent

(E) the former attitude is sardonic; the latter is also sardonic

11. On the issue of slavery in America, which of the following best describes the perspectives of these two authors?

(A) Thoreau is a social observer and philosopher who is ardently opposed to slavery; Washington has actually experienced slavery.

(B) Thoreau covertly advocates slavery; Washington overtly opposes slavery.

(C) Thoreau dislikes all slavery leaders; Washington dislikes only slave owners who "erased" his personal history.

(D) Thoreau is a detached historian; Washington is also detached and is numb from an overabundance of personal trauma.

(E) Thoreau is a retired judge; Washington aspires to become a political representative.

ANSWERS AND EXPLANATIONS

1. A	**5.** E	**9.** D
2. A	**6.** C	**10.** C
3. B	**7.** B	**11.** A
4. E	**8.** D	

1. HARD INFERENCE QUESTION **Consider "would smile" in its broader context for clues about why members of Congress smiled.** From "if any believed me to be in earnest," we can understand that Congress would think the author was jesting and, therefore, would not take his proposition seriously. They would react to this nonsensical or *ludicrous* idea with a smile; **(A)** is the answer. There are no context clues to support (B), *conceal their inner scorn;* (C), *demonstrating their consent;* (D), *mocking the author's demeanor,* that is, his behavior and conduct; or (E), *smiling to mask their belief that the author is somewhat deranged* (crazy.) On the basis of the passage, (E) is too extreme an answer choice.

2. TRICKY ALL/EXCEPT QUESTION **Find clues to the meaning and the relevance in context of "making a distinction without a difference."** Context clues in the vicinity of this phrase include "foolishness and intellectual incapacity" (line 12). All choices except (A) reflect these clues, so **(A)** is the correct answer. Potentially challenging vocabulary in the answer choices include *judicious* (fair and just), *obtuseness* (vacuity, stupidity), and *ineptness* (lack of skill.)

3. HARD ROMAN-NUMERAL-LIST QUESTION **Just like ALL/EXCEPT questions, Roman-numeral-list questions are time-consuming to answer, requiring a good deal of passage revisiting and reviewing.**
I. The Fugitive Slave Law (referred to as "this law" in line 15) is personified: the context clues are *"its natural habitat"* and *"It was born and bred."* (lines 18 and 19);
II. "Hearsay" is rumor. Context clue to support II is "I hear a good deal said about . . ." (line 15)
III and IV. No textual evidence.
The answer is **(B)**.

4. TRICKY EXPLANATION FOR A WORD-IN-CONTEXT QUESTION **Skim up and down and around the word "shuddered" to get clues about precisely why the friends of slaves shuddered.** Not (A), since there's no evidence that they feared becoming slaves themselves. Not (B), since there's no mention of *cold and stern emotions*. Not (C), because there's no mention of *crooked juries or judges*. (D) is out because an uncertain future is not confirmed. The correct answer is **(E)** since it is the closest paraphrasing of "the friends of the slave, have <u>shuddered</u> when they have understood that his fate was left to the legal tribunals [courts] of the country to be decided. Free men have no faith that justice will be awarded in such a case" (lines 30–34).

5. WORD-IN-CONTEXT QUESTION **Reread the complete sentence that contains "precedents," and predict what the word means.** No doubt, you recognize the prefix *pre-*, so you know you need an answer that relates to *before*. The answer choices are challenging, though, because (A), (B), (D), and (E) all relate to *before* in one way or another. The broad context of the word (reproduced below) shows that precedents have something to do with how judges have decided cases. But (A), *retired judges;* (B), *predecessors;* (C), *legal rivals;* and (D), *previous colleagues* have more to do with persons and less to do with (E), *prior legal decisions*, which is the answer. Notice that "precedents" is preceded by the possessive pronoun "his," clarifying that precedents are prior decisions of the judge. Choice **(E)** makes the most sense.

30   . . . the friends of the slave, have <u>shuddered</u>
when they have understood that his fate was left to the
legal tribunals of the country to be decided. Free men
have no faith that justice will be awarded in such a
case. The judge may decide this way or that; it is a
35 kind of accident, at best. It is evident that he is
not a competent authority in so important a case.
It is no time, then, to be judging according to his
<u>precedents</u>, but to establish a precedent for the future.
I would much rather trust to the sentiment of the people.
40 In their vote you would get something of some value, at
least, however small; but in the other case, only the
trammeled judgment of an individual, of no significance,
be it which way it might.

Sometimes, as in this case, tough word-in-context questions require you to reread and reconsider a broad context in order to settle on the meaning that makes most sense.

6. PURPOSE QUESTION **Reread "a sixth part of a nation" in context to get a sense of the main purpose it serves.** The italic blurb that precedes the passage tells you that the author is Thoreau, who was "a social thinker," not a mathematician or physicist; therefore, there's no reason for him to (A) *demonstrate his mathematical prowess* or (D) *show his ability to manipulate ratios and statistics.* The phrase does not indicate a *ratio of slave owners to slaves,* so (B) is out. The purpose of this sentence is not to portray *the slave population and its general characteristics,* so cross off (E). The most sensible answer is **(C)**.

7. GETTING THE GIST OF A PARAGRAPH QUESTION **Skimming the paragraph for details about Booker T. Washington's birth and early life reveals that few, if any, solid details are known.** In fact, everything from the place of his birth to the date of his birth is vague and sketchy. The answer is **(B)**. You're sharp, but perhaps *opaque* (dark, obscure) and *ambiguous* (unclear; vague) are potentially challenging words that appear in this answer choice. (A) is unsupported because there's no evidence to support a description of his birth and his upbringing as *distasteful and disdainful.* Likewise, there's no proof that the author's interest in his birth is *very low,* so (D) is out. (C) is off since the unknowns about his youth are not confirmed as *disturbing.* Lastly, there's no passage evidence to support (E), that his *beginnings were more like those of a free-spirited vagabond.* . . .

8. TIME-CONSUMING ROMAN-NUMERAL-LIST QUESTION **To ace this demanding question, diligently skim the four line references given in items I–IV.** A quick overview of lines 92 and 93 and line 70 will reveal that I and II have nothing to do with information about the Lincoln campaign being passed on orally from one slave to another. Skim around lines 108 and 129, however, and you'll readily pick up on how *the grapevine telegraph* and the *mail carrier* were both conduits of political information. The correct answer is **(D)**. You need to work quickly on list questions, so you don't lose time.

9. TRICKY DECODING-OF-TERMS QUESTION THAT INVOLVES BOTH PASSAGES **Delve back into the passages and read up, down, and around each of the very visual terms, "sausages" and "horse or cow."** You're sharp, so you'll see that these terms are symbolic or figurative, rather than literal, in their meanings. Considering the contexts of these terms, you find nothing about the *value* (monetary or otherwise) of *processed foods and that of natural livestock,* so cross (A) off with your active pencil and move on! You're savvy enough to understand that sausages and horses/cows are mentioned for more than comic relief, so (B) is out. This passage isn't about the marketplace of the 1800s, so bye-bye (C). Choice (E) is too broad; this passage does not encompass the role of women during this period of American history. The answer is **(D)**; certainly, thinking of a human being as a sausage, horse, or cow is *dehumanizing* and *demeaning* that individual.

10. CHALLENGING QUESTION ON PAIRED PASSAGES AND THEIR AUTHORS' ATTI-TUDES **Questions on attitude, mood, or tone require you to have absorbed the overall sense and feel of the passages** so that you can answer questions, such as this one, that require you to consider the passages on a holistic level. The Passage 1 author is writing on the topic of American slavery, so how could he be *apathetic?* (A) is out. Also, the Passage 1 author is neither *resigned* (accepting) when it comes to slavery nor *mocking*; he obviously considers slavery to be a serious issue worth writing about. Cross off (B) and (D). Overall, these authors do not have a *sardonic* (sarcastic) tone; bye-bye (E). The correct answer is **(C)**.

11. PAIRED-PASSAGE PERSPECTIVES QUESTION—YIKES! **Reflect on all of the reading and rereading and thinking you have done so far on this passage.** You should be in tip-top shape to probe into this paired-passage point-of-view question. It is not true that Thoreau *advocates slavery*, covertly or openly. He opposes it, so cross off (B). (C), Thoreau *dislikes all slavery leaders; Washington dislikes only slave owners who have "erased" his personal history.* Neither author is *detached*; each has an opinion and strong feeling toward the topic of slavery, so (C) and (D) are invalid. There is no passage evidence to support the statement that *Thoreau is a retired judge* or that *Washington aspires to become a political representative*, so (E) is also out. The correct answer is **(A)**. The evidence: The italic blurb identifies Thoreau as a "social thinker." It is clear that Washington has experienced slavery because he uses the first-person point of view, "I," to relate his experiences.

Chapter 4

2400 CLUB GRAND MIXTURE

On the SAT, the critical reading sections include 19 sentence-completion questions and a total of 48 reading-passage questions. Each short passage (1 or 2 paragraphs) and pair of paragraphs may have anywhere from 2 to 6 questions; each of the longer passages, as many as 13 questions.

 Familiarize yourself with the directions ahead of time.

The practice test questions that follow are a mixture of the medium to hard questions discussed in the critical reading sections of this book. If you can ace these questions, you are headed for 800 on the critical reading portion of the SAT.

PRACTICE TEST QUESTIONS

> **Directions:** Each of the following sentences contains one or two blanks; each blank indicates that a word or set of words has been left out. Below the sentence are five words or phrases, lettered (A) through (E). Select the word or set of words that best completes the sentence.

1. Though Paul's view of the world was softened by _____, he quickly became _____ when he attended an urban college campus and experienced the cynical nature of many of his peers.

   (A) romanticism..disinterested
   (B) saccharine..dissatisfied
   (C) hysteria..disheartened
   (D) paranoia..dismissive
   (E) naiveté..disillusioned

2. Although the host of the home-decorating show touted uniformity of adornments when decorating a Christmas tree, Lucida preferred a(an) _____ assortment of ornaments, for each one—unique and special—held a warm memory.

   (A) homogeneous
   (B) unvarying
   (C) mixing
   (D) dispersed
   (E) eclectic

3. To balance her sons' _____ schedules that include an endless bustle of
schoolwork, sports, religion, and play
dates, as well as a bevy of birthday parties, Susie tries to foster "down time"
during the week.

(A) furious
(B) frenetic
(C) kinetic
(D) mellow
(E) mad

4. Gabriella's _____ sense is so keen that,
in one whiff, she can detect whether the
goat cheese is topped with mango-
chutney or pineapple salsa.

(A) visceral
(B) auditory
(C) tactile
(D) olfactory
(E) visual

5. After much soul searching and _____,
Pamela realized that she is predominantly self-serving and self-indulgent,
the _____ of June, who epitomizes
altruism.

(A) rendezvous..parallel
(B) divulging..mainstay
(C) aggravation..provocation
(D) extrovertion..adversary
(E) introspection..antithesis

6. Regardless of a weekend of ceaseless fiascos, one _____ relentlessly following
the next until her problem-solving
energy was completely _____, Ava
remained sanguine.

(A) conundrum..gratified
(B) infusion..precluded
(C) debacle..dissipated
(D) gaffe..malfunctioned
(E) diversion..expunged

7. The candidate's speech was filled with
_____ instead of substance; Alexa's oratory was crafted _____, veiling the little
straightforward information that her
speech contained.

(A) conjecture..expertise
(B) promises..delivery
(C) veracity..duplicity
(D) pomposity..pragmatism
(E) bombast..rhetoric

8. Peter is sprightly and jovial, even though
his closest friends describe his disposition
as _____ and _____.

(A) lugubrious..melancholic
(B) downcast..prescient
(C) austere..incriminating
(D) jubilant..demonstrative
(E) histrionic..lackadaisical

> **Directions:** Read each passage below, and then answer the questions that follow. The correct response may be stated outright or merely suggested in the passage.

Questions 9 and 10 are based on the following passage.

This paragraph, taken from a letter the author writes to her sister, is from Mary Shelley's science fiction novel, Frankenstein.

Will you smile at the enthusiasm I express
concerning this divine wanderer? You would not if
you saw him. You have been tutored and refined by
books and retirement from the world, and you are
Line
5   therefore somewhat fastidious; but this only renders
you the more fit to appreciate the extraordinary merits
of this wonderful man. Sometimes I have endeavored
to discover what quality it is which he possesses that
elevates him so immeasurably above any other person
10   I ever knew. I believe it to be an intuitive discernment,
a quick but never-failing power of judgment, a penetration
into the causes of things, unequalled for clearness and
precision; add to this a facility of expression and a
voice whose varied intonations are soul-subduing music.

9. In line 5, "renders" most closely means

(A) portrays
(B) provides
(C) makes
(D) rends
(E) entreats

10. Lines 10–14 suggest that which of the following pairs of qualities are most admired about the "divine wanderer" first mentioned in line 2?

(A) adventurous and intrepid spirit
(B) magnanimity and overall kindness
(C) perspicacity and eloquence
(D) strength and innocence
(E) arrogance and perseverance

> **Directions:** The questions that follow the two passages in this section relate to the content of both, and to their relationship. The correct response may be stated outright in the passages or merely suggested.

Questions 11–14 are based on the following passages.

Passage 1 is taken from Olaf the Glorious: A Story of the Viking Age *by Robert Leighton.*
Passage 2 is from Homer's The Odyssey, *translated into English prose by Samuel Butler.*

Passage 1

Now although Olaf had spoken of his wish
to return to the land of his fathers, yet now
that he was upon his own dragonship, and
free to follow where fortune should lead him,
Line
5   he showed no haste to make a landing in Norway.*
He bent his course across the Gulf of Finland,
and then westward among the many green islands
and rocky holms that lie in the mid sea between
Finland and Sweden, and for many sunny days
10 and calm starry nights simply enjoyed the idle
pleasures of his new life of freedom. It was the
summer season, when all the channels of the sea
were clear of ice, and there were many trading
ships abroad which might have been an easy
15 prey had Olaf so chosen to fall upon them. But
although he was a Viking, and had all the Viking's
lust for war and plunder, he yet remembered the
time when his own mother had been taken by
Klerkon and sold into bondage. So he determined
20 to let all peaceful merchant ships alone, and to join
battle only with such vessels as were intent upon
warfare.

Passage 2

Now all the rest, as many as fled from sheer
destruction, were at home, and had escaped both
25 war and sea, but Odysseus only, craving for his
wife and for his homeward path, the lady nymph
Calypso held, that fair goddess, in her hollow caves,
longing to have him for her lord. But when now
the year had come in the courses of the seasons,
30 wherein the gods had ordained that he should return
home to Ithaca, not even there was he quit of labours,
not even among his own; but all the gods had pity

---

* Olaf's homeland

on him save Poseidon,* who raged continually against godlike Odysseus, till he came to his own country.

35   Poseidon had now departed for the distant Ethiopians . . . the uttermost of men, abiding some where Hyperion sinks and some where he rises.

11. Both passages emphasize which aspect of the sea?

(A) Its fertility and bounty
(B) Its profound depth
(C) Its seasonal rhythm
(D) Its steadfast calm
(E) Its potential to present struggle or conflict

12. It can be inferred that Odysseus (Passage 2), compared to Olaf (Passage 1), regards returning "homeward" (line 26) with more

(A) zeal and disdain
(B) intensity and hesitance
(C) ferocity and vigor
(D) fervor and nostalgia
(E) restiveness and apathy

13. Unlike the author of Passage 1, the author of Passage 2 does which of the following?

(A) characterizes Greek gods as inherently belligerent
(B) alludes to seamen who have returned home safely
(C) uses a first-person narrative point of view
(D) portrays the sea as unconditionally tranquil
(E) stereotypes a group of people

14. Which of the following expresses a main contrast between voyagers Olaf and Odysseus?

(A) while the former engages in missionary work, the latter commits himself to "his own" (Passage 2, line 32)
(B) while the former is a revolutionary, the latter is an unadventurous spirit who wishes to remain in the "hollow caves" (Passage 2, line 27)
(C) while the former experiences wanderlust, the latter experiences an intense longing for "his homeward path" (Passage 2, line 26)
(D) while the former seeks to forgive Klerkon (Passage 1, line 19), the latter seeks to overtake Poseidon (Passage 2, line 33)
(E) while the former has a desultory voyage to Norway, the latter makes a halfhearted "return home to Ithaca" (Passage 2, lines 30 and 31)

---

* *According to Greek mythology, Poseidon is god of the sea.*

Questions 15–20 are based on the following passage.

This passage is taken from the writings of English nurse Florence Nightingale.

The very first canon of nursing, the first
and the last thing upon which a nurse's attention must
be fixed, the first essential to a patient, without which
all the rest you can do for him is as nothing, with which

Line
5   I had almost said you may leave all the rest alone, is
this: to keep the air he breathes as pure as the external
air, without chilling him.

Yet what is so little attended to? Even where it is
thought of at all, the most extraordinary misconceptions

10   reign about it. Even in admitting air into the patient's
room or ward, few people ever think, where that air comes
from. It may come from a corridor into which other wards
are ventilated, from a hall, always unaired, always full
of the fumes of gas, dinner, of various kinds of mustiness;

15   from an underground kitchen, sink, washhouse, water-closet,
or even, as I myself have had sorrowful experience, from
open sewers loaded with filth; and with this the patient's
room or ward is aired, as it is called—poisoned, it should
rather be said. Always, air from the air without, and that,

20   too, through those windows, through which the air comes
freshest. From a closed court, especially if the wind do
not blow that way, air may come as stagnant as any from a
hall or corridor.

Coaching
*Hey, 2400 Club
members, once again
dotted lines illustrate
how you might
downsize this long
passage by reading in
pieces.*

*Some like their pieces
small; others like
them big. You're
motivated and self-
directed, so break the
passage down in a
way that suits you
personally as a reader.*

Again, a thing I have often seen both in private

25   houses and institutions. A room remains uninhabited; the
fireplace is carefully fastened up with a board; the windows
are never opened; probably the shutters are kept always
shut; perhaps some kind of stores are kept in the room;
no breath of fresh air can by possibility enter into that

30   room, nor any ray of sun. The air is as stagnant, musty,
and corrupt as it can by possibility be made. It is quite
ripe to breed small-pox, scarlet-fever, diphtheria, or anything else you please.

Yet the nursery, ward, or sick room adjoining will

35   positively be aired by having the door opened into that room.
Or children will be put into that room, without previous
preparation, to sleep.

A short time ago a man walked into a back-kitchen in
Queen Square, and cut the throat of a poor consumptive

40   creature, sitting by the fire. The murderer did not deny

the act, but simply said, "It's all right." Of course he
was mad.

But in our case, the extraordinary thing is that
the victim says, "It's all right," and that we are not mad.
45 Yet, although we "nose" the murderers, in the musty unaired
unsunned room, the scarlet fever which is behind the door,
or the fever and hospital gangrene which are stalking
among the crowded beds of a hospital ward, we say,
"It's all right."

----

50 With a proper supply of windows, and a proper supply
of fuel in open fire places, fresh air is comparatively easy
to secure when your patient or patients are in bed. Never
be afraid of open windows then. People don't catch cold
in bed. This is a popular fallacy. With proper bed-clothes
55 and hot bottles, if necessary, you can always keep a patient
warm in bed, and well ventilate him at the same time.

15. In context, the word "reign" (line 10)
most closely means

(A) overshadow
(B) rule
(C) influence
(D) prevail
(E) hover

16. According to the author, "previous preparation" (lines 36 and 37) would most
likely involve which of the following?

  I. Serving convalescents ample fluids
and broths
 II. Providing the patient with warm
sleepwear and hot bottles
III. Opening windows and shutters
IV. All of the above

(A) I only
(B) II only
(C) I and II only
(D) II and III only
(E) IV

17. The anecdote in paragraph 5 (lines
38–49) serves primarily to

(A) interject a dose of comic relief
tinged with irony
(B) validate Nightingale's apprehension
about open-door policies at hospitals
(C) digress from a topic that is too heavy
and care-laden
(D) compare individuals' motives surrounding their destructive actions
(E) juxtapose people's reactions to a
common murder and their reactions
to negligent caretakers

18. In context, the words "the scarlet fever
which is behind the door . . . of a hospital
ward" (lines 46–48) create which figurative language effect?

(A) extended metaphor
(B) personification
(C) dramatic irony
(D) humorous exaggeration
(E) symbolic imagery

19. On the basis of the passage as a whole, the "victim" in line 44 most likely refers to

(A) "few people" (line 11)
(B) "children" (line 36)
(C) "a poor consumptive creature" (lines 39 and 40)
(D) "the murderer" (line 40)
(E) "a patient" (line 55)

20. In developing her first-person narrative, Nightingale does all of the following EXCEPT

(A) exaggerate a literary allusion
(B) include a snippet of dialogue
(C) digress onto a brief personal reflection
(D) offer some troubleshooting and a solution
(E) pose a question and then answer it

Directions: The questions that follow the two passages in this section relate to the contents of both and to their relationship. The correct response may be stated outright or merely suggested.

Questions 21–32 are based on the paired passages that follow.

The first passage is excerpted from Joseph Conrad's Typhoon. *The second passage is excerpted from* The Black Cat, *a short-story thriller by Edgar Allan Poe.*

Passage 1

CAPTAIN MACWHIRR, of the steamer Nan-Shan, had a physiognomy that, in the order of material appearances, was the exact counterpart of his mind: it presented no marked characteristics of firmness or stupidity; it had no pronounced characteristics

Line
5 whatever; it was simply ordinary, irresponsive, and unruffled.

The only thing his aspect might have been said to suggest, at times, was bashfulness; because he would sit, in business offices ashore, sunburnt and smiling faintly, with downcast eyes. When he raised them, they were perceived to be direct in their glance

10 and of blue colour. His hair was fair and extremely fine, clasping from temple to temple the bald dome of his skull in a clamp as of fluffy silk. The hair of his face, on the contrary, carroty and flaming, resembled a growth of copper wire clipped short to the line of the lip; while, no matter how close he

15 shaved, fiery metallic gleams passed, when he moved his head, over the surface of his cheeks. He was rather below the medium height, a bit round-shouldered, and so sturdy of limb that his clothes always looked a shade too tight for his arms and legs.

Having just enough imagination to carry him through each

20 successive day, and no more, he was tranquilly sure of himself; and from the very same cause he was not in the least conceited. It is your imaginative superior who is touchy, overbearing, and difficult to please; but every ship Captain MacWhirr commanded was the floating abode of harmony and peace. It was, in truth,

25   as impossible for him to take a flight of fancy as it would be
for a watchmaker to put together a chronometer with nothing
except a two-pound hammer and a whip-saw in the way of tools.
Yet the uninteresting lives of men so entirely given to the
actuality of the bare existence have their mysterious side. It
30   was impossible in Captain MacWhirr's case, for instance, to
understand what under heaven could have induced that perfectly
satisfactory son of a petty grocer in Belfast to run away to sea.
And yet he had done that very thing at the age of fifteen. It
was enough, when you thought it over, to give you the idea of an
35   immense, potent, and invisible hand thrust into the ant-heap of
the earth, laying hold of shoulders, knocking heads together, and
setting the unconscious faces of the multitude towards
inconceivable goals and in undreamt-of directions.

Passage 2

   From my infancy I was noted for the docility and humanity
40   of my disposition. My tenderness of heart was even so conspicuous
as to make me the jest of my companions. I was especially fond of
animals, and was indulged by my parents with a great variety of pets.
With these I spent most of my time, and never was so happy as when
feeding and caressing them. This peculiarity of character grew with my growth,
45   and in my manhood, I derived from it one of my principal sources of
pleasure.
   To those who have cherished an affection for a faithful and
sagacious dog, I need hardly be at the trouble of explaining the nature
or the intensity of the gratification thus derivable. There is something
50   in the unselfish and self-sacrificing love of a brute, which goes directly
to the heart of him who has had frequent occasion to test the paltry
friendship and gossamer fidelity of mere Man. I married early, and
was happy to find in my wife a disposition not uncongenial with my
own. Observing my partiality for domestic pets, she lost no opportunity
55   of procuring those of the most agreeable kind. We had birds, gold-fish,
a fine dog, rabbits, a small monkey, and a cat. This latter was a remarkably
large and beautiful animal, entirely black, and sagacious to an astonishing
degree. In speaking of his intelligence, my wife, who at heart was not a
little tinctured with superstition, made frequent allusion to the ancient
60   popular notion, which regarded all black cats as witches in disguise. Not
that she was ever serious upon this point—and I mention the matter at
all for no better reason than that it happens, just now, to be remembered.
   Pluto—this was the cat's name—was my favorite pet and playmate.
I alone fed him, and he attended me wherever I went about the house.
65   It was even with difficulty that I could prevent him from following me
through the streets. Our friendship lasted, in this manner, for several years,

during which my general temperament and character—through the instrumentality of the Fiend Intemperance—had (I blush to confess it) experienced a radical alteration for the worse. I grew, day by day, more moody, more

70   irritable, more regardless of the feelings of others. I suffered myself to use intemperate language to my wife. At length, I even offered her personal violence. My pets, of course, were made to feel the change in my disposition. I not only neglected, but ill-used them. For Pluto, however, I still retained sufficient regard to restrain me from maltreating him, as I made no scruple

75   of maltreating the rabbits, the monkey, or even the dog, when by accident, or through affection, they came in my way.

But my disease grew upon me . . . and at length even Pluto, who was now becoming old, and consequently somewhat peevish—even Pluto began to experience the effects of my ill temper. One night, returning home, much

80   intoxicated, from one of my haunts about town, I fancied that the cat avoided my presence. I seized him; when, in his fright at my violence, he inflicted a slight wound upon my hand with his teeth.

21. Which of the following descriptive phrases testifies to Captain MacWhirr's "bashfulness" (line 7)?

(A) "no marked characteristics of firmness" (lines 3 and 4)
(B) "irresponsive and unruffled" (line 5)
(C) "downcast eyes" (line 8)
(D) "the surface of his cheeks" (line 16)
(E) "round-shouldered" (line 17)

22. A "clamp" (line 12) and "copper wire" (line 13) serve primarily

(A) as color imagery
(B) as metaphors that describe Captain MacWhirr's hair
(C) to simulate the captain's fiery temper
(D) to contrast the captain's two personalities
(E) to emphasize the captain's mental tension

23. It can be inferred from the final sentence of Passage 1 that the author recognizes

(A) an ubiquitous, influential higher power
(B) a universal, hyperactive imagination
(C) how people see themselves in others
(D) a grand-scale chaotic, pernicious force
(E) how parents are unable to influence their children's destinies

24. In context, the term "shade" (line 18) in Passage 1 most closely means

(A) thread
(B) shadow
(C) hue
(D) hair
(E) tint

25. In line 70 (Passage 2), the phrase "regardless of" most nearly means

(A) remiss in
(B) unrelated to
(C) indifferent toward
(D) irreverent toward
(E) irregular toward

26. The narrator's confession in line 73 (Passage 2), "I not only neglected, but ill-used them," most directly contradicts his

(A) maltreatment of rabbits and monkeys (line 75)
(B) wife's superstition (lines 59 and 60)
(C) being indulged by his parents (line 42)
(D) "affection for a faithful and sagacious dog" (lines 47 and 48)
(E) "partiality for domestic pets" (line 54)

27. In Passage 2, an individual who becomes the "jest of my companions" (line 41) is most analogous to

(A) a pariah who has been banished from his or her hometown
(B) a sentimental person who feels an intense nostalgia
(C) a scapegoat who is alienated by his peers
(D) a recluse who, unexpectedly and suddenly, craves social interaction
(E) a youngster who is the source of jokes among his contemporaries

28. In context, "consequently" (line 78) most closely means

(A) as a result
(B) habitually
(C) inconsequentially
(D) appropriately
(E) discordantly

29. "The immense, potent, and invisible hand" (line 35) of Passage 1 is most analogous to which of the following in Passage 2?

(A) "manhood" (line 45)
(B) "Man" (line 52)
(C) "witches in disguise" (line 60)
(D) "Fiend Intemperance" (line 68)
(E) "Pluto" (line 73)

30. Which aspect of character portrayal matters more in Passage 1 than in Passage 2?

(A) the character's preoccupation with outward appearance
(B) the character's uncanny, obsessive nature
(C) the character's indecisive personality
(D) the character's inner turmoil
(E) the character's physical description

31. Captain MacWhirr (Passage 1) differs most from the narrator in Passage 2 in that the former is more

(A) likely to indulge in his whimsical desires
(B) prone to violence
(C) skillful in terms of interpersonal relationships
(D) equipped with a vivid imagination
(E) stable in temperament

32. Passage 1 and Passage 2 share a general tone of

(A) self-possessed indignation
(B) severe acrimony
(C) quizzical humor
(D) basic forthrightness
(E) righteous aloofness

ANSWERS AND EXPLANATIONS

1. E	**9.** C	**17.** E	**25.** D
2. E	**10.** C	**18.** B	**26.** E
3. B	**11.** E	**19.** E	**27.** E
4. D	**12.** D	**20.** A	**28.** A
5. E	**13.** B	**21.** C	**29.** D
6. C	**14.** C	**22.** B	**30.** E
7. E	**15.** D	**23.** A	**31.** E
8. A	**16.** D	**24.** D	**32.** D

1. Why it's tough: two blanks; context clues are subtle; all possible answer choices for the second blank share the prefix *dis-* (meaning not)
   Your strategies: Assign a positive (+) to the first blank and a negative (–) to the second blank since Paul's world view was initially softened but became negative (–), *disillusioned*, once he encountered his *cynical* peers.
   Your word (possibilities): In this case, you may find yourself tongue-tied when it comes to bringing your word to the blank.
   Challenging vocabulary: *cynical, saccharine, dismissive, naiveté*
   Best answer: **(E)**; *naiveté* is an inexperienced and unsophisticated view of the world.

2. Why it's tough: long sentence starting with the opposite-indicating *Although*.
   Your strategies: Let *although* cue you into the fact that the second half of the sentence is in contrast to the first half. The opposite of *uniformity* (first half) would be *an eclectic assortment*. (A) and (B) are opposites of *eclectic*. (C), *mixing*, doesn't work; it's awkward. (D), *dispersed*, means spread out.
   Your word: *varied?*
   Challenging vocabulary: *touted, adornments, homogeneous, eclectic*
   Best answer: **(E)**; *eclectic* means collected from various sources.

3. Why it's tough: cumbersome comma series; the answer choices, as is often the case, contain the correct answer and one of its antonyms.
   Your strategies: Find an adjective to modify *schedules*. Since the boys' schedules involve *an endless bustle*, these schedules must be very "busy" or "crazy." (Would you have brought those words, or similar ones, to the blank?) Decide on the better of the two best choices, *frenetic* and *mad. Mad* is out—too casual and colloquial; *frenetic* is the answer. Even though Susie may feel *furious* sometimes, that word does not describe the schedules.
   Your word: *hectic? crazy? fast-paced? frantic?*
   Challenging vocabulary: *bevy, frenetic, kinetic?*
   Best answer: **(B)**, *frenetic* means frenzied or frantic.

4. Why it's tough: challenging vocabulary in answer choices

   Your strategies: Pick up on the context clue *in one whiff*, which has to do with the sense of smell.

   Your word: *smelling?*

   Challenging vocabulary: *keen, visceral, tactile, olfactory*

   Best answer: **(D)**; *olfactory* means relating to the sense of smell.

5. Why it's tough: two-blankers are often challenging; tricky sentence structure with its two commas; first comma separates prepositional phrase from the main clause of the sentence; second comma introduces an adjective clause.

   Your word (possibilities): In this case, you may find yourself tongue-tied when it comes to bringing your word to the blank.

   Your strategies: (1) Use the conjunction *and* to realize that the word for the first blank has to be related to *soul searching*; (2) assuming you understand that *altruism* means showing concern for mankind, you can predict that the second blank needs the opposite (*antithesis*).

   Challenging vocabulary: *epitomizes, altruism, rendezvous, divulging, antithesis*

   Best Answer: **(E)**; *introspection* means looking inward.

6. Why it's tough: tricky two-blanker that starts with the opposite-indicating phrase *Regardless of*.

   Your word (possibilities): Again, you may find yourself tongue-tied when it comes to bringing your word to the blank.

   Your strategies: Pick up on the negative (–) value of the first blank: *Regardless of . . . fiascos, one* (negative value) *following the next. . . , Ava remained sanguine* (cheerful). Also, always read with your eyes peeled for context clues such as *fiascos* and *problem-solving* (clues for the first blank).

   Challenging vocabulary: *sanguine, conundrum, debacle, dissipated, gaffe, diversion, expunged*

   Best answer: **(C)**; a *debacle* is a big problem, a total collapse or failure; *dissipated* means spent, as in "depleted of energy."

7. Why it's tough: two-blanker; compound sentence separated by a semicolon; challenging vocabulary

   Your word (possibilities): And again, you may find yourself tongue-tied when it comes to bringing your word to the blank.

   Your strategies: The words *filled with _____ instead of substance* indicate that the missing word means the opposite of *substance*. *Bombast* and *pomposity* both work, but the second blank also needs a negative word since Alexa's oratory was *crafted* and is *veiling...information*. Eliminate (B), since these words are too basic for an upper-level question. (Keep level-headed.)

   Challenging vocabulary: *conjecture, veracity, pomposity, bombast, rhetoric*

   Best answer: **(E)**; *bombast* and *rhetoric* both connote windblown language that is insincere and lacks substance.

8. Why it's tough: two-blanker; challenging vocabulary in sentence and answer choices
   Your strategies: Pick up on the opposite-indicating *even though* so that you understand the blanks must be opposites of *sprightly* and *jovial*. Also, the conjunction *and* tells you that the blanks need similar words.
   Your words: *sluggish? sad?*
   Challenging vocabulary: *sprightly, jovial, disposition, lugubrious, melancholic, prescient, histrionic, lackadaisical*
   Best answer: **(A)**; *lugubrious* and *melancholic* mean sad, gloomy.

9. VOCABULARY WORD-IN-CONTEXT QUESTION **To get a sense of the word's contextual meaning, reread the full sentence in which the word appears.** Predict a meaning for the word, then plug in the answer choices to find the match that makes the most sense. To be a prudent 2400 Club member, reread the sentence in its entirety to ensure that the sentence flows smoothly with your answer selection. In this case, the answer is **(C)**, *makes*. *Rends* is a decoy for the distracted test taker. *Rends* only sounds and looks like *renders*; *rends* means tears up, as in "The tiger *rends* its prey."

10. INFERENCE QUESTION; NOTICE KEY WORD *SUGGESTS* **Peruse lines 10–14, sniffing out context clues that indicate admirable traits of the mysterious personage, the "divine wanderer."** Lines 10–14 are reproduced below, with context clues in italics:

    10   I believe it to be an *intuitive discernment,*
            a quick but never-failing power of judgment, a penetration
            into the causes of things, unequalled for clearness and
            precision; add to this a *facility of expression* and a
            voice whose varied intonations are soul-subduing music.

    The first set of italics indicates "perspicacity" (keen perceptiveness); the second set indicates "eloquence" (effective and/or artful speech). The answer is **(C)**.

11. FINDING A PARITY BETWEEN THE PARAGRAPHS **Quickly and carefully skim the passages for references to the *sea*.**

                            So he determined
    20 to let all peaceful merchant ships alone, and to join
        <u>battle only with such vessels as were intent upon</u>
        <u>warfare</u>. (Passage 1, final line)

        and

                            as many as <u>fled from sheer</u>
        <u>destruction</u>, were at home, and had <u>escaped both</u>
    25 <u>war and sea</u> (Passage 2, lines 23–25)

                <u>Poseidon,* who raged continually</u> against
        godlike Odysseus (Passage 2, lines 33 and 34)

The underscored parts especially reveal how the sea is depicted as having the *potential to present struggle or conflict*. The best answer is **(E)**.

12. PAIRED-PARAGRAPH PERSPECTIVE QUESTION **Reflect on how the homeward voyage is depicted in both passages.** Textual evidence tells us that Odysseus feels a "craving for his wife and for his homeward path" (Passage 2, lines 25 and 26). A *craving* is a deep-seated desire or affection. These are all positive longings, so eliminate (A) and (C), which contain negative terms like *disdain* and *ferocity*. Odysseus cannot wait to see his wife and homeland, so eliminate (B), *hesitance*, and (E), *apathy*. The correct answer is **(D)**. *Fervor* means intense emotion, and *nostalgia* means homesickness.

13. BROAD QUESTION THAT REQUIRES YOU TO HAVE A SENSE OF WHAT'S BEING WRITTEN BY THE AUTHORS OF THE PARAGRAPHS **Find evidence in Passage 2 to support only one choice.** There's no passage proof for (A) or (C)—where's the first-person *I*?—so cross them off. Active pencil! The Passage 2 author tells about how Poseidon, god of the sea, *raged continually*, so eliminate (D). If anyone is stereotyping, it's the Passage 1 author: "he was a Viking, and had all the Viking's lust for war and plunder" (lines 16 and 17). Eliminate (E). Based on passage evidence, the answer is **(B)**: "Now all the rest, as many as fled from sheer destruction, were at home, and had escaped both war and sea" (Passage 2, opening line).

14. TRICKY QUESTION THAT INVOLVES SEVERAL TERMS AND PHRASES USED IN THE PASSAGES **To answer this question successfully, you need to notice the key word, *contrast*, in the question and have an understanding of the words *former* and *latter*. Skim the passages for details that portray Olaf and Odysseus to get a sense of the ways in which they *differ*.** With tough, time-consuming questions, do not rely on your memory alone. Instead, use the line references provided in the answer choices, and refer back to the passage as needed. Nowhere does it say that Olaf is involved in *missionary work* or that he is a *revolutionary*, so eliminate (A) and (B). Furthermore, (B) is wrong because the passage implies that Odysseus is being held in the *hollow* caves against his will. Klerkon and Poseidon are figures who are mentioned, but nowhere is it said that Olaf wishes to forgive Klerkon or that Odysseus wants to overtake the sea god. Eliminate (D). Active pencil! The first part of (E) is supported, since Olaf has a *desultory* (aimless, unfocused) voyage to Norway; in fact, he takes his sweet time (lines 5–11). The second part of choice (E) is inaccurate. Odysseus by no means makes a *halfhearted* return to Ithaca; he has a "craving for his . . . homeward path" (lines 25 and 26). To be valid, the entire answer choice must be supported by the passage. *Wanderlust*, that feeling of itchy feet one has coupled with the desire to travel around, indeed describes Olaf. The answer is **(C)**.

15. CHALLENGING WORD-IN-CONTEXT QUESTION **First, reread the sentence and predict what "reign" should mean:** "Yet what is so little attended to? Even where it is thought of at all, the most extraordinary misconceptions reign about it." To get the gist of this sentence, you need to know what *it* refers to . . . . Look back earlier in

the passage, and you'll notice that *it* must refer to keeping air around the patient pure (line 6). Second, consider the answer choices carefully. The meaning should fit into the context perfectly. Note that "reign" is found in the second sentence of paragraph two, which functions as a topic sentence. The ideas in paragraph two are about how, even when caretakers admit air into a patient's room, they don't think about where the air is coming from. Paraphrase sentence two: *Even when caretakers think about letting in clean and pure air, there are bizarre misunderstandings (or fallacies) regarding how to do this.* "The most extraordinary misconceptions *reign* about it," (that is, the proper way to let in pure air). The connotation of "reign" is strength and power; a king or monarch, for example, *reigns* over his land. Tempting choices would be (B), *rule*, and (C), *influence*. Keeping in mind that the word substitution has to flow smoothly, however, you see that the best choice is **(D)**, *prevail*, which is a word of strength, meaning to predominate. Choice (E), *hover*, does fit, but lacks the connotative value of power that characterizes *reign*.

16. TIME-CONSUMING ROMAN-NUMERAL-LIST QUESTION **Based on your memory of what you have read and by skimming the passage, find evidence (or the lack thereof) to support or discredit each item in the Roman-numeral list.**
I. *Serving convalescents ample fluids and broths* is good common sense but is never mentioned in this excerpt.
II. *Providing the patient with warm sleepwear and hot bottles* is mentioned at the very end.
III. *Opening windows and shutters* is mentioned in lines 26–28.
The correct answer is **(D)**.

17. QUESTION ON UNDERSTANDING THE FUNCTION OF ONE PART OF THE PASSAGE TO THE WHOLE PASSAGE **Reread the anecdote in paragraph five, and consider its role or purpose in the passage.** The anecdote tells that a murderer is thought of as "mad" when he kills a convalescent, but a patient victimized by negligent caretakers pardons them and says that they are not "mad." Here's the essential part on which you should focus:

40   The murderer did not deny the act, but simply said, "It's all right." Of course he
       was mad.
       But in our case, the extraordinary thing is that
       the victim says, "It's all right," and that we are not mad.

So there's a difference (contrast) between the reactions to a cold-blooded murderer and to neglectful caretakers, who, in Nightingale's opinion, practically commit murder by their remiss ways. The correct answer is **(E)**. To *juxtapose* is to consider two things, side by side, for the purposes of comparing and contrasting them.

18. A QUESTION THAT EVOKES YOUR KNOWLEDGE OF FIGURATIVE LANGUAGE **For this rather rare type of question, you will not only need to know the meanings of the figurative terms in the answer choices (*personification*,**

metaphor, *irony*, *allusion*, *humorous*, *exaggeration*, and *symbolic imagery*), **but also need to be aware of how to spot these terms in a passage.** In context, "the scarlet fever which is behind the door . . . of a hospital ward" (lines 46–48) creates which rhetorical effects? The answer is **(B)**. If you visualize scarlet fever as stealthily "hiding" behind the hospital-room door, or if you imagine seeing the "gangrene" *stalking* (as surreptitious people might do) amid the hospital beds, then you can see how these words personify these ailments as they sneak up on and hunt down their victims.

19. CONSIDER TO WHOM A WORD REFERS IN CONTEXT **Skim around each answer choice to see which entity most likely fills the shoes of the "victim."** According to the anecdote in paragraph five, the "victim" must be someone who is not blatantly murdered, but rather is "killed" by nurses (caretakers, in general) since Nightingale (a nurse) says, "But in *our case*, the extraordinary things is that . . . " (lines 43 and 44). The only answer that makes sense is **(E)**, *a patient*.

20. TIME-CONSUMING ALL/EXCEPT QUESTION **Find evidence to validate all but one answer choice.** In line 41, a *snippet of dialogue* appears, so (B) is out. In lines 16 and 17, Nightingale *digresses onto a brief personal reflection*, eliminate (C). In the last paragraph, she offers *some troubleshooting and a solution*; cross off (D). The author *poses a question* in line 8 and *then answers it*, good-bye to (E). The answer is **(A)**. A *literary allusion* is a reference, usually to some work of literature; there is none in this passage.

21. TIME-CONSUMING QUESTION THAT REQUIRES YOU TO UNDERSTAND THE SIGNIFICANCE OF SEVERAL PHRASES FROM THE PASSAGE AND HOW THEY MAY OR MAY NOT RELATE TO A CHARACTER'S "BASHFULNESS." **Quickly and carefully skim around the five phrases listed so that you get a sense of their meanings in context.** (A) and (B) refer to the Captain's outward "material appearances" (line 2), so these answer choices are out. (D), "the surface of his cheeks" relates to the "metallic" hair that remains on his face even after he has shaved, so (D) is out. (E), "round-shouldered," contributes to the description of the captain's stature. The answer is **(C)**, "downcast eyes," an indicator of shyness or bashfulness.

22. PURPOSE QUESTION **Reread these two terms as they are used in context (lines 10–14) to get a sense of their purpose.** (A) is incorrect because the "clamp" has nothing to do with color. (C) is out because nowhere is it said that the Captain has a fiery temper. This might be a tempting choice, though, since "fiery" and "flaming" appear in the vicinity. No evidence points to the Captain's dual personality or mental tension, so (D) and (E) are out (though these two traits, to an extent, characterize our "pet lover" in Passage 2). Careful rereading reveals that "clamp" and "copper wire" are metaphors (figurative speech devices used to make direct comparisons) to describe the Captain's hair. The answer is **(B)**.

23. MAKING AN INFERENCE BASED ON A "MOUTHFUL" OF A SENTENCE THAT BOR-
DERS ON THE INSCRUTABLE **Reread that challenging final sentence very
carefully to ascertain its meaning. Don't be daunted; focus on what you *do*
understand.** Let's paraphrase to cut this mouthful down to size: ". . . a big, powerful, and invisible hand forcefully pushed into the earth . . . grabbing people's shoulders and knocking their heads together, and moving unaware people toward goals
and places that they never would have thought of or dreamed of." It sounds like
some "higher power" that makes things happen to people on Earth. (C) and (E) do
not coordinate with this paraphrasing. (E) relates to the Belfast boy discussed in
prior lines. Though (D) mentions a "grand-scale . . . force," nothing in the final line
points to this force being pernicious (very destructive or harmful). (B) is not supported here. **(A)** is the best answer. An *ubiquitous* (omnipresent) power fits many
people's sense of a higher power, although this varies from one individual to
another.

24. WORD-IN-CONTEXT QUESTION **The 2400 Club is open-minded when it
comes to what a word might actually mean *in* context.** Reread the pertinent
lines: "He was rather below the medium height . . . and so sturdy of limb that his
clothes always looked a **shade** too tight for his arms and legs." (lines 16–18) (A),
thread, relates to clothing, but the word does not work in context. (B), *shadow*,
resembles *shade*, but doesn't fit either. Cross these choices off with an active pencil.
(C) and (E), *hue* and *tint*, relate to shades of color, but that's not how the Captain's
clothes are being described. Reread the pertinent lines again, if you need to. Now
make a prediction for what you think *shade* means. A *bit* too tight? A *smidgen* too
tight? The word that fits these predictions best and flows smoothly is *hair*, a *hair* too
tight. The answer is **(D)**.

25. PHRASE-IN-CONTEXT QUESTION **Embed the expression "regardless of" in a
wide enough context so you can ascertain its meaning within the passage.**
(A) does not work because *remiss* means negligent in fulfilling one's responsibilities.
(B) does not flow, and (C) makes no sense because *indifferent* means showing no con-
cern. Choice (E) is tempting, since *regardless* and *irregular* might seem similar at first.
Irreverent means disrespectful, so choice **(D)** works best and flows most smoothly.
The narrator's harsh language and violence directed at his wife (lines 71 and 72)
are *irreverent* to an extreme.

26. TOUGH QUESTION THAT ALLUDES TO SEVERAL TERMS AND PHRASES USED
THROUGHOUT THE PASSAGE **Using the given line references, refer back to
the passage to see which answer choice *contradicts* (key word) the narrator's maltreatment of his pets.** This type of question takes time, so work quickly
but diligently. Certainly (A) is in line with the maltreatment. (B) and (D) are out
since (B), the wife's superstition, is directed at the cat alone and (D) is directed at a
dog—the quote you're asked about, "I not only neglected, but ill-used them," pertains to all of his pets. (C) is incorrect because it has more to do with the parents'
actions than the narrator's. The answer is **(E)**, since *partiality* would be the narrator's "soft spot" or adoration of his pets.

27. DRAWING A PARALLEL BETWEEN AN INDIVIDUAL DESCRIBED IN THE PASSAGE AND SOME HYPOTHETICAL INDIVIDUAL **The 2400 Club pays attention to key words in the question, like *analogous*.** The word *jest* tells you that the narrator was the "joke" among his friends. He is the one they made fun of. Which of the people described would be most similar? The best answer is **(E)**.

28. WORD-IN-CONTEXT QUESTION **The 2400 Club knows that each word listed should be plugged in to find the one that fits and flows most smoothly in the sentence.** There's no evidence to support Pluto's being peevish (irritable) on a regular basis, so (B), *habitually*, is out. (C) looks like a cousin of *consequently*, but *inconsequentially* means irrelevantly or insignificantly. Cross off these bogus choices using your active pencil. (D) and (E) also do not work—*discordantly* means clashingly or acrimoniously (bitterly). The answer that fits best is **(A)**.

29. TRICKY DECODING OF TERMS INVOLVING BOTH PASSAGES **Delve back into both passages and read up/down/around each term listed. Determine which term is most *analogous* (similar to) "The immense, potent, and invisible hand" of Passage 1.** (A) and (B) are out because *manhood* simply refers to the narrator's adulthood, and *Man* is preceded by the word *mere*, making *Man* seem measly. Neither correlates to a hand that is *immense and potent* (powerful, effective, strong). Eliminate (A) and (B) with your active pencil. (C), *witches in disguise*, refers to a superstitious view of black cats. (E), *Pluto*, is the name of the narrator's black cat. (C) and (E) are out. The correct answer is **(D)**. Line 68 reveals that a force called *Fiend Intemperance* (which might be decoded to mean "beastly lack of moderation" or "beastly excess") plays a role in the narrator's radical change. Why does Poe capitalize *Fiend Intemperance*? Perhaps it is the proper *name* of some entity, some unseen but influential power force.

30. PAIRED-PASSAGE PERSPECTIVE QUESTION **Reflect on all of the reading and thinking you have done so far on these passages.** There's no passage evidence to support that Captain MacWhirr is *preoccupied* (obsessed) with his outward appearance or that his nature is *obsessive*. Cross off (A) and (B). There is also no proof that he has an *indecisive personality* or suffers from *inner turmoil* (the latter sounds more like the Passage 2 narrator), so cross off (C) and (D), also. The answer is **(E)**, since a physical description of the Captain spans lines 1 through 18.

31. CHARACTERIZATION QUESTION THAT DEALS WITH BOTH PASSAGES **Skim around the passages for details that illustrate these two characters— Captain MacWhirr and the Passage 2 narrator (pet lover)—to get a sense of how they *differ*.** Note that in the question, "the former" refers to Captain MacWhirr. (A) is wrong because the passage says the opposite about MacWhirr: "It was impossible for him to take a flight of fancy . . ." (lines 24 and 25). There's no proof that he's *prone to violence* or *skillful interpersonally*; out go (B) and (C). In fact, (B) describes the pet lover. (D) is incorrect because lines 19 and 20 contradict this answer choice: "Having just enough imagination to carry him through each successive day, and no more . . ." The answer is **(E)**.

32. GLOBAL QUESTION ON AUTHORS' MUTUAL TONE **Questions on attitude, mood, and tone require you to absorb the overall sense and feeling of the passages.** Regardless of when these types of questions appear, prudent test takers save these global questions for last. Usually, you can eliminate "extreme" tones, like (A) and (B), since most authors want to come across as levelheaded. *Indignation* means anger; *acrimony*, bitterness. There's no trace of *humor*, so cross off (C). There's no evidence of *righteous aloofness*, so cross off (E). Active pencil! The best answer is **(D)**, *basic forthrightness*, since both passages plainly tell it like it is.

PART 2

THE WRITING SECTIONS

WRITING THE 25-MINUTE ESSAY

ENGLISH GRAMMAR AND USAGE

IMPROVING SENTENCES

IDENTIFYING SENTENCE ERRORS

IMPROVING PARAGRAPHS

Chapter 5

WRITING THE 25-MINUTE ESSAY

2400 Club Comprehensive Strategies

Strategy 1: **T**ake a side.

Strategy 2: **H**ave a timing plan.

Strategy 3: **E**ngage your reader.

Strategy 4: **E**dit, using the 2400 Club Checklist.

Strategy 5: **S**upport your thesis with examples.

Strategy 6: **S**entence and vocabulary variety

Strategy 7: **A**ssess what you have written.

Strategy 8: **Y**our voice

Writing is a life skill! You're motivated to do well in school and to perform brilliantly on your college entrance exams. Surely, you are driven also to do well in the vocation you eventually choose. Writing well is a lifelong skill that is pertinent to everyday living and to work situations. Psyche yourself to learn how to write well—not simply for the SAT, but also for your real life.

STRATEGY 1: TAKE A SIDE

On the SAT, the essay "Assignment" is posed as a question. For example, the sample test that the College Board released on its website in the fall of 2004 featured an Assignment that asked, "Do people have to be highly competitive in order to succeed?"

First, decide whether your answer to the assignment question is *yes* or *no*. Do not argue on both sides of the fence; no one respects a writer without a backbone. You must take a side and stand firmly, selecting specific examples that support your point of view. Just imagine a litigating attorney for the defense who believes her client is innocent, but also, at the same time, can see how he could be guilty. Yikes!

Once you read the question, you do not have the luxury of spending lots of time deliberating the topic. This essay is due *now*, not next week! The bottom line is that you need to

> **Essay Coaching:**
> *Insightfully explore* **relevant examples** *that develop and support a* **coherent point of view**. *Yes, it's okay to use the first-person pronoun "I."*

decide, as quickly as possible, whether your answer to the assignment question is *yes* or *no*. Just for practice, read the statements below and check the box that applies.

 Time Saver: Read the essay Assignment (usually posed as a question), and be a quick decision maker. The sooner you decide *yes* or *no*, the sooner you can start brainstorming, selecting supporting examples, and writing your essay.

Sharpening Skills—Quick Decision Making

Do you think that the individual good outweighs the common good?   ❑ yes   ❑ no

Is intellectual strength inferior to physical stamina?   ❑ yes   ❑ no

Is an individual's effect on those who are closest to him or her the
    primary indicator of that individual's integrity and character?   ❑ yes   ❑ no

Is superior wisdom more valuable than supreme kindness?   ❑ yes   ❑ no

Train yourself to be a quick decision maker. Read a bunch of famous quotations (many Internet sites feature them) and decide, speedily, whether you agree or disagree with each one. Read newspaper headlines, and decide how you feel about the issues addressed. Listen to political commentators on television, and hastily decide whether you agree or disagree with their viewpoints. In real life, rash decision making is undesirable. On a timed test, however, quick thinking is pragmatic and advantageous.

STRATEGY 2: HAVE A TIMING PLAN

Essay Tip
Timing is key.
Think
3-20-2.

A timing plan keeps you in control. Testing centers usually provide clocks or digital time displays in clear view. In some cases, proctors write the *start* time and the *stop* time on the blackboard and announce midway points so that you have a sense of how much time has elapsed and, more important, how much time you have left.

You have 25 minutes to serve up a three-course meal: an appetizer (the introductory paragraph), a zesty entrée (two or three body paragraphs), and a memorable dessert (the concluding paragraph.)

The 2400 Club timing plan is **3-20-2**. This timing plan is a guide, so it is *flexible*. You, personally, may need only 1 minute, for example, for stage 1; in this case, you will have an extra 2 minutes for stage 2.

Essay Practice and Timing

Schedule jam-packed?

No time to write the 25-minute essay?

 Time Saver: Allot *half* the time (12–13 minutes) to write *half* an essay. Write about one single-spaced page, containing an introduction and one solid body paragraph. Next time you have another 12–13 minutes to spare, write the second half of your essay: about one single-spaced page, containing a second body paragraph and a conclusion. In general, write longer body paragraphs and relatively shorter introductory and concluding paragraphs.

Ask a parent, older sibling, trusted relative, teacher, or tutor to read and critique your essay so that you may benefit from some constructive feedback. With practice, rest assured that writing the 25-minute essay will get easier and easier, particularly within the time constraints given.

THE ESSAY—STAGE 1: *ABOUT* 3 MINUTES

Read the "think box." The purpose of this boxed text, usually a paragraph or two in length, is to warm you up, to acclimate you to the topic at hand.

Next, carefully read the writing **Assignment** that follows the think box and, as you have learned, is typically posed as a question. Brainstorm. Formulate your ideas. Brainstorm some more. If you have time, you can *roughly* sketch a lean "concept map" or "web." Or simply jot down a list of ideas (write words, phrases, and abbreviations, not complete sentences).

Time Saver
Jot down your brainstorming/ prewriting notes in phrases and abbreviations.

Example

Assignment: Is wisdom superior to kindness?

> *No, kindness gr8er.*
> *- charitable orgs—Red Cross, Big Br/Big Sis, comm'y outreach*
> *- kind figs in lit:*
>> *- husb & wife, sh story, "Gift of Magi" O'Henry*
>> *- Linda L., Miller's Death of Salesman*

Practice can make you a pro at spontaneous essay writing. Use Barron's big SAT preparation book to find myriad think boxes, essay topic, and sample essays. Read each think box and assignment. Is your answer to the Assignment *yes* or *no*? Don't deliberate—*yes* or *no*? Your essay is due in 25 minutes, not next week.

FAST-FORWARD ESSAY WRITING

Once you've worked through a good number of practice essays, you may want to try a fast-forward, time-saving approach: *read just the Assignment.* This approach may sound radical, but you may find that skipping over the think box gives you extra time to use on the actual composing and revising of your essay. Try the fast-forward approach, and decide for yourself whether you are able to think directly about the Assignment, without first having read the think box.

Time Saver
Do you consider yourself quick-minded and decisive? If so, try the "fast-forward" approach to get a jump-start on your essay writing.

If you fast-forward to the Assignment question and you don't quite get where it's coming from, you can always go back to the think box. Try both approaches, and see which one works better for you.

THE ESSAY—STAGE 2: *ABOUT* 20 MINUTES

Write. Write. Write. Don't sweat the small stuff now. Just get your ideas out of your head and onto the two sheets of lined paper provided on your answer sheet. Let your thoughts flow. You're shooting for an exemplary 12, so try to write a four- to five-paragraph essay that is well developed and clearly expressed. You should write an introductory paragraph, two or three body paragraphs, and a concluding paragraph.

If you have written two solid body paragraphs and see that you have time to write more, press on and add a third body paragraph, for a total of five paragraphs. But don't add just for the sake of adding. Write more only if you have another insightful point to make or relevant example to discuss. Length matters less than quality; still, it is very unlikely that two paragraphs will earn you a high score on the essay.

THE ESSAY—STAGE 3: *ABOUT* 2 MINUTES

Proofread and polish. (See the 2400 Club Checklist of Errors to Avoid, page 115.) Realistically, the 25 minutes allotted to the essay do not give you enough time to write a complete first draft and then a final copy. You'll be happy to know, however, that the readers are asked to evaluate your essay as if it were a *draft*. Breathe a sigh of relief.

If there are changes that you wish to make, use single-line cross-outs for deletions. Do not litter your essay with sloppy scratch-offs and unsightly scribble-scrabble. A messy essay could be a turnoff to the evaluators.

Abridged Essay Practice

No doubt, you're superbusy: schoolwork, sports, college planning, part-time job, family, friends, volunteer work. . . . If a 25-minute block of uninterrupted time is an unimaginable luxury, you can practice essay writing in an abridged form. Cut the time allotted for writing the essay; give yourself 10 minutes to write two paragraphs. You can use one of these combinations:

10-Minute Combo

Example 1	*Example 2*	
Write the appetizer and half the entrée:	Write the full entrée:	**Time Saver**
■ Introductory paragraph and body paragraph 1	■ Two or three body paragraphs	*Try "abridged essay practice" when you have a spare 10 minutes.*

Know the Directions Cold

Notice that no time is allotted in this timing plan for reading the twelve or so lines of directions that precede the think box. The reason is that you should *know* them cold ahead of time.

 Know your essay directions. Read and study them now, making sure to include the finer details of the essay guidelines. Then, on test day, you can circumvent these lengthy directions, saving precious writing time.

Study the directions that follow now so that on test day you can skip them. These directions are not taken verbatim from an actual SAT, but they tell you everything you need to know.

ESSAY

Time—25 minutes

Go to page 2 of the answer sheet to write the ESSAY.

Time Saver
Read and know these essay directions here and now so that on test day, you can skip them.

This essay section allows you to show that you can develop and express ideas in an effective way. Therefore, take care to state your point of view, indicate your ideas soundly and clearly, and use language appropriately.

Essay Tip
Read between the lines: what they're telling you is that yes, to an extent, neatness counts.

Write the essay on the lined paper provided in your answer booklet; this is the only paper on which you may write. Write on every line, and avoid wide margins. Make sure your handwriting is a reasonable size. Remember that the essay readers are not familiar with your handwriting, so write or print neatly and legibly.

You have 25 minutes to compose an essay on the given assignment. DO NOT WRITE ON A DIFFERENT TOPIC. AN OFF-TOPIC ESSAY RECEIVES A ZERO.

Carefully consider the issue presented in the excerpt below and the Assignment that follows it.

> The think box contains the thought-provoking excerpt or quotation on which the Assignment is based.

Assignment: The assignment or prompt is usually posed as a question.

Write an essay that expresses your point of view. Include supporting examples and analysis taken from your studies, reading, life experience, or personal observations.

DO NOT WRITE YOUR ESSAY IN YOUR TEST BOOKLET. Credit is given only for what you write on the lined paper provided on your answer sheet.

Now that you are familiar with the essay directions, you should be able to answer the straightforward questions below. If you're not sure of an answer, reread the preceding directions more carefully.

Sharpening Skills—Getting Essay Directions Down Pat

1. Does neatness of penmanship count?
    - ☐ yes   ☐ no   ☐ not sure

2. Should I write in print or script?
    - ☐ print   ☐ script   ☐ however I write more neatly

3. Should I write on every line, or should I double-space my essay?

    ☐ every line   ☐ double space   ☐ not sure

4. Should I write on the black lines of the essay paper that is provided, or should I indent, making wider margins?

    ☐ write on lines given   ☐ indent   ☐ not sure

5. If I run out of time before I've written my complete essay, will the evaluators read my "brainstorming" notes that I jotted down on the left or at the bottom of the Assignment page?

    ☐ yes   ☐ no   ☐ not sure

6. Should I use personal examples or nonpersonal examples, the latter being examples taken from my reading of literature, history books, science, or reputable newspapers and newsmagazines?

    ☐ personal   ☐ nonpersonal   ☐ either is fine

7. If I finish another writing skills or a critical reading section with time to spare, may I return to my essay to work on it?

    ☐ yes   ☐ no   ☐ not sure

Essay Directions Answers

1. *Yes*, neatness counts. You want your essay to be very legible.
2. *Print* and *script* are both fine. Use the form in which you write more neatly.
3. Write on *every line*.
4. *Write on lines given*. Essay evaluators will not think highly of gaping margins.
5. *No*, the evaluators will read only what is written on the lined paper provided.
6. In theory, *personal* and *nonpersonal* examples are both fine. But as a 2400 Clubber, you're eager to give this test everything you've got. Using examples from your reading could put a feather or two in your cap! The essay is your chance to tout your learning. Give yourself every possible advantage.
7. *No*, if you finish a section before the allotted time is up, you may go back and work on that section only.

STRATEGY 3: ENGAGE YOUR READER

Strong writers reel 'em in fast. Your introductory paragraph should be crisp, clear, and fairly brief. It should include a statement or two that relates to the topic. (Remember: The topic is set forth by the Assignment, not necessarily by the think box.) From there on, the introduction becomes focused on the topic itself. To keep things simple, plainly restate the given statement and tell whether you agree or disagree with it.

Essays in which the introductory paragraph was merely two or three sentences have been known to earn ratings of a 5 or 6. Introductions are simple and formulaic. The substance—the meat and potatoes—of your essay is made up of the body paragraphs.

Traditionally, the final sentence of the introductory paragraph is the thesis. Once the reader has read your thesis, there should be no question about your point of view.

STRATEGY 4: EDIT, USING THE 2400 CLUB CHECKLIST

Good writers know that editing is an ongoing process. Good writers know that editing can make the difference between writing that is clear and writing that is obfuscated (cloudy; opaque). As you write your sentences and paragraphs, scrutinize them with an editor's eye. The 2400 Club checklist below helps you to be aware of the types of errors to avoid. You can edit and revise throughout the writing process, but it's smart to spend about 2 minutes more at the end in a more focused effort at improvement. Use these 2 minutes as your chance to show, for example, that you're competent with commas and adept with parallel form.

Okay—you can't do everything in 2 minutes (see Strategy 2). Still, you can achieve some polishing of your prose. Polishing involves more than crossing your *t*'s and dotting your *i*'s. For example, look for wordiness, repetition, and weak vocabulary. Also, as you edit your essay, make sure you haven't made any of the grammatical errors that the grammar portion of the SAT tests you on!

Good Writers Know It's Important to Also Be Good Editors

The checklist that follows is handy, but you can't take it with you—on test day, that is. Use it regularly as you proofread your essays for English and history classes. Eventually, the list will become second nature to you and will serve as a "mental editor's checklist" on test day.

2400 Club Checklist of Errors to Avoid
- ❏ Spelling errors
- ❏ Capitalization errors
- ❏ Punctuation errors: commas, semicolons, colons, apostrophes, quotation marks, end marks
- ❏ Verb errors: form, tense, agreement with subject
- ❏ Pronoun errors: form, agreement with antecedent, ambiguity
- ❏ Wordiness and superfluous language
- ❏ Redundancy
- ❏ Stale, repetitive vocabulary
- ❏ Lack of parallelism
- ❏ Double negatives
- ❏ Poor diction (word choice) and usage
- ❏ Lack of paragraph indentation
- ❏ Lack of coherence

Clean Editing

Yes, in two concentrated minutes, you can add polish and clarity to your prose and bring your essay closer to that pristine score of 12. In editing, avoid sloppy crossouts and ink blots that make your essay look messy. Here are a few basic proofreading marks to give you that editor's edge and to keep your editing clean:

∧   the caret, for inserting a letter, word, or phrase

*   the asterisk, to show where long phrases or sentences should be added

—   the clean, single-line crossout, to replace a word with the more effective word that you'll write neatly on top

¶   the paragraph symbol, to show where you want to indent

↓   the delete symbol, to remove material; for example, a redundant word or expression. Remember: extraneous language is never preferable; economy of language is.

STRATEGY 5: SUPPORT YOUR THESIS WITH EXAMPLES

The "stuff" of your essay, the supporting examples, should be discussed in the body paragraphs. Three body paragraphs make for a very solid essay. You have to decide the length with which you are comfortable. Two well-supported body paragraphs can suffice and earn a perfect score.

To catapult your essay to a perfect 12, select examples that allow you to discuss the essay assignment in insightful ways. **Insight** is that special ingredient that moves "pretty good" essays closer to the level-12 ranks. Pertinent examples are ones that lend themselves to juicy and perceptive discussion of the topic. To a great extent: the more salient your examples, the stronger your insight.

Essay Coaching:
You aspire to achieve a perfect 12 on the essay. In addition to insightfully discussing your supporting examples, strive to fill all 46 lines of the essay paper provided. Every word should contribute to the development of pertinent examples; there should be no "filler."

Use This "Handy Reminder" to Write a Body Paragraph

Think of your hand, with its five fingers, as a body paragraph. This may sound strange, but it is a visual mnemonic device. Hold your left hand in front of you, and pretend that it is one of the two or three body paragraphs that you should write on your SAT essay. This device is a great writing tool since your hand is always with you, a "handy reminder."

Your pinky represents a concise topic sentence that will begin a paragraph.

Your ring, middle, and pointer (index) fingers represent three body sentences that support your topic sentence. Body sentences should illustrate specific examples or details. As you write, be sure that each paragraph has unity. Do not go off on tangents. Do not digress from your topic. To keep yourself focused, frequently reread your topic sentence.

Your thumb represents the closing sentence, which affirms or restates your point. To make things simple, you can reread your topic sentence and just tweak it a bit to come up

Essay Coaching:
Think of a body paragraph as your hand, with each finger representing one part of the paragraph structure.

with your closing sentence. This sentence, which is sometimes called the concluding sentence or the "clincher," can simply be a rephrasing of the topic sentence.

Your palm represents the unifying idea that gives coherence and focus to each body paragraph.

Give yourself a thumbs-up! You have written an organized and substantial body paragraph.

STRATEGY 6: SENTENCE AND VOCABULARY VARIETY

Have you heard a CD "skip," playing the same part of a song over and over again? Well, that's how your essay will sound if all of your sentences are long, or if all of them are short. Don't put your reader to sleep. Refrain from writing sentences that are all more or less the same length.

Writing a good essay is a balancing act. You need some short sentences and some longer ones. Too much of one type makes the essay resemble either a choppy sea or a rambling, runaway train.

Vocabulary variety is also important. Too much of a good thing is not a good thing anymore. Too much use of the word *conflict* in your essay is boring. Too much use of the word *change* or *freedom* in your essay is boring. ZZZzzz . . .

Does the paragraph below sound like part of an essay that will impress the evaluators? Or does it sound like an essay that might irritate them or—horrors!—put them to sleep?

> *Change is good for everyone. Change is a dynamic force from which all can benefit. Without change, life would be an endless drone of the same old routine. Change separates thinkers from nonthinkers. Above all, change is the only way to ensure commercial development and the changing for the better of mankind. The future calls for change. Change is the key.*

Boring! Some good ideas but boring just the same because the word *change*, like the figurative horse, is beaten to death. . . See the chart below for some other words the writer could have used in place of *change*.

From the Assignment you are given, get a sense of the words that you might use often in your essay. Then, brainstorm alternative words that you can sprinkle throughout so that you don't come across as a writer with a limited vocabulary.

Let's look again at the Assignments below. This time the words and/or phrases in three of the questions that you might be inclined to overuse are in boldface type.

Do you think that the **individual good** outweighs the **common good**?
Is **intellectual strength** inferior to **physical stamina**?
Is superior **wisdom** more valuable than supreme **kindness**?

Essay Coaching:
*Strong writers use **vocabulary variety** to avoid sounding like broken records.*

*Strong writers spice up their essays with a handful of **upper-level vocabulary** words that fit and flow smoothly in context.*

Underline the key words that you might be tempted to overuse as you write your essay. The 2400 Club strives for rich, effective diction and vocabulary variety.

Brainstorm other words that you can use to express these ideas. Varying your vocabulary will avoid repetition and redundancy in your writing. For example:

Key Words in Writing Topic That You're Tempted to Use ad Nauseum	Alternative Words to Use So You Sound as Though You Have a Brain and So the Reader Does Not Fall Asleep
• Conflict	• strife, discord, struggle, dispute, friction
• Change	• development, evolution, transformation, modification, variation
• Freedom	• autonomy, independence, choice, free will, self-determination, liberty
• Wise	• sagacious, prudent, astute, keen-minded

Sharpening Skills—Vary Your Vocabulary

Now it's your turn. Fill in the right-hand column of the chart below with at least three alternatives for each given word.

Key Words in Writing Assignment That You Might Be Tempted to Use Ad Nauseum	Alternative Words to Use So You Sound as Though You Have a Brain and So the Essay Reader Does Not Fall Asleep
Power	
Inequity	
Kindness	
Competition	
Equality	

STRATEGY 7: ASSESS WHAT YOU HAVE WRITTEN

Writing is a recursive process, so you should frequently assess what you have written. Reread your output after every three sentences or so. In this way, you will refresh your memory in terms of the points you have made and the examples you have provided. Reading will also help you to avoid redundancy—a common plague in writing.

Writing is a recursive process. Going back over what you've written is a smart strategy for writing well.

Revision shouldn't just happen at the end. If, after every few sentences, you take a few seconds to reread and "re-see" what you have written, you will have an essay that flows more smoothly. Frequent assessment also eliminates wordiness. As you assess, you may even spot usage errors, spelling errors, or omission of words. Revising as you write also cuts down the time required to look over the essay in its entirety. Find a revision rhythm that works well for you.

Make sure that you have given the essay evaluators a hearty, three-course meal: appetizer (clear introductory paragraph), entrée (two or three well-supported body paragraphs), and dessert (a concluding paragraph). Even at this stage, you can add a sentence or two by using an asterisk and neatly writing the addition at the bottom of your essay.

Good news: This essay will be evaluated as if it were a draft. That's keeping things real because a draft is all even the best writers can accomplish in a mere 25 minutes. Two evaluators will read your essay, each scoring it on a scale of 0 to 6. A perfect score is a 12.

STRATEGY 8: YOUR VOICE

Scholarly and erudite are out. So are cynical and convoluted. Overcasual is taboo also. Your voice should be straightforward, reasonable, and persuasive. When in doubt, err on the side of being more conversational and natural, less formal.

Fluff is out, too. Avoid phrases that say nothing: "in my opinion," "I believe that," "it is my truest estimation that," "to my way of thinking," "it seems only reasonable that," and so on. These phrases constitute "verbal clutter."

Quality, not quantity, is in.

Cut the fluff, slang, verbal clutter, and awkward, "put-on" vocabulary.

What About Vocabulary?

You're determined to reach the ranks of the 2400 Club, so you're making a serious effort to learn high-frequency SAT words (like those in *Barron's Hot Words for the SAT*) and you're resolute about learning some harder, off-the-bell-curve words as well. (Study the word lists in Appendix A at the end of this book.)

Since you have an upper-level, mental word bank to call upon, challenge yourself to strengthen your essay with strong vocabulary words that you can use with *accuracy* and *comfort*. Avoid highfalutin words that mystify you when it comes to their precise definitions, spellings, and proper usages. If you use big words merely for the sake of adornment, your essay will come across as artificial, inflated, and unnatural.

A final note about the writing section . . .

As you know, two evaluators will read your essay. You want your essay to read clearly and smoothly. You don't want the readers to be distracted by mechanical and spelling errors. You don't want the readers to stumble over your errors. Careless errors—ones that you can easily eliminate in your editing—can leave a bad taste in the mouths of the readers, resulting in a lower score for you.

More 2400 Club Strategies:

ELIMINATE SMOG

Don't let **SMOG** cloud your essay!

What is **SMOG** ?

SMOG is an acronym that stands for **S**pelling, **M**echanics, **O**veruse, and **G**rammar. If you keep SMOG in mind as you write and edit, your essay will be clear and will reflect your command of the English language.

Spelling errors contribute to smog. It's true that misspelled words aren't the biggest deal when it comes to effective writing. Nevertheless, the fewer spelling errors in your essay, the more competent you will come across as a writer. At the present time, SAT essays are handwritten in pencil. You will not be typing your essay on a personal computer, so good old "spell check" will not be at your disposal.

To become a better speller, read more and pay close attention to the spellings of tricky words as you read. Make mental pictures of the tricky words that you encounter in good novels, newspapers, and textbooks. Reading and becoming a talented speller go hand-in-hand. No doubt, you're very busy, but look at this suggestion as multitasking and making the best use of your limited time.

Sharpening Skills—Spelling

The following is a list of twenty frequently used words that are spelling demons for many writers. Circle the correct spelling of each word.

1. accummulate	accumulate	acummulate
2. intresting	interesting	intaresting
3. successful	sucessful	succesfull
4. beautiful	beuatifull	beautyful
5. arguement	argeument	argument
6. beginning	beggining	begginning
7. therfor	therefore	theirfor
8. disagreement	disaggrement	disagreemint
9. ocurrence	ocurrance	occurrence
10. respectabel	respectable	respecttable
11. possibility	posibility	possabiluty
12. posessions	possetions	possessions
13. confrence	conference	conference
14. unnecessary	unneccessary	unnecceseery
15. dissapointment	disappointment	disappointmint
16. sufficcient	suffcent	sufficient
17. delibratly	deliberratley	deliberately
18. acsessible	accesible	accessible
19. extraordinary	extraordinry	extrordinary
20. fullfilling	fulfiling	fulfilling

Spelling Drill Answers

1. accumulate	6. beginning	11. possibility	16. sufficient
2. interesting	7. therefore	12. possessions	17. deliberately
3. successful	8. disagreement	13. conference	18. accessible
4. beautiful	9. occurrence	14. unnecessary	19. extraordinary
5. argument	10. respectable	15. disappointment	20. fulfilling

Mechanical errors contribute to smog. Some writers are comma-phobic, neglecting to insert commas where they belong. Other writers are comma-happy, sprinkling them here, there, and everywhere! A command of punctuation doesn't make you an awesome writer, but it does make you a writer who is proficient in one of the conventions of writing.

Lack and overuse of apostrophes, commas, and semicolons are examples of mechanical errors in punctuation. Other such errors involve end marks and quotation marks. Incorrect capitalization is another type of mechanical error.

Mechanical errors can adversely affect your writing. A misplaced comma or apostrophe may even significantly change the meaning of a sentence. Since you're probably a strong English student, the following drills will seem like child's play—a cinch! The point is, however, that even the best students are sometimes guilty of sloppy errors. Mechanical oversights can make a student come across as a "sleepy writer."

Sharpening Skills—Mechanics

Don't be punctuation-phobic. Insert commas, apostrophes, and semicolons where they belong:

1. Before leaving for Florida Ms. Peach cleaned her house from top to bottom and tidied up her vegetable garden.

2. The post and beam fence blocks the childrens access to the forest beyond this is crucial since the woods are filled with poison ivy.

Insert capital letters, quotation marks, and end marks where they belong:

3. Have you read Edgar Allan Poe's gruesome and eerie short story titled the black cat

4. I am so excited to have memorized the names of the five great lakes: Huron, Ontario, Michigan, Erie, and Superior

Mechanics Drill Answers

1. Before leaving for Florida, Ms. Peach cleaned her house from top to bottom and tidied up her vegetable garden.

2. The post and beam fence blocks the children's access to the forest beyond; this is crucial since the woods are filled with poison ivy.

3. Have you read Edgar Allen Poe's gruesome and eerie short story titled "The Black Cat"?

4. I am so excited to have memorized the names of the five great lakes: Huron, Ontario, Michigan, Erie, and Superior!

<u>Overuse</u> of "empty phrases" contributes to smog. Do you use "filler" when you write? "Filler" always gets a bad rap—just think of a hot dog. Do you write a lot without saying much? Yada-yada-yada . . . . Is your writing sluggish? Do you use "empty phrases" that slow down your essay?

Here are some examples of empty phrasing:

It is my opinion that . . .	It seems to me that . . .
It likely holds true that . . .	I truly believe that . . .
As it is often said . . .	For all intents and purposes . . .
I feel that . . .	It has been said that . . .

These kinds of phrases come across as hedging, giving your writing a spineless aura of uncertainty. Say what you want to say, and say it firmly, without equivocation.

Empty phrasing contributes to *smog*, making your ideas not only foggy but also flimsy.

Sharpening Skills—Eliminate Empty Phrasing

Cross off the empty phrases in the paragraph below:

> For the most part, motivation comes from within. Each of us has the power and ability to put his or her thoughts into action. I believe that, for all intents and purposes, our innermost desires fuel our actions. By and large, external motivation is weak and really, really short-lived. What we are told to do and what we witness are far less motivating than what our inner sense propels us to accomplish. When you want to change your intentions into actions, it is said that you should look within for the stimulus. You will find it deep within you, just waiting to take shape. This is truly what I believe.

Empty Phrasing Answers

> ~~For the most part,~~ motivation comes from within. Each of us has the power and ability to put his or her thoughts into action. ~~I believe that, for all intents and purposes,~~ our innermost desires fuel our actions. ~~By and large,~~ external motivation is weak and short-lived. What we are told ~~to do~~ and what we witness are far less motivating than what our inner sense propels us to accomplish. When you want to change your intentions into actions, ~~it is said that~~ you should look within for the stimulus. You will find it deep within you, just waiting to take shape. ~~This is truly what I believe.~~

Here is the flab-free, succinct paragraph. Unlike the original paragraph, this one is lean and has a backbone.

> Motivation comes from within. Each of us has the power and ability to put his or her thoughts into action. Our innermost desires fuel our actions. External motivation is weak and short-lived. What we are told and what we witness are far less motivating than what our inner sense propels us to accomplish. When you want to change your intentions into actions, you should look within for the stimulus. You will find it deep within you, just waiting to take shape.

Grammatical errors contribute to smog. A fair portion of the SAT tests you on your ability to recognize and correct grammatical errors. It makes sense, then, that your essay should be as free of grammatical errors as possible. Turn to the Hierarchy of Grammar Glitches on page 138. Avoid these grammar glitches in your essay.

Sharpening Skills—Grammatical Errors

Can you spot grammatical errors in the paragraph below? Use the "Grammar Error Bank" below to help you find four errors. The errors in the paragraph do not necessarily appear in the order in which they are listed in this box:

Grammar Error Bank

1. Subject-verb agreement error
2. Pronoun-antecedent agreement error
3. Ambiguous pronoun error: pronoun lacks a clear reference
4. Run-on (also known as comma splice)
5. Lack of parallelism

A backyard lawn is a wondrous place. It's a place to pitch a badminton net, it's a place to play bocci ball. You can even sunbathe there in a lounge chair when the sun is warm. If one desires, you can rake up piles of leaves in autumn and jump! You can collect pinecones in the yard and use them for crafts projects, scented fireplace crackle, or arranging natural centerpieces. A backyard, with its natural greenery and open spaces, offer a private place where the imagination can roam free.

Here is the paragraph, now free of grammatical errors.

A backyard lawn is a wondrous place. It's a place to pitch a badminton net, **and** it's a place to play bocci ball. You can even sunbathe there in a lounge chair when the sun is warm. If **you** desire, you can rake up piles of leaves in autumn and jump! You can collect pinecones in the yard and use them for crafts projects, scented fireplace crackle, or ~~arranging~~ natural centerpieces. A backyard, with its natural greenery and open spaces, **offers** a private place where the imagination can roam free.

SUMMARY: HIGH SCORER'S STRATEGY ACRONYM

- Do you like puzzles, acrostics, or anagrams?
- Do you like to remember things by making lists of items that spell out a word or name? In other words, do you find acronyms helpful?
- Do you like to picture things in your mind's eye?
- Do you daydream in detail or vivid color?

If so, visualize the "word picture" below. The initial letters of the eight strategies for writing an essay spell out "THE ESSAY."

T	**ake** a side.
H	**ave** a timing plan.
E	**ngage** your reader.
E	**dit**, using the 2400 Club Checklist.
S	**upport** your thesis with examples.
S	**entence** and vocabulary variety
A	**ssess** what you have written.
Y	**our** voice

Take a mental snapshot of the acronym above. Save it in your mind's eye, and call it up on test day as a reference. Probably, several of the boldface words will pop into your mind, and you'll remember a critical step in the writing process

PRACTICE ASSIGNMENTS

The 2400 Club leaves nothing to chance, knowing that preparation is key to achievement. You can use the practice assignments below in a number of ways. For example, you can read them and see whether you can come up with historical and/or literary examples to support them. Or you can try jotting down a list of ideas. If your motto is "practice makes perfect," you can time yourself and practice writing a four- or five-paragraph essay in 25 minutes. If you're so busy that you can't devote that much time to one sitting, just write one or two body paragraphs.

The following is a list of hypothetical Assignments. Notice that they are posed as questions. Most of them are brief but juicy. Time yourself: give yourself about 3 minutes to read the Assignment, decide on your position, and come up with two or three supporting examples. It's not feasible to write a detailed, Roman numeral outline on test day. Likewise, there's not enough time to create a detailed, baroque concept map or web diagram. Instead, simply jot down a list of notes in the form of short phrases, not complete sentences.

Train yourself to be a quick decision maker. Read the essay Assignment, and decide quickly whether your answer to the question is *yes* or *no*.

Be a quick decision maker; deliberation is a luxury you cannot afford on test day. Check *yes* or *no* for each Assignment:

1. Is envy a strong motivator for personal success? ☐ yes ☐ no
2. Does imitation demonstrate a sluggish imagination? ☐ yes ☐ no
3. Is health a direct function of an individual's lifestyle? ☐ yes ☐ no
4. Is leisure reading a luxury that only the privileged can enjoy? ☐ yes ☐ no
5. Is anger a manifestation of a person's insecurity? ☐ yes ☐ no
6. Do people change more to please others than to please themselves? ☐ yes ☐ no
7. By practicing kindness toward others, do we give a gift to ourselves? ☐ yes ☐ no
8. Is wisdom a more valuable personal asset than kindheartedness? ☐ yes ☐ no
9. Does an individual's vocation predominantly define his or her character and moral fiber? ☐ yes ☐ no
10. Is what people say as influential as what people do? ☐ yes ☐ no

Remember, if you're not quite sure what the question is asking of you or where the question is coming from, go to the "think box" (located just above the Assignment) for help. Be careful, however, not to simply write about a topic or idea discussed in the rectangular box. You must respond to the Assignment; an off-topic essay gets a zero.

ESSAY SCORING GUIDE

Scoring Level 6

Essays on this level demonstrate a clear command of writing and thinking skills, despite the occasional, infrequent minor error. Characteristics of essays on this level include:

1. intelligent, convincing development of a position on the issue
2. selection of relevant examples and other evidence to support its position
3. smooth, well-orchestrated progression from idea to idea
4. use of varied sentence types and appropriate vocabulary
5. freedom from most technical flaws (mistakes in grammar, usage, diction)

These essays are *insightful*.

Scoring Level 5

Essays on this level exhibit a generally dependable command of writing and thinking skills, despite some mistakes along the way. Characteristics of essays on this level include:

1. proficient, coherent development of a position on the issue
2. selection of basically relevant evidence to support its position
3. relatively well-ordered progression from idea to idea
4. reasonably varied sentence structure
5. relative freedom from technical flaws

These essays are *effective*.

Scoring Level 4

Essays on this level exhibit a generally adequate command of writing and thinking skills, although they are typically inconsistent in quality. Characteristics of essays on this level include:

1. workmanlike development of a position on the issue
2. selection of reasonably appropriate evidence to support its position
3. acceptable progression from idea to idea
4. somewhat varied sentence structure
5. some flaws in mechanics, usage, and grammar

These essays are *competent*.

Scoring Level 3

Essays on this level exhibit an insufficient command of writing and thinking skills, although they do show some signs of developing proficiency. Characteristics of essays on this level include:

1. sketchy development of a position on the issue
2. selection of weak or inappropriate evidence to support its position
3. erratic progression from idea to idea

4. somewhat limited vocabulary
5. inadequately varied sentence structure
6. multiple flaws in mechanics, usage, and grammar

These essays are *inadequate*.

Scoring Level 2

Essays on this level exhibit a quite flawed command of writing and thinking skills. Characteristics of essays on this level include:

1. limited development of a position on the issue
2. selection of weak or inappropriate evidence to support its position
3. tendency toward incoherence
4. highly limited vocabulary
5. numerous problems with sentence structure
6. errors in mechanics, usage, and grammar serious enough to interfere with the reader's comprehension

These essays are *seriously flawed*.

Scoring Level 1

Essays on this level exhibit an acutely flawed command of writing and thinking skills. Characteristics of essays on this level include:

1. absence of evidence to support a point of view
2. lack of a position on the issue
3. absence of focus and organization
4. rudimentary vocabulary
5. severe problems with sentence structure
6. extensive flaws in mechanics, usage, and grammar severe enough to block the reader's comprehension.

These essays are *fundamentally deficient*.

Scored sample essays appear at the end of this chapter.

Both your essay subscore (that is, your combined score of 2 to 12) and your multiple-choice writing subscore will go into making up your eventual writing skills score, with the essay subscore counting as one-third of your total writing score.

SAMPLE ESSAYS: 11–12 RANGE, 10–11 RANGE, AND 8–9 RANGE

Your essay will be read, evaluated holistically, and scored by two trained readers. Each reader will give your essay a rating of 1 to 6, so your combined score will range from 2 to 12. Therefore, a 12 is a perfect score on the essay portion of the SAT writing section. The sample essays that follow provide examples of essays that would most likely score within a particular ability range.

You're a high-achieving student, so be confident that you can and will write an essay in the 9–12 range on test day. The essays that follow are paragons or paradigms, models of competency that you can emulate.

Sample Essay #1
11–12 Score Range

> "Truth is more of a stranger than fiction."
> —Mark Twain's Notebook
>
> This quotation stresses the elusive nature of truth. Self-knowledge is a personal type of truth that, for some, is a known. For others, it is as elusive as the "stranger" in Twain's quote.

Think Box; known as the essay prompt

Assignment: Do we need to be faced with hard choices in order to understand the truth about who we are?

Write an essay that expresses your point of view. Include supporting examples and analysis taken from your studies, reading, life experience, or personal observations.

Difficult decisions are critical in the task of discovering ourselves. While for inconsequential choices our persona does not need to be uncovered, tough decisions reflect our true nature because deep thinking is necessary. In both literature and history, our hardest choices and dilemmas illuminate our characteristics and qualities, for better or for worse.

In Arthur Miller's adaptation of Henrik Ibsen's An Enemy of the People, the protagonist Dr. Thomas Stockmann must make a gigantic, life-threatening decision to confront his town over their renowned springs. The doctor believes that the town's springs, which are thought to heal, are dangerously polluted and have the potential to kill people. But the springs are the center of the town's economy, and the doctor would have to confront the local press, government, and populace in his fight to clean the city. Dr. Stockmann's brother, Mayor Peter Stockmann, and the independent press warned him that an attack on the springs is an attack on the town, and that he would be punished for his disloyalty. But even without the support of people with power, the doctor decides he must struggle to expose the true status of the springs. In his resistance, this simple doctor learns more than just about the evils of the powerful, who convince the public that he is a traitor, but that while he may have an ego, he also has the spirit and heart to find justice and the will to not let any other person repress and intimidate him as he refuses to leave the town even when mobs shell his house and torment his family.

Historical examples also point to the reflection of one's personality through hard decision making. Michael Collins was a revolutionary Irishmen who led the fight against the British in the Irish War of Independence. It is never easy for a militant rebel to negotiate and compromise with his opponents, but

Collins went to London to make peace with the government of Lloyd George. Knowing that his followers would detract him as a sell-out and a turncoat, Collins wanted to spare Ireland of more blood and violence and made a settlement with the British, which ended the war but did not give Ireland total independence. Many of his allies in Ireland, as expected, turned against him, without understanding the fact that the treaty was the best deal Collins could attain. And during the brief civil war that followed the treaty's establishment, Collins was assassinated by Irish hardliners. His decision to talk and make peace with the British despite calls of treason prove that Collins was not looking out for himself and his own power, but for the safety and future of the Irish people.

These uneasy choices of Dr. Stockmann and Collins show that it is the toughest decisions which reveals character. Granted that there are many other hard choices that may bring out quite different behavior, as literary and historical examples demonstrate, hard decisions show the true nature of a person.

—*Brian T.*

Essay strengths: This essay insightfully develops a point of view using relevant literary and historical examples. The writer's discussion flows logically and includes a significant amount of detail: authors' names, literary titles, characters' names, Irish War of Independence, historical figures. The author shows finesse with writing topic sentences. The topic sentence for paragraph 3 even contains the transitional word *also*: "Historical examples also point to the reflection of one's personality through hard decision making."

The author uses simple, compound, and complex sentence structures that demonstrate excellent sentence variety. The length of the essay is impressive, and the quality is there. Strong and effectively used vocabulary includes *inconsequential, illuminate, protagonist, renowned, retract,* and *turncoat.*

Essay weaknesses: An 11 or 12 essay does not have to be flawless; in fact, this essay contains a subject-verb agreement error: "the toughest decisions which reveal<u>s</u> character."

Sample Essay #2
11–12 Score Range

The author of *The 7 Habits of Highly Effective People,* Stephen R. Covey, advises, "Live out of your imagination, not your history." Covey urges us to go beyond our pasts and to create something new in our lives. Some of us live by evoking the past, and some of us live by imitating others. Both styles of living may be considered uninspired, since both depend on reproducing the past or that which already exists.

Think Box; known as the essay prompt

Assignment: Does imitation demonstrate a sluggish imagination?

Write an essay that expresses your point of view. Include supporting examples and analysis taken from your studies, reading, life experience, or personal observations.

The age-old adage, "Imitation is the sincerest form of flattery," asserts that imitation is a positive trait, not a negative quality. Imitation certainly does not demonstrate a sluggish imagination. Rather, people learn by imitating and imitation stimulates imagination.

Have you ever seen a young child, deep in concentration, construct a LEGO model? The instructions for LEGO designs are simple: Copy the diagram exactly as illustrated. It is through duplication that the youngster is able to reproduce the model. In turn, the youth learns about relationships between colored blocks of different sizes and shapes. Similarly, beginning writers may learn about writing by replicating, or imitating, writing strategies. For example, beginning an essay with a lead—a quote, question, or statistic—engages the reader. To emphasize, imitation is an appropriate and effective learning tool.

Imitation stimulates imagination. After a child learns how to successfully recreate a LEGO design for a space shuttle, aircraft carrier, or other intricate object, he or she is then empowered to produce original creations. As a matter of fact, inspired after building the LEGO Apollo 13 space station, my nine-year-old cousin Phillip designed and created his very own "Intergalactic Space World 2005!" In the same way, once a young writer masters the structure of the essay, he is then free to write creatively. Science fiction author Andrew Benz, commented, "My imagination soared after I internalized the conventions of writing." In this way, imitation fosters the development of a creative imagination.

To conclude, the confidence and competency gained through imitation encourages imagination. Listlessness and lethargy are byproducts of inactive minds, not of imitation. Simply put, imitation lays the groundwork for a healthy imagination.

—*by Dana J. G.*

Essay strengths: Very well organized; excellent use of transitional phrases, such as "*In turn,*" "*Similarly,*" and "*In the same way.*" Effective topic sentences are used in the body paragraphs, such as the engaging rhetorical question, "*Have you ever seen a young child, deep in concentration, construct a LEGO model?*" and the crisp, "*Imitation stimulates imagination.*" These first-rate topic sentences introduce paragraphs that are well supported by examples based on the author's personal experience and observation. This author also uses strong and fitting vocabulary, such as *adage, asserts, trait, replicating, intricate, fosters, competency, listlessness, lethargy.* To put the icing on the cake, this author demonstrates great competency with both punctuation and conventions of English grammar.

Essay weaknesses: There are no weaknesses, really. Even though the examples are not taken from literature, they are insightful and well developed.

Sample Essay #3
10–11 Score Range

> Work informs us about people's character. For those in the workforce, the majority of their hours are taken up by playing various work roles in society. To an extent, which roles they play and how those roles are played reveals their nature.

Think Box; known as the essay prompt

Assignment: Does an individual's profession define his or her character and moral fiber?

Write an essay that expresses your point of view. Include supporting examples and analysis taken from your studies, reading, life experience, or personal observations.

Are morals victims of success? Is conscience ignored on the climb up the corporate ladder? Both classic pieces of literature and challenges encountered in careers prove that an individual's profession molds one's character and morality.

Many great novels contain protagonists whose senses of self are influenced by their occupations. In I Am the Cheese by Robert Cormier, David Farmer, a journalist, accidentally becomes aware of confidential government information. Therefore, he is forced to use an alias and create an entirely new identity. Without a doubt, his job causes him to betray his own integrity by keeping secrets from his son. Another well-known book that fits this idea is Animal Farm by George Orwell. The tale depicts the propagandist Squealer, a complacent pig who sacrifices his morals by manipulating the truth to persuade others. Both Cormier and Orwell understand the concept that one's job may cause one to suspend his own sense of right and wrong.

Did you know that the average model, dancer, or actor is thinner than 95% of the general population? This statistic raises the question, what will one give up for success? Many supermodels jeopardize their health to keep a size 0–2 figure. Other models become self-absorbed about their appearance. As a result of their careers, these stars demonstrate the undesirable traits of unhealthy lifestyles and selfish attitudes. Similarly, some pro athletes surrender fair play to the desire to win. The "it's not about winning or losing, but how you play the game" attitude has been replaced by a "win at all costs" mindset. Unfortunately, the price has been honesty and good sportsmanship. Therefore, jobs present dilemmas that test one's character.

Clearly, profession affects character and moral fiber. Not only is this proven through textual references, but it is also obvious when challenges erupt in one's profession that test one's personal nature. Carrying ethics and morality from one's private life to one's professional life is essential for right to triumph wrong in society.

—by Andrea B. G.

Essay strengths: This essay is interesting, insightful, and logically organized. Each body paragraph is substantial and supported by suitable, illustrative examples. The author uses engaging rhetorical questions at the opening of the essay to draw the reader in: "Are morals victims of success? Is conscience ignored on the climb up the corporate ladder?" The author also uses a catchy question as the topic sentence for the second body paragraph: "Did you know that the average model, dancer, or actor is thinner than 95% of the general population?"

The writer also uses effective and fitting vocabulary, demonstrating a winning variety of good words: *alias, propagandist, complacent, suspend, jeopardize, traits, erupt.*

The concluding paragraph effectively reinforces the central ideas of this essay.

Essay weaknesses: Even an essay that demonstrates competency may have a couple of errors. Did you detect the error in plural/singular inconsistency in the following sentence: "Many supermodels jeopardize their health to keep a size 0–2 figure."? The plural noun, supermodels, requires the corresponding plural noun, figures, so the sentence should read: "Many supermodels jeopardize their health to keep size 0–2 figures."

Sample Essay #4
8–9 Score Range

> "He enjoys true leisure who has time to improve his soul's estate," according to author Henry David Thoreau. Those who would agree with this statement would have different ideas about how one can best "improve his soul's estate." Among many other pastimes, reading for pleasure is one satisfying path to self-improvement. Some would say, however, that to an extent only a fortunate minority enjoys leisure reading.

Think Box; known as the essay prompt

Assignment: Is leisure reading a luxury that only the privileged can enjoy?

Write an essay that expresses your point of view. Include supporting examples and analysis taken from your studies, reading, life experience, or personal observations.

Where is the best place to get a book? Barnes and Noble? A neighborhood yard sale? Or, the public library? Reading is a pleasurable activity that anyone can choose to enjoy. After all, access to books is free and reading appeals to people of all ages and places.

People who can afford to buy books can shop at the local bookstore or visit Amazon.com. Those on a budget can pick up bargain-priced books at church bazaars and garage sales. Better yet, public libraries loan books for free, and a library card doesn't cost a dime! My town library has thousands of books on the shelves. There is a section for biographies, another for fiction, and there is even a magazine and newspaper alcove in the back. So, reading is not just for a privileged few.

Reading is a great equalizer that transcends socio-economic barriers. Take J.K. Rowling's <u>Harry Potter</u> books. This series has been published in a dozen languages and is available for sale worldwide. The latest release, <u>Harry Potter and the Half-Blood Prince</u> is expected to be the fastest-selling novel in history. The popular retail chain, ABC Books, reported first hour sales of 13 books per second! <u>Reading Lolita in Tehran</u> by Azar Nafisi is an example of literature mirroring real life. Nafisi's story is about a group of woman from different religious sects who overcome obstacles and gather weekly to discuss great novels. Clearly, reading does not discriminate based on native language, culture, or geographical location.

In conclusion, reading is a luxury that doesn't cost money and is available to everyone in the world. Why not check out a good book from your area library today?

—by Jean B. G.

Essay strengths: The opening engages the reader with its attention-getting series of questions. The essay is packaged neatly in four distinct paragraphs. This essay contains solid examples, such as those relating to book authors and their works in paragraph 3. Snazzy details such as "published in a dozen languages" and "first hour sales of 13 books per second", add interest to the essay. Although the essay does not contain an extensive assortment of glittering vocabulary, some good words can be found, such as *alcove, equalizer, transcends, mirroring,* and *native,* that are appropriately used.

    Essay weaknesses: This rather uncomplicated essay is organized neatly. Body paragraph one, however, contains a digression in which the author shifts from third-person point of view to first person: "My town library has thousands of books on the shelves." Also, some of the details in this paragraph ("a section for biographies, another for fiction, and there is even a magazine and newspaper alcove") do not support the main idea (books are free/cheap).

    In addition, the essay contains some punctuation and grammatical errors. First, this sentence requires another comma: "The latest release, Harry Potter and the Half-Blood Prince is expected to be the fastest-selling novel in history." Second, "group of woman" is a careless error. Last, the conclusion is a bit abrupt. In all, the essay would not qualify as terribly "insightful"; it is more casual and straightforward, keeping it in the 8–9 range.

Chapter 6

ENGLISH GRAMMAR AND USAGE

Let's face it—for many students, grammar is an arcane and boring subject. How interesting are mismatched correlative conjunctions and misplaced participles? Some English teachers dislike teaching grammar because of students' facial reactions to the comments, "Now let's discuss comma usage as it relates to restrictive and nonrestrictive subordinating clauses." Yikes!

On the SAT the 49 objective, multiple-choice questions on English grammar and usage come in three varieties:

Improving sentences	25 questions
Identifying sentence errors	18 questions
Improving paragraphs	6 questions
Time allotted	35 minutes (one 25-minute section; one 10-minute section)

TIMING PRACTICE WHEN YOU'RE CRUSHED FOR TIME

Multiple-Choice Writing Sections

The first section is 25 minutes; the second (Section 10) 10 minutes. Not enough free time to time yourself on the longer of the two writing sections? Simply time yourself on Section 10, the shorter section. The ratio of questions to minutes is the same:

Longer Section: 35 questions / 25 minutes = Shorter Section: 14 questions / 10 minutes

$$\frac{35}{25} = \frac{14}{10}$$
$$1.4 = 1.4$$

If you find that you manage well the timing for Section 10, be confident that you can manage the timing for the longer section, which is typically Section 5 or Section 6.

The good news: None of these sections requires you to draw intricate sentence diagrams or to label parts of speech, so wipe the sweat off your brow. More good news: You don't have to rewrite grammatically flawed sentences and transform them into grammatically flawless ones. In short, the English grammar and usage questions, as unappealing as they sound, are not *that* intense.

The not-so-good news: The objective grammar questions hold you to a high standard of proper written English. Don't fight it; go with it, even though the correct form may sometimes sound strange. To ace this portion of the test, psyche yourself to take pride in expressing the English language in a grammatically sound and pristine way. To approach a perfect 800 on the writing sections, you need to develop a high regard and sensitivity for the conventions of standard, written, grammatically correct English. Language that is considered conversational or colloquial does not fit the requirements of written English.

Unfortunately, our fast-paced world, with its text messaging, instant messaging, has desensitized many of us to what standard written English actually sounds like. We live in a world of quick chats and brief notes. We live in a world of verbal and written shorthand: *k, lol, g2g, brb, ttyl, sup, . . .*

Now imagine your loving parent hovering over your PC, asking, "*To whom* are you speaking?" or "Is that your user profile *in which* you listed your favorite music groups?" Now imagine your parent sitting down for a chat and saying, "I am disappointed in *your impatience* with your brother." You might ask yourself, "*Whence* did this person come?" Or maybe not. (Every italicized phrase or word is absolutely correct.) The point is, standard written English tends to be so butchered in everyday usage that it's hard to know whether certain grammatically correct phrases are actually right or wrong.

To make matters worse, for the most part, you can't rely on newscasters, politicians, and highly regarded talk-show hosts to model exemplary English usage. Multitudinous grammatical errors come across the television and radio airwaves every hour.

Remember: the SAT is about standard *written* English, not *spoken* English.

NEW WRITING STRATEGY! GRAMMAR COUNTING: 1, 2, 3

Grammar counts on the SAT. You have to answer 49 multiple-choice objective grammar questions, contributing to your writing score ranging on a scale from 200 to 800. Because your writing sample is scored holistically, the conventions of standard written English grammar and usage also count when you write your essay.

Count your way to a competitive multiple-choice writing score!

Grammar counting helps you recognize inconsistencies within sentences so that you can make the necessary corrections. As you read the sentences, conduct an internal dialogue of "counts."

As easy as *1, 2, 3* . . . Count subjects. Count nouns. Count people. Count pronouns. Use your Active Pencil to indicate the count. Jot down *1* for singular; jot down *2* for plural.

Illustrations of Grammar counting, using snippets from sentences:

         2   1   2
. . . **Gary and Lillian . . . conducted an extensive poll about the spending habits . . .**

      1   *2*

The poem's allusions and creative expressions . . . (Compound subject . . . that's *2*! If the poem itself is referenced, the singular pronoun "it" would agree, and singular verb forms would be required.)

              1   *2*

. . . the consumption of natural herbal remedies . . . (Singular subject . . . that's *1*! If the remedies are referred back to, the count for resources is 2, indicating plural.)

                 2

. . . Governor Gary and Congresswoman Lillian . . . (That's *2* for two people! To agree with *2*, a plural verb must follow. Likewise, Gary and Lillian would be referred back to using plural personal pronouns such as "they" and "them." The singular "it" would not agree.)

           2   *2*

The chronological records of artifact findings . . . (That's a plural subject . . . indicated by *2*; as the findings are plural, plural pronouns such as "they" or "them" would be used to refer back to the findings.)

To illustrate grammar counting, consider the following three hard identifying sentence errors questions:

                                   2   *2*

If <u>it is</u> confirmed <u>empirically</u>, the hypotheses of Regina Vander and Randi
  A   B

                             2   *1*

Stiles <u>will be among</u> the <u>greatest</u> progressive strides in science of the past several
            C   D

  2

decades. <u>No error</u>
        E

Noticing that "hypotheses" is plural will help alert you to the inconsistency between "hypotheses" and the singular pronoun "it." Therefore, the correct answer is choice A.

               1   *2*

The galloping speed of both science and computer technology <u>have forced</u> many
                                               A

     2   *2*   *1*

graduates <u>to consider</u> questions that <u>formerly</u> <u>were the</u> singular realm of
          B   C   D

    2

sociologists. <u>No error</u>
          E

Noticing that the subject "speed" is singular will help alert you to the subject–verb agreement error between "speed" and "have." Therefore, the correct answer is choice A.

2   1   2

The vivid red and blue wings of the monarch butterfly <u>cautions</u> predators <u>that</u>
                                                      A   B

the creature <u>is</u> poisonous <u>if consumed</u>. <u>No error</u>
        C   D   E

Noticing that the subject "wings" is plural (indicated by 2), you will more likely detect the subject–verb agreement error between "wings" and "cautions." Therefore, because of this agreement error, the correct answer is choice A.

2400 Club Grammar-Savvy Tips:

These four tips apply to all three objective grammar sections: identifying sentence errors, improving sentences, and improving paragraphs.

- **T**ake care to read the original versions of sentences or paragraphs very carefully.
- **I**dentify, first, all verbs and pronouns that are underlined.
- **Pa**y close attention to the nonunderlined portions of sentences and paragraphs.
- **S**elect "No error" approximately 15–20 percent of the time.

TAKE CARE TO READ THE ORIGINAL VERSIONS OF SENTENCES OR PARAGRAPHS VERY CAREFULLY

This tip is important. Read through the original version of each sentence or paragraph to absorb the meaning. The new sentence version that you select must maintain this original meaning. A revision that sounds good or is attractively concise is not the correct answer if that version distorts the original meaning.

Also, reading and internalizing the meaning of the original can help you to detect overall sentence errors such as faulty comparison and lack of parallelism, which are discussed later.

IDENTIFY, FIRST, ALL VERBS AND PRONOUNS THAT ARE UNDERLINED

Pronoun and verb errors are among the most pervasive on the SAT. Be a savvy grammarian who works smart: examine verbs and pronouns first. If these check out, then start looking for other types of errors: faulty diction, lack of parallel form, and comma splices.

Once you've identified a verb, make sure that it is in the correct tense and form *and* is in agreement with the subject. Ask yourself:

Time Saver

First scrutinize verbs and pronouns in the sentence.

Keep your eye on them since a bevy of errors surround these parts of speech.

Working this way is time-efficient.

Is the verb in the right tense?	If not, there is an error in *verb tense*.
Is the verb in the right form?	If not, there is an error in *verb form*.
Does the verb agree with the subject?	If not, there is an error in *subject-verb agreement*.

Also, be prudent about pronouns because multifarious (numerous and varied) errors involve these pesky little words: ambiguous pronouns, pronoun shifts, pronouns without antecedents, wrong pronoun case, misused pronouns. All of these errors will be addressed in detail later.

PAY CLOSE ATTENTION TO THE NONUNDERLINED PORTIONS OF SENTENCES AND PARAGRAPHS

This is one of the most effective tips for the objective grammar sections. Intuitively, test takers focus in very closely on the underlined portions of sentences and paragraphs. However, you need to focus as closely, *if not more closely,* on the nonunderlined portions. The reason: *Nonunderlined portions dictate the form of the underlined portions!*

Here are examples to illustrate this dynamic:

Nonunderlined Portions	Indications for Underlined Portions
In the early seventeenth century	Need past tense
Mia and her aunt Hillary	Plural subject
Either of the two pies	Singular subject
Either	Need *or*
Not only	Need *but* or *but also*
Next September	Need future tense
The young tennis enthusiasts	Need plural pronouns: *they, them, their*
Neither of the candidates	Need singular pronouns: *he, she, him, her, his, hers*
Swimming, jogging	Need a parallel gerund; *fishing, hiking*

Naturally, you'll focus in on the underlined parts of sentences. It's the nonunderlined portions, however, that tell you how the underlined portions need to be, whether they should be changed somehow or remain as they are. Start noticing the form of the nonunderlined portions, and you will be better equipped to see whether or how the underlined portions should be rewritten.

SELECT "NO ERROR" APPROXIMATELY 15–20 PERCENT OF THE TIME

"No error" occurs approximately 15–20 percent of the time in the objective grammar questions. One or two of every ten sentences in the section on identifying sentence errors are correct as written; select choice (E) to indicate "No error." In the improving sentences section, select choice (A), the original form of the sentence, to indicate "No error." When offered as a choice in the improving paragraphs section, "No error" is choice (A), indicated as *"(As it is now)."* Get this quirky disparity down pat now, so on test day you'll know the ropes.

Do some aspects of English grammar sound like Greek (Swahili?) to you? Don't worry. This section covers every grammar glitch, one by one, with plenty of examples for each. After you study the examples, try the Sharpening Skills exercises to see how well you've grasped that particular error type. Think of the Hierarchy of Grammar Glitches below as an overview of the test designers' pet peeves in regard to grammatical errors. As you can see, spelling and capitalization errors are not addressed.

One effective way to improve your writing and vocabulary is to read good books, good newspapers, and good periodicals. Specifically, read to improve your grammar skills. You'll be amazed at how much you can learn, in terms of writing mechanics and grammar, when you read with a mindset for grammar. For example, you can glean insight into how to use a semicolon and how to express logical comparisons. You can also pick up on parallel form and appropriate verb tenses. Try this focus next time you read; you can brush up on grammar and peruse a good book or news article at the same time. Multitasking—a beautiful thing!

HIERARCHY OF GRAMMAR GLITCHES

Higher Frequency Errors

↑

Verb Errors

Pronoun Errors

Faulty Idioms

Lack of Parallelism

Diction Errors

Misplaced Modifiers

Adjective Versus Adverb Errors

Plural–Singular Inconsistency

Redundancy and Wordiness

Faulty Comparisons

Run-ons (Comma Splices) and Fragments

↓

Lower Frequency Errors

Let's review these grammatical topics, one by one:

Verb Errors

Verb errors: wrong verb tense, wrong verb form, verb does not agree with subject

Chances are, you're an Honors English student or a student who typically achieves high Bs and As. In this case, you can readily spot the subject and verb of a sentence. You understand that the subject and verb work together. You also understand that singular subjects require singular verbs, which (unlike singular nouns) end in *s*. Yada-yada-yada . . . You know the basics.

Once you've spotted the verb, make sure that it is in the correct tense and form *and* in agreement with the subject.

Be vigilant about verbs because a multitude of errors surround these action and being words. Check out any underlined verbs first. Once you've found a verb, ask yourself these questions:

■ Is the verb in the right tense? If not, there is an error in *verb tense*. Example: When we rode the chair lift to the top of the mountain, Julia *cries* out, "Here at last!" (*cried*)

Time Saver
First check out verbs and pronouns in the sentence.

Keep your eye on them since a bevy of errors surround these parts of speech.

Working this way is time efficient.

■ Is the verb in the right form? If not, there is an error in *verb form*.
Example: Every morning, Joanna takes a walk to clear her mind, to tone her body, and *thinking* about the day ahead. (*to think*)

■ Does the verb agree with the subject? If not, there is an error in *subject–verb agreement*.
Example: Around the track *runs* Sheila and Gus. (*run*)

To detect errors in subject–verb agreement, it is a good idea to "downsize" or simplify the sentence by crossing off prepositional phrases, appositives, and modifiers. The following examples illustrate downsizing. Read each sentence with only the words that are *not* crossed out. See how basic the downsized version sounds? A simpler sentence form allows you to detect subject–verb agreement errors more quickly.

Illustrations of Downsizing Sentences to Reveal the Simple Subject and Verb

1. Original version: Between the corner fruit market and Parkside Deli is the old-time barber shop that my dad took me to when I was a young boy.

    Downsized version: ~~Between the corner fruit market and Parkside Deli~~ is the ~~old-time~~ barber shop ~~that my dad took me to when I was a young boy~~.

    The subject and verb are in inverted order, yet they agree with each other. Both the subject and the verb are in singular form. (The barber shop *is*.)

2. Original version: The scenic pond that is surrounded by towering cypress trees were there ever since I can remember.

    Downsized version: The ~~scenic~~ pond ~~that is surrounded by towering cypress trees~~ were there ~~ever since I can remember~~.

    The subject and verb are in regular order, yet this sentence contains a subject–verb agreement error. The sentence should read *The pond _was_ there*.

3. Original version: With its chilling sound track and mind-blowing special effects, "Raising Ducklings" are one of the zany movies that I will never forget.

   Downsized version: ~~With its chilling sound track and mind-blowing special effects,~~ "Raising Ducklings" are one ~~of the zany movies that I will never forget~~.

   This sentence contains a subject-verb agreement error. Despite the plural words *special effects and movies*, the sentence should read *"Raising Ducklings" is one...*

4. Original version: Before leaving Puerto Rico, Evan, an enthusiastic and brawny sixteen-year-old, wanted to rent a moped and take it for a ride along the scenic side streets.

   Downsized version: ~~Before leaving Puerto Rico,~~ Evan~~, an enthusiastic and brawny sixteen-year-old,~~ wanted to rent a moped and take it ~~for a ride along the scenic side streets~~.

5. Original version: Alec, hardworking and charity-minded, readily accepted invitations to fundraising events and philanthropy dinners.

   Downsized version: Alec~~, hardworking and charity-minded, readily~~ accepted ~~invitations to fundraising events and philanthropy dinners~~.

Sharpening Skills—Verb Forms

Using your ability to isolate the verb and the subject of a sentence, circle the verb error in each of the following sentences. Then write the correct form of the verb on the line provided. Detailed answer explanations follow.

1. Around the circus ring walks Miranda and her majestic white horses. _____

2. According to the band leader, neither the outdoor café nor the amphitheaters located outside the strip mall provides a good spot for the band to make its community debut. _____

3. The snowman, wearing a boldly striped hat and purple fleece gloves that stick out on his sides, add a whimsical addition to the backyard. _____

4. The purpose of the annual Career Night is illustrating the many professions that high school students may one day choose. _____

5. Before the Jansens left the lakeside cabin, they take a roll of group photos, capturing the natural beauty of this idyllic setting. _____

Verb Forms Answers

1. Subject–verb agreement error; should be *walk* to agree with the plural subject *Miranda* and *horses.*

2. Subject–verb agreement error; what makes this especially hard is that the two subjects are linked by correlative conjunctions (*neither . . . nor*). In this case, the verb agrees with the latter subject; should be *provide* to agree with *amphitheaters.* What makes this question even more difficult is that the subjects and the verb are interrupted by the phrase *located outside the strip mall.* If a sentence has a compound subject (think of this as a "double subject" or two subjects joined together by a conjunction), the plural form of the verb should follow. For example, "Grilled chicken and a feta cheese omelet *are* Phillip's favorite post-workout meals." The compound subject (plural) is *Grilled chicken and a feta cheese omelet.*

3. Subject–verb agreement error; should be *adds* to agree with the subject, *snowman.* What makes this hard is that the subject and the verb are separated by the gerund phrase *wearing a boldly . . . his sides.*

4. Verb form error; should be the infinitive, *to illustrate*

5. Verb tense error; should be the past tense *took,* which is indicated by the introductory adverbial clause *Before the Jansens left the lakeside cabin.*

Pronoun Errors

Pronoun errors: ambiguous pronouns; pronoun shifts; pronouns without antecedents; wrong pronoun case; misused pronouns

Be prudent about pronouns because multifarious (numerous and varied) errors involve these tricky words. After coping with verbs, high scorers check out underlined pronouns next. Study the box below to be sure you are familiar with singular and plural personal pronouns.

Singular Pronouns	Plural Pronouns
I, me	we, us
my, mine	our, ours
you, your, yours	you, your, yours
he, she, him, her	they, them
her, hers, his	their, theirs
it, its	

When you see a pronoun that is underlined in the section on identifying sentence errors, ask yourself:

■ Does the pronoun agree in number and gender with its antecedent (word to which it refers)?

If not, there is an error in *pronoun agreement.*
Example: A good skier is aware of *their* surroundings.
(The singular noun *skier* takes the singular possessive *his.*)

■ Is the pronoun reference clear?

If not, there is an *ambiguous pronoun* error.
Example: Tom and Phillip went on their annual hiking trip, even though *he* was suffering from a sprained ankle.
(*He* is ambiguous since this pronoun can refer to either *Tom* or *Phillip.* Change *he* to *Tom* or *Phillip.*)

■ Has the pronoun point of view shifted?

If so, there is an error called *pronoun shift.*
Example: You know you're in trouble when *one feels* butterflies racing in your stomach and chills crawling up your spine.
(Since this sentence is written basically in the second-person *you,* to be grammatically consistent change *one feels* to *you feel.*)

■ Is the pronoun in the correct case, objective versus subjective?

If not, there is a *pronoun case* error.
Example: Hank and Andrew offered their old scooters to my sister and *I,* but we politely refused.
(Since the italic pronoun is the <u>object</u> of the prepositional phrase *to my sister and I,* change *I* to the objective case *me.*)

Subjective-Case Pronouns	Objective-Case Pronouns
(function as *subjects*)	(function as *direct objects, indirect objects,* or *objects of prepositional phrases*)
I	me
we	us
he, she	him, her
you	you
they	them
who	whom

Know the W pronouns:

WHO ➔ refers to a person.
There is the gentleman *who* helped us change our flat tire.

WHAT ➔ refers to an event or inanimate thing.
What is that gigantic, green creature lurking beyond the fence?

WHEN ➔ refers to a date or time period
August 2007 is *when* he was born.

WHERE ➔ refers to a place
The festival at the beach is *where* we met.

WHY ➔ refers to a reason or cause
Please tell your brother *why* you wish to borrow his baseball mitt.

Faulty Idioms

People don't worry *over* their futures; they worry *about* their futures. One thing is not different *than* another thing; one thing is different *from* another thing. Connor does not excel *with* lacrosse; he excels *in* lacrosse. After waiting on line, visitors do not walk *in* the museum, they walk *into* the museum. Jenna has a sweet tooth; she doesn't have a preoccupation *on* dark chocolate, she has a preoccupation *with* dark chocolate.

You might think that *being* raised in an English-speaking home would suffice to prepare one to use idioms correctly in speaking and in writing. However, idiom errors are so rampant (television is a predominant culprit), and faulty English assaults the ear so frequently that even the best students can stumble into the idiom trap.

The 2400 Club counters this problem by actively studying correct usage. One of the best ways is to learn common verb-preposition pairs, which are tested frequently in the grammar and usage portions of the writing section of the SAT. When working on the identifying sentence errors section, pay close attention to prepositions that are underlined. The wrong preposition in a phrase produces an *idiom error.* As you know, prepositions are rather small words that show direction, location, or association: *to, toward, above, behind, onto, near, under, over, on, in, by, about, up, of, for, with,* and many more.

Sharpening Skills—Preposition Pairs

Study the abridged list below of common verb-preposition pairs. Train your ear to *hear* which prepositions commonly follow which verbs.

Know these verb-preposition pairs:

accuse of	consist of	hide from
agree to/with/on	contribute to	hope for
apologize for	cover with	insist on/upon
apply to/for	decide on/upon	participate in
approve of	depend on/upon	prevent from
believe in	dream about/of	protect from
care about/for	escape from	recover from
compare to/with	excuse for	release from
complain about	forget about	succeed in
confide in	free from	wait for/on

Fony Abs

To connect items or ideas within a sentence, speakers and writers use connecting words called "conjunctions." To remember the most commonly used conjunctions, think of some body-conscious type flaunting a fake six-pack! Let Fony Abs be your silly mnemonic (memory-assisting device) for seven common conjunctions:

Fony = *for, or, nor, yet*   Abs = *and, but, so*

Peanut Butter and Jelly

To be a top scorer, you should know *not only* your Fony Abs *but also* your **correlative conjunctions**, hard-working pairs that go together like peanut butter and jelly. (Check out the correlative conjunctions that appear in the preceding sentence.) As pairs, correlatives hook up words, phrases, and clauses within a sentence. *Just as* some things go together, such as peanut butter and jelly, *so* correlative conjunctions work together in pairs. Know your correlative conjunctions. If you spot one in a sentence, look for its mate, which should also be in the sentence.

neither . . . nor . . .

either . . . or . . .

not only . . . but also . . .

as . . . as . . .

just as . . . so . . .

both . . . and . . .

Grammar Coaching:
The 2400 Club knows correlative conjunction pairs cold.

These pairs are basic, easy to memorize, and pervasive on the multiple-choice grammar questions.

Memorize them.

Here are examples of how correlative pairs are used to connect items of information in sentences:

According to Aunt Lexi, **neither** raspberry pie **nor** chocolate-covered pretzels make a suitable dessert.

You can select **either** the blue trench coat **or** the beige tweed jacket.

In my opinion, you look **not only** fit **but also** radiant!

Since no one bothered to make a cozy fire, it is **as** cold in the log cabin **as** it is outdoors.

Just as quietly as he entered the room, **so** he left without a sound.

As you have learned, **both** steady concentration **and** a methodical approach can bring you into the ranks of the 2400 Club.

Memorize Some Idioms

The hardest (level 4 and level 5) multiple-choice grammar questions are often about idioms. These language expressions of standard, written English may appear on the multiple-choice identifying sentence error questions, improving sentences questions, or improving paragraphs questions of the Writing section. In everyday use, idioms are toyed with and denatured a bit, straying from their pure and eloquent form based on standard and proper, written English.

Most often, hard idiom questions lurk among the questions that just precede the Improving Paragraphs exercise. Here are some examples that have appeared on real tests; these examples are worthwhile to read, read aloud, read again, and remember:

A person is *regarded as* a hero . . . NOT *regarded to be* a hero.

Jack *prefers* hot dogs *to* hamburgers . . . NOT hot dogs *over* hamburgers and NOT hot dogs *more than* hamburgers.

Cardiovascular exercise is *necessary for* weight loss . . . NOT *necessary with* weight loss.

The Native American museum is the *only one of its kind* . . . NOT only *one of a kind*.

As intellectual beings, we *draw upon* resources . . . we do NOT *draw from* resources . . .

One person's idea of an enjoyable evening is often *different from* . . . NOT *opposite to* another person's sense of a pleasurable evening.

Some birds are more *particular about* their nesting sites . . . NOT *particular in* their nesting sites.

The baseball pitcher *thought it wise* to wear a heart protector . . . NOT *thought it as wise* to wear a heart protector.

A neighbor may bring up an issue *with regard to* your boisterously barking dog . . . NOT *in regards to* your boisterously barking dog.

An unabridged list of common English idioms would be so extensive as to take up a bevy of pages. You're most likely a sharp-shooter when it comes to surfing the Internet. Search English idiomatic language, and you will find numerous listings of common usage. Lists of English idioms provide good study material if idioms are challenging for you. Also, most grammar and composition textbooks contain lists of idioms; just check the table of contents.

Lack of Parallelism

Cross off the one that doesn't belong:	Cross off the one that doesn't belong:
grapes, filet mignon, cantaloupe	to enjoy music, to eat fine food, resting
tennis, football, sneakers	magazine editor, publishing, advertising copywriter

In standard written English, certain components of a sentence should be expressed in the same way. Keeping these parts similar is called "parallelism," or parallel form. Without parallelism, clarity and logic within a sentence are compromised. Here's a tip-off for parallelism: a listing of items in a comma series appears in the sentence. Your job is to make sure that each member of the comma series is expressed in the same way. Although parallelism errors often occur within a comma series, they can occur if only two terms within a sentence are expressed in dissimilar ways. **Example:** Jenna looked forward to sleep-away camp mostly because she couldn't wait *to water-ski* and *hiking* the nature trails. The italicized terms are not parallel. To correct this error, change *hiking* to *to hike*.

Did you find the terms that don't belong in the box above? Answers: filet mignon, resting, sneakers, publishing. Use your ability to spot the odd-man-out in the the grammar questions on the SAT by making sure that items being compared or listed are parallel to one another.

Basic Examples of Parallelism

To get a sense of parallel form, consider these examples:

jogging, boating, and parasailing
(gerund, gerund, and gerund)

to eat, to sleep, and to watch television
(infinitive, infinitive, and infinitive)

investigated, followed, and captured
(past-tense verb, past-tense verb, and past-tense verb)

to find long sticks and to toast marshmallows
(infinitive-direct object and infinitive-direct object)

More Advanced Examples of Parallelism

barked loudly, growled angrily, and ran quickly
(past-tense verb-adverb, past-tense verb-adverb, and past-tense verb-adverb)

eating pizza, munching popcorn, and sipping soda
(gerund-object, gerund-object, and gerund-object)

Sharpening Skills—Parallel Form

On the line provided, rewrite the part of the sentence that is not parallel to the other part or parts.

1. To increase your fitness level, you should not only stretch every day but also cardio-vascular exercise.

   _____

2. Far from the ideal dinner guest, Gus would regularly belch, chew with his mouth open, and to pick his teeth at the dinner table.

   _____

3. Hillary's favorite pastimes include shopping at the mall, the latest movies, and instant-messaging her friends.

   _____

4. For birthdays and other special occasions, Petronella likes to give her brothers-in-law gloves, jewelry to her sisters, and electronic toys to her young sons.

   _____

5. For enthusiasts of the outdoors, either hiking or a bicycle—if done on a regular basis—can significantly increase one's cardiovascular endurance.

   _____

Parallel Form Answers

1. *do* cardiovascular exercise
2. *pick* (delete *to* since the preceding verbs are not infinitives)
3. *seeing* the latest movies
4. *gloves to her brothers-in-law*
5. *bicycling*

Diction Errors

If a toddler throws a temper tantrum in front of the toy store, is he causing a "scenario" or a "scene" at the mall?

If you wish to bypass the quicksand pit, do you "circumnavigate" or "circumvent" it?

If you wish to tell your history teacher that you investigated myriad sources for your research paper, is it more appropriate to tell him that you did "exhaustive" or "exhausting" research?

Diction errors result from inappropriate word choice. When words are underlined in the identifying sentence errors section, be sensitive to their spellings and, therefore, their precise meanings. You need to consider, not whether a word is misspelled, but *how* it is spelled. (Spelling errors have historically been very rare on the SAT.) Spelling counts in the sense that you need to know which homophone appears in a sentence: *stationary* or *stationery*? *principle* or *principal*? *whether* or *weather*? *reign* or *rain*?

The acid test: Does the word sound "off"?

Ask yourself, "Is this the precise word that fits the context of this sentence?" If you think the word is "off," you may have spotted a diction error. Top scorers amass a strong and varied upper-level vocabulary. Top scorers are also sensitive to words that sound and/or look alike but have different meanings and usages. Study the lessons titled "Tricky Twins and Triplets" in Barron's *Hot Words for the SAT*. In these lessons, you will find words often confused, such as *indignant/indigenous/indigent*, *aesthetic/ascetic/atheistic*, and *coalesce/convalesce*. Knowing the precise meanings and spellings of words will help you spot diction errors in the section on identifying sentence errors in the SAT.

Sharpening Skills—Diction Errors

For each of the following sentences, circle either "No error" or "Diction error." 2400 Club challenge: If you spot a diction error, replace the faulty word with a word that makes sense in the context.

1. Now that the clearance sale is over, I could kick myself; I should of bought the pool toys that were 75 percent off!

   No error   Diction error   →   Replace _____ with _____.

2. Andrew is taking antibiotics and trying his best to rest. Please do not exacerbate him with your taunting and teasing!

   No error   Diction error   →   Replace _____ with _____.

3. Despite our forgoing frivolous expenditures and unnecessary frills, we still cannot amass a sizable savings account.

   No error   Diction error   →   Replace _____ with _____.

4. To determine on the duration of their stay at Snow Lodge Mountain, the Miltons took a family vote, deciding to prolong their stay from 7 days to 2 weeks instead of protracting it from 7 days to 5.

   No error   Diction error   →   Replace _____ with _____.

5. I'm tired of you feigning malaise; that's just your way of getting out of helping with the housework.

   No error   Diction error   →   Replace _____ with _____.

6. Hank, the fact is that the more I ascent to your demands, the more presumptuous you become with your requests.

No error   Diction error   → Replace _____ with _____.

7. Because of the author's concerns regarding her intellectual work being protected, the project editor ensured her repeatedly that her original work was copyright protected.

No error   Diction error   → Replace _____ with _____.

8. Because of a life-changing car accident, the young lady lost her short-term memory and was subsequently unable to sustain any new information.

No error   Diction error   → Replace _____ with _____.

9. Marcus is an assiduous student whose papers are always on time and whose test scores are among the highest; in fact, he is a model specimen of a conscious work ethic.

No error   Diction error   → Replace _____ with _____.

10. We are not exactly close friends, so why are you offended by me not inviting you to join us for dinner?

No error   Diction error   → Replace _____ with _____.

Diction Answers

1. Diction error   →   Replace *of* with *have.*
2. Diction error   →   Replace *exacerbate* with *exasperate.*
3. No error
4. Diction error   →   Replace *protracting* with *curtailing.*
5. Diction error   →   Replace *you* with *your.*
6. Diction error   →   Replace *ascent* with *assent.*
7. Diction error   →   *assured* fits this context better.
8. Diction error   →   Replace *sustain* with *retain.*
9. Diction error   →   Replace *conscious* with *conscientious.*
10. Diction error   →   Replace *me* with *my.*

Misplaced Modifiers

To avoid ambiguity, modifying phrases need to be placed in close proximity to the word that they modify. Errors occur when modifiers are "misplaced," usually meaning that they are set apart from the noun or pronoun to which they refer.

The modifying phrases are italicized in the examples that follow. Notice how the meaning of the sentence changes when the modifying phrase and the word modified are in close proximity.

Who's hanging in the tree? Who's looking at whom?
Hanging from the highest branch, the man with binoculars eyed the monkey.
Hanging from the highest branch, the monkey eyed the man with binoculars.

Who's carefree, the girl or the shoreline?
Lola strolled along the Tappen Beach shoreline, *without a care in the world*.
Without a care in the world, Lola strolled along the Tappen Beach shoreline.

Adjective Versus Adverb Errors

Those who help cheerful are more appreciated than those who help unwillingly.

Despite saying "no" constant to her pleading children, Mom is besieged with the same question over and over again.

Did you detect any grammatical errors in the sentences above? Each has an adjective/adverb error. Here are the corrected sentences:

Those who help *cheerfully* are more appreciated than those who help unwillingly.

Despite saying "no" *constantly* to her pleading children, Mom is besieged with the same question over and over again.

Sharpening Skills—Adjective/Adverb Errors

Each sentence contains an adjective/adverb error. Replace the faulty adjective with the correct adverb.

1. Melvin, the shabby dressed man who walked his three shaggy dogs every day, rested with a cup of coffee at the corner of Forest Avenue and School Street.

2. Hank knows that, even though he did badly on his PSAT, he will perform more strong on the SAT.

3. Despite his sore calf muscle and sprained ankle, Augie performed miraculous in the 20-meter dash.

4. Comforting, Nanna Rose lulled baby Jean to sleep with a sonorous rendition of "Mary Had a Little Lamb."

5. We love you and miss you so much that we hope you return home quick!

Adjective/Adverb Answers

1. *shabbily* dressed man
2. more *strongly*
3. performed *miraculously*
4. *Comfortingly*, Nanna Rose
5. return home *quickly*

Plural–Singular Inconsistency

Can two children grow up and merge into one adult artist?
Can college classmates share the same GPA?

Reasonably, you know not. In the following sentences, however, these two logic-defying phenomena are not as easily spotted.

Mia and Maggie, the six-year-olds who attend the Museum Art School, dream of becoming a famous sculptor one day and sharing their own studio. (Can two young girls become one renowned sculptor?)

Popularity with the freshmen girls is not the only goal that Ralph and Rich share; these ambitious juniors also want to earn a GPA that will award them honor roll status. (Can two guys earn a single grade point average?)

When sentences lack consistency between plural and singular components that go together, the resulting sentences are illogical. It's as if magic occurs in these unsound sentences.

Redundancy and Wordiness (Relatives of Flabby Phrasing)

Have you ever heard of the expression "beating a dead horse"?

Redundancy is like that; redundancy is saying the same thing over again, . . . or over again . . . and again.

The redundancy is boldfaced in this sentence:

Although he looks like a slugger, the guy at the plate **still** hasn't made contact with the ball **yet**.

You need one or the other, *yet* or *still*. Using both words is overkill. Wordiness is flabby writing that uses too many words to say something that can be expressed with brevity. Your mantra: "Concise is nice; wordy is out!" Keep this mantra in mind when you write your essay.

Sharpening Skills—Redundancy and Wordiness

Trim the fat in the following sentences by crossing off redundant and/or wordy expressions.

1. Ever since I was young, I wanted, from an early age, to pursue a career in either the performing arts or the fashion world.

2. Simultaneously talking on the telephone while writing a business letter is very challenging to do at the same time.

3. Although I sensed an atmosphere of instability, Ms. Hanna reassured me kindly and with gentle assurance that my senior position with the company was solid and secure.

4. All together, the dog barking, the television blaring, and the boys chattering created a crescendo of clamor that rivaled the roar of a hurricane itself, with all of these three noisy things happening at once.

5. Sluggishly walking from the couch to the dessert buffet, slow-moving Jim appeared less than enthusiastic to be at yet another holiday cocktail party even though he seemed to be enjoying the decadent walnut truffle.

6. Ravenous Harold ate both three croissants as well as two hunks of Fontina cheese.

Redundancy and Wordiness Answers

For each sentence, this answer key shows one way that you can eliminate redundancy and wordiness. These answers do not illustrate all possibilities.

1. Ever since I was young, I wanted, ~~from an early age,~~ to pursue a career in either the performing arts or the fashion world.
2. ~~Simultaneously~~ talking on the telephone while writing a business letter is very challenging to do at the same time.
3. Although I sensed an atmosphere of instability, Ms. Hanna reassured me kindly ~~and with gentle assurance~~ that my senior position with the company was solid and secure.
4. All together, the dog barking, the television blaring, and the boys chattering created a crescendo of clamor that rivaled the roar of a hurricane itself, ~~with all of these three noisy things happening at once~~.
5. Sluggishly walking from the couch to the dessert buffet, ~~slow-moving~~ Jim appeared less than enthusiastic to be at yet another holiday cocktail party even though he seemed to be enjoying a decadent walnut truffle.
6. Ravenous Harold ate ~~both~~ three croissants as well as two chunks of Fontina cheese.

Faulty Comparisons

Danny's off-road vehicle is cooler than Jackie.
Hannah's parents require more household chores than Mia and Ashton combined.
A summer getaway to Martha's Vineyard appeals more to Laura than Disney World.

Did you detect faulty logic in the sentences above? Each illustrates a faulty comparison. Can an apple be sweeter than some other produce market? No! Can the lyrics of one musician be more sensitive than another musician? No! These comparisons do not make sense either. When you see that things are being compared, be sure that *like things are being compared:*

people compared to *people*

a *type of thing* compared to the *same type of thing*

an *activity* to another *activity*

Here's an equation to remember:

Faulty comparison = Faulty logic

Look at it this way: If you're amazed that one bird's beak is much shinier than another bird's beak, would you compare one bird to the other bird's beak, or would you compare one beak to the other beak? Obviously, the latter is correct. But if you're not concentrating when you read, you're apt to miss errors in faulty comparison.

Logic breaks down when dissimilar things are compared, as in the examples that follow.

Example 1

The yellow cockatiel's beak is much shinier than the grey cockatiel. (faulty comparison)

The yellow cockatiel's beak is much shinier than that of the grey cockatiel. (correct)

The yellow cockatiel's beak is much shinier than the grey cockatiel's. (also correct)

Example 2

By reading a bar graph that they found on an Internet site about nutrition, the curious couple discovered that the water content of a chestnut is similar to an apple. (faulty comparison)

By reading a bar graph that they found on an Internet site about nutrition, the curious couple discovered that the water content of a chestnut is similar to *that of* an apple. (correct)

By reading a bar graph that they found on an Internet site about nutrition, the curious couple discovered that a chestnut's water content is similar to an apple*'s*. (also correct)

Comparative Form	Superlative Form
Use to compare two things: *er* ending Example: Of the two puppies, the small*er* one has the fuzz*ier* coat and the *more* playful disposition.	Use to compare three or more things: *est* ending Example: Of the whole litter of pups, the small*est* one has the fuzz*iest* coat and the *most* playful disposition.
Taller, shorter, smarter, faster *better, more*	*Tallest, shortest, smartest, fastest* *best, most*

Let the 2400 Club's catchy mnemonic device work for you:
The *two*-letter ending *-er* is used to compare *two* items;
the *three*-letter ending *-est* is used to compare *three or more* items.

Sharpening Skills—Faulty Comparisons

For each sentence, indicate whether there is a faulty comparison by circling "Error" or "No error."

1. A voracious nonfiction reader, Julian couldn't decide which of the four sports biographies he favored more.   Error   No error

2. The dark plaid wallpaper in the boys' bathroom is much more masculine than the powder room, which is conveniently situated off the kitchen.   Error   No error

3. Both on the playing field and off, Hugo's sportsmanship is far more admirable than that shown by Peter's.   Error   No error

4. Of all the Christmases she can remember, Julia decided that this past one was the greatest of them all in terms of the festivity and gratitude shown by her loved ones.   Error   No error

5. Hands down, the warm and mouth-watering cinnamon buns sold at Rosefeld Mall are much more scrumptious than Good Ole Bakery.   Error   No error

6. Full of comic humor and whimsy, Hank delightfully announced that his life is as inane and unpredictable as a circus clown.   Error   No error

7. Which roller coaster is the cooler one, Tricky Twister or Crazy Cyclone?   Error   No error

8. Hard Rock Hotel's waterslide or Portofino Bay Hotel—which slide do you think is the fastest?   Error   No error

Faulty Comparisons Answers

1. Error; should be *he favored most.*
2. Error; should be *than the wallpaper in the powder room.*
3. Error; should be *than that shown by Peter.*
4. No error
5. Error; should be *than Good Ole Bakery's* or *those sold at Good Ole Bakery.*
6. Error; should be *that of a circus clown* or *a circus clown's.*
7. No error
8. Error; should be *Portofino Bay Hotel's*; *faster* should be used because only two slides are being compared.

Run-ons (Comma Splices) and Fragments

Run-ons

For the improving sentences portion of the SAT, you will need to spot run-on sentences and, in each case, to select the answer choice that most effectively eliminates the run-on. Also, for the essay portion of the SAT, you want your writing to be run-on-free! Most important, in your personal and professional life you want your written communications to be free of run-ons (comma splices).

Using shorthand notations, the chart below explains the basic rules of semicolon and comma use to punctuate compound sentences. There are many additional uses for semicolons and commas, but these are the ones that apply most frequently to the writing sections of the SAT

Attention, Grammar Gurus
Top scorers learn the hard and fast rules about how to use semicolons correctly.

Shorthand	Meaning	Run-ons	Sound Compound Sentences
IC	Independent Clause	IC , IC = comma splice	IC ; IC
		IC IC = fused sentence	IC, conjunction* IC

* Fony Abs

Here's the hard and fast rule for the types of run-ons that appear most frequently on the SAT: *The part of the sentence that precedes a semicolon must be an independent clause; the part of the sentence that follows the semicolon must also be independent.*

Fragments

A dependent clause or a phrase on its own is a sentence fragment. Notice in the examples that follow that fragments can be short or long.

> **Because everybody else at the amusement park was wearing rain ponchos.**
> **Nothing but silence.**
> **Deciding to be the most prolific cartoonist who ever lived.**

Sharpening Skills—Sentence Errors

For each of the following, indicate on line *a*, whether the item is a sentence, a fragment, or a run-on. 2400 Club members: for an added challenge, if the item is a fragment or a run-on, indicate on line *b* precisely what the sentence error is. If the item is a sound sentence, leave *b* blank.

1. Beyond the rustic post-and-beam fence and encroaching on the church parking lot that is just off of Glen Cove Road.

    a. _____ *b.* _____

2. Justin likes the chocolate biscotti he also likes the cinnamon-pecan cookies.

    a. _____ *b.* _____

3. Do you like the Mets, or do you like the Jets?

    a. _____ *b.* _____

4. Early on weekday mornings, before she runs on her treadmill for 45 minutes, Beth meditates.

    a. _____ *b.* _____

5. Without even looking back for a final glimpse of his aunt's puzzling facial expression.

    a. _____ *b.* _____

6. Since Jeremy would not acknowledge his responsibility with regard to the impending debacle.

    a. _____ *b.* _____

7. Because of Kurt's disrespectful tone, Myra would not look at him neither would Dave.

    a. _____ *b.* _____

8. Dissillusioned, I left.

    a. _____ *b.* _____

9. Hanging onto every word, an ancient talisman that originated in India.

    a. _____ *b.* _____

10. Janice's humor was trenchant so was Doug's.

    a. _____ *b.* _____

11. Without a word and without looking back, Frederick left the tranquil place where he had spent many afternoons composing earnest letters to his ex-girlfriend.

    a. _____ *b.* _____

12. The sterling silver ring features an elaborate scroll design, it is named the Diva.

    a. _____ *b.* _____

Sentence Errors Answers

    1. *a.* fragment   *b.* couple of phrases followed by an adjective clause

    2. *a.* run-on   *b.* fused sentence (add semicolon after *biscotti*)

    3. *a.* sentence (compound sentence)

    4. *a.* sentence (complex sentence)

    5. *a.* fragment   *b.* series of prepositional phrases

6. *a.* fragment   *b.* subordinate adverbial clause followed by prepositional phrases

7. *a.* run-on   *b.* fused sentence (add semicolon after *him*)

8. *a.* sentence (simple sentence)

9. *a.* fragment   *b.* gerund clause followed by a noun (*talisman*) modified by a subordinate adjective clause (*that originated in India*)

10. *a.* run-on   *b.* fused sentence (add semicolon after *trenchant*)

11. *a.* sentence (complex sentence)

12. *a.* run-on   *b.* comma splice (replace the comma with a semicolon to create a compound sentence)

A Final Note on Grammar and Usage Errors

Just because something seems wrong doesn't mean that it is wrong. Sometimes hard questions feature sentences that contain words and/or phrases that sound or look wrong but are actually fine. Don't get trapped by these "false positives." The sentences that follow contain parts (italicized) that are likely to appear wrong to even the brightest students. Keep in mind that, just because you, your peers, and your teachers may not speak or write this way, the italicized parts are sound when it comes to standard written English.

Is this the picnic table *on which* you supposedly left your compact disc player?
(It may jar your ear, but *on which* is perfectly all right. Even though most people don't speak or write this way, the phrase is grammatically sound. In the real world of conversation, we would probably ask:
Is this the picnic table where you supposedly left your compact disc player?
(According to the conventions of standard written English, *where* is not used correctly here.)
or:
Is this the picnic table you supposedly left your compact disc player on?

This is the scene *in which* the tornado rips through the unsuspecting village.
Conversational English might go something like this:
This is the scene where the tornado rips through the unsuspecting village.
(According to the conventions of standard written English, *where* is not used correctly here.)

***Because* my purse had been stolen at the ballfield, I carried *neither* valuables *nor* sentimental items with me again.**
(Maybe you were once told that a sentence may not start with *Because*. Provided that the sentence culminates in an independent clause, however, the sentence is grammatically acceptable.)

Chapter 7

IMPROVING SENTENCES

For this section of the SAT, you must select the sentence version that is grammatically correct and most effectively written. You are given an "original sentence" in which a part or the entire sentence is underlined. Then you are given four ways to rewrite the underlined portion. Choice (A) repeats the original. If you think the original is better than any other version, select (A); otherwise, select one of the other answer choices.

 If you don't like the original sentence version, quickly skip over answer choice (A), since (A) is always a reproduction of the original.

For this section you need to select not only the choice that rectifies the error but also the choice that expresses the original meaning most clearly and succinctly. Also, you are more likely to have to contend with two *or more* errors at a time. You may need to eradicate a pronoun-agreement error while moving a misplaced modifier to its correct location—all the while being careful to select the sentence version that is most concise.

2400 Club Strategies: The 4Cs of Improving Sentences

When shopping for the perfect diamond, consumers concern themselves with 4Cs: clarity, cut, carat, and carbon factor. When shooting for the perfect grammar score, test takers concern themselves with these 4Cs:

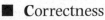

Coaching:
Working smart, the 2400 Club knows to first consider the two most concise sentence versions.

The 2400 Club also knows, however, that grammatical soundness always ranks above succinctness.

- Correctness
- Clarity
- Conciseness
- Colloquialisms

Let's discuss these C factors. Each is accompanied by a brief mantra (*in italics*) that can help you recall a grammar tip.

CORRECTNESS

"Concise is nice, but grammatical <u>correctness</u> ranks above brevity."

"Correctness" means that the sentence is grammatically sound. When selecting the best sentence version, follow the conventions of standard written English. This part of the SAT is not about which sentences you understand or which sentences could "fly" in conversational English. This is about *standard written English*, which doesn't have much about it that's casual. As discussed before, unfortunately your ears may not hear many examples of the level of standard written English that you are expected to uphold on this section of this test. In fact, you may not hear grammatically and idiomatically sound, conventional English even from the mouths of well-reputed newscasters, talk-show hosts, politicians, and business leaders. In short, on this part of the SAT you're held to a higher standard of language than almost anyone also (except university professors of English, good SAT verbal coaches, and your fellow test takers).

In this section you are more likely to encounter sentence-level errors such as run-ons, comma splices, fused sentences, and sentence fragments than you are in the section on identifying sentence errors.

CLARITY

"<u>Clarity</u> ranks above conciseness."

"Clarity" means lucidity, intelligibility, lack of ambiguity. The best sentence version is the one that produces the most effective sentence—a sentence that has clarity, lacks awkwardness, *and* uses the conventions of standard written English.

If the nonunderlined portion of a sentence mentions *Jake* and *Justin*, and the underlined portion mentions *he*, then you have ambiguity—Jake or Justin?

If the nonunderlined portion mentions *Paris* and *Athens*, and the underlined portion mentions *there*, you again have ambiguity—Paris or Athens?

Lack of clarity also occurs when a sentence is awkwardly constructed or confusing.

CONCISENESS

"For sentences twice as nice, trim the fat and be <u>concise</u>."

Get this concept down cold: *concisely written sentences are preferred*. However, astute test takers do not robotically pick the shortest sentence versions. If a concise sentence is vague, ambiguous, or confusing, then a *longer* sentence that is precise and clear will be preferred.

Deciding on the best sentence version is a balancing act that requires a firm hold on grammar and your keen judgment. Many factors have to be taken into consideration when selecting the most effective sentence, including grammatical soundness, conciseness, and clarity. Without a doubt, conciseness is favored, provided that it does not come at the expense of grammatical correctness or clarity of meaning.

Flabby/awkward	Concise
During the hour that I had for lunch . . .	During my lunch hour . . .
Not having even a bit of hesitation . . .	Without hesitation . . .
Hardly any time ago . . .	Recently . . .

You get the idea. Flabby is out; concise is in.

Knowing that conciseness is key, high scorers save time by *first* zeroing in on the two most concise sentence versions. More often than not, one of these two versions is the correct choice. The SAT favors economy of language.

COLLOQUIALISMS

"*Colloquial* and slang go out with a bang."

Colloquialisms are out! Read the sentence versions very carefully, making sure that your ear picks up on any words or phrases like the crossed-off language below. If only one word or phrase in a sentence version does not sound to you like standard written English (grammatically perfect, formal language), cross out that choice. Process of elimination works great in improving sentences.

Here are examples of types of language, some general and some specific, that you should cross out.

~~Casual language~~	~~Conversational language~~
~~Slang~~	~~Trendy language~~

When it comes to outdoor sports, I like ~~tons of things~~.

There's ~~lots and lots~~ of information about medieval archers.

That Black Diamond ski trail is ~~a beauty~~!

The town supervisor should ~~of~~ made a speech at the fund-raising dinner.

At MGM studios, the teen tourists were ~~really into~~ the demonstration on cinematic special effects.

Get the idea? The bottom line is that you have to train your ear to hear words and phrases that fall short of standard written English.

The 2400 Club knows that the best sentences are expressed in standard written English.

If phrases or words are very casual or conversational, chances are they're out.

Be Alert to Introductory Phrases

As you work through this section, try to develop sensitivity to introductory phrases, which start off a sentence and are followed by a comma. The introductory phrases are italicized in the sentences below. Notice that the person, place, or thing that the introductory phrase modifies immediately follows the phrase.

Standing six feet tall and acing every test, Alex is not only handsome but also highly intelligent. (The introductory phrase modifies *Alex*.)

Twenty minutes from town center and a short walk from the beach, the picturesque neighborhood is a beach lover's dream. (The introductory phrase modifies *picturesque neighborhood*.)

Constructed of dense alloy, bundles of wire, and rustproof hinges, the robot represents the culmination of the mad scientist's life work. (The introductory phrase modifies *robot*.)

When introductory phrases are followed by something that the phrase is *not* intended to modify, the sentence is flawed. Here are examples of grammatically flawed sentences that contain misplaced modifiers.

Standing six feet tall and acing every test, handsomeness and intelligence distinguish Alex. (Incorrect—misplaced modifying phrase)

Twenty minutes from town center and a short walk from the beach, a beach lover's dream can be found in the picturesque neighborhood. (Incorrect—misplaced modifying phrase)

Constructed of dense alloy, bundles of wire, and rustproof hinges, the mad scientist created a robot that represented the culmination of his life's work. (Incorrect—misplaced modifying phrase)

Be sensitive to introductory phrases; keep your eyes peeled for them. Make sure each one is followed by what it's supposed to modify.

Be a Grammar Guru—Know Your Mantras

You're on your way to becoming a grammar guru. Review those important mantras, and let them play in your head as you work through the improving sentences section. You can sing them pop style, rap style, or opera style—doesn't matter. Internalize them so that they ring in your ear on test day and always. Let them guide you:

> *"Concise is nice, but grammatical soundness ranks above brevity."*
> *"Clarity ranks above conciseness."*
> *"For sentences twice as nice, trim the fat and be concise."*
> *"Colloquial and slang go out with a bang."*

Even if the original sentence is grammatically sound, don't automatically select choice (A). There may be another version that is also grammatically sound but expresses the meaning more clearly and succinctly. In that case, choice (A) is overshadowed by this *better* version.

Most often, one of the two most concisely worded sentences is the correct answer. By the same token, for most of the questions in the improving sentences section, you can easily eliminate two or more answer choices that are *wordy* and/or *awkward* in their phrasing.

Follow Through

Follow through is vital for that winning swing of the baseball bat or tennis racquet. Follow through is imperative for keeping the soccer ball out of the goal. Follow through, which takes both discipline and practice, is also key on the SAT. Even if you find a tempting sentence version that is grammatically sound and well expressed, you should follow through and prudently consider all remaining choices before selecting your final answer.

PRACTICE TEST QUESTIONS

As a 2400 Club member, you do not receive silver-platter service here. You are not given groups of practice exercises that fall under a particular category of error. Instead, you get just what you will encounter on test day: a miscellaneous grouping of errors. With these practice exercises, you will get a mix of sentence errors, the added brain challenge that a sharp shooter like you requires.

Here are the directions for the questions on improving sentences. Learn them now so that on test day you won't even have to read them.

Directions: The underlined sections of the sentences below may contain errors in standard English, including awkward or ambiguous expression, poor word choice (diction), incorrect sentence structure, and faulty grammar, usage, and punctuation. In some cases, the entire sentence may be underlined. Read each sentence carefully, and identify which of the five alternative versions most effectively and correctly expresses the meaning of the original. Choice (A) always repeats the original. Choose (A) if none of the other choices improves the original sentence. Indicate your choice by filling in the corresponding space on your answer sheet.

SAMPLE QUESTION:

Ultimately, the truth about <u>people's natures and motives eventually come out</u>.

(A) people's natures and motives eventually come out
(B) people's natures and motive eventually will come out
(C) peoples natures and motives eventually comes out
(D) peoples' natures and motives eventually coming out
(E) people's natures and motives comes out

Correct answer: (E)

1. At Mount Snow the family of four <u>drove snowmobiles, skiing for hours, and enjoyed an afternoon of ice-skating</u>.

(A) drove snowmobiles, skiing for hours, and enjoyed an afternoon of ice-skating
(B) driving snowmobiles, skiing for hours, and enjoying an afternoon of ice-skating
(C) went snowmobiling, skied for hours, and had enjoyed skiing for all of the afternoon
(D) drove snowmobiles, skied for hours, and enjoyed an afternoon of ice-skating
(E) snowmobiled, skied, and enjoyed an afternoon of ice-skating

2. Even though Haley claimed dessert was her favorite course of any meal, she <u>ate hardly none of the apple pie or cookies that was</u> laid out before her.

(A) ate hardly none of the apple pie or cookies that was
(B) hadn't eaten none of the cookies or of the apple pie that were
(C) had eaten hardly a none of the apple pie or cookies that had been
(D) eats hardly any of the apple pie or cookies that was
(E) ate hardly any of the apple pie or cookies that were

3. Either Mike or Joe <u>wanted to be sports-casters when they grew up</u>.

(A) wanted to be sportscasters when they grew up

(B) wants to be a sportscaster when he grows up

(C) had wanted to get into sportscasting as their professions as elders

(D) they wanted to be sportscasters growing up

(E) wanted to be a sportscaster when they grow up

4. <u>A pragmatic woman, purchasing a gold-and-silver-tone watch was a smart idea since she can wear it with her silver jewelry as well as her gold</u>.

(A) A pragmatic woman, purchasing a gold-and-silver-tone watch was a smart idea since she can wear it with her silver jewelry as well as her gold

(B) A smart idea, a pragmatic woman purchased a gold-and silver-tone watch that she can wear with her silver jewelry as well as her gold

(C) The pragmatic woman purchased a gold-and silver-tone watch, which was a smart idea, she can wear it with her silver as well as her gold jewelry

(D) Not only a pragmatic woman, she is a smart woman, too, and so she bought a silver-and gold-tone watch that matches her jewelry

(E) A pragmatic and smart woman, she purchased a gold-and silver-tone watch that she can wear with both her silver and gold jewelry

5. Under construction for nearly six months, <u>the frazzled homeowners were continually presented</u> with renovation challenges and vital decisions that would affect the overall feel of what they hoped to be their lifelong home.

(A) the frazzled homeowners were continually presented

(B) the homeowners, frazzled, were presented over and over

(C) the fixer-upper home continually presented the homeowners

(D) the fixer-upper home continually presented him

(E) continually presented

6. Hector enjoys movies more <u>then theater going since the latter do</u> not have the distractions associated with set changes and intermission.

(A) then theater going since the latter do

(B) then going to the theater since the latter do

(C) than theater since the former do

(D) then the performances at the theater being that the latter does

(E) than theater since the former does

7. <u>During the fall months of September, October, and November,</u> Ernest's soccer schedule is in full swing; there are State Cup competitions as well as Junior League tournaments.

(A) During the fall months of September, October, and November,

(B) During September, October, and November,

(C) During September, November, and October,

(D) During September up and through November,

(E) In the fall, during September through November,

8. During late October, <u>because of its lush and colorful foliage, Drew decided to take his family for a ride up to Vermont</u>.

(A) because of its lush and colorful foliage, Drew decided to take his family for a ride up to Vermont

(B) on account of its lushness and its colorfulness, Vermont was the place to which Drew decided to take a ride with his family.

(C) Drew's family decided to take him for a ride up to Vermont, because of its lush and colorful foliage.

(D) Drew decided to take his family for a ride up to Vermont, because of its lush and colorful foliage.

(E) Because of its lush and colorful foliage, Drew having decided on taking his family for a ride up to Vermont

9. Just as a home theater was a dream come true for the Benson family, <u>so a backyard tennis court was a dream come true for the Janice family</u>.

(A) so a backyard tennis court was a dream come true for the Janice family

(B) so was a backyard tennis court was a dream come true for the Janice family

(C) as a dream came true for the Janice family with its backyard tennis court

(D) so a tennis court, in the backyard, was a dream that the Janices realized

(E) and, as such, a backyard tennis court was a dream come true for the Janice family

10. Since Mom wanted a miniature poodle and Dad wanted a Labrador retriever, the <u>perfect compromise being</u> a mini Labradoodle, a cross between a miniature poodle and a modest-sized Labrador retriever.

(A) perfect compromise being

(B) perfection of compromising was

(C) perfect compromise was

(D) compromise that seemed just perfect to both of them was

(E) perfect compromise was planned on being

11. Now that there are only two summer employment options available, you must decide between <u>becoming a highly paid golf caddy or to be a computer intern who learns a great deal but who is paid meagerly</u>.

(A) becoming a highly paid golf caddy or to be a computer intern who learns a great deal but who is paid meagerly

(B) becoming a highly paid golf caddy or becoming a computer intern who learns a great deal but who is paid meagerly

(C) whether you should become a highly paid golf caddy and whether, instead, you should become a computer intern who, while learning a great deal, but who is paid meagerly

(D) becoming a highly paid golf caddy and interning in the computer field, you will learn a great deal but you will be paid meagerly

(E) becoming a golf caddy who is highly paid and becoming a computer intern who learns a great deal but who is paid meagerly

12. Brimming with outerwear, sneakers, library books, and bulging backpacks, the mudroom, situated between the garage and the kitchen, serves as a clearing house for the hustle-bustle of daily life.

    (A) the mudroom, situated between the garage and the kitchen, serves as
    (B) in the mudroom and situated between the garage and the kitchen, serves as
    (C) the mudroom, situated between the garage and the kitchen, serving as
    (D) the mudroom is situated between the garage and the kitchen, it serves as
    (E) the garage and the kitchen have the mudroom in between them so that the latter serves as

13. Always think for yourself, for when somebody says that they like one ski lodge over another, for example, it's merely their opinion.

    (A) that they like one ski lodge over another, for example, it's merely their opinion
    (B) that they like one ski lodge over another, for example, it's merely his or her opinion
    (C) that they like one ski lodge over another, for example, it's merely just their opinion
    (D) that he likes one ski lodge over another, for example, it's merely his opinion
    (E) that he likes one ski lodge over another, for example, its merely his opinion

14. To the boys' delight, the party bags contained cool sunglasses, candies that are sweet and sour, and pocket-sized flashlights.

    (A) candies that are sweet and sour, and
    (B) candies that are sweet as well as sour, and
    (C) sweet and sour candies, and they contained
    (D) sweet and sour candies, and
    (E) candies, being sweet and sour, additionally

15. If Phillip had to decide between playing shortstop or first base, he would choose shortstop because that is the position he enjoys most.

    (A) or first base, he would choose shortstop because that is the position he enjoys most
    (B) or first base, he would choose shortstop, being the one he most enjoys
    (C) and playing first base, he would choose shortstop because that is the position he enjoys more
    (D) and first base, he would choose shortstop because that is the position he enjoys most
    (E) and first base playing, he would be choosing shortstop while that being the position he is most enjoying

ANSWERS AND EXPLANATIONS

1. D	**6.** E	**11.** E
2. E	**7.** B	**12.** A
3. B	**8.** D	**13.** D
4. E	**9.** A	**14.** D
5. C	**10.** C	**15.** C

Although there may be more than one error in a sentence, only one error may be indicated below for each incorrect version.

1. *Correct answer:* **(D)**

(A) Lack of parallelism: "drove"/ "skiing"/"enjoyed"
(B) Sentence fragment
(C) Final third of sentence is wordy
(E) Loss of info. Enjoyed what?

2. *Correct answer:* **(E)**

(A) Double negative: "hardly none"
(B) Double negative: "hadn't eaten none"
(C) awkward construction: "hardly a none"
(D) Verb tense should be consistent with "claimed"; need "were" to agree with "cookies."

3. *Correct answer:* **(B)**

(A) "Either Mike or Joe" is a singular construction. "Sportscasters" and "they" disagree since these terms are plural.
(C) Awkward and wordy
(D) The pronoun "they" is unnecessary; "sportscasters" does not agree with the singular subject "Mike" or "Joe"; "growing up" distorts original meaning of sentence.
(E) The singular "sportscaster" and the plural pronoun "they" are not in agreement.

4. *Correct answer:* **(E)**

(A) Misplaced modifying phrase
(B) Misplaced modifying phrase
(C) Comma splice
(D) Very wordy

5. *Correct answer:* **(C)**

(A) Misplaced modifying phrase
(B) Wordy and awkward
(D) The singular "him" does not agree with the plural "their home."
(E) Sentence fragment

6. *Correct answer:* **(E)**

(A) Faulty diction; "than" is used to make a comparison. Like (B) and (D), "latter" refers incorrectly to the theater instead of the movies.
(B) Faulty diction; "than" is used to make a comparison.
(C) Subject-verb agreement error
(D) Wordy

7. *Correct answer:* **(B)**

(A) Redundancy; "fall months" is obvious.
(C) Wrong order of months
(D) Awkward phrasing
(E) Redundancy

8. *Correct answer:* **(D)**

   (A) Misplaced modifying phrase; "because of its lush and colorful foliage" should be positioned next to Vermont
   (B) Wordy and awkward
   (C) Original meaning is changed.
   (E) Misplaced modifying phrase; awkward verb phrasing

9. *Correct answer:* **(A)**

   (B) Meaningless repetition of "was"
   (C) Lack of parallelism
   (D) Lack of parallelism
   (E) As a correlative, idiomatic pair, "Just as"...should be followed by "so."

10. *Correct answer:* **(C)**

    (A) Results in a fragment
    (B) Awkward
    (D) Wordy and awkward
    (E) Wordy and awkward

11. *Correct answer:* **(E)**

    (A) Lack of parallelism; also diction error: between x *and* y
    (B) Diction error: between x *and* y
    (C) Wordy and awkward
    (D) Run-on sentence (comma splice)

12. *Correct answer:* **(A)**

    (B) The introductory modifying phrase, "Brimming with outerwear, sneakers, library books, and bulging backpacks," should be placed immediately before "mudroom" since that's what the phrase modifies. The words "in the" should be eliminated.
    (C) Sentence fragment
    (D) Run-on sentence (comma splice)
    (E) Misplaced modifying phrase, as in (B); awkwardly worded

13. *Correct answer:* **(D)**

    (A) Pronoun-agreement error; "somebody" is a singular pronoun, so "they" cannot refer to it
    (B) Same explanation as (A)
    (C) The expression "merely just" is redundant.
    (E) The word "its" is a possessive pronoun; should be the contraction "it's" (it is).

14. *Correct answer:* **(D)**

    (A) Lack of parallelism; each member of this series consists of *adjective-noun*
    (B) Lack of parallelism; "as well as" is unnecessarily wordy
    (C) The words "they contained" are superfluous.
    (E) Lack of parallelism; "additionally" is awkward

15. *Correct answer:* **(C)**

    (A) Faulty correlative conjunction; "between" goes with "and"
    (B) Same explanation as (A)
    (D) The word "more" is needed to compare two positions.
    (E) Wordy and awkward

Chapter 8

IDENTIFYING SENTENCE ERRORS

For this component of the writing section of the SAT, you will need only to identify the grammar or usage error in the sentence. At the same time, you have to keep in mind that about 15–20 percent of the sentences will have no error.

THE OVERPREPARATION METHOD: FIND THE ERROR, NAME THE ERROR, FIX THE ERROR

Be ready to ace the identifying sentence errors section. Just over-prepare yourself as you work through the warm-up exercises on pages 170–172, using the ambitious find it–name it–fix it method.

Think of this section as a version of "eye-spy." You're a grammar private eye, and as a grammar sleuth you must spot the errors.

2400 Club Coaching: *Grammar gurus overprepare, using the Find-Name-Fix method.*

What You Must Do on Test Day	**What the 2400 Club Does to Overprep**
Find the error	Find the error
	Name the error
	Fix the error

As stated above, your overpreparation method goes like this: "Find error–name error–fix error." Naming the error is the hardest part, but remember that you do not have to give the error a name on test day. Naming will become easier once you have read through all of the grammar tips in this book.

For now, refer to the Hierarchy of Grammar Glitches (reproduced below) to help you name the error. On test day, of course, you will not be provided with an error list as a reference.

Remember: in the real world, only English teachers need worry about the fine line of distinction between a diction and an idiom error, the difference between a comma splice and a fused run-on, or the distinction between lack of parallelism and faulty comparison.

To work *efficiently, first scrutinize any verbs and pronouns that are underlined.*

A plethora of errors surrounds these ubiquitous parts of speech.

To name the error, choose one of the following:

Verb Error   →   Subject–verb agreement; verb tense; verb form

Pronoun Error   →   Ambiguous pronoun; pronoun shift; pronoun case

Faulty Idiom

Lack of Parallelism

Diction Error

Misplaced Modifier

Adjective Versus Adverb Errors

Plural–Singular Inconsistency

Redundancy and Wordiness

Faulty Comparison

Run-Ons and Fragments

> *Keep your eye on verbs and pronouns. A bevy of errors surrounds these parts of speech.*

WARM-UP EXERCISES

Just for this **sharpening skills** exercise, you are given hints (indicated by arrows) for some of the sentences. The arrows emphasize a very important tip about the identifying sentence errors section of the SAT:

> **2400 Club Coaching:** To attain a perfect 800 on the writing section of the SAT, pay as close attention to the *non*underlined portions of the sentences as you do to the underlined portions.

This tip may sound counterintuitive, but it works.

> **Directions:** The following sentences test your ability to recognize grammar and usage errors. Each sentence contains either a single error or no error at all. No sentence contains more than one error. The error, if there is one, is underlined and lettered. If the sentence contains an error, select the one underlined part that must be changed to make the sentence correct. If the sentence is correct, select choice E. In choosing answers, follow the requirements of standard written English.

> *The arrows clue you in on what is imperative for you to notice in the nonunderlined portions.*

1. A glossary of terms, a section on clauses,
       A   B
and using idiomatic expressions are
    C   D
included in the new grammar textbook.

No error
  E

Find the error: _____
Name the error: _____
Fix the error: _____

2. According to veterinarian Jim Silver,
                 ↓
of all the breeds of dogs, poodles learn
  A   B
tricks like "sit" and "roll over" more
     C   D
quickly. No error
          E

Find the error: _____
Name the error: _____
Fix the error: _____

3. Too busy for her <u>own</u> good, Nadine
                  A

<u>was</u> negligent about drinking enough
 B

water<u>, in fact</u>, she was dehydrated so
      C

badly that she suffered <u>daily</u> from
                D

headaches and irritability. <u>No error</u>
                        E

Find the error: _____
Name the error: _____
Fix the error: _____

4. Feeling awkward <u>about</u> the bold asser-
                 A

tions he had made in his public address,

Jake decided to <u>resign</u> his harshly stated
            B

declaration about the <u>prevalent</u> injustices
                C

<u>between</u> male and female athletes.
  D

<u>No error</u>
  E

Find the error: _____
Name the error: _____
Fix the error: _____

5. A motorcade of celebrities <u>compacted</u>
                     A

the early morning traffic, which was

<u>already</u> flooded with commuters <u>who</u>
 B   C

were trying <u>to beat</u> the rush-hour clock.
          D

<u>No error</u>
  E

Find the error: _____
Name the error: _____
Fix the error: _____

6. ↓
The bubbly toddlers <u>around</u> the scenic
               A

park <u>was</u> walking, hoping <u>to find</u> a
     B   C

colorful jungle gym before their mothers

decided <u>it</u> was time to return home.
       D

<u>No error</u>
  E

Find the error: _____
Name the error: _____
Fix the error: _____

7. <u>When</u> tackling reading comprehension
   A

on the SAT, test takers should answer

questions based on <u>what's</u> stated or
              B

implied in the passages and <u>not based</u> on
                  C

what <u>she knows</u> to be fair or reasonable.
      D

<u>No error</u>
  E

Find the error: _____
Name the error: _____
Fix the error: _____

8. Their sailing certificates hung side

<u>by side</u> in the living room <u>in symbolizing</u>
 A   B

their commitment <u>to</u> trying new things
            C

in life and to inspire their young children

to try new sports and <u>activities</u>. <u>No error</u>
               D   E

Find the error: _____
Name the error: _____
Fix the error: _____

9. <u>As</u> group leader, Jean is very <u>incisive</u>
   A   B

   when it comes to determining how staff

   outings should be arranged<u>; typically</u> she
                                            C

   needs to ponder something <u>for only</u> a few
                                          D

   minutes before she decides on the details.

   <u>No error</u>
     E

   Find the error: _____
   Name the error: _____
   Fix the error: _____

10. Last week Gary went <u>to the</u> ski club meet-
                                      A

    ing with <u>his</u> daughters where they <u>receive</u>
               B   C

    a brochure on the mountain trails and a

    schedule <u>of</u> ski school clinics and ice-
                 D

    skating times. <u>No error</u>
                     E

    Find the error: _____
    Name the error: _____
    Fix the error: _____

ANSWERS AND EXPLANATIONS

1. *Did you notice the comma series, which often indicates an error in parallel form?*
   Find error: C   Name error: lack of parallelism   Fix error: *a list of*

2. Find error: D   Name error: faulty comparison; superlative "most" is needed because "all the breeds" are being compared   Fix error: *most*

3. Find error: C   Name error: run-on (comma splice)   Fix error: *water; in fact*

4. Find error: B   Name error: diction error   Fix error: *retract (disavow)*

5. Find error: A   Name error: diction error   Fix error: *compounded (added to)*

6. *Did you notice that the subject of the sentence, "toddlers," is plural?*
   Find error: B   Name error: Subject–verb agreement error; verb and subject are in reverse order   Fix error: *were*

7. *Did you notice that the subject of the sentence, "test takers," is plural?*
   Find error: D   Name error: pronoun agreement error   Fix error: *they know*

8. Find error: B   Name error: verb-form error   Fix error: *to symbolize*

9. Find error: B   Name error: diction error   Fix error: *decisive* (incisive means harsh or vitriolic)

10. *Did you notice the first two words of the sentence? "Last week" indicates the past tense.*
    Find error: C   Name error: verb-tense error   Fix error: *received* ("went" also indicates past tense)

What makes the following practice questions particularly hard? Some prep books serve up practice exercises on a silver platter. You are told, for instance, that a set of exercises is on subject-verb agreement or on parallel form. Or you are told that the exercises are on double negatives or on faulty comparisons. Then the error type is a no-brainer; you simply have to *find* an error of the given type. These types of exercises are too easy for a smart young adult like you because half of the job is already done.

A smorgasbord of errors is represented in the exercises that follow, just as on test day. You are not given the error type. Also, error types are intermingled, making them harder to spot. You need to read the sentence, determine whether or not something is wrong, consider the various errors pertaining to grammar and usage, and then find the error—if there is one.

To add an extra challenge, most of the sentences contain a hard vocabulary word, so you'll be on "double-duty": sharpening your grammar skills while strengthening your vocabulary. These exercises have the same format as the ones you'll see on the SAT. You need to select a letter in order to identify the sentence error. Since you're a motivated student, you may want to challenge yourself. You may want not only to find the error but also to fix the error and name the error.

> **Coaching**
> *Top scorers know the myriad grammatical error types cold. The 2400 Club understands that the form of the non-underlined portions of the sentence dictates the form of the underlined portions.*

PRACTICE TEST QUESTIONS

Students: This book contains more identifying sentence error questions than improving sentences questions. The balance of these questions will be different on the SAT; you will answer 25 improving sentences questions and 18 sentence error questions. Grammar is grammar, so knowing how to identify sentence errors will greatly help you with the longer improving sentences questions.

Directions: The following sentences test your ability to recognize grammar and usage errors. In each sentence five parts are underlined and lettered. Each sentence contains either a single error or no error at all. No sentence contains more than one error. The error, if there is one, is underlined and lettered. If the sentence contains an error, select the one underlined part that must be changed to make the sentence correct. If the sentence is correct, select choice E. In choosing answers, follow the requirements of standard written English.

---

1. Although Melissa vehemently <u>claims</u> <u>that</u>
                       A   B

 she speaks <u>truthful</u> to me, I still am not
         C

 sure <u>whether</u> or not I can trust her fully.
     D

 <u>No error</u>
  E

2. When <u>interrogated</u> <u>about</u> his recent
          A   B

 promotion to director of publicity,

 Harrison <u>recanted</u> that he could not con-
         C

 ceive <u>of being</u> more excited or grateful.
     D

 <u>No error</u>
  E

3. In this heartbreaking case that involved
   A

several cousins, Judge Klein pointed out

that the inauspicious outcomes have
         B

been determined largely by her earlier,
            C   D

foolhardy actions. No error
              E

4. Despite the coach's spirited pep talk,
   A   B

every one of the players were feeling
                C

deeply defeated by the landslide loss

endured at the regional tournament.
      D

No error
  E

5. Badminton, ping-pong, and volleyball

are among the many popular activities
     A

that the children enjoy outdoors and
 B   C

indoors at the diversified summer camp.
           D

No error
  E

6. For art and woodworking enthusiasts,
   A   B

making a wooden sailboat and sculpting
  C

with papier mâché provides hands-on,
           D

creative fun. No error
         E

7. Furnished with an eclectic style
             A

of decor, the home features three
 B

distinct fireplaces, each of which are
                C

dressed in a different style: English,
           D

rustic, and contemporary. No error
              E

8. Although Jared, a hard-hitting athlete

and loyal team player, impresses others

as passive and easygoing, he
 A B

underscores his opponent at every
  C

chance he gets. No error
     D   E

9. Not only are fireplace tools such as a
  A   B

broom, a poker, and tongs decorative,

but they are also functional as well.
 C   D

No error
  E

10. Situating along the scenic Adriatic coast
    A

in central Italy, Francavilla al Mare is the
 B

town where the family will vacation
      C   D

during the summer. No error
           E

11. If Luke follows the written directions in

the instruction booklet <u>and focuses</u> on
                         A

the sketches, he should <u>be</u> able to
                        B

assemble the aluminum goalie net

<u>really</u> <u>easy</u>. <u>No error</u>
  C   D   E

12. Billy <u>can't</u> find his baseball <u>mitt</u>, so he
            A   B

decided that either Daddy or Tom <u>are</u>
                                  C

using it at the ball field <u>behind</u> the
                           D

community center. <u>No error</u>
                      E

13. Before dinner was served <u>during</u> the
                               A

American Airlines flight from New York

to Rome, the brothers <u>began</u> to watch
                       B

"Scary Movie 3" <u>on</u> <u>their</u> dad's laptop
                C   D

DVD player. <u>No error</u>
                 E

14. <u>Some</u> college graduates make career
       A

decisions based <u>on</u> salary and prestige,
                B

<u>irregardless</u> of their true desires and
   C

intellectual <u>aptitudes</u>. <u>No error</u>
             D   E

15. Quotidian <u>pastimes</u> <u>of</u> the family include
                  A   B

strolling along the shoreline, <u>to shop</u> the
                                C

beach vendors<u>, and</u> listening to the
             D

jukebox at the snack bar. <u>No error</u>
                              E

16. <u>After</u> climbing the rocks that led to the
       A

150-feet-long breakers, the children

walked along the full length of the

<u>prodigious</u> and slippery stones, from <u>one</u>
   B   C

end of <u>it</u> to the other. <u>No error</u>
       D   E

17. Some parents <u>coerce</u> <u>their</u> children <u>in</u>
                    A   B   C

playing one particular sport or another,

without proper consideration of the

<u>youngsters'</u> genuine interests and
   D

talents as individuals. <u>No error</u>
                            E

18. The ancient African and Asian game

mancala, with <u>its</u> playing board of
              A

wooden bowls, its colorful, gemstone

playing pieces, and its <u>myriad</u> strategy
                        B

possibilities, happily <u>bemused</u> the family
                       C

<u>for days</u>. <u>No error</u>
   D   E

19. Their children <u>having had</u> experienced
                   A

    the <u>malaise</u> of car sickness one <u>too</u>
       B   C

    many times, so the couple decided it was

    best not to venture <u>into</u> a cramped car
                      D

    for a six-hour journey along uncertain

    roads. <u>No error</u>
           E

20. With bittersweet <u>nostalgia,</u> the woman
                  A

    noticed <u>that</u> the bronze lion's head
           B

    knocker that adorned the heavy wooden

    door looked just <u>like</u> the one belonging
                C

    to <u>her aunt's</u>. <u>No error</u>
       D   E

21. At Tivoli Gardens, just <u>outside</u> Rome,
                     A

    fountains and waterfalls feature

    sculptures of Greek and Roman gods

    and goddesses, zoomorphic animal

    faces, and <u>even</u> <u>show</u> winged dragons,
            B   C

    contributing to a tantalizing experience

    <u>that blends</u> fantasy and nature. <u>No error</u>
     D   E

22. The full-length <u>feature</u> films that <u>will be</u>
                  A   B

    shown during the eight-<u>hour</u> trans-
                       C

    Atlantic flight <u>includes</u> "Paycheck,"
                 D

    starring Ben Affleck, and "Runaway

    Jury," featuring Martin Sheen. <u>No error</u>
                            E

23. <u>Comprised</u> of an accordion player, a
      A

    bongo <u>drum</u>, and a saxophonist, the
          B

    musical <u>trio</u> <u>traveled</u> across the sand,
           C   D

    playing lighthearted melodies for the

    sunbathers. <u>No error</u>
              E

24. Although Pedro's plan initially seemed

    <u>ingenuous</u>, <u>it</u> soon turned <u>out</u> to be a
     A   B   C

    <u>debacle</u> of unparalleled proportion and
     D

    great consequence. <u>No error</u>
                   E

25. <u>Since</u> the clear water remains relatively
     A

    shallow all the way to the breakers,

    which <u>are</u> about 250 feet from shore,
         B

    when the sea is very placid, beachgoers

    feel as if they are swimming in a pool

    rather <u>than</u> <u>the sea</u>. <u>No error</u>
         C   D   E

26. Despite Mitchell's <u>steadfast</u> attempts to
                    A

mitigate his <u>friends'</u> ongoing rivalry, <u>he</u>
           B   C

was ultimately unable to mediate <u>their</u>
                                D

long-overdue reconciliation. <u>No error</u>
                                 E

27. The indefatigable beach vendor <u>from</u>
                                A

Bangladesh carries a 12-foot-long, steel

clothes bar, <u>to brim</u> with beaded cover-
            B

ups, <u>fringed</u> shawls<u>, and</u> long Hawaiian-
      C   D

style sundresses. <u>No error</u>
                 E

28. How can one pass judgment on the

habits and <u>preoccupations</u> of others
               A

when <u>they have</u> never experienced the
         B

daily responsibilities and routines that

<u>characterize</u> the pace of <u>their</u> everyday
    C   D

lives? <u>No error</u>
       E

29. I hope that <u>after</u> <u>you</u> give me the keys to
              A B

the Jeep you'll offer <u>lending</u> me twenty
                     C

dollars to boost my chances of having a

memorable night <u>out</u> on the town.
               D

<u>No error</u>
 E

30. After eating <u>their</u> <u>ice-cream cone</u> and
             A   B

playing their fifth game of foosball, the

invigorated boys joined <u>in</u> on a volleyball
                     C

<u>match at</u> the net on the sand. <u>No error</u>
   D   E

ANSWERS AND EXPLANATIONS

1. C	**7.** C	**13.** E	**19.** A	**25.** D
2. C	**8.** C	**14.** C	**20.** D	**26.** C
3. D	**9.** D	**15.** C	**21.** C	**27.** B
4. C	**10.** A	**16.** D	**22.** D	**28.** B
5. E	**11.** D	**17.** C	**23.** B	**29.** C
6. D	**12.** C	**18.** C	**24.** A	**30.** B

1. C Adverb versus adjective error. To modify the verb "speaks," the adjective "truthful" should be changed to the adverb *truthfully*.

2. C Diction error. Wrong word; should be *stressed, repeated,* or a similar word. "Recant" means to take back a statement that was made.

3. D Ambiguous possessive pronoun. "Her" lacks a clear antecedent.

4. C Subject–verb agreement error. The singular pronoun "every one" requires the singular verb *was*. "Players" is the object of the prepositional phrase, not the subject of the sentence.

5. E No error

6. D Subject–verb agreement error. *Provide* is needed to agree with the compound subject.

7. C Subject–verb agreement error. *Is* is needed to agree with the singular pronoun "each."

8. C Diction error. Wrong word. Should be *undermines* or *undercuts*.

9. D Redundancy. Eliminate *as well*.

10. A Idiom error. Should be *Situated*.

11. D Adverb versus adjective error. To modify the infinitive "to assemble," the adjective "easy" should be changed to the adverb *easily*.

12. C Subject–verb agreement error. The verb *is* should be used to agree with the singular "Tom," which is the closer of the two subjects that are joined by the conjunction "or."

13. E No error

14. C Diction error. Wrong word. Should be *regardless*.

15. C Lack of parallelism. "To shop" should be *shopping* to agree with the two gerunds in the series, strolling and listening.

16. D Pronoun-agreement error. The plural pronoun *them* is needed to agree with the antecedent, "stones."

17. C Idiom. *Coerce into* is standard English.

18. C Diction error. Wrong word. *Amused* works in this sentence. "Bemused" means befuddled or confused.

19. A Verb-form error. The correct verb for this introductory clause is *having*.

20. D Redundancy. Should be *her aunt*.

21. C   Lack of parallelism. Delete "show" to maintain parallel form in the comma series: noun, noun, and noun.

22. D   Subject–verb agreement error. The plural verb *include* is needed to agree with the subject, "films."

23. B   Lack of parallelism. To maintain parallel form in the comma series, the instrument, "drum," should be changed to the person, *drummer*.

24. A   Diction error. Wrong word. "Ingenuous" means honest. Should be *ingenious*. For the record, "<u>dis</u>ingenuous" means insincere.

25. D   Lack of parallelism. A gerund (known as a verbal noun form) is needed to match the previous gerund, "swimming." Should be *swimming* (or perhaps *cavorting*) *in the sea*.

26. C   Pronoun error. Pronoun *he* lacks an antecedent. "Mitchell's" is a possessive adjective and, therefore, not a proper antecedent.

27. B   Verb-form error. Should be the gerund *brimming*.

28. B   Pronoun-agreement error. The singular *he has* (*she has, he or she has*) is needed to agree with the singular pronoun "one" that appears earlier in the sentence.

29. C   Verb-form error. The gerund "lending" should be the infinitive *to lend*.

30. B   Plural/singular consistency error. The singular "ice-cream cone" should be *ice-cream cones* to agree with the plural "boys." It's very doubtful that the boys are sharing one ice cream cone!

Chapter 9

IMPROVING PARAGRAPHS

YOU BECOME THE EDITOR

At first glance, this section on paragraphs might look like more critical reading—yikes! Don't panic, though; it's not. This section does not deal with reading comprehension; it's about proofreading, editing, and revising. When you work on improving paragraphs, unlike when you tackle long critical reading passages, you do *not* have to do any of the following:

The Good News: What You Do *Not* Have to Do

- Do *not* first skim the questions for line references.
- Do *not* mark the text with sidebars or line references.
- Do *not* read the questions first.
- Do *not* read the passage in pieces; read the whole thing in one gulp.
- Do *not* read the passage with great focus; read it in a cursory fashion.
- Do *not* anticipate questions on tone or mood as you read.

So what *do* you have to do? You are asked to read a short essay, usually two to four paragraphs in length. The essay is straightforward and easy to understand; the vocabulary is basic. For you, that part's a cinch. Next you are asked questions about how to revise and edit the essay. In other words, you're coming in at stages 3 and 4 of the writing process: (1) brainstorming/prewriting, (2) drafting/free-writing, (3) revising, (4) editing/polishing, and (5) publishing.

Peer Editing

Let's cut this section of the SAT down to size. Simply visualize a peer-editing session that you most likely have participated in during English class. Imagine yourself looking over a classmate's piece of writing. In fact, the essays on the test resemble hasty drafts written by students in junior high school, not polished pieces of prose. As you quickly read through the essay, you will stumble upon a variety of sentence errors and awkward phrasing. In fact, these essays are riddled with errors to be ironed out! To make this section even less intimidating, imagine that you are editing a draft written by a fourth or fifth grader. No big deal—right?

Your Job in a Nutshell

The bottom line is that your writing expertise is being called upon to clean up a messy piece of writing. As you work on improving paragraphs, imagine yourself engaged as a helpful and skillful peer editor, an English teacher, or a magazine, or newspaper editor.

You will be asked to do one or more of the following.

What You *Do* Have to Do

- Combine sentences so that they flow smoothly.
- Clear up ambiguous or awkward sentences.
- Revise sentences so that they are concise.
- Streamline long-winded phrases and sentences.
- Determine which sentence should be eliminated from a paragraph.
- Understand which strategies the writer uses.
- Edit parts of sentences, using correct punctuation, including semi-colons.
- Eliminate superfluous words and phrases.
- Determine how paragraphs might be reordered.
- Determine which change would **NOT** be an improvement to an essay. This is a counterintuitive question type because it asks you to find something that actually makes the sentence less effective. Just be savvy to this question type. Knowing that these types of questions exist is half the battle; spotting them will make you a sharp test taker.
- Predict what the author is most likely to write about next. Reread the final paragraph to get a sense of the author's "next step," where he or she might go from here.

2400 Club Strategy:

- **Read.**
- **Read.**
- **Reread.**

- <u>**Read**</u> **the first paragraph carefully** to get a sense of the essay's main idea and point of view. Then skim the rest of the essay. Most essays consist of two to four short paragraphs, so reading the whole thing is no big deal. You should read the entire essay because usually one or two questions will require you to have a holistic sense of the essay as a unified whole.
- <u>**Read**</u> **each question**, paying close attention to the part that is underlined. Before returning to the essay, *predict* the best rewording from the available answer choices.
- <u>**Reread**</u> **the context** that surrounds the sentence or sentences about which you are being asked. To get a sense of context, you need some idea of what comes *before and after* the sentence at hand.

This strategy is very important. Since the test makers reproduce, in italics, the sentence or sentences that you are asked to work on, you may be tempted to consider these sentences alone, in isolation. As a member of the 2400 Club, though, you should prudently go back to the passage and consider the italicized portion in context.

Note: *There's no need to refer to the questions first since the essays are basic and easy to understand. By the same token, there's no need to mark the passage ahead of time with sidebars and line references, as you do with long-passage critical reading.*

PRACTICE TEST QUESTIONS

Directions: The passage below is the unedited draft of a student essay. Some of the essay needs to be rewritten to make the meaning clearer and more precise. Read the essay carefully.

The essay is followed by questions about changes that might improve all or parts of its organization, development, sentence structure, use of language, appropriateness to the audience, or use of standard written English. In each case, choose the answer that most clearly and effectively expresses the student's intended meaning. Indicate your choice by filling in the corresponding space on the answer sheet.

(1) Some parents feel that having a child focus on one sport at an early age is a good idea. **(2)** Others feel that pigeon-holing a child at an early age is bad. **(3)** The middle ground believes that exposing children to a variety of sports while young is the best idea, still these parents believe that having a child maintain some consistency with a particular sport, whether soccer or baseball, for example, is also advisable.

(4) Why not take the lead from your child? **(5)** Let him or her indicate to you whether he enjoys the hustle-bustle and challenge involved with participating in a variety of team or individual-oriented sports, or let him show you how he prefers sticking to that tennis game or to keep on with that swim team. **(6)** Whichever the case, be sure that three golden rules apply to your child's game; good sportsmanship, good attitude, and making a solid effort. **(7)** Think back to your childhood and the sports and activities you really liked or disliked. **(8)** Trust your child's feelings about the sports that are best for him.

(9) One should keep foremost in mind the reasons why sports involvement is important. **(10)** Team membership offers a child a sense of belonging and unity. **(11)** Team membership also teaches a child discipline and commitment. **(12)** More than this, being on a team fosters a healthy sense of working with others. **(13)** Of course, physical fitness is another strong reason to encourage your child's participation in sports. **(14)** Overarching, the positives of team-sports participation far outweighs the negatives.

1. Which of the following is the best revision of the underlined portion of sentence 5 (reproduced below)?

   Let him or her indicate to you whether he enjoys the hustle-bustle and challenge involved with participating in a variety of team or individual-oriented sports, or let him show you how he prefers sticking to that tennis game or to keep on with that swim team.

   (A) (As it is now)
   (B) or let them show you how they prefer sticking to that game of tennis or keeping on with that team for swimming
   (C) or let her show you how she prefers sticking to that tennis game or keeping on with the swim team
   (D) why not let him show you how he prefers sticking to that tennis game or keeping on with that swim team
   (E) having them show you how or why not preferring tennis or swimming is their thing

2. Which of the following is the best revision of the underlined portion of sentence 6 (reproduced below)?

   Whichever the case, be sure that three golden rules apply to your child's game; good sportsmanship, good attitude, and making a solid effort.

   (A) (As it is now)
   (B) in your child's game; good sportsmanship, good attitude and making a solid effort.

   (C) for your child's game: good sportsmanship, good attitude and making a good and solid effort.
   (D) to your child's game: good sportsmanship, good attitude, and solid effort.
   (E) to your child's game, which are the qualities of being a good sport, having a good attitude, and making a solid effort

3. To maintain paragraph cohesiveness, which sentence should be deleted from paragraph 2?

   (A) sentence 4
   (B) sentence 5
   (C) sentence 6
   (D) sentence 7
   (E) sentence 8

4. Which is the best version of sentence 14 (reproduced below)?

   Overarching, the positives of team-sports participation far outweighs the negatives.

   (A) (As it is now)
   (B) Overall, the positives of team-sports participation far outweigh the negatives.
   (C) Overall, the positives of participating in team-sports far outweigh the negatives.
   (D) Overally, the positive elements of team-sports participating far outweigh the negative aspects.
   (E) Overall, the positiveness of team sports majorly outweigh the negativity.

ANSWERS AND EXPLANATIONS

1. C   **2.** D   **3.** D   **4.** C

1. (C)

  (A): Lacks parallel form

  (B): The plural "them" does not agree with the singular "him or her."

  (C): Singular pronoun "her" is correct; "sticking to" and "keeping on" are parallel gerunds

  (D): Creates a run-on (comma splice) sentence

  (E): Very awkward

2. (D)

  (A) and (B): A semicolon should not be used to introduce a list.

  (C): Members of comma series are not parallel

  (D): Is concise and correct

  (E): Unnecessarily wordy

3. (D)

  (A): Sentence 4 is an effective, rhetorical question that serves as a topic sentence.

  (B) and (C): Sentences 5 and 6 develop the topic.

  (D): Sentence 7 is nostalgic, yet not cohesive with (logically related to) the rest of the paragraph

  (E): Sentence 8 is an effective closing sentence.

4. (C)

  (A): Subject–verb agreement error

  (B): The term "team-sports participation" is a mouthful.

  (C): Smooth and clear. Replace "overarching" with "overall." "Overarching" is an adjective meaning "encompassing" or "comprehensive."

  (D): "Overally" is not a word.

  (E): Subject–verb agreement error and awkward

Chapter 10

2400 CLUB GRAND MIXTURE

On the SAT test, the balance of questions in the writing section will be different from what you see here. There will be 25 improving sentences questions, 18 identifying sentence errors questions, and 6 improving paragraphs questions.

 Familiarize yourself with the directions ahead of time.

PRACTICE TEST QUESTIONS

The practice test questions that follow present a mixture of the various types of grammar and usage questions. If you can ace these questions, you are headed for 800 on the writing portion of the SAT.

Directions: The underlined sections of the sentences below may contain errors in standard English, including awkward or ambiguous expression, poor word choice (diction), incorrect sentence structure, and faulty grammar, usage, and punctuation. In some cases, the entire sentence may be underlined. Read each sentence carefully, and identify which of the five alternative versions most effectively and correctly expresses the meaning of the original. Choice (A) always repeats the original. Choose (A) if none of the other choices improves the original sentence. Indicate your choice by filling in the corresponding space on your answer sheet.

---

1. September 9, 2009, <u>marks the day where we met</u> at the Harbor Festival.

   (A) marks the day where we met
   (B) marking the day where we met
   (C) marks the day on which we met
   (D) marks the day where we had met each other
   (E) is marking the day during which we had met

2. One of the many self-defeating traits of the people-pleaser <u>is the disability to say "no" to peoples requests</u>.

   (A) is the disability to say "no" to peoples requests
   (B) are the inabilities of saying "no" to peoples requests
   (C) is the disability to say "no" to the requests of people
   (D) is the inability to say "no" to people's requests
   (E) are the inability with saying "no" to peoples requests

3. <u>Phillip's grandfathers had been black-smiths in Italy, and so, he pretended to be one, and this he did at his school's Colonial Village Exhibition</u>.

(A) Phillip's grandfathers had been blacksmiths in Italy, and so, he pretended to be one, and this he did at his school's Colonial Village Exhibition.

(B) Phillip's grandfathers, being black-smiths in Italy, made him pretend to be one; this he did at his school's Colonial Village Exhibition.

(C) Because Phillip's grandfathers had been blacksmiths in Italy, he pretended to be a blacksmith during the Colonial Village Exhibition, which was held at his school.

(D) Blacksmiths long ago in Italy, Phillip's grandfathers had him pretend to be one, and this he did at his school's Colonial Village Exhibition.

(E) At his school, during their Colonial Village Exhibition, since Phillip's grandfathers were black-smiths in Italy, this he did too, pretending to be the same.

4. Editing is more than just a stage in the writing <u>process, for it being</u> the time to polish and hone a piece of writing.

(A) process, for it being
(B) process, being it's
(C) process: it being
(D) process, for its
(E) process; it is

5. Perennials and evergreens, centerpieces of an appealing <u>landscape, contribute to</u> a home's natural beauty.

(A) landscape, contribute to
(B) landscape, they contribute to
(C) landscape, and it contributes to
(D) landscape, contributing to
(E) landscape; contribute to

6. <u>When Sheila opens gifts, the givers should receive a gesture of thanks</u>.

(A) When Sheila opens gifts, the givers should receive a gesture of thanks
(B) When Sheila opens gifts, the givers should receive thanks from her.
(C) Sheila opens gifts, the givers should receive her gestures of thanks
(D) Opening gifts, Sheila should make the givers recipients of thanks
(E) When Sheila opens gifts, she should thank those who gave her the presents.

7. The puppy scratches himself <u>vigorously, and he probably has fleas</u>.

(A) vigorously, and he probably has fleas.
(B) vigorously, and since he probably has fleas
(C) vigorously; he probably has fleas
(D) probably, because he vigorously has fleas
(E) vigorously, with having fleas, probably

8. Mr. Hinton's employees agree that <u>it is loudly and rapidly that he barks out orders</u>.

(A) it is loudly and rapidly that he barks out orders
(B) he barks out orders loudly and rapidly
(C) loudly and rapidly, his barking out orders
(D) he barks out orders, he does this loudly and rapidly
(E) orders are barked out loudly and rapidly by him

9. Ten arborvitae trees <u>are planted along-side the house an arbor is situated in between them</u>.

(A) are planted alongside the house an arbor is situated in between them

(B) are planted alongside the house with an arbor situating between them

(C) are planted alongside the house, an arbor is situated in between them

(D) between which is situated an arbor, planted alongside the house

(E) are planted alongside the house; an arbor is situated between them

10. <u>Because Gus is a health nut, he eats only organic foods, drinks</u> eight bottles of water a day, and works out religiously.

(A) Because Gus is a health nut, he eats only organic foods, drinks

(B) Because Gus is a health nut: eats organic foods, drinks

(C) Eating only organic foods, since Gus is a health nut, he's drinking

(D) Because Gus is a health nut, eating organic foods, drinking

(E) Gus is a health nut; that is the reason why he eats only organic foods, drinks

---

Directions: The following sentences test your ability to recognize grammar and usage errors. Each sentence contains either a single error or no error at all. No sentence contains more than one error. The error, if there is one, is underlined and lettered. If the sentence contains an error, select the one underlined part that must be changed to make the sentence correct. If the sentence is correct, select choice E. In choosing answers, follow the requirements of standard written English.

---

11. <u>It's</u> difficult to imagine how one can
   A

<u>contrive</u> of vivid, picturesque details
    B

<u>about</u> an exotic and distant place that <u>he</u>
  C   D

has never once visited. <u>No error</u>
                E

12. The woman found that her <u>brisk,</u> early
                A

morning walk through Sunset Park and

along the boardwalk, lined with

sycamore trees, that stretched along the

quiet harbor had become an <u>enervating</u>
                              B

<u>ritual</u> that would keep her alert and
  C

<u>refreshed</u> for the remainder of her day.
    D

<u>No error</u>
  E

13. With <u>their</u> rhythmic and <u>hypnotic</u>
        A   B
    movements, the orange, turquoise, and

    yellow buoys that <u>dot</u> the seascape
                        C
    playfully skip and <u>they</u> jump over the
                        D
    undulating waves. <u>No error</u>
                        E

14. <u>Large,</u> lush geraniums in sunny reds
        A
    and bright corals <u>cascade</u> down from <u>the</u>
                        B   C
    third-floor balcony, reaching three and

    four feet <u>toward</u> the earth. <u>No error</u>
                D   E

15. The vivacious children, <u>after</u> much
                            A
    pleading from <u>their</u> weary parents, put
                    B
    away their toys <u>and</u> made their beds
                    C
    <u>themself.</u> <u>No error</u>
        D   E

16. Available <u>in</u> tropical flavors <u>such as</u>
                A   B
    lime, coconut, and peach, the snow

    cones that <u>are sold</u> at the beach by the
                    C
    jaunty man who pushes along his

    colorful, rolling cart are tastier than

    <u>the pizzeria sells.</u> <u>No error</u>
            D   E

17. According to <u>their</u> fond recollections,
                    A
    the seaside resort offered leisurely

    summer days <u>to</u> take in natural beauty,
                    B
    to eat fresh <u>food,</u> and to escape the
                    C
    responsibilities of <u>everyday</u> life. <u>No error</u>
                        D   E

18. The couple <u>bought</u> a set of four hand-
                    A
    painted, ceramic plaques <u>where</u> each
                            B
    features pastoral scenes that depict the

    labors and harvests associated with each

    of the <u>four</u> <u>seasons:</u> winter, spring,
            C   D
    summer, and fall. <u>No error</u>
                        E

19. The cacophonous drone <u>of a</u> yellow
                            A
    seaplane <u>interrupted</u> the <u>sonorous</u> and
                B   C
    breezy rhythm of the coastal <u>waves.</u>
                                    D
    <u>No error</u>
        E

20. The shiny, black stretch limousine <u>and</u>
A

leather seats was <u>equipped</u> with a pop-
B

up flat screen television, a DVD player,

and recessed water coolers <u>that</u> glowed
C

with light effects, changing color every

ten seconds from lavender to orange,

<u>then</u> from red to green. <u>No error</u>
D   E

21. <u>A regular</u> amount of <u>uninterrupted,</u> free
A   B

time is necessary <u>to</u> the pursuit of daily
C

exercise <u>and</u> leisure reading. <u>No error</u>
D   E

22. Although the office measures <u>only</u> ten
A

feet by thirteen <u>feet;</u> it holds two book-
B

shelves, two desks, two computers<u>, and</u>
C

a <u>commodious</u> file cabinet. <u>No error</u>
D   E

23. Soon <u>to turn</u> ten years old, Phillip
A

thought about <u>having</u> a 3D <u>party:</u> eating
B   C

dinner, dancing under the strobe light,

and <u>the movie "Dodgeball"</u> with Ben
D

Stiller would provide the entertainment

for him and his friends. <u>No error</u>
E

24. <u>Julian,</u> please <u>get me</u> that Harry Potter
A   B

book <u>quick</u> <u>so</u> we can read some of it
C   D

together on the family-room couch.

<u>No error</u>
E

25. Since the <u>newly constructed</u> shower stall
A

in the basement was rather large, Sheila

<u>bought</u> the <u>largest of</u> the two sizes of
B   C

curtain rods <u>that</u> were available at the
D

hardware store. <u>No error</u>
E

26. Grandma<u>, affectionately</u> called
A

"Gramm," encouraged her grandson's

reading <u>by</u> <u>assuring</u> him that the words
B   C

he <u>hesitated</u> are the same ones she
D

would have stumbled upon. <u>No error</u>
E

27. I <u>have</u> tried every shawl, shrug, and
A

scarf with this maroon dress <u>but,</u> to my
B

<u>consternation</u>, none of them <u>seem</u> right
C   D

for the casual yet put-together look I

desire. <u>No error</u>
E

28. <u>Upon</u> receiving my friend's Christmas
    A

card this year, I am <u>so</u> happy <u>to see</u> that
               B   C

her three young children are as beautiful

and radiant <u>like I</u> remember them.
            D

<u>No error</u>
  E

29. After <u>mulling</u> <u>over</u> long lists of dog
         A   B

names that they printed off the Internet,

the Mardis <u>had finally</u> narrowed down
           C

the choices for their chocolate-brown

puppy to their <u>three</u> favorites: Mocha,
           D

Coco, and Baci. <u>No error</u>
          E

30. To rejoice in the holiday season, the

fourth graders assembled <u>in</u> the
             A

computer lab to put on a marvelous

presentation for <u>their</u> parents that
          B

<u>includes</u> a power-point presentation,
  C

portraying a family tradition, followed <u>by</u>
                   D

a family cookie exchange in the cozy

library. <u>No error</u>
     E

Directions: The passage below is the unedited draft of a student essay. Some of the essay needs to be rewritten to make the meaning clearer and more precise. Read the essay carefully.

The essay is followed by questions about changes that might improve all or parts of its organization, development, sentence structure, use of language, appropriateness to the audience, or use of standard written English. In each case, choose the answer that most clearly and effectively expresses the student's intended meaning. Indicate your choice by filling in the corresponding space on the answer sheet.

(1) Only a Mother knows the highs and lows of child-rearing today.
(2) Raising loving, unspoiled, balanced children who have desirable attributes these days can be an overwhelming enterprise. **(3)** It requires consistent devotion to tender feelings, routines, school work, and growing friendships. **(4)** Caring for children who require endless energy, yet nothing comes close to glimpsing the look of contentment and self-worth that can be seen in your children's eyes, if you take the time to notice, at the end of an enjoyable day spent together.
(5) A motherhood memoir should not breed a litany of complaints.
(6) Likewise it should not construct an image of perfection: daily routines

that are perfectly planned, neatly wrapped, prepackaged, and leisurely waiting its flawless execution.

(7) If I were to compose one, mine would be those of an ordinary and devoted mother who, despite exhaustion and a weary voice brought on by endless communication with her young children, cannot sleep—for the highlights of her day spent with her children flash like summer night fireflies in her mind's eye.

(8) Since I am a dedicated optimist, I would choose to focus on the highs of our days, and not the lows of our days. **(9)** Let's not lose sight of the profusion of smiles and excited ideas that outweigh kids' meltdowns and strident voices. **(10)** Rejoice in the carefree flutter of summer play, long days of recreation that used to be ours when we were very young.

(11) I feel privileged to have the time and the desire to run through a backyard sprinkler with my boys, to fill smooth and cool water balloons, then to have a catch, to enjoy raspberry and lime ice pops together, then seeing which one of us can throw the stick the farthest. **(12)** I feel lucky to have a sunny deck to lounge out on, listening to dance music pump through the outdoor speakers.

(13) After all, despite being on the go and on call all day long, I relish the late evening when my boys are finally asleep at night and, as always, they appear to me as "perfect little angels," just as on the day they were born.

31. Which of the following is the best revision of sentence 2 (reproduced below)?

Raising loving, unspoiled, balanced children who have desirable attributes these days can be an overwhelming enterprise.

(A) (As it is now)
(B) Children who have desirable attributes like lovingness, unspoiledness, and balance can be an overwhelming enterprise these days.
(C) Raising loving, unspoiled, balanced children who have desirable attributes can be an overwhelming enterprise.
(D) When it comes to raising children with attributes to be desired, a loving and unspoiled and balanced nature, its an overwhelming enterprise today.
(E) These days, raising loving, unspoiled, balanced children can be an overwhelming enterprise.

32. Of the following, which is the best revision of the underlined portion of sentence 4 (reproduced below)?

Caring for children who require endless energy, yet nothing comes close to glimpsing the look of contentment and self-worth that can be seen in your children's eyes, if you take the time to notice, at the end of an enjoyable day spent together.

(A) (As it is now)
(B) *who requires endless energy, yet*
(C) *that are requiring endless energy, and*
(D) *requires endless energy, yet*
(E) *requiring endless amounts of energy, and yet*

33. Which of the following demonstrates the best way to revise the underlined portion of sentence 6 (reproduced below)?

    Likewise it should not construct an image of perfection: daily routines that are perfectly planned, neatly wrapped, prepackaged, and leisurely waiting its flawless execution.

    (A) (As it is now)
    (B) *and, all the while, leisurely awaiting their flawless execution*
    (C) *and leisurely waiting execution, flawlessly*
    (D) *and leisurely waiting their flawless execution*
    (E) *and, with leisure, awaiting its flawless execution*

34. Which of the following best replaces the word "one" in sentence 7?

    (A) a well-adjusted child
    (B) an honest memoir
    (C) a sense of self-esteem
    (D) a reality check
    (E) a novel

35. Which of the following represents the best way to deal with sentence 11 (reproduced below)?

    I feel privileged to have the time and the desire to run through a backyard sprinkler with my boys, to fill smooth and cool water

balloons, then to have a catch, to enjoy raspberry and lime ice pops together, then seeing which one of us can throw the stick the furthest.

(A) Leave it as it is.
(B) Delete it.
(C) Elaborate on how the mother makes her free time.
(D) Divide it into two sentences and change "seeing" to "to see."
(E) Move it to the introductory paragraph, and explain what it means to "feel privileged."

36. Which of the following represents the best way to deal with sentence 13 (reproduced below)?

    After all, despite being on the go and on call all day long, I relish the late evening when my boys are finally asleep at night and, as always, they appear to me as "perfect, little angels," just as on the day they were born.

    (A) Leave it as it is.
    (B) Connect it to the preceding paragraph (paragraph 4).
    (C) Break it down into two sentences, and delete some wording.
    (D) Delete it entirely.
    (E) Break it down into three sentences by using two semicolons.

ANSWERS AND EXPLANATIONS

1. C	7. C	13. D	19. E	25. C	31. E
2. D	8. B	14. E	20. A	26. D	32. D
3. C	9. E	15. D	21. C	27. D	33. D
4. E	10. A	16. D	22. B	28. D	34. B
5. A	11. B	17. A	23. D	29. C	35. D
6. E	12. B	18. B	24. C	30. C	36. C

1. *Correct answer:* **(C)**

   (A) The word "where" should be used to refer to a place, not a date or time
   (B) Sentence fragment
   (D) The term "each other" is superfluous
   (E) Wordy and awkward

2. *Correct answer:* **(D)**

   (A) Diction error; "Disability" is wrong word choice.
   (B) Subject-verb agreement error; ("disability") "one" takes a singular verb.
   (C) Diction error
   (E) Subject-verb agreement error; "peoples" lacks an apostrophe

3. *Correct answer:* **(C)**

   (A) Cumbersome and wordy; an oversupply of commas
   (B) Distorts original meaning; grandfathers are no longer blacksmiths
   (D) The pronoun "one" lacks a clear antecedent.
   (E) The pronoun "their" is ambiguous.

4. *Correct answer:* **(E)**

   (A) Awkward
   (B) Awkward; rather colloquial
   (C) Misuse of colon; colons are used to introduce lists or examples
   (D) The possessive pronoun "its" does not work in this sentence

5. *Correct answer:* **(A)**

   (B) Comma splice (a specific type of run-on)
   (C) The singular "it" does not agree with the plural "perennials and evergreens."
   (D) Sentence fragment
   (E) Faulty use of semicolon; in a compound sentences, the semicolon divides two independent clauses if no conjunction is used

6. *Correct answer:* **(E)**

   (A) Improper shift between active and passive voices
   (B) Improper shift between active and passive voices
   (C) Comma splice
   (D) Awkward construction

7. *Correct answer:* **(C)**

   (A) Ineffective coordination of clauses that should show a cause–effect relationship
   (B) The expression "and since" is awkward.
   (D) Awkward construction; "vigorously" is misplaced
   (E) Choppy and awkward

8. *Correct answer:* **(B)**

   (A) Wordy; modifying adverbs are ineffectively placed
   (C) Awkward; misplaced modifiers, "loudly and rapidly"
   (D) Comma splice; two independent clauses cannot be joined by a comma
   (E) Ineffective passive voice; "by him" tacked on at the end is awkward

9. *Correct answer:* **(E)**

   (A) Fused sentence (run on)
   (B) Misplaced modifier; "with an arbor situated between them" is an adjective clause that should follow arborvitae trees
   (C) Comma splice
   (D) Sentence fragment

10. *Correct answer:* **(A)***

    * Yes, a sentence may start with a subordinating conjunction such as "Because," provided that an independent clause follows the introductory dependent clause.

    (B) The subordinating (dependent) clause is incorrectly followed by a colon.
    (C) Misplaced modifier; "eating only organic foods" should immediately precede "Gus"
    (D) Sentence fragment
    (E) Ineffectively wordy

11. B Diction error. Wrong word. The correct word is *conceive.*

12. B Diction error. Wrong word. The correct word is *energizing.* "Enervating" means weakening or draining of energy.

13. D Unnecessary word. Delete *they.*

14. E No error

15. D Faulty word. "Themself" is not a word. The plural pronoun *themselves* is needed to agree with "children."

16. D Faulty comparison. Snow cones should be compared to snow cones: *than those the pizzeria sells.*

17. A Pronoun error. "Their" lacks an antecedent.

18. B Diction error. Should be *in which;* the adverb "where" indicates a place.

19. E No error

20. A Diction error. Should be *with.*

21. C Idiom error. Should be *for.*

22. B Punctuation error. Replace the semicolon with a comma. Remember: a semi-colon divides two independent clauses.

23. D Lack of parallelism. Change to *watching the movie "Dodgeball"* so that each introductory member of the comma series is a gerund, an *-ing* ending verb form.

24. C Adjective/adverb error. Replace "quick" with *quickly* to modify the verb *get*.

25. C Faulty comparison. Since "two sizes of curtain rods" are being discussed, the comparative form *larger* should be used. Remember: the two-letter ending *-er* is used when comparing two things; the three-letter ending *-est*, when comparing three or more things.

26. D Idiom error. Should be *hesitated on.*

27. D Subject–verb agreement error. The singular verb form *seems* is needed to agree with the singular subject "None." Think of *none* as a contraction for *not one.* Remember: every pronoun that ends in *-one* or *-body* is singular.

28. D Correlative conjunction error. To express comparison, the sentence should read *as beautiful and radiant as.*

29. C Incorrect verb tense. Eliminate "had."

30. C Incorrect verb tense. Should be *included* to agree with the past-tense verb "assembled."

31. E
(A): The expression "these days" is misplaced.
(B): distorts intended meaning of sentence
(C): The clause "who have desirable attributes" is superfluous.
(D): Confusing and wordy
(E): Concise and clear

32. D
(A): Distorts intended meaning of sentence
(B): The singular verb "requires" does not agree with "children," the plural
(C): Antecedent of "who." "*Who*" is the relative pronoun that should be used to refer to people
(D): Clear and concise
(E): "Requiring' is the wrong verb form

33. D
(A) and (E): The singular "its" does not agree with the plural "routines" to which it refers.
(B): "All the while" is flabby phrasing.
(C): Awkward
(D): The best answer

34. B

(A): No one can "compose" a child; "compose," in the context of this paragraph, means to write.

(B): The best choice, since "one" refers to the "motherhood memoir" mentioned in sentence 5.

(C): No proof or prior reference for this choice.

(D): A tricky decoy answer, not quite right.

(E): A fair answer, but a "memoir," which has been specifically mentioned, is a better choice than the broader term *novel*

35. D

(A): cannot leave this sentence as is because it is rambling

(B): No; the ideas fit into the paragraph.

(C): This information is not necessary.

(D): Here is the correct answer:

> *I feel privileged to have the time and the desire to run through a backyard sprinkler with my boys, to fill smooth and cool water balloons, then to have a catch. I feel lucky to enjoy raspberry and lime ice pops together, then to see which one of us can throw the stick the furthest.*

(E): No; this sentence is appropriate in this paragraph.

36. C

(A): Don't leave the sentence as is; it's rambling.

(B): This sentence works nicely as a conclusion line that's set off on its own.

(C): Yes, the best effective choice:

> *After all, despite being on the go and on call all day long, I relish the late evening when my boys are finally asleep. As always, they appear to me as "perfect little angels," just as on the day they were born.*

(D): Do not delete the sentence; it makes a reflective conclusion.

(E): Two semicolons would be overkill.

PART 3

THE MATH SECTIONS

GETTING STARTED

STRATEGIES FOR SOLVING SAT MATH PROBLEMS

TOPICS IN ARITHMETIC

TOPICS IN ALGEBRA

TOPICS IN GEOMETRY

TOPICS IN STATISTICS

WORD PROBLEMS

2400 CLUB GRAND MIXTURE

Chapter 11

GETTING STARTED

This book is aimed at students who aspire to a score of 2400—the 2400 Club. The fact that you are in this group means that you are good at math and can probably answer most of the SAT math questions without too much exertion. To join the 2400 Club, however, you need to crack those tricky little zingers at the end of the math sections. This part of the book provides strategies and practice for doing just that.

Before you even start the test, you can take steps to increase your chances of a perfect score.

2400 Club Strategies Before and During the Test . . .

Strategy 1: **S**tudy the basics and know each topic in this book.

Strategy 2: **T**rain yourself on grid-ins. Learn the do's and don'ts.

Strategy 3: **R**eview the formulas that precede the math sections.

Strategy 4: **A**cquire awareness of question difficulty in the spectrum of questions.

Strategy 5: **T**reat the test booklet as your own. Feel free to scribble in it.

Strategy 6: **E**ducated guessing is a must if you don't know the answer.

Strategy 7: **G**raphing calculators rule. Practice on the calculator you will use for the SAT.

Strategy 8: **Y**es to practicing! Answer every question in this book.

MATH ON THE SAT

Altogether there are 70 minutes of math on the SAT: two 25-minute sections and one 20-minute section. The questions are either multiple-choice, where you select an answer, or grid-in, where you provide an answer in a small grid (more later). Graphing calculators are allowed.

The math sections include much of the algebra and introductory statistics that you learn in high school. Many of the math questions are like brain teasers—enjoy!

EASY VERSUS HARD QUESTIONS

Here are some "bread and butter" questions, the type that 2400 students must get right, no *ifs, ands,* or *buts.* Try them.

Questions

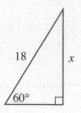

1. The value of x in the figure shown above is

   (A) $18\sqrt{3}$ (B) $9\sqrt{3}$ (C) $\frac{9}{2}\sqrt{3}$ (D) 9 (E) $6\sqrt{3}$

2. If $y^3 = 64$, what is the value of $y^{-\frac{1}{2}}$?

   (A) $-\frac{1}{2}$ (B) -2 (C) $\frac{1}{2}$ (D) 2 (E) $2\sqrt{2}$

3. What is the solution set for the equation $\frac{2x+1}{x-3} = 0$?

   (A) $\{\ \}$ (B) $\left\{\frac{1}{2}\right\}$ (C) $\left\{-\frac{1}{2}\right\}$ (D) $\left\{-\frac{1}{2}, 3\right\}$ (E) $\left\{\frac{1}{2}, 3\right\}$

4. The spinner in the diagram above randomly stops in any of the numbered regions shown. Given that the regions are equally likely, what is the probability that the spinner will land in 2, 3, or 4?

   (A) $\frac{1}{512}$ (B) $\frac{1}{4}$ (C) $\frac{1}{2}$ (D) $\frac{3}{8}$ (E) $\frac{1}{3}$

Solutions

1. The answer is **(B)**.

   This is a 30–60–90° triangle, where the relationships between the sides are as shown below:

   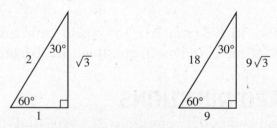

   For the given triangle, 18 is the hypotenuse, so the length opposite the 30° angle is 9, and opposite the 60° angle is $9\sqrt{3}$.

2. The answer is **(C)**.

$$y^3 = 64 \Rightarrow y = 4$$

$$4^{-\frac{1}{2}} = \frac{1}{4^{\frac{1}{2}}} = \frac{1}{\sqrt{4}} = \frac{1}{2}$$

3. The answer is **(C)**.

$$\frac{2x+1}{x-3} = 0$$

$$\Rightarrow 2x + 1 = 0 \quad \text{Multiply both sides by } (x-3).$$

$$\Rightarrow x = -\frac{1}{2}$$

$$\therefore \text{Solution set} = \left\{-\frac{1}{2}\right\}.$$

4. The answer is **(D)**.

For any one region, the probability that the spinner will land there is $\frac{1}{8}$, since each of the eight regions is equally likely. The probability of landing in 2, 3, or 4 is therefore given by

$$P(2, 3, \text{ or } 4) = P(2) + P(3) + P(4)$$

$$= \frac{1}{8} + \frac{1}{8} + \frac{1}{8}$$

$$= \frac{3}{8}$$

What makes these questions easy is that each deals with one clearly defined topic that should long ago have been mastered. The more difficult questions involve more than one topic and require that you apply what you know, often in tricky ways.

Here are four questions that are similar to those above, but considerably harder. Try them!

Questions

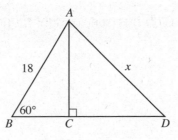

1. In the figure shown above, given that $\overline{AC} \cong \overline{DC}$, the value of x is

    (A) $18\sqrt{6}$ (B) $18\sqrt{2}$ (C) $9\sqrt{2}$ (D) $9\sqrt{3}$ (E) $9\sqrt{6}$

2. Let $f(x) = 2^{-x}$ and $g(x) = 4 \cdot 2^{-x}$. Which is true?

   (A) $g(x) = f(x - 2)$
   (B) $g(x) = f(x + 2)$
   (C) $g(x) = f(x) - 2$
   (D) $g(x) = f(x) + 2$
   (E) $g(x) = f(2x)$

3. Find all real values of x for which $\dfrac{1}{x - 3} \le 1$.

   (A) $x \ge 4$
   (B) $x > 4$
   (C) $x \le 3$ or $x \ge 4$
   (D) $x < 3$ or $x \ge 4$
   (E) $3 < x \le 4$

4.

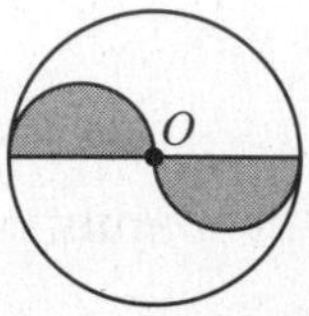

   In the figure shown above, O is the center of the circle, and each shaded region is a semicircle with O as the endpoint of a diameter. A point is chosen at random inside the circle. What is the probability that the point lands in the shaded region?

   (A) $\dfrac{1}{2}$ (B) $\dfrac{1}{3}$ (C) $\dfrac{1}{4}$ (D) $\dfrac{1}{5}$ (E) $\dfrac{1}{6}$

   Solutions

   1. The answer is **(E)**.

      $\triangle ABC$ is a 30–60–90° triangle.

      $\therefore BC = 9$ and $AC = 9\sqrt{3}$.

      $\triangle ADC$ is a 45–45–90° triangle.

      $\therefore AD = AC\sqrt{2} = (9\sqrt{3})\sqrt{2} = 9\sqrt{6}$.

   The 2400 Club has special right triangles down cold.

2. The answer is **(A)**.
   Try each choice to see which one gives $g(x) = 4 \cdot 2^{-x}$. For choice (A):

   $$f(x-2) = 2^{-(x-2)}$$
   $$= 2^{2-x}$$
   $$= 2^2 \cdot 2^{-x}$$
   $$= 4 \cdot 2^{-x} = g(x) \quad \text{Yes!}$$

3. The answer is **(D)**.
   The one thing you cannot do here is blithely multiply both sides of the inequality by $x - 3$. Remember: if $x - 3$ is negative, the inequality sign switches!

   Here are two methods of solving.

   Coaching:
   Resist the urge to multiply both sides of an inequality by a quantity that could be negative.

   <u>Method I</u>: Plug-In Strategy
   Plug in one value from the region $x > 4$ (choose 5) and another value from the region $x < 3$ (choose 2). Notice that both numbers work. Any number in the region between 3 and 4 fails, suggesting that the answer is (C) or (D).

   Notice that 3 cannot be a solution (it gives a zero in the denominator), so the answer must be (D).

   <u>Method II</u>: Algebra

   $$\frac{1}{x-3} \le 1$$
   $$\Rightarrow \frac{1}{x-3} - 1 \le 0$$
   $$\Rightarrow \frac{1}{x-3} - \frac{x-3}{x-3} \le 0 \quad \text{Get a least common denominator.}$$
   $$\Rightarrow \frac{4-x}{x-3} \le 0$$
   $$\Rightarrow \frac{x-4}{x-3} \ge 0 \quad \text{Multiply both sides by } -1.$$

   Signs analysis yields $x \le 3$ or $x \ge 4$. However, notice that x cannot be 3 because 3 is not in the domain of $\frac{1}{x-3}$. Thus the answer is $x < 3$ or $x \ge 4$ (D).

   Look at the two methods shown for solving this problem. Method II, the "pure" algebraic solution, may earn you a gold star from your math teacher, but it is not recommended for the SAT: it is too time-consuming.

You should constantly be on the lookout for a quick plug-in solution, such as Method I.

The 2400 Club looks for a time-saving solution to every problem.

4. The answer is **(C)**.

Put the two shaded halves together; you get a smaller, shaded circle whose radius is half the radius of the original circle.

Method I: Ratios in Similar Figures

Here is a neat time-saving fact: For any two similar figures, if the ratio of the corresponding linear dimensions is $\dfrac{a}{b}$, then the ratio of the areas is $\left(\dfrac{a}{b}\right)^2$.

Thus, in the given problem,

$$\frac{\text{Radius of shaded circle}}{\text{Radius of original circle}} = \frac{1}{2}.$$

$$\therefore \frac{\text{Area of shaded circle}}{\text{Area of original circle}} = \left(\frac{1}{2}\right)^2 = \frac{1}{4}.$$

$$\therefore P(\text{point in shaded circle}) = \frac{1}{4}.$$

Method II: An Alternative, Slower Method That Doesn't Use Ratios in Similar Figures

Let r be the radius of the original circle. Then the shaded circle has radius $\dfrac{r}{2}$.

$$P(\text{point in shaded circle}) = \frac{\text{Area of shaded region}}{\text{Area of original circle}}$$

$$= \frac{\pi\left(\dfrac{r}{2}\right)^2}{\pi r^2} = \frac{1}{4}$$

GRID-INS

What Are They?

Ten of the math questions are termed "student-produced response questions." There are no choices; you produce the answer. These questions are also called "grid-ins" because each one comes with a small grid, on which you bubble in your answer.

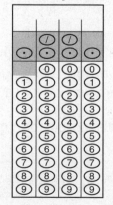

What the Answers Cannot Be

Notice on the grid above that the only symbols are the digits 0–9, the decimal point, and the slash. This means that the correct answer will never be negative, contain a variable, or contain a π or % symbol. Nor will the answer ever exceed 9999 or have a zero before the decimal point.

 The top row is for you to enter your answer before gridding it in. Don't try to save time by omitting this step.

> The 2400 Club avoids a careless mistake by writing the answer at the top of the grid.

Gridding-in Rules

The machine that scores your SAT test will look only at what you bubble in on the grid; so be sure you fill in the grid correctly.

- ■ Stay left! Start your answer in the leftmost column of the grid. This ensures that you will always have room for your answer, and you won't lose precision in decimal answers.
- ■ For each digit that you wrote in the top row, darken the corresponding oval.
- ■ If you have a decimal answer between 0 and 1, for example .72885, don't start with zero. Start with the decimal point, and fill in as many digits as you can. You will get full credit for either .728 or .729. Since you don't need to round your answer, don't do it! Note that both .72 and .73 will be scored as incorrect. You must write as much of the answer as fits on the grid.
- ■ If your answer is a fraction such as $\dfrac{12}{8}$, you can enter 12/8, 6/4, 3/2, or 1.5. Given that you don't need to reduce fractions, don't bother!

  What you may *not* do is bubble in your answer as a mixed number. For $\dfrac{3}{2}$ you may not enter 11/2, which the machine will read as $\dfrac{11}{2}$.
- ■ If you get a range of answers for a grid-in question, pick one and enter it. Often a question has more than one correct answer.

Question Difficulty

The grid-in questions are numbered 9–18 in a math section of the test. Typically, questions 9–11 are easy, 12–15 are medium, and 16–18 are hard. This information is helpful to 2400 scorers. If the answer to question 18 seems obvious to you at first glance, reread the question to spot what you're missing.

Scoring

There is no penalty for a wrong answer, so guess if you can.

Final Tip

Don't commit the crime of getting the answer right and the gridding-in wrong.

> 2400 Club members concentrate as if their lives depend on gridding-in their answers correctly.

Example 1

Three consecutive terms in a geometric sequence are $\dfrac{16}{27}, \dfrac{32}{81}, \dfrac{64}{243}$.
If $\dfrac{64}{243}$ is the sixth term of the sequence, find the second term.

Solution: The answer is $\dfrac{4}{3}$.

Method I: Look for a Pattern

Here are the given terms, starting with the sixth term and working backward.

$$\frac{64}{243}, \frac{32}{81}, \frac{16}{27}.$$

Look for a pattern, and then extend it. Notice that the numerators are being halved, and the denominators are being divided by 3. Continuing with this pattern yields $\dfrac{4}{3}$ as the second term:

$$\underset{\text{6th}}{\frac{64}{243}}, \underset{\text{5th}}{\frac{32}{81}}, \underset{\text{4th}}{\frac{16}{27}}, \underset{\text{3rd}}{\frac{8}{9}}, \underset{\text{2nd}}{\frac{4}{3}}.$$

Method II: Find the Common Ratio

Recall that the next term in a geometric sequence is found by multiplying the preceding term by a common ratio, r. Therefore, you can always find r by dividing any term by the preceding term. For the given sequence,

$$r = \frac{32}{81} \div \frac{16}{27} = \frac{32}{81} \cdot \frac{27}{16} = \frac{2}{3}.$$

Since $\dfrac{16}{27}$ is the fourth term, the third term is $\dfrac{16}{27} \div \dfrac{2}{3} = \dfrac{8}{9}$ and the second term is

$\dfrac{8}{9} \div \dfrac{2}{3} = \dfrac{4}{3}.$

Grid-in 4/3 or 1.33.

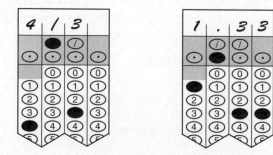

Example 2

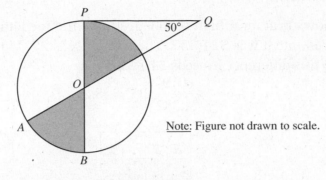

Note: Figure not drawn to scale.

In the figure above, the circle with center O has $\overline{PQ}$ tangent to it at P. Find the ratio of the shaded area to the area of the circle.

Solution: The answer is $\dfrac{2}{9}$.

Since $\overline{PQ}$ is a tangent and $\overline{OP}$ is a radius, $\overline{PQ} \perp \overline{OP}$. Therefore, $m\angle POQ = 40°$ and $m\angle AOB = 40°$ (vertical angles are congruent). Each shaded sector is $\dfrac{40}{360} = \dfrac{1}{9}$ of the circle area. Therefore, the ratio of the shaded area to the area of the circle is $2\left(\dfrac{1}{9}\right) = \dfrac{2}{9}$.

Grid-in either 2/9 or .222.

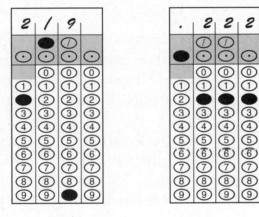

Example 3

The following table, from the U.S. Census Bureau, shows the median annual earnings in 1999 of workers with different levels of education.

Median Annual Earnings (Ages 21–64)

Level of Education	Median Annual Earnings ($)
Not a high school graduate	21,332
High school graduate	27,351
Some college	31,988
Bachelor's degree	42,877
Advanced degree	55,242

By what percent did the median annual earnings of a high school graduate (with no further education) exceed those of someone who was not a high school graduate?

Solution: The answer is 28.2.

The table shows that for a high school graduate the median earning was \$27,351, while for a nongraduate it was \$21,332. The difference is $27{,}351 - 21{,}332 = 6019$. The percent by which this difference exceeds 21,332 is

$$\frac{6019}{21{,}332} \cdot 100 = 28.2 .$$

Grid-in 28.2.

TIPS FOR THE SAT MATH SECTIONS

Question Difficulty

The SAT math questions in a given 25-minute section get incrementally harder from start to finish. Thus questions 1–3 are considered easy, 4–7 are medium, and 8–10 are hard. As stated previously, for the grid-ins, 9–11 are easy, 12–15 are medium, and 16–18 are hard. Since all the questions are worth the same, it makes sense to start at question 1 and then proceed in order.

Keep track of where you are in the spectrum of questions. Picking an intuitive answer for an "easy" question is probably right. Doing so for a "hard" question is almost certainly wrong.

Don't get bogged down on any one question. Circle it in your booklet, and return to it if you have time.

> The 2400 Club warms up on the easy questions, gathers steam on the medium ones, and leaves time to crack the hard ones at the end.

Guessing

For every multiple-choice question that you get wrong, the Educational Testing Service deducts $\frac{1}{4}$ point. The purpose of this penalty is to discourage you from guessing. Since there are four wrong answers for every right answer, making random choices will give you an average score of zero. The fact that you're reading this book, however, means that you're smart enough to eliminate at least one of the choices and thus increase your odds of guessing the correct answer. For you it pays to guess!

Be aware that to get an 800 score for math you need to answer just about every question correctly. Leaving more than one answer blank gives you no chance.

Suppose you're bogged down on one of the "hard" multiple-choice questions and just can't see a way to solve it. You can improve your guessing odds by eliminating any answer choice that seems obvious. Also eliminate an answer choice that contains a number given in the problem statement. These choices are distracters, meant to trap you.

A wrong answer on a grid-in does not carry a penalty, so you might as well guess. Unfortunately, the probability of a correct guess when you really have no clue is very low. It may not pay you to use valuable time to grid-in something that is almost certainly wrong.

Suppose you know, however, that the answer is an integer in a given range. Then you should guess—you have nothing to lose.

Finally, if you must guess, don't dither. Guess and move on.

The Test Booklet

The test booklet is yours, so use it! Cross off the wrong choices in the multiple-choice questions. Circle the questions you need to return to. Make diagrams where relevant. Write on the diagrams that are provided. (Don't waste time redrawing!)

After your booklet has been collected, no one will look in it again.

Your Answer Sheet

The answer sheet, unlike the test booklet, is all important.

Since the scoring machine is very sensitive, beware of stray marks on your answer sheet. When you erase an answer, be sure to do it thoroughly.

Now consider the following nightmare scenario: You leave out a question, circle it in your answer booklet, and move on. You get so involved in the remaining problems that you fail to leave a blank on your answer sheet for the omitted question. *As a result, every subsequent answer is off by 1 in the grid.*

You are smart enough to understand what a disaster this would be. You must make sure that it doesn't happen.

One way of avoiding this problem is to transfer your answers in groups of five. Toward the end of the set, enter one at a time to guarantee that every question you answered gets bubbled on the answer sheet.

> The 2400 Club really, really concentrates when filling in the answer sheet.

Calculators

The official SAT guide tells you that you don't need a calculator for any of the questions. And being a good math student, you probably won't use a calculator for most of the questions. But make no mistake—the graphing calculator that you've been using in your math classes these past couple of years will be a huge asset on the SAT. It can save you time and effort.

If you've never used a graphing calculator before, then bring your scientific calculator. The important thing is to use a calculator that you're comfortable with.

How to Use the Graphing Calculator

The discussion below refers to the TI-84 Plus graphing calculator. All graphing calculators, however, have similar features. Be sure to know your own calculator!

What follows is not a comprehensive manual. It assumes that you are familiar with your own graphing calculator and summarizes features that may be useful for the SAT. You probably know a lot more than what is presented here!

1. The MODE button shows all the default settings highlighted on the left. You should select Degree (instead of Radian) for the angle mode, since any trig question on the SAT will have angles in degrees.

2. The "top" level of the calculator is where you will do arithmetic calculations and work with trig functions.

3. The y = button accesses the window where you will type the formulas for functions whose graphs you want to view. The functions must be in the form $y =$. For example, if you want to graph $2x - y = 5$, you need to rewrite the equation as $y = 2x - 5$ before you can type it in. You must use the X, T, θ, n button for x and the − button for subtraction. The (−) button is for negation.

   Example: Here's how you would type in $y = -(x-4)^2$:
   y =, (−), (, X, T, θ, n, −, 4,), x².

4. The 2nd button allows you to access the "blue" functions. Thus, 2nd x² gets you the radical sign, $\sqrt{\ }$, since it appears in blue above the x² button.

   Example: Here's how you would enter $y = \sqrt{2x-3}$:
   y =, 2nd, x², 2, X, T, θ, n, −, 3.
   No closing parenthesis is required.

5. The GRAPH button gives you the graphing window, with both x- and y-axes ranging from −10 to 10. Your graph should appear.

6. The WINDOW button allows you to change the range of numbers on the x- and y-axes. Be sure to use the negation key, (−), for negative numbers.

7. The TRACE button allows you to use the right- and left-arrow keys to get values for points on the graph.

8. The CALC menu allows you to carry out some very useful operations after you've sketched a graph. Since CALC appears in blue above the TRACE button, you need 2nd TRACE . Here's what the CALC menu allows:

   - value: Enter any x, and you'll get the corresponding y value.
   - zero: This gives a zero of the function, that is, an x-intercept of the graph. Use the left- and right-arrow keys to "bracket" the root. Just to the left of the root, hit ENTER . Then move just to the right, and hit ENTER twice. The graphing calculator will give you that x-intercept.
   - minimum or maximum: This gives any minimum or maximum point on the graph. Again, you bracket the desired point. Get close to it on the left, ENTER , get close to it on the right, ENTER twice, and the calculator will give you the coordinates of the desired point.

9. The MATH menu allows you to get cubes, cube roots, and absolute values.

   Example: Find $\sqrt[3]{625}$. Go to the top level of the calculator. (2nd MODE is the way to QUIT and go there.) Then MATH 4 selects $\sqrt[3]{\ }$. Now type 625 ENTER , and you get the answer, 8.549879733.

   Example: Graph $y=|x+4|$. MATH NUM abs gets you $y = $ abs, and you can now enter $x + 4$.

Some Final Tips

The 2400 Club prepares ahead of time.

Here are some steps you should take to maximize your chances for success.

1. Before leaving home, put new batteries in your calculator and an extra set of fresh batteries in your pocket. Being a calculator wizard won't help if your batteries are dead.

2. At the start of a math section, don't use precious time studying the formulas at the top of the page. By the time you take the test, facts about special triangles, areas, volumes, and the Pythagorean theorem should be part of your bloodstream.

3. Know the formulas in Appendix B at the back of this book. Recognizing a situation that can be solved with a quick plug-in to a formula can save you time and effort.

4. At the start of the grid-in questions, don't waste time reading the extensive instructions for filling in the grids correctly. If you do all the grid-in questions in this book, the instructions will be second nature to you by the time you take the test.

Chapter 12

STRATEGIES FOR SOLVING SAT MATH PROBLEMS

You've set your sights on an 800 for math, so it's a good bet that you can set up an equation and solve it with the best of them. If this is the solution that immediately strikes you, go for it. However, be aware that there are test-taking strategies—some of them unorthodox—that can lead to fast and accurate solutions, even for "difficult" problems.

2400 Club Strategies for Math Problems . . .

Strategy 1: **P**lug-in answer choices, rather than solve the problem.

Strategy 2: **L**earn to pick good numbers for problems with percents or fractions.

Strategy 3: **U**se a graphing calculator for maximum or minimum problems.

Strategy 4: **G**raphing calculators work for intersection of graphs.

Strategy 5: **G**raphing calculators work for transformations.

Strategy 6: **I**nequalities? A graphing calculator works here too!

Strategy 7: **N**eat way to visualize sets: Venn diagrams.

Strategy 8: **G**ood way to find shaded areas: subtraction.

PICK A NUMBER

What types of problems are candidates for this strategy?

- Problems involving variables rather than numbers

- Percent problems

- Problems with fractions

- Any problem for which your math teacher would suggest that you select variables and translate the English into algebra

Which numbers should you try?

- For percent problems, start with 100.

- For problems with fractions, start with the least common denominator (LCD) of all the fractions.

- If possible, pick simple integers, even if they're unrealistic in the context of the problem.

■ Pick different numbers for different quantities.
■ Don't choose a number in the problem statement. If you do, you may introduce a special case.

What is the technique? If there are variables in the answer choices, pick easy integer numbers (as mentioned above) for the variables. Find the answer to the problem using your numbers. Then plug your numbers into the answer choices, and see which choice gives you the answer that you got. Be sure to try all of the answer choices. If more than one choice gives the right answer, then you need to try other numbers.

Example 1

In a certain election, several students collected signatures to place a candidate on the ballot. Of these signatures, 25 percent were thrown out as invalid. Then a further 20 percent of those remaining were eliminated. What percent of the original number of signatures were left?

(A) 40%   (B) 45%   (C) 50%   (D) 55%   (E) 60%

Solution: The answer is **(E)**.
This is a percent problem, so start with 100 signatures. If 25 percent of 100 are thrown out, 75 are left. If 20 percent of 75 are thrown out, 60 are left. Therefore, 60 of the original 100 signatures, or 60 percent, are left.

Example 2 Grid-In

Three consecutive odd integers are such that three times the middle integer is 25 more than the sum of the smallest and largest. Find the largest of the integers.

Solution: The answer is 27.
If you pick the simplest set of consecutive odd integers, namely 1, 3, and 5, you can see at a glance that 3×3 is not 25 more than $1 + 5$. Notice that:

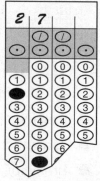

3(middle number) ≈ sum of the 3 numbers.
∴ 25 + (first + third) ≈ sum of the 3 numbers.
This suggests trying numbers in the twenties.
Try 21, 23, 25.

Is (3×23) 25 more than $21 + 25$; that is,
is 69 equal to $25 + (21 + 25) = 71$?   No, but close!
Try 23, 25, 27.

$3 \times 25 = 75$, and $75 = 25 + (23 + 27)$.   Yes!
Grid-in 27.

By the way, there's no rule that says you can't use algebra! Be sure to let x be the number you need to find, namely, the largest of the three odd integers. Then the consecutive odd numbers are $x - 4$, $x - 2$, and x. Now translate into math: "3 times the middle is 25 more than the sum of the smallest and largest":

$$3(x - 2) = 25 + [(x - 4) + x]$$
$$\Rightarrow 3x - 6 = 25 + 2x - 4$$
$$\Rightarrow x = 27.$$

Example 3

If $a = b^2c$, where $a \neq 0$ and $b \neq 0$, then $\dfrac{b}{c} =$

(A) $\dfrac{a}{c}$ (B) $\dfrac{a}{b}$ (C) $\dfrac{a}{bc}$ (D) $\dfrac{a}{b^2c}$ (E) $\dfrac{a}{bc^2}$

Solution: The answer is **(E)**.

Suppose you pick $b = 2$ and $c = 3$. Then a must be 12, since $a = 2^2(3)$. Therefore $\dfrac{b}{c} = \dfrac{2}{3}$. This is what you must get when you plug your values into the answer choices.

(A) $\dfrac{a}{c} = \dfrac{12}{3} = 4$ No, not equal to $\dfrac{2}{3}$ (D) $\dfrac{a}{b^2c} = \dfrac{12}{12} = 1$ No

(B) $\dfrac{a}{b} = \dfrac{12}{2} = 6$ No   (E) $\dfrac{a}{bc^2} = \dfrac{12}{18} = \dfrac{2}{3}$ Yes!

(C) $\dfrac{a}{bc} = \dfrac{12}{6} = 2$ No

Example 4

Mary has d dollars to spend and goes on a shopping spree. First she spends $\dfrac{2}{5}$ of her money on shoes. Then she spends $\dfrac{3}{4}$ of what's left on a few books. Finally she buys a raffle ticket that costs $\dfrac{1}{3}$ of her remaining dollars. What fraction of d is left?

(A) $\dfrac{1}{10}$ (B) $\dfrac{3}{20}$ (C) $\dfrac{1}{5}$ (D) $\dfrac{3}{10}$ (E) $\dfrac{23}{60}$

Solution: The answer is **(A)**.

This is similar to the percent problem (Example 1), but now fractions are used. Pick the LCD of the fractions to replace d, the original number of dollars. The LCD of 3, 4, and 5 is 60.

$\dfrac{2}{5}$ of 60, that is, 24, is spent, leaving 36.

Then $\dfrac{3}{4}$ of 36, that is, 27, is spent, leaving 9.

Then $\dfrac{1}{3}$ of 9 that is, 3, is spent, leaving 6.

$\therefore \dfrac{6}{60} = \dfrac{1}{10}$ is the fraction of the original amount left.

Example 5

If x is not equal to 2 or -2, which is equivalent to $\dfrac{3x^2 - 8x + 4}{x^2 - 4}$?

(A) $3 - 8x$ (B) $4 - 2x$ (C) $\dfrac{3x-2}{x-2}$ (D) $\dfrac{3x+2}{x+2}$ (E) $\dfrac{3x-2}{x+2}$

Solution: The answer is **(E)**.

You are given that x can be any number except 2 or -2. Nothing in the problem suggests that x can't be 0. Since 0 is an easy number to substitute, try it in the given fraction:

$$\frac{3x^2 - 8x + 4}{x^2 - 4} = \frac{4}{-4} = -1.$$

Now plug $x = 0$ into the answer choices to find which one equals -1.

(A) $3 - 8x = 3$ No, not equal to -1

(B) $4 - 2x = 4$ No

(C) $\dfrac{3x-2}{x-2} = 1$ No

(D) $\dfrac{3x+2}{x+2} = 1$ No

(E) $\dfrac{3x-2}{x+2} = -1$ Yes!

Again, if you're good at algebra, solve this problem algebraically by factoring the numerator and denominator and then canceling:

$$\frac{3x^2 - 8x + 4}{x^2 - 4} = \frac{(x-2)(3x-2)}{(x-2)(x+2)} = \frac{3x-2}{x+2}.$$

Example 6

A man has x dollars to be divided equally among p people. If n newcomers join the group, how many fewer dollars does each person get than each of the original people would have received?

(A) $\dfrac{xn}{p+n}$ (B) $\dfrac{x}{p+n}$ (C) $\dfrac{xn}{p^2+pn}$ (D) $\dfrac{-xn}{p^2+pn}$ (E) $\dfrac{-xn}{p+n}$

Solution: The answer is **(C)**.

The key to doing this problem by plugging in numbers is to realize that x dollars will be divided among various numbers of people. Pick x to be a number with lots of factors: 36 is a good choice, and so is 20. Try $x = 20$, $p = 4$ (the original number of people), and $n = 6$ (the number of newcomers). When \$20 is divided by 4, each person gets \$5. When \$20 is divided by $6 + 4$, each person gets \$2. The answer to the question is \$5 − \$2 = \$3. Now plug your numbers into the answer choices to see which one gives you 3.

(A) $\dfrac{xn}{p+n} = \dfrac{(20)(6)}{10} = 12$ No

(B) $\dfrac{x}{p+n} = \dfrac{20}{10} = 2$ No

(C) $\dfrac{xn}{p^2 + pn} = \dfrac{(20)(6)}{16+24} = 3$ Yes!

Note: You can eliminate choices (D) and (E) without plugging in. The statement of the problem calls for a positive answer. You can see at a glance that the expressions in (D) and (E) are negative.

The algebraic solution of the problem is to say that p people would each get $\dfrac{x}{p}$ dollars, while $p + n$ people would each get $\dfrac{x}{p+n}$. The difference is

$$\frac{x}{p} - \frac{x}{p+n} = \frac{x(p+n) - xp}{p(p+n)} = \frac{xn}{p^2 + pn}.$$

PLUG-IN

The plug-in strategy is a huge time-saver on the SAT. Instead of solving a problem from scratch and then optimistically searching for your answer among the choices, try plugging the values given in choices (A) through (E) into the problem to find the one that works. Remember: one of those choices is the correct answer! Your job is to use an efficient method to find it.

Plugging-in works whenever you're asked to find a specific numerical value, and you're given five numbers from which to choose. Since the answer choices are invariably arranged in increasing or decreasing order, starting with (C), the middle choice, sometimes saves time and effort. Even if (C) doesn't work, you may be able to see whether to try a higher or lower value. In that case, you'll be able to eliminate two more choices.

Example 7

Which is a solution to $(8^x)(2^4) = \left(\dfrac{1}{2}\right)^x$?

(A) -2 (B) -1 (C) $-\dfrac{1}{12}$ (D) 0   (E) $\dfrac{1}{2}$

Solution: The answer is **(B)**.

A solution to the equation will give a true statement when you plug it in. Here, starting with choice (C) is not wise; plugging in $-\dfrac{1}{12}$ is much harder than plugging in 0 or -1. Also, if $-\dfrac{1}{12}$ doesn't work, can you really tell whether to make x bigger or smaller? Instead, start with choice (D) and plug in 0, an easy number. Recall that $a^0 = 1$.

$$(8^0)(2^4) \stackrel{?}{=} \left(\frac{1}{2}\right)^0$$

$$\Rightarrow (1)(16) \stackrel{?}{=} 1 \quad \text{False}$$

Try choice (B): plug in −1. Recall that $a^{-1} = \frac{1}{a}$ and $\left(\frac{1}{a}\right)^{-1} = a$.

$$(8^{-1})(2^4) \stackrel{?}{=} \left(\frac{1}{2}\right)^{-1}$$

$$\Rightarrow \left(\frac{1}{8}\right)(16) \stackrel{?}{=} 2 \quad \text{True!}$$

Again, there's no rule that says you can't use algebra if you know how to do it. The idea is to write everything with the same base, in this case 2:

$$(8^x)(2^4) = \left(\frac{1}{2}\right)^x$$

$$\Rightarrow (2^3)^x 2^4 = (2^{-1})^x$$

$$\Rightarrow 2^{3x} \cdot 2^4 = 2^{-x}$$

$$\Rightarrow 3x + 4 = -x$$

$$\Rightarrow x = -1.$$

Example 8

If $\dfrac{x^2 - x - 6}{x^2 - 4x + 3} = \dfrac{4}{3}$, find x.

(A) −10   (B) −2   (C) 2   (D) 10   (E) 100

Solution: The answer is **(D)**.

Plug in choice (C), $x = 2$:

$$\frac{4-2-6}{4-8+3} \stackrel{?}{=} \frac{4}{3} \quad \text{No}$$

Try choice (D), $x = 10$:

$$\frac{100-10-6}{100-40+3} \stackrel{?}{=} \frac{4}{3} \quad \text{Yes!}$$

The method shown is a mindless way of solving the problem, but it has the virtue of always working. You can, however, use your knowledge of algebra and combine strategies to find the solution.

Notice that the trinomials in the given expression factor easily:

$$\frac{x^2 - x - 6}{x^2 - 4x + 3} = \frac{(x-3)(x+2)}{(x-3)(x-1)} = \frac{x+2}{x-1}.$$

Now plugging-in becomes a lot simpler, and you can quickly eyeball your way through the answer choices.

If you get as far as factoring and simplifying, solving the final equation becomes quite easy:

$$\frac{x+2}{x-1} = \frac{4}{3}$$

$$\Rightarrow 3x + 6 = 4x - 4 \quad \text{(Cross-multiply)}$$

$$\Rightarrow x = 10.$$

> The 2400 Club uses every tool in its toolkit, including algebra.

Example 9

Line segment $\overline{AB}$ has midpoint $(7, -1)$. If point A has coordinates $(2, 6)$, then point B has coordinates

(A) $\left(\dfrac{9}{2}, \dfrac{5}{2}\right)$ (B) $\left(\dfrac{19}{2}, -\dfrac{9}{2}\right)$ (C) $(12, -8)$ (D) $(14, -8)$ (E) $\left(12, \dfrac{5}{2}\right)$

Solution: The answer is **(C)**.

Draw a picture. The coordinates of M, the midpoint of $\overline{AB}$, are given by

$$\left(\frac{x_A + x_B}{2}, \frac{y_A + y_B}{2}\right).$$

<u>Method I</u>: Plug-In

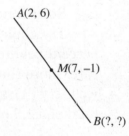

Notice that the average of the endpoints' x-coordinates is 7, and the average of the endpoints' y-coordinates is -1. Plug in the integer answer choices first.

(C): point $B = (12, -8)$. Since $A = (2, 6)$,

$$M = \left(\frac{12+2}{2}, \frac{-8+6}{2}\right) = (7, 1), \text{ the given midpoint.}$$

<u>Method II</u>: Slope

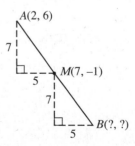

Notice that to get from point A $(2, 6)$ to midpoint M $(7, -1)$, the x-coordinate of A goes up 5 and the y-coordinate of A goes down 7:

$$2 + 5 = 7 \quad \text{and} \quad 6 - 7 = -1.$$

The three points A, M, and B are collinear, and M is the midpoint of $\overline{AB}$.

Therefore, to get from M to B, the x-coordinate of M should go up 5, and the y-coordinate of M should go down 7:

$$7 + 5 = 12 \quad \text{and} \quad -1 - 7 = -8.$$

Therefore, B is point $(12, -8)$.

Example 10

The sides of a triangle are in the ratio 4:3:2. If the perimeter of the triangle is 792, what is the length of the smallest side?

(A) 88   (B) 176   (C) 200   (D) 264   (E) 352

Solution: The answer is **(B)**.

You're given a choice of five numbers, so try the plug-in strategy, starting with choice (C). If the smallest side is 200, the biggest side is double this length, or 400. The middle side is somewhere between these values. Even if you take a number only slightly larger than 200, you get a perimeter over 800—too big. Now you can also eliminate choices (D) and (E): 200 is too big, and 264 and 352 are even bigger! You can eliminate choice (A) with similar reasoning. If the smallest side is approximately 90, then the biggest side is 180 and the middle side is somewhere in between. The resulting perimeter is quite a bit less than 792, the given value. The answer must be choice (B).

This is a case where a direct solution is actually easier, if you see it. If the sides are in the ratio 4:3:2, then there are 9 "parts." If the perimeter is 792, each part is $792/9 = 88$. The smallest side is 2 parts, and $2 \times 88 = 176$.

Example 11

Ten pounds of mixed nuts contain 50 percent peanuts. How many pounds of peanuts must be added so that the final mixture has 60 percent peanuts?

(A) 2.5   (B) 5   (C) 6   (D) 10   (E) 12.5

Solution: The answer is **(A)**.

Try choice (C): 6 pounds of peanuts. The original 10-pound mixture contained 50 percent peanuts, or 5 pounds. Now you have 11 pounds of peanuts in a 16-pound mixture, more than 60 percent. This result automatically eliminates choices (D) and (E) as well. Try (A): adding 2.5 pounds of peanuts to 5 pounds gives 7.5 pounds of peanuts for a total of 12.5 pounds.

$$\frac{7.5}{12.5} = 0.6 = 60\% \quad \text{Yes!}$$

Example 12

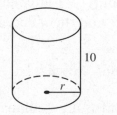

Note: Figure not drawn to scale.

If the volume of the cylinder shown above is $1{,}000\pi^3$, then the value of r, the radius of the base, is

(A) π (B) $\sqrt{10}$ (C) 10   (D) 10π (E) 100π

Solution: The answer is **(D)**.

The volume of a cylinder is

$$V = (\text{area of base}) \times \text{height} = \pi r^2 h.$$

Here, the height is 10, so $V = 10\pi r^2$. Set V equal to $1,000\pi r^3$ (given):

$$1,000\pi r^3 = 10\pi r^2.$$

One of the answer choices is a value of r that makes the two sides equal. Don't blindly plug in $r = 10$, choice (C)! You can see that to end up with π^3 in the answer, you need to get two factors of π from r^2, so the answer must have a π. Try (D), $r = 10\pi$, which works.

THE GRAPHING CALCULATOR

Be aware that every time you push a calculator button, you're using valuable time. Still, there are some situations where you should consider a graphing calculator solution.

Identifying a Graph

 Suppose that you are given an equation and then asked about its graph. Sometimes the calculator can provide instant gratification.

Example 13

Which is the graph of $y = -(x - 2)^2$?

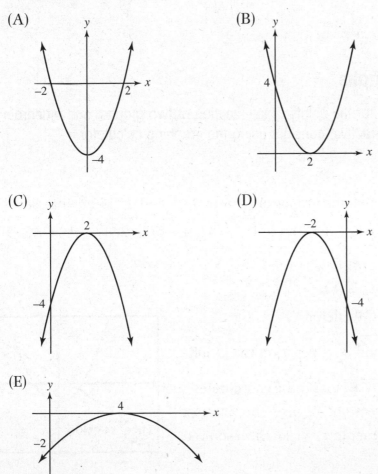

Solution: The answer is **(C)**.

Method I: Graphing Calculator

Use the graphing calculator to sketch the graph of $y = -(x - 2)^2$. The graphing window clearly shows a graph that matches choice (C)! End of story.

Of course, there are ways to solve this problem without a graphing calculator.

Method II: Logical Reasoning

Since the coefficient of x^2 is negative, the graph is concave down, eliminating choices (A) and (B). Also, since the constant term is –4, the y-intercept of the graph is –4, eliminating choice (E). Solving $-(x - 2)^2 = 0$ yields $x = 2$ as a double root, eliminating choice (D). Therefore, the answer is (C).

Method III: Transformations

If $f(x) = -x^2$, the given equation, $y = -(x - 2)^2$, represents $f(x - 2)$. Then, as shown below, the graph of $f(x)$ is shifted 2 units to the right, resulting in choice (C).

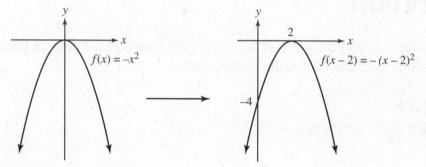

Intersection of Two Graphs

 When you are asked for the points of intersection of two graphs, and algebraic or plug-in solutions are unattractive, consider using the graphing calculator.

Example 14

Find the points at which the graphs of $y = \frac{1}{2}x^2 - 3$ and $y = x + 1$ intersect.

(A) (–2, –3) (4, 5)   (B) (–1, –2) (5, 4)   (C) (–4, –3) (–2, 4)   (D) (–4, –3) (2, 3)
(E) (–2, –1) (4, 5)

Solution: The answer is **(E)**.

Method I: Graphing Calculator

Graph $y_1 = \frac{1}{2}x^2 - 3$ and $y_2 = x + 1$ on the graph-

ing calculator. Either [TRACE] to get the coordinates of the points of intersection, or use the intersect option in the [CALC] menu to yield the required points. The answer is (E).

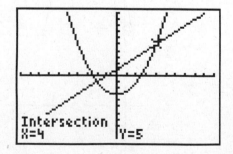

Again, you may prefer an algebraic or plug-in solution.

Method II: Algebra

Solve $y = \frac{1}{2}x^2 - 3$ and $y = x + 1$ simultaneously. Substitute $x + 1$ for y in the first equation:

$$x + 1 = \frac{1}{2}x^2 - 3$$
$$\Rightarrow 2x + 2 = x^2 - 6$$
$$\Rightarrow x^2 - 2x - 8 = 0$$
$$\Rightarrow x = 4 \text{ or } -2.$$

Substituting $x = 4$ in $y = x + 1$ yields $y = 5$, and substituting $x = -2$ yields $y = -1$. Thus the coordinates where the graphs intersect are $(-2, -1)$ and $(4, 5)$, choice (E).

Method III: Plug-In

Since a point of intersection lies on both graphs, its coordinates must satisfy both equations. Go through each answer choice, plugging in the coordinates, until you find the points that satisfy both equations. If you start at choice (A), you find that you need to go all the way to choice (E):

$(-2, -1)$	$(4, 5)$
Plug into $y = \frac{1}{2}x^2 - 3$:	
$-1 = \frac{1}{2}x^2 - 3$	$5 = \frac{1}{2}(4)^2 - 3$
$\Rightarrow -1 = -1$ True	$\Rightarrow 5 = 8 - 3$ True
Plug into $y = x + 1$:	
$-1 = -2 + 1$ True	$5 = 4 + 1$ True

Transformations

 When you are given a transformation on a "mystery" function and can't remember the formula for the resulting graph, consider using the graphing calculator.

Example 15

The graph of $f(x)$ is shown below:

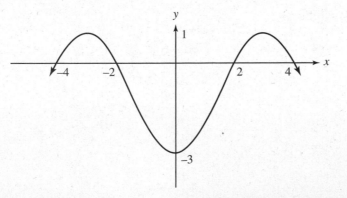

A transformation is applied that results in the following graph:

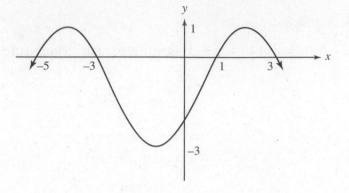

Which of the following functions describes this graph?

(A) $f(x-1)$ (B) $f(x+1)$ (C) $f(x)-1$ (D) $f(x)+1$ (E) $f(-x)$

Solution: The answer is **(B)**.

Notice that the graph of $f(x)$ has been shifted 1 unit to the left, a move that always transforms $f(x)$ into $f(x+1)$. You should know this—but suppose you're not certain. A backup strategy is to graph an easy function like $y = x^2$ on the graphing calculator. Now graph $y = (x-1)^2$, which is $f(x-1)$, then $y = (x+1)^2$, which is $f(x+1)$, and so on, until you find the formula that shifts the graph of $y = x^2$ to the left.

Inequalities

You should consider using the graphing calculator in the solution of an inequality that seems tricky.

Example 16

The solution to the inequality $|2x-1| < 6$ is

(A) $x < -\dfrac{5}{2}$ or $x > \dfrac{7}{2}$ (B) $x < -\dfrac{7}{2}$ or $x > \dfrac{5}{2}$ (C) $-\dfrac{5}{2} < x < \dfrac{7}{2}$ (D) $-\dfrac{7}{2} < x < \dfrac{5}{2}$

(E) $\dfrac{5}{2} < x < \dfrac{7}{2}$

Solution: The answer is **(C)**.

<u>Method I</u>: Algebra

$$|2x-1| < 6$$
$$\Rightarrow -6 < 2x - 1 < 6$$
$$\Rightarrow -5 < 2x < 7$$
$$\Rightarrow -\frac{5}{2} < x < \frac{7}{2}.$$

<u>Method II</u>: Graphing Calculator
Graph

$$y_1 = \text{abs}\,(2x - 1)$$
$$y_2 = 6.$$

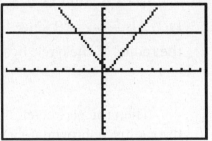

The question asks for x-values such that $y_1 < y_2$, namely, x-values such that the graph of y_1 is below the graph of y_2. A quick glance at the screen shows that this is true for the x-values in choice **(C)**.

A final note:

> The 2400 Club is familiar with a graphing calculator and knows when to use it, and when *not* to use it, to save time.

SOME ADDITIONAL TIPS

Certain types of questions immediately suggest a place to start or a strategy to try.

Geometry

In a geometry question where the figure is provided, mark all the given data and anything else you can deduce on the diagram in the test booklet. If necessary, add helpful line segments. When you find the answer, check that it seems reasonable if the diagram is drawn to scale: the answer can't be 7 if the longest segment in the diagram is 5.

Be warned: Many figures on the SAT are purposely not drawn to scale. (A note below the figure will state that the figure is not drawn to scale.) In such cases, any answer choice that appears reasonable is almost certainly wrong!

Example 17 Grid-In

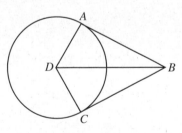

In the figure above, a circle with center D has tangents $\overline{BA}$ and $\overline{BC}$ at points A and C, respectively. If $\overline{BD}$ has length 17 and $\overline{BC}$ has length 15, find the perimeter of quadrilateral $ABCD$.

Solution: The answer is 46.

Mark the diagram as shown.

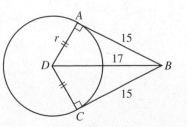

$\overline{DA} \perp \overline{BA}$ and $\overline{DC} \perp \overline{BC}$ since a radius is perpendicular to a tangent at the point of contact. Also, $\overline{BA} \cong \overline{BC}$ since tangents to a circle from an external point are congruent. Find the radius of the circle by using the Pythagorean theorem in say, $\triangle ABD$:

$$r^2 = 17^2 - 15^2 \Rightarrow r^2 = 17^2 - 15^2 \Rightarrow r = 8.$$

Then the perimeter of quadrilateral $ABCD$ is $2(15 + 8) = 46$. Notice that length 8 for the radius, approximately half of the length of $\overline{BC}$, looks reasonable on the diagram.

Grid-in 46.

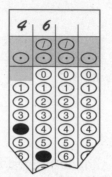

Simultaneous Equations

If you're given two equations in x and y and are asked to find $x + y$, $x - y$, xy, or x/y, then add, subtract, multiply, or divide the given equations. The result may pleasantly surprise you.

Example 18

Given that $x^2 + y^2 = 4$ and $x^2 + y^2 - 4x - 4y = -4$, then $x + y =$

(A) 1   (B) 2   (C) 3   (D) 4   (E) 8

Solution: The answer is **(B)**.

$$x^2 + y^2 = 4 \quad (1)$$
$$x^2 + y^2 - 4x - 4y = -4 \quad (2)$$

$$(1) - (2): 4x + 4y = 8$$
$$\Rightarrow x + y = 2.$$

Alternatively, since $x^2 + y^2 = 4$, replace $x^2 + y^2$ in equation (2) with 4:

$$4 - 4x - 4y = -4$$
$$\Rightarrow 4x + 4y = 8$$
$$\Rightarrow x + y = 2.$$

Shaded Areas

Subtract areas to find shaded regions.

Example 19

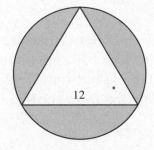

An equilateral triangle with side 12 is inscribed in a circle. Find the shaded area.

(A) $12\pi - 36\sqrt{3}$ (B) $36\pi - 48\sqrt{3}$ (C) $36\pi - 36\sqrt{3}$ (D) $48\pi - 48\sqrt{3}$ (E) $48\pi - 36\sqrt{3}$

Solution: The answer is **(E)**.

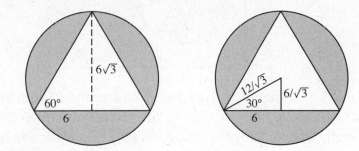

Area of $\triangle = \left(\dfrac{1}{2}\right)(12)(6\sqrt{3})$

$\qquad = 36\sqrt{3}.$

Radius of circle $(\bigcirc) = \dfrac{12}{\sqrt{3}}.$

$\therefore$ Area of $\bigcirc = \pi\left(\dfrac{12}{\sqrt{3}}\right)^2$

$\qquad = 48\pi$

$\therefore$ Shaded area $= \bigcirc$ area $- \triangle$ area

$\qquad = 48\pi - 36\sqrt{3}.$

Sets

 Use Venn diagrams to solve problems with sets.

Example 20

At John Adams High School, 120 students take programming, and 200 students take statistics. Of these, 50 students take both programming and statistics. An additional 80 students take neither programming nor statistics. If a student at this school is picked at random, what is the probability that he or she takes programming but not statistics?

(A) $\dfrac{1}{7}$ (B) $\dfrac{7}{45}$ (C) $\dfrac{1}{5}$ (D) $\dfrac{4}{15}$ (E) $\dfrac{12}{35}$

Solution: The answer is **(C)**.

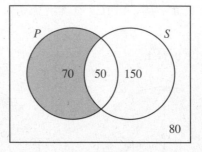

Let P be the set of students taking programming, and S the set taking statistics. Draw a Venn diagram as shown. Start by placing 50, the number who take both programming and statistics, in the intersection of P and S. Since 120 students take programming, there are 70 left in P. Also, since 200 students take statistics, there are 150 left in S. Place 80, the number of students who take neither class, outside P and S. The total number of students in the school is $70 + 50 + 150 + 80 = 350$.

The probability that a student takes programming only is

$$\frac{\text{Number who take programming only}}{\text{Total number of students}} = \frac{70}{350} = \frac{1}{5}.$$

One final piece of advice: Every problem on the SAT is designed to be solved within a reasonable amount of time. If, after some thought, you can't come up with a reasonable way to tackle a problem, circle it in your test booklet and move on. Don't allow yourself to become bogged down in endless, futile calculation.

Chapter 13

TOPICS IN ARITHMETIC

Doing arithmetic may evoke warm, fuzzy memories of elementary school, but don't be complacent about SAT arithmetic. The problems can be challenging.

Some 2400 Club Strategies for Tackling Arithmetic . . .

Strategy 1: **P**ick-a-Number for problems with fractions or percents.

Strategy 2: **R**emember to plug-in answer choices.

Strategy 3: **O**ne, two, three! Know those counting rules.

Strategy 4: **B**rush up on the number sets. Know the different sets of numbers.

Strategy 5: **L**earn formulas for sequences and series.

Strategy 6: **E**xpress exponential growth as a geometric sequence.

Strategy 7: **M**ake a tree for probability.

Strategy 8: **S**et up a proportion for percent and rate problems.

SETS

Sets of Numbers

Many SAT questions involve nothing more than manipulation of numbers, yet these questions can be tricky. For starters, you need to be clear about which numbers belong to which sets.

Integers = $\{\ldots, -4, -3, -2, -1, 0, 1, 2, 3, 4, \ldots\}$
Nonnegative integers = $\{0, 1, 2, 3, 4, \ldots\}$
Positive integers = $\{1, 2, 3, 4, \ldots\}$
Negative integers = $\{-1, -2, -3, -4, \ldots\}$
Even integers = $\{\ldots, -4, -2, 0, 2, 4, \ldots\}$
Odd integers = $\{\ldots, -5, -3, -1, 1, 3, 5, \ldots\}$

Consecutive Integers

Consecutive integers are two or more integers that directly follow each other. For example, 10, 11, 12 are consecutive integers. If n is an even integer, then $n, n + 2, n + 4$ are *consecutive even integers*. Notice that if n is odd, then $n, n + 2, n + 4$ represent *consecutive odd integers*.

Factors and Multiples

The *factors* of a positive integer n are the positive integers that can be divided into n without a remainder. For example, the factors of 18 are 1, 2, 3, 6, 9, 18.

The *multiples* of n are the positive integers that have n as a factor. For example, the multiples of 7 are 7, 14, 21, 28, 35, . . .

The *greatest common factor* or *greatest common divisor* of two integers is the largest integer that is a factor of both. The *least common multiple* of two integers is the smallest integer that is a multiple of both. For example, the greatest common factor of 12 and 30 is 6, whereas the least common multiple of 12 and 30 is 60.

Prime Numbers

A *prime number* has exactly two factors, 1 and itself. This statement means that 1 is not a prime number, and 2 is the only even prime number.

The *prime factorization* of an integer is the product of its prime factors. For example, the prime factorization of 45 is $3^2 \times 5$.

Rational Numbers

The *set of rational numbers* is the set of all numbers that can be written as a fraction $\frac{a}{b}$, where a and b are integers and $b \neq 0$. Here are some examples of rational numbers:

$2 \quad$ (since $2 = \frac{2}{1}$)

0.68 (since $0.68 = \frac{68}{100}$)

$0.\overline{6}$ (since $0.\overline{6} = \frac{2}{3}$)

 Notice that the *decimal equivalent* of a fraction can be obtained by dividing the numerator (top) by the denominator. Your calculator will do this for you in the blink of an eye. Your calculator can also find the fractional equivalent of a decimal. Type the decimal, or if you already have it displayed as the answer to a calculation, follow the decimal with MATH Frac ENTER, and you'll see the equivalent fraction displayed on the screen.

> The 2400 Club knows that every integer, terminating decimal, and nonterminating *repeating* decimal is a rational number.

Sets and Elements

A *set* is a collection of objects, usually related. Each object is a *member* or *element* of the set. You need to know correct set notation for the SAT. For example, if $S = \{2, 7, 9, 12\}$, you can say that $7 \in S$ ("7 is an element of S"), but $4 \notin S$ ("4 is not an element of S").

Union and Intersection

Suppose that $P = \{2, 5, 8, 11\}$ and $Q = \{2, 4, 6, 8, 10\}$. The *union* of P and Q, denoted as $P \cup Q$, is the set of elements that are in either P or Q (or both), that is,

$$P \cup Q = \{2, 4, 5, 6, 8, 10, 11\}.$$

The *intersection* of P and Q, denoted as $P \cap Q$, is the set of elements that are in both P and Q, that is,

$$P \cap Q = \{2, 8\}.$$

Example 1

Let A be the set of integer remainders when eight consecutive integers are divided by 8. Let B be the set of prime factors of 36. Let C be the set of all numbers of the form $2m + 1$, where m is an integer. Which represents $A \cap B \cap C$?

(A) $\{1, 2, 3, 4, 5, 6, 7\}$ (B) $\{1, 3, 5, 7\}$ (C) $\{1, 2, 3\}$ (D) $\{1, 3\}$ (E) $\{3\}$

Solution: The answer is **(E)**.

$$A = \{0, 1, 2, 3, 4, 5, 6, 7\}, \quad B = \{2, 3\}, \quad C = \{\ldots, -3, -1, 1, 3, 5, \ldots\}.$$

$A \cap B \cap C$ is the intersection of the three sets, namely, the elements that are common to A, B, and C. The number 3 is the only element that fits the bill, so $\{3\}$ is the answer.

Eliminate choices (A)–(D) because they all contain the number 1, which is not prime!

Squares and Square Roots

Perfect squares pop up frequently on the SAT. Even though your calculator can help you here, you should recognize the first twenty perfect squares: 1, 4, 9, 16, 25, 36, 49, 64, 81, 100, 121, 144, 169, 196, 225, 256, 289, 324, 361, 400.

Every positive number has two *square roots:* a positive and a negative number. Thus the square root of 64 is 8 or −8. The symbol $\sqrt{64}$ represents the positive root, 8, while $-\sqrt{64}$ represents the negative root, −8. The solution to the equation $x^2 = 64$ is ±8.

> The 2400 Club does not forget the negative root when solving equations that require square roots on both sides.

Beware of questions that involve negative numbers, fractions, squares, and inequalities. These are a poisonous brew.

Example 2

If a and b are nonzero numbers such that $a < b$, which of the following must be true?

$\quad$ I. $\dfrac{1}{a} > \dfrac{1}{b}$

$\quad$ II. $a^2 < b^2$

$\quad$ III. $b^2 \geq 1$

(A) None $\qquad$ (B) I only $\qquad$ (C) II only $\qquad$ (D) III only $\qquad$ (E) I and II only

Solution: The answer is **(A)**.

Look for a counterexample that shows each choice is false. Don't forget fractions and negative numbers!

$\quad$ I: $-2 < 2$ does not imply that $-\dfrac{1}{2} > \dfrac{1}{2}$.

$\quad$ II: $-2 < 1$ does not imply that $4 < 1$.

$\quad$ III: Let $b = \dfrac{1}{2}$. Notice that $b^2 = \dfrac{1}{4}$, which is less than 1.

> The 2400 Club knows that a *single counterexample* shows that a statement is false.

Ratio, Proportion, Percents

A *ratio* is a quotient of two quantities. For example, suppose that the ratio of boys to girls at a school is 4 to 5; that is, for every 4 boys there are 5 girls. Another way of expressing this is:

$$\frac{\text{Number of boys}}{\text{Number of girls}} = \frac{4}{5}.$$

The ratio can also be denoted as:

$$\text{Number of boys : Number of girls} = 4 : 5.$$

In the picture on the right, $AB = BC$.

The ratio of AC to $AB = \dfrac{2}{1}$ or 2:1 or 2 to 1.

A *percent* is a ratio in which the second quantity is 100. For example,

$$23\% = \frac{23}{100} = 0.23.$$

A *proportion* is an equation that sets two ratios equal to each other. For example,

$$\frac{2}{5} = \frac{6}{15}.$$

Proportions are often used in the solution of SAT problems.

Example 3 Grid-In

The price of a toaster was originally x dollars. Later, the toaster went on sale at a 20 percent discount, and was eventually sold for $50.40 after an additional 10 percent discount off the sale price. What was x, the original price, in dollars, of the toaster?

Solution: The answer is 70.

This is a tricky problem that can be simplified by using the pick-a-number strategy. Instead of working backward from the actual price, note that the problem deals with percents, so start with $x = \$100$. Now work through the problem to see what percent of the original price, x, was actually paid:

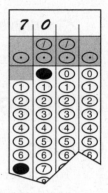

The 20 percent discount gives a sale price of $80.

The additional 10 percent discount leaves a final price of $72, which is 72 percent of $100.

Therefore $50.40, the actual final price paid, was 72 percent of x, the original price.

Set up the following proportion: $\dfrac{72}{100} = \dfrac{50.40}{x}$.

Cross-multiply to solve for x: $x = \dfrac{(50.40)(100)}{72} = 70$.

Grid-in 70.

Percent Increase and Decrease

Some of the more challenging problems on the SAT involve *percent increase* or *percent decrease*.

The percent increase of a quantity equals

$$\frac{\text{amount of increase}}{\text{original amount}} \cdot \frac{100}{1}$$

The percent decrease of a quantity equals

$$\frac{\text{amount of decrease}}{\text{original amount}} \cdot \frac{100}{1}$$

Example 4

The following chart shows the cost of one DVD player at a discount store during each of the first 6 months of the year.

Month	January	February	March	April	May	June
Cost	$200.99	$195.99	$150.00	$150.00	$135.99	$120.85

The percent decrease in the cost of the DVD player from January to June was closest to

(A) 12%   (B) 40%   (C) 50%   (D) 60%   (E) 66%

Solution: The answer is **(B)**.

Actual decrease = cost in January – cost in June = \$200.99 – \$120.85 = \$80.14.

Percent decrease = $\dfrac{80.14}{200.99} \cdot 100 \approx 40\%$.

High scorers don't waste time using a calculator for the final calculation. You can see that the fraction is approximately $\dfrac{80}{200}$, which is $\dfrac{40}{100}$ or 40%.

COUNTING AND PROBABILITY

Counting

To answer the question "How many ways can . . . ?" sounds simple: you just count. These problems, however, can be tricky.

The Basic Rule of Counting: If event 1 can happen in k different ways, and an independent event, event 2, can happen in m different ways, then the total number of ways in which both events can happen is km.

A typical problem is the "outfit" problem. If you have 3 pairs of jeans and 10 T-shirts, you have a choice of $3 \times 10 = 30$ different outfits, where an outfit consists of a pair of jeans and a T-shirt.

Note that the basic rule can be extended to more than two events. If, in addition to your jeans and T-shirts, you have 4 hats, the number of different possible outfits increases to $10 \times 3 \times 4 = 120$, where an outfit consists of a pair of jeans, a T-shirt, and a hat.

This is all you'll need to solve counting problems on the SAT test. However, knowing the formulas for permutations and combinations (in the following section) can lead to a speedier solution.

Permutations and Combinations

A *permutation* is the number of arrangements of n objects, where each different ordering of the objects counts as one permutation. For example, how many arrangements are there of the letters E,X,A,M? Imagine having four slots:

You have 4 choices for the first slot, 3 choices for the second slot, and 2 choices for the third slot. By the time you get to the fourth slot, there is no choice: just 1 letter is left. Therefore, the total number of arrangements is $4 \times 3 \times 2 \times 1 = 24$. It is important to understand that EXAM and MAXE, for example, are different permutations.

In general, the number of permutations of n items taken r at a time is given by the formula

$$_nP_r = \frac{n!}{(n-r)!}$$

Now consider the problem of calculating the number of 3-person committees that can be formed from 6 people who are willing to serve. There are $6 \times 5 \times 4$ ways of selecting 3 people. If the order of their selection, however, is irrelevant—for example, Mary-Tom-Nick is the same committee as Nick-Mary-Tom—you must divide by $3 \times 2 \times 1$ because each group of 3 people can be chosen in 6 different ways. When the order of choosing is not important, each arrangement is called a *combination*.

In general, the number of combinations of n items taken r at a time is given by the formula

$$_nC_r = \frac{n!}{(n-r)!r!} = \frac{_nP_r}{r!}$$

Probability

Events

Suppose that an experiment is performed. An *event E* is a set of particular outcomes of this experiment. If S is the set of all possible outcomes of the experiment, then E is a subset of S. For example, consider the experiment of flipping a fair coin and tossing a fair six-sided die. The set S of all possible outcomes is

$$S = \{H1, H2, H3, H4, H5, H6, T1, T2, T3, T4, T5, T6\}$$

Here are some events for the above experiment:

A = {Getting a prime number and tails} = {T2, T3, T5}
B = {Getting a head on the coin} = {H1, H2, H3, H4, H5, H6}
C = {Getting a 4 on the die} = {H4, T4}

Probability of an Event

The *probability* of an event E, $P(E)$, is given as follows: If E can occur in m ways out of a total of n equally likely ways, then

$$P(E) = \frac{m}{n} = \frac{\text{Number of outcomes in event } E}{\text{Total number of possible outcomes}}$$

For the coin/die experiment above, all 12 outcomes in set S are equally likely, so the probabilities of events A, B, and C (described above) are

$$P(A) = \frac{3}{12} = \frac{1}{4}, \quad P(B) = \frac{6}{12} = \frac{1}{2}, \quad P(C) = \frac{2}{12} = \frac{1}{6}$$

Note that:

■ If event E is the empty set, it represents an *impossible event*, and $P(E) = 0$.
■ If $E = S$, it represents a *certain event*, and $P(E) = 1$.
■ Therefore, if E is a nonempty, nonequal subset of S, then $0 < P(E) < 1$.
■ E', the *complement* of E, is the set containing all the elements of S that are not in E. Thus the probability that event E will *not* happen is given by $P(E') = 1 - P(E)$.
  In the coin/die experiment, the probability of getting a 4 on the die, $P(C)$, is $\frac{1}{6}$.

The probability of *not* getting a 4 on the die = $P(C') = 1 - P(C) = 1 - \frac{1}{6} = \frac{5}{6}$.

Mutually Exclusive Events

In the coin/die experiment, recall that

A = {Getting a prime number and tails} = {T2, T3, T5}
B = {Getting a head on the coin}= {H1, H2, H3, H4, H5, H6}
C = {Getting a 4 on the die} = {H4, T4}

Events A and B are *mutually exclusive*. In other words, they cannot occur simultaneously in one run of the experiment. They are disjoint sets. To find the probability of getting tails with a prime number *or* heads on the coin, the probabilities are additive:

$$P(A \text{ or } B) = P(A \cup B) = P(A) + P(B)$$

$$= \frac{1}{4} + \frac{1}{2} = \frac{3}{4}$$

Contrast this with the problem of finding the probability of getting either a head on the coin (event B) or a 4 on the die (event C). Again you want to find $P(B \cup C)$. But in this case, events B and C are not mutually exclusive, since outcome H4 is in both events. The addition rule for finding the probability of B or C must be adjusted since the intersection of the two sets is nonempty: (You don't want to count the common element, H4, twice.)

$$P(B \cup C) = P(B) + P(C) - P(B \cap C)$$

$$= \frac{1}{2} + \frac{1}{6} - \frac{1}{12}$$

$$= \frac{7}{12}.$$

Independent Events

In the coin/die experiment, the probability of getting a head on the coin (event B) *and* a 4 on the die (event C) is given by the multiplication rule:

$$P(B \cap C) = P(B) \times P(C) = \left(\frac{1}{2}\right)\left(\frac{1}{6}\right) = \frac{1}{12}.$$

Events B and C are *independent*. This statement should feel intuitively correct to you: P({Getting a 4 on the die}) is independent of what happens on the coin toss.

In general: The probability that both A *and* B occur is given by

$$P(A \cap B) = P(A) \times P(B).$$

Event B is independent of event A if and only if the probability of event B is not influenced by whether A has or has not occurred. If P(B) changes after A has occurred, then A and B are *dependent* events.

In this case $P(A \cap B) = P(A) \cdot P(B|A)$, where $P(B|A)$ means "the probability of B given that A has occurred."

Example 5

A small bag contains 4 white and 3 red marbles. Two marbles are randomly removed from the bag. Find the probability that a white marble is removed, followed by a red.

(A) $\dfrac{1}{7}$ (B) $\dfrac{2}{7}$ (C) $\dfrac{3}{7}$ (D) $\dfrac{4}{7}$ (E) $\dfrac{12}{49}$

Solution: The answer is **(B)**.

$$P(WR) = P(W) \cdot P(R\,|\,W)$$

$$= \frac{4}{7} \cdot \frac{1}{2}$$

$$= \frac{2}{7}$$

Notice that in a vacuum $P(W) = \dfrac{4}{7}$ and $P(R) = \dfrac{3}{7}$. But since "removing a white marble"

and "removing a red marble" (without replacement) are dependent events, these probabilities must be adjusted if one of the events has already happened.

Example 6

A hat contains the integers 1 to 100, inclusive. If a number is drawn at random from the hat, what is the probability that a multiple of 5 or a multiple of 8 is drawn?

(A) $\dfrac{3}{5}$ (B) $\dfrac{33}{100}$ (C) $\dfrac{8}{25}$ (D) $\dfrac{31}{100}$ (E) $\dfrac{3}{10}$

Solution: The answer is **(E)**.

The events in this experiment are:

A = {Getting a multiple of 5} = {5, 10, 15, . . . , 100}.
B = {Getting a multiple of 8} = {8, 16, 24, . . . , 96}.

<u>Method I</u>: Find Number of Successful Outcomes

The total number of outcomes is 100, the number of integers that can be drawn. The "successful" outcomes are the numbers that are either multiples of 5 or multiples of 8.

Number of multiples of $5 = \dfrac{100}{5}$ or 20.

Number of multiples of $8 = \dfrac{100}{8}$ or 12 (The remainder is irrelevant.)

But beware: The integers 40 and 80 are multiples of both 5 and 8. Don't count them twice! Thus the number of successful outcomes is $20 + 12 - 2 = 30$.

The required probability is $\dfrac{30}{100} = \dfrac{3}{10}$.

<u>Method II</u>: Find $P(A$ or $B)$

A and B are not mutually exclusive events, since each set contains 40 and 80.

$$P(A \text{ or } B) = P(A \cup B)$$
$$= P(A) + P(B) - P(A \cap B)$$
$$= \frac{20}{100} + \frac{12}{100} - \frac{2}{100}$$
$$= \frac{3}{10}.$$

Example 7

In a batch of 10 light bulbs, 2 are defective. If 3 of the bulbs are chosen at random, what is the probability that at least 1 of the chosen bulbs is defective?

(A) $\dfrac{8}{15}$ (B) $\dfrac{7}{15}$ (C) $\dfrac{3}{10}$ (D) $\dfrac{1}{4}$ (E) $\dfrac{1}{5}$

Solution: The answer is **(A)**.

A good way to save time here is to use the complement rule:

P (at least 1 bulb is defective) = $1 - P$ (none of the bulbs is defective).

In this way you need to deal with just one event: none of the 3 chosen bulbs is defective.

<u>Method I</u>: Find Number of Successful Outcomes

To find P (none of the 3 chosen bulbs is defective):

Total number of ways to pick 3 of the 10 bulbs = $\dfrac{(10)(9)(8)}{(3)(2)(1)} = 120$.

(You need to divide by the number of arrangements of those 3 bulbs, since the order of picking them is irrelevant.)

There are $10 - 2 = 8$ nondefective bulbs.

Total number of ways to pick 3 nondefective bulbs = $\dfrac{(8)(7)(6)}{(3)(2)(1)} = 56$.

$\therefore P$ (none of the bulbs is defective) = $\dfrac{56}{120} = \dfrac{7}{15}$.

P(at least 1 defective) = $1 - P$(none defective)

$$= 1 - \frac{7}{15} = \frac{8}{15}$$

Method II: Tree Diagram

A tree diagram provides a snapshot of a multistage experiment. At each stage all possible outcomes are shown. Each "branch" of the tree represents one composite outcome of the completed experiment.

Below is a tree diagram for the light bulb problem. Think of the problem as a three-stage experiment in which each stage involves choosing 1 bulb. At each stage, either a defective bulb (D) or a nondefective bulb (N) is chosen.

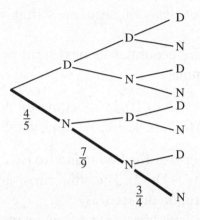

Only one branch leads to an outcome in which none of the bulbs is defective. The probabilities are shown at each stage along this branch: The probability of picking a nondefective bulb the first time is $\frac{8}{10} = \frac{4}{5}$, since 8 bulbs are not defective. The probability of picking a nondefective bulb the second time is affected by the fact that a nondefective bulb is already gone: there are 9 bulbs left, of which 7 are nondefective. Similarly, at the third stage there are 8 bulbs left, of which 6 are nondefective. Notice that the following are dependent events, since the probabilities at each stage are affected by the result of the previous stage:

Drawing a nondefective bulb at the first stage
Drawing a nondefective bulb at the second stage
Drawing a nondefective bulb at the third stage

In a tree diagram, to find the probability of any branch, multiply the probabilities along the way:

$$P \text{ (no defective bulb)} = \left(\frac{4}{5}\right)\left(\frac{7}{9}\right)\left(\frac{3}{4}\right) = \frac{7}{15}$$

Now use the complement rule, as in the above method of solving:

$$P \text{ (at least 1 defective)} = 1 - P \text{ (none defective)}$$

$$= 1 - \frac{7}{15} = \frac{8}{15}.$$

Coaching:
To find the probability that "at least 1 ..." occurs, it is usually much easier to find 1 − the probability that "none ..." occurs.

Note: In a tree diagram, if more than one branch leads to a required outcome, add the probabilities for all of the successful branches.

SEQUENCES AND SERIES

A sequence is a list of numbers that generally follow a pattern, for example, 2, 5, 10, 17, 26, . . .

The pattern for the kth term is "square k and add 1." Thus the next term in the sequence is 37.

Arithmetic and Geometric Sequences and Series

There are two particular types of sequences that you should know, arithmetic and geometric.

An *arithmetic sequence* generates its next term by adding a *common difference* to the preceding term. For example:

$$-2, 2, 6, 10, \ldots \quad \text{common difference} = 4$$
$$10, 8, 6, 4, \ldots \quad \text{common difference} = -2$$

Notice that the nth term of the first sequence is $-2 + (n-1)4$, and the nth term of the second sequence is $10 + (n-1)(-2)$. The nth term of an arithmetic sequence is always the first term plus $(n-1)$ common differences.

A *geometric sequence* generates its next term by multiplying the preceding term by the same number, called a *common ratio*. For example:

$$3, 9, 27, 81, \ldots \quad \text{common ratio} = 3$$
$$4, \frac{4}{3}, \frac{4}{9}, \frac{4}{27}, \ldots \quad \text{common ratio} = \frac{1}{3}$$

Notice that the nth term of the first sequence is $(3)(3)^{n-1}$, and the nth term of the second sequence is $(4)\left(\dfrac{1}{3}\right)^{n-1}$. The nth term of a geometric sequence is always the first term multiplied by the $(n-1)$th power of the common ratio.

Sequences Involving Exponential Growth

The growth of a geometric sequence is called *exponential growth*. It is illustrated in Example 8.

Example 8 Grid-In

A colony of bacteria numbers 2,000 at 1 PM and increases 20 percent per hour. What is the population at 4 PM that same day?

Solution: The answer is 3,456.

An increase of 20 percent means that the second term in the sequence is

$$2{,}000 + 20\% \text{ of } 2{,}000$$

$$= 2{,}000 + \left(\frac{1}{5}\right)(2{,}000) = 2{,}000\left(1+\frac{1}{5}\right) = 2{,}000\left(\frac{6}{5}\right).$$

Coaching:
High scorers should know that if a number x increases by $\frac{1}{5}$, it becomes $\frac{6}{5}x$.

Here is the sequence of population numbers for the colony:

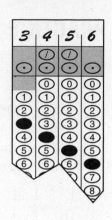

1 PM	2 PM	3 PM	4 PM
2,000	$2{,}000\left(\dfrac{6}{5}\right)$	$2{,}000\left(\dfrac{6}{5}\right)^2$	$2{,}000\left(\dfrac{6}{5}\right)^3$

This is a geometric sequence with common ratio $\dfrac{6}{5}$.

The answer is $2{,}000\left(\dfrac{6}{5}\right)^3 = 3{,}456$.

Grid-in 3456.

PRACTICE TEST QUESTIONS

1. Points A and B are on the number line in such a way that A corresponds to 0.625 and B corresponds to 0.637. If P is the midpoint of $\overline{AB}$, and Q is on the number line two-thirds of the distance from A to B, what is the ratio of PQ to AQ?

   (A) $1:4$
   (B) $1:3$
   (C) $1:2$
   (D) $2:3$
   (E) $4:3$

2.

   Population in Region R by Towns
   ♀ = 10,000 people

Town A	♀♀
Town B	♀♀♀♀
Town C	♀♀♀♀♀
Town D	♀♀♀♀♀♀♀♀♀

   If the four towns shown in the graph are the only towns in Region R, the combined populations of which two towns account for exactly 45 percent of the population of Region R?

   (A) A and B
   (B) B and C
   (C) A and C
   (D) A and D
   (E) B and D

3. Let A = {all 3-digit positive integers with the digit 1 in the ones place}, and let B = {all 3-digit positive integers with the digit 2 in the tens place}.

   How many elements are there in $A \cup B$ that are not in $A \cap B$?

   (A) 162
   (B) 171
   (C) 180
   (D) 182
   (E) 191

4. Yan needs $2.37 in postage to mail a letter. If he has 60-cent, 37-cent, 23-cent, 5-cent, and 1-cent stamps, at least 10 of each, what is the *smallest* number of stamps he can use to get the exact postage he needs?

   (A) 6
   (B) 7
   (C) 8
   (D) 9
   (E) 13

5. Ali is in a minivan with x children. Let y be the average (arithmetic mean) of the children's ages. If Ali's age is 6 times y, then her age is what fraction of the total ages of all the people in the minivan?

   (A) $\dfrac{6}{6+y}$

   (B) $\dfrac{6}{6+x}$

   (C) $\dfrac{6}{x+y}$

   (D) $\dfrac{x}{6y}$

   (E) $\dfrac{y}{6x}$

6. If x and y are integers whose least common multiple is a perfect square and whose greatest common divisor is a prime number, which could represent the ordered pair (x, y)?

   (A) $(9, 1)$
   (B) $(16, 25)$
   (C) $(16, 3)$
   (D) $(9, 2)$
   (E) $(18, 4)$

7. For the expression $x\sqrt{x}$, where $-100 \le x \le 100$, how many x values are there such that the expression is an integer?

(A) 100
(B) 21
(C) 20
(D) 11
(E) 10

8. Consider the following statement: If n^2 is divisible by k, then n is divisible by k, where n and k are positive integers. When is this statement true?

　　I. Whenever k is even
　　II. Whenever k is odd
　　III. Whenever k is prime

(A) I only
(B) II only
(C) III only
(D) II and III only
(E) I, II, and III

Questions 9–11 are grid-in questions.

9.　　　　**10.**　　　　**11.**

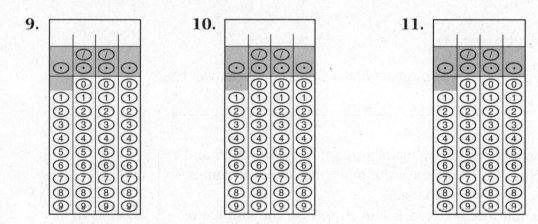

9. A population of bacteria doubles every 2 hours. What is the percent increase after 4 hours?

10. Six chairs are placed in a row to seat six people. How many different seating arrangements are possible if two of the people insist on sitting next to each other?

11. Let x, y, and z be consecutive even integers. If the product of 3 and y is 32 more than the sum of x and z, what is the median of the numbers in set $S = \{x, y, z, 2x, 2y, 2z\}$?

ANSWERS AND EXPLANATIONS

The difficulty level for each question is specified in parentheses: (M) = Medium, (H) = Hard.

1. A (M)	**4.** B (H)	**7.** D (M)	**10.** 240 (H)
2. B (M)	**5.** B (H)	**8.** C (H)	**11.** 47 (M)
3. A (H)	**6.** E (M)	**9.** 300 (M)	

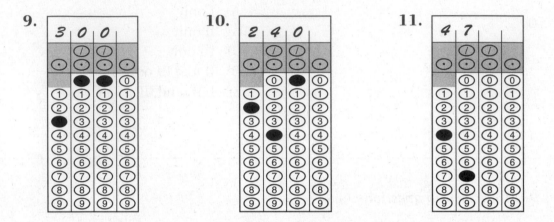

9.   10.   11.

1. The answer is **(A)**.

Draw a picture of the points on the number line:

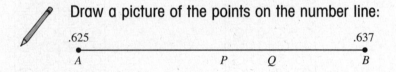

.625   .637
A   P   Q   B

Imagine blowing up the picture so that *A* is at 625 and *B* is at 637. Now solve the problem without decimals. The ratios won't change!

P is midway between *A* and *B*, so take the average of 625 and 637:

Coaching:
It is always easier to work with whole numbers than with decimals or fractions.

$$\frac{625+637}{2}=631$$

Distance $AB = 637 - 625 = 12$. Point *Q* is $\frac{2}{3}$ of the distance from *A* to *B*, and $\frac{2}{3}$ of 12 is 8. Therefore *Q* is 8 units from *A*, at 633.

Here is the picture:

625   631   633   637
A   P   Q   B

$$\frac{PQ}{AQ}=\frac{2}{8}=\frac{1}{4}, \text{ so the ratio is } 1:4.$$

Note that you don't even need the given values:

P is $\dfrac{1}{2}$ the distance from A to B, and Q is $\dfrac{2}{3}$ the distance from A to B.

Using common denominators

$$AP : AQ = \frac{3}{6} : \frac{4}{6}$$

$$\therefore PQ : AQ = \frac{1}{6} : \frac{4}{6} = 1 : 4$$

2. The answer is **(B)**.

   Since each little symbol represents the same number of people, you can reduce the problem: Which combination of two towns accounts for 45 percent of the symbols? You don't need to multiply by 10,000 at any stage! Count the number of symbols: 20; 45% of 20 = $0.45 \times 20 = 9$. The only two towns that have a total of 9 symbols are B and C.

3. The answer is **(A)**.

   Draw a picture of a 3-digit integer in set A.

h	t	o

There are 9 choices for the hundreds place and 10 choices for the tens place. (Remember: the number can't start with 0.) The ones place must contain 1, so that is the only choice. Therefore:

number of permutations $= (9)(10)(1) = 90$ elements in A.

Now draw a picture of a 3-digit integer in set B.

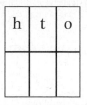

h	t	o

There are 9 choices for the hundreds place, 1 choice for the tens place, and 10 choices for the ones place. (Again, remember that the number can't start with 0.) Therefore:

number of permutations $= (9)(1)(10) = 90$ elements in B.

Each element in $A \cap B$ has both a 1 in the ones place and a 2 in the tens place: $121, 221, 321, \ldots, 921$. There are 9 such elements in $A \cap B$. To avoid counting those elements twice in $A \cup B$, you must subtract 9.

Thus $A \cup B$ contains $90 + 90 - 9 = 171$ elements.

Therefore, the number of elements in $A \cup B$ *not* in $A \cap B = 171 - 9 = 162$.

4. The answer is **(B)**.

The fewest number of stamps is seven:

$2(60 \text{ c}) + 3(37 \text{ c}) + 1(5 \text{ c}) + 1(1 \text{ c})$

Notice that if Yan uses three 60-cent stamps, there is a remainder of 57 cents. He will then need eight stamps:

$3(60 \text{ c}) + 1(37 \text{ c}) + 4(5 \text{ c})$

OR

$3(60 \text{ c}) + 2(23 \text{ c}) + 2(5 \text{ c}) + 1(1 \text{ c})$

If Yan uses one 60-cent stamp or no 60-cent stamps, he will need at least eight stamps. Try it!

Your strategy should be trial and error, trying to use three 60-cent stamps, then two, then one. You should realize that you want to include at least one 60-cent stamp in your solution because using the smaller denominations increases the number of stamps.

5. The answer is **(B)**.

Method I: Pick-Convenient-Numbers Strategy

Try 10 children whose average age is 5. Then, sum of ages = 50, and Ali's age = $(6)(5) = 30$.

The fraction $\dfrac{\text{Ali's age}}{\text{total of ages}} = \dfrac{30}{50 + 30} = \dfrac{3}{8}$.

Go through the answer choices using $x = 10$ and $y = 5$ to see which expression gives $\dfrac{3}{8}$. The only answer choice that works is $\dfrac{6}{6+x}$.

Method II: Logical Reasoning and Algebra

You have y = average age of children and x = number of children.

Let S = sum of ages of children.

Let A = Ali's age.

By the definition of arithmetic mean, $y = \dfrac{S}{x}$, so $S = xy$.

Also, $A = 6y$ (given).

$$\text{Ali's age as fraction of total ages } = \frac{A}{S + A}$$

$$= \frac{6y}{xy + 6y} = \frac{6y}{(x+6)y} = \frac{6}{6+x}$$

6. The answer is **(E)**.

Check through each ordered pair until you find the one that works. Don't be fooled by choices (A)–(D): In each case the greatest common divisor is 1, and 1 is not a prime number!

The least common multiple of 18 and 4 is the smallest integer that divides them both; 18 doesn't work. Try multiples of 18 until you find one that works; 36, which is a perfect square, fits the bill. The greatest common divisor of 18 and 4 is the largest integer that divides exactly into each of them; 4 doesn't work, but 2 does and 2 is prime. Therefore the required ordered pair is (18, 4).

7. The answer is **(D)**.

Recall that the integers are . . . , –3, –2, –1, 0, 1, 2, 3, ...

The expression $x\sqrt{x}$ will be an integer only if x is an integer perfect square. Then x could be 1, 4, 9, 16, 25, . . . ,100. But, of course, you shouldn't forget 0, which gives you 11 possible values of x. Don't even *think* of including negative numbers for x. The square root of a negative number is not a real number.

8. The answer is **(C)**.

Look for counterexamples for I, II, and III. In each case look for values of k that are *not* prime.

    I: $n = 2$, $k = 4$

        $(2)^2$ is divisible by 4, but 2 is not.

    II: $n = 3$, $k = 9$

        $(3)^2$ is divisible by 9, but 3 is not.

    III: You can't find a counterexample for III because the statement is true! Think about it this way: If n^2 is divisible by k, where k is prime, n^2 must have a factor k^2. (Otherwise you won't be able to get an exact square root.) Therefore, n must have a factor k.

9. The answer is 300.

Use the pick-a-convenient-number-for-percent-problems strategy.

Let 100 be the initial population. Then:

After 2 hours: population = 200.

After 4 hours: population = 400.

$$\text{Percent increase} = \frac{\text{actual increase}}{\text{original amount}} \times 100$$

$$= \frac{400 - 100}{100} \times 100 = 300\%.$$

Grid-in 300.

10. The answer is 240.

    Draw a picture of the chairs and the possible placements of the two people who must sit together.

The picture above shows 5 possible placements: 1–2, 2–3, 3–4, 4–5, or 5–6. In each of these cases there are 4 seats left. The number of permutations for seating the remaining 4 people is $(4)(3)(2)(1) = 24$. Multiply this number by the 5 possible two-together placements, and you get $(24)(5) = 120$. Don't pat yourself on the back yet: did you remember to multiply 120 by 2, because there are 2 ways of arranging the 2 people sitting together? Final answer $= (2)(120) = 240$.

Grid-in 240.

11. The answer is 47.

Let the consecutive even integers be x, $x + 2$, and $x + 4$, where $y = x + 2$ and $z = x + 4$.

Translate what is given into math:

$$3(x + 2) = 32 + (x + x + 4)$$
$$\therefore 3x + 6 = 2x + 36$$
$$\therefore x = 30$$
$$\therefore x = 30, y = 32, z = 34, \text{ and } S = \{30, 32, 34, 60, 64, 68\}.$$

The median of the set of numbers is the middle number when the numbers are arranged in order, or the average of the two middle numbers when the number of elements is even. In this case the median $= \dfrac{34 + 60}{2} = 47$.

Grid-in 47.

Chapter 14

TOPICS IN ALGEBRA

It goes without saying that you need to know your algebraic basics. However, whereas a beautiful algebraic solution may be the gold standard on a high school math test, on the SAT you should aim for a time-saving "quick and dirty" solution wherever possible.

2400 Club Strategies in Algebra . . .

Strategy 1: **A**lmost all equations and inequalities: plug-in the answer choices when solving.

Strategy 2: **L**inear and quadratic functions: standard form is the key.

Strategy 3: **G**raphing calculators: use for

domain and range,

max/min problems,

transformations,

intersection of graphs,

solution of inequalities.

Strategy 4: **E**xponential equations: solve with the same base on both sides.

Strategy 5: **B**oth positive and negative roots: remember these when solving $x^2 = k$.

Strategy 6: **R**adical equations: solve by isolating the radical.

Strategy 7: **A**wkward, unfamiliar function definitions: handle by applying operations to "first number" and "second number."

EXPONENTS

The laws of exponents should be second nature to high scorers.

$$a^x \cdot a^y = a^{x+y}.$$
$$a^x \div a^y = a^{x-y}.$$
$$(a^x)^y = a^{xy}.$$
$$a^0 = 1.$$

Negative exponents are also fair game on the SAT:

$$a^{-n} = \frac{1}{a^n} \text{ and } a^n = \frac{1}{a^{-n}}.$$

So are fractional exponents:

$a^{\frac{1}{n}} = \sqrt[n]{a}$, the nth root of a.

$a^{\frac{m}{n}} = \sqrt[n]{a^m} = \left(\sqrt[n]{a}\right)^m .$

Example 1

$16^{-\frac{3}{4}}$ is equal to

(A) $\dfrac{1}{12}$ (B) -8 (C) 8 (D) $-\dfrac{1}{8}$ (E) $\dfrac{1}{8}$

Solution: The answer is **(E)**.

$$16^{-\frac{3}{4}} = \frac{1}{16^{\frac{3}{4}}} = \frac{1}{\left(\sqrt[4]{16}\right)^3} = \frac{1}{2^3} = \frac{1}{8} .$$

Scientific Notation

Scientific notation is a convenient way of representing very small or very large numbers. The number is written as a number between 1 and 10 multiplied by a power of 10. For example,

$6.235 \times 10^6 = 6{,}235{,}000$ (move the decimal point 6 places to the right).
$2.08 \times 10^{-4} = 0.000208$ (move the decimal point 4 places to the left).

Example 2

If $x = 2.4 \times 10^6$ and $y = 6.0 \times 10^{-8}$, express xy in scientific notation.
(A) 1.44×10^{-1} (B) 14.4×10^{-2} (C) 1.44×10^{-2} (D) 1.44×10^{-3} (E) 14.4×10^{-3}

Solution: The answer is **(A)**.

<u>Method I</u>: Multiplication

$$
\begin{aligned}
xy &= (2.4 \times 10^6)(6.0 \times 10^{-8}) \\
&= (2.4 \times 6.0)(10^6 \times 10^{-8}) \\
&= 14.4 \times 10^{-2} .
\end{aligned}
$$

If you think choice (B) is the correct answer, look again! In scientific notation the number multiplied by the power of 10 must be between 1 and 10. You need to rewrite 14.4×10^{-2} as $(1.44 \times 10^1) \times 10^{-2} = 1.44 \times 10^{-1}$.

<u>Method II</u>: Graphing Calculator

 Set the $\boxed{\text{MODE}}$ to **Sci** (Scientific Notation) and type in $2.4 \times 10\char`^6 \times 6.0 \times 10\char`^(-8)$.

Your calculator will tell you that the answer is 1.44E–1, which means 1.44×10^{-1}. If you don't use Scientific Notation mode, you will need to convert the decimal answer, .144, to scientific notation, namely, 1.44×10^{-1}.

Monomials

You may need to use the laws of exponents to simplify a *monomial*, an algebraic expression with just one term.

Example 3

If $x^2 b^4 = ab^{-1}$, what is a in terms of b and x?

(A) $x^2 b^3$ (B) $x^2 b^5$ (C) $x^2 b^{-3}$ (D) $x^2 b^{-5}$ (E) $x^2 b^4$

Solution: The answer is **(B)**.

The question means: Solve for a.

$$x^2 b^4 = ab^{-1}$$

$$\Rightarrow \frac{a}{b} = x^2 b^4$$

$$\Rightarrow a = x^2 b^5. \quad \text{(Multiply both sides by } b.)$$

POLYNOMIALS

A *binomial* has two terms, while a *trinomial* has three. You need to be able to add, subtract, and multiply monomials and binomials.

Factoring

You also need to know the following *factored forms* or products:

$x^2 - y^2 = (x + y)(x - y)$ (Difference of perfect squares)

$x^2 + 2xy + y^2 = (x + y)^2$ (Perfect square trinomial)

$x^2 - 2xy + y^2 = (x - y)^2$ (Perfect square trinomial)

You may be expected to factor simple trinomials, For example, $x^2 - x - 12 = (x \quad)(x \quad)$.

You must find factors of -12 whose sum equals the middle coefficient, namely, -1.

Answer: $x^2 - x - 12 = (x - 4)(x + 3)$.

> **Coaching:**
> *High scorers do not make careless mistakes when factoring. They always check a factored form by taking a minute to mentally multiply the two binomials of their answer. The result must equal the given polynomial.*

Example 4

If $x^2 - y^2 = 40$, and $x - y = 4$, then $x^2 + y^2 =$

(A) $2xy$ (B) $-2xy$ (C) $100 + 2xy$ (D) $100 - 2xy$ (E) $10 - xy$

Solution: The answer is **(D)**.

<u>Method 1</u>: Algebra

$$x^2 - y^2 = (x + y)(x - y)$$

$$\Rightarrow 40 = 4(x + y)$$

$$\Rightarrow x + y = 10.$$

Now square both sides:

$$x^2 + 2xy + y^2 = 100$$
$$\Rightarrow x^2 + y^2 = 100 - 2xy.$$

<u>Method II</u>: Pick-Some-Numbers Strategy

The numbers are small enough for you to find values of x and y that satisfy the given equations, $x^2 - y^2 = 40$ and $x - y = 4$.

If you take a moment to try some of the perfect squares under 100, you can hit the jackpot with $x = 7$ and $y = 3$. (Check that these numbers work: $49 - 9 = 40$, and $7 - 3 = 4$.) You can now calculate that $x^2 + y^2 = 49 + 9 = 58$. Plugging your x and y values into the choices shows that (D) gives the right value:

$$100 - 2xy = 100 - 2(7)(3) = 100 - 42 = 58.$$

<u>Method III</u>: Algebra and Pick-Some-Numbers Strategy

$$x + y = 10 \quad \text{(See Method I.)}$$
$$x - y = 4 \quad \text{(Given.)}$$
$$\therefore 2x = 14 \quad \text{(Add the equations.)}$$
$$\therefore x = 7 \text{ and } y = 3.$$

Once you have x and y, proceed with plugging in, as shown in Method II.

RATIONAL EXPRESSIONS

A *rational expression* is a quotient of two polynomials. Typically, you simplify a rational expression by factoring the numerator and denominator and canceling common factors. For example:

$$\frac{2x^2 - 98}{x^2 + 4x - 21} = \frac{2(x^2 - 49)}{(x + 7)(x - 3)} = \frac{2(x + 7)(x - 7)}{(x + 7)(x - 3)} = \frac{2(x - 7)}{(x - 3)}.$$

ABSOLUTE VALUE

The *absolute value* of a quantity x, denoted as $|x|$, equals x if $x \geq 0$, and $-x$ if $x < 0$. For example, $|-2.3| = 2.3$, and $|10| = 10$. The answer is always positive or zero. You can think of the absolute value of a number as being its distance from 0 on a number line. Also, $|a - b| = |b - a| =$ the distance from a to b.

DIRECT AND INDIRECT VARIATION

The quantity y is *directly proportional* to a quantity x if $y = kx$, where k is constant. You can also say that y *varies directly with* x. Informally: As x increases, y increases. Notice that $\frac{y}{x}$ is constant; and if (x_1, y_1) and (x_2, y_2) satisfy the equation $y = kx$, then $\frac{y_1}{x_1} = \frac{y_2}{x_2}$.

Rate Problems

Rate problems are usually applications of direct variation; they can be solved by setting up a proportion and solving for a missing quantity.

Example 5 Grid-In

A runner covers a distance of 1 mile in 20 minutes. If he runs at the same speed the next day, how many miles will he cover in $1\frac{1}{2}$ hours?

Solution: The answer is $\frac{9}{2}$.

You've seen the familiar equation linking distance, speed, and time: $d = st$. If s, the speed, is constant, as it is in the given problem, then the equation represents a direct variation between distance d and time t. Thus $\frac{d}{t}$ is constant, and you can set up a proportion. There is, however, a pitfall: you can't use minutes in one fraction and hours in the other! Here is the correct proportion: $\frac{1}{20} = \frac{x}{90}$, where the numerator represents miles and the denominator represents minutes. Cross-multiply:

$$x = \frac{90}{20} = \frac{9}{2} \text{ miles}.$$

Grid-in 9/2 or 4.5.

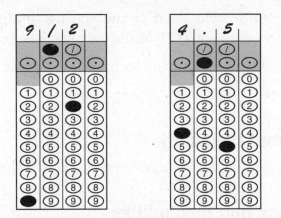

| | The 2400 Club uses the same units for all fractions in a rate problem. | |

The quantity y is *inversely proportional* to a quantity x if $y = \frac{k}{x}$, where k is constant. You can also say that y *varies indirectly with* x. In this case, as x increases, y *decreases*. Problems that involve indirect variation cannot be solved with a proportion. If (x_1, y_1) and (x_2, y_2) satisfy the equation $y = \frac{k}{x}$, then the quantity xy is constant, and $x_1 y_1 = x_2 y_2$.

Example 6

A family has enough birdseed to feed 6 parakeets for 2 weeks. For how many days would this food last if there were 7 parakeets?

(A) 11   (B) 12   (C) $\frac{12}{7}$ (D) $\frac{7}{3}$ (E) $\frac{49}{3}$

Solution: The answer is **(B)**.

Be on the lookout for this kind of problem. The situation is not direct variation: the number of days goes *down* as the number of parakeets goes *up*. You start with 14 days and can therefore eliminate choice (E) right off the bat. If you're forced to guess, choose (A) or (B); either seems reasonable. But the calculation is easy if you realize that the problem is an example of indirect variation between number of days and number of parakeets. (Parakeets) × (days) = constant; therefore, if x is the number of days, $(6)(14) = 7x \Rightarrow x = 12$.

SOLVING EQUATIONS AND INEQUALITIES

Some general rules:

1. The same quantity can be added to both sides of an equation or inequality without changing it. For example, if $x - 4 < 8$, then $x < 12$.

2. Both sides of an equation can be multiplied or divided by the same nonzero quantity. For example, if $-5x = 37$, then $x = -\dfrac{37}{5}$.

3. If both sides of an inequality are multiplied by a negative quantity, the inequality sign flips around. For example, if $-2x < 12$, then $x > -6$.

4. Fractions can be eliminated by multiplying throughout by the least common denominator (LCD) of the fractions. For example, if $\dfrac{x}{5} - \dfrac{2}{3} = 2x + \dfrac{1}{2}$, multiplying both sides by 30, the LCD, yields $6x - 20 = 60x + 15$.

Linear Equations and Inequalities

These are solved by getting the variables on one side, and the numbers on the other.

Quadratic Equations and Inequalities

These are solved by inspecting the graph on the graphing calculator or by factoring. (You will not be required to use the quadratic formula on the SAT.) For example,

$$x^2 - 6x + 8 = \Rightarrow (x - 4)(x - 2) = 0$$
$$\Rightarrow x = 4 \text{ or } 2.$$

To solve $x^2 - 6x + 8 > 0$:

$$x^2 - 6x + 8 > 0$$
$$\Rightarrow (x - 4)(x - 2) > 0.$$

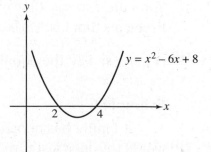

The roots are 2 and 4.

Notice that the y-values in the graph are positive outside the roots. Thus the answer is $x < 2$ or $x > 4$. If asked to solve $x^2 - 6x + 8 < 0$, note that y is negative for x-values between the roots, namely, $2 < x < 4$.

Equations with Radicals

To solve equations with radicals, isolate the radical, that is, get it by itself on one side. Then square both sides. For example:

$$\sqrt{x} - 5 = 2 \Rightarrow \sqrt{x} = 7 \Rightarrow x = 49.$$

Equations with x^2

To solve equations where x is squared, don't forget the negative root. For example:

$$x^2 = 16 \Rightarrow x = \pm 4.$$

Exponential Equations

Exponential equations on the SAT can always be written with the same base b on each side, where $b > 0$ and $b \neq 1$. You can then equate the exponents:

$$b^m = b^n \Rightarrow m = n$$

For example, to solve $3^{2x} = 27^{x-2}$, write both sides with base 3:

$$3^{2x} = 27^{x-2}$$
$$\Rightarrow 3^{2x} = \left(3^3\right)^{x-2}$$
$$\Rightarrow 3^{2x} = 3^{3x-6}$$
$$\Rightarrow 2x = 3x - 6$$
$$\Rightarrow x = 6.$$

It goes without saying that high scorers remember the distributive property when multiplying the exponents in the second line!

Equations with Rational Expressions

These equations look a lot easier when you multiply both sides by the least common denominator of the fractions. For example:

$$\frac{x-5}{x+3} = 2 \Rightarrow x - 5 = 2(x + 3)$$
$$\Rightarrow x = -11.$$

Inequalities with Rational Expressions

Tricky stuff! What you cannot do is mindlessly multiply both sides by a quantity that may be negative. See Example 8 on page 258.

Equations and Inequalities with Absolute Value

In the examples that follow, visualizing $|x|$ as the distance on the number line from x to 0 can be helpful.

Solve $|x| = 2$. Here, you want values of x whose distance from 0 is 2.

Answer: $x = 2$ or -2, as shown on the number line.

Solve $|x| < 2$. Here, you want x-values whose distance to 0 is less than 2.

Answer: $-2 < x < 2$.

Solve $|x| > 2$. Here, you want x-values whose distance to 0 is greater than 2.

Answer: $x < -2$ or $x > 2$.

Here is a useful framework to remember for the type of question on absolute value that you will encounter on the SAT:

$$|x - a| = k \Rightarrow x - a = k \text{ or } x - a = -k.$$
$$|x - a| < k \Rightarrow -k < x - a < k.$$
$$|x - a| > k \Rightarrow x - a > k \text{ or } x - a < -k.$$

Example 7

For a large Thanksgiving dinner, Mr. Gonzalez will cook a turkey that weighs at least 12 pounds but no more than 20 pounds. If x represents the weight of a turkey, in pounds, which of the following represents all possible values of x?

(A) $|x - 16| \geq 4$ (B) $|x - 16| \leq 4$ (C) $|x - 12| \leq 20$ (D) $|x - 20| \leq 16$
(E) $|x - 20| \geq 12$

Solution: The answer is **(B)**.

You need to find which of the given inequalities is equivalent to $12 \leq x \leq 20$. Choice (B) is the one that works:

$$|x - 16| \leq 4$$
$$\Rightarrow -4 \leq x - 16 \leq 4$$
$$\Rightarrow 12 \leq x \leq 20$$

Example 8

Which is the solution to $\dfrac{x - 5}{x + 3} < -1$?

(A) $x < 1$ (B) $x < -3$ or $x > 5$ (C) $-3 < x < 5$ (D) $x < -3$ or $x > 1$ (E) $-3 < x < 1$

Solution: The answer is **(E)**.

Method 1: Plug-in Strategy
Take some easy-to-plug-in numbers from the range in each answer choice. Just one number that doesn't satisfy the given inequality invalidates that choice.

Choice (A): Try $x = -10$. $\dfrac{-15}{-7} < -1$. No.

🕐 Think about what you're doing here, and notice that any number that produces a negative value in the numerator and denominator will result in a positive quantity, which can't be less than −1. Therefore, you should try a negative number whose magnitude is sufficiently large.

Can you see that $x = -10$ can be used to pull the plug on choices (B) and (D) too? You must now choose between choices (C) and (E). Try $x = 4$, which is in (C) but not in (E):

$\dfrac{4-5}{4+3} = -\dfrac{1}{7}$, which is not less than −1. The answer must be (E).

<u>Method II</u>: Algebra

Beware! You can't just multiply both sides by $x + 3$. If $x + 3$ is negative, the inequality sign must flip. Here is a solution that uses signs analysis.

$$\frac{x-5}{x+3} < -1 \Rightarrow \frac{x-5}{x+3} + 1 < 0$$

$$\Rightarrow \quad \frac{x-5}{x+3} + \frac{x+3}{x+3} < 0$$

$$\Rightarrow \quad \frac{2x-2}{x+3} < 0$$

$$\Rightarrow \quad \frac{x-1}{x+3} < 0. \quad \text{(Divide both sides by 2.)}$$

Use signs analysis, as shown below, to see that the expression is negative when $-3 < x < 1$.

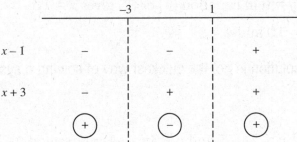

🕐 Method I is much better than Method II because it saves time. Wherever possible, use plug-in instead of tricky algebra!

Example 9

If $p + 2\sqrt{x-1} = q$, and $q > p$, what is $x - 1$ in terms of p and q?

(A) $\dfrac{\sqrt{q-p}}{2}$ (B) $\sqrt{\dfrac{q-p}{2}}$ (C) $\dfrac{q-p}{2}$ (D) $\dfrac{(q-p)^2}{2}$ (E) $\dfrac{(q-p)^2}{4}$

Solution: The answer is **(E)**.

This is an equation with a radical, so your plan should be to isolate the radical and then square both sides.

$$p + 2\sqrt{x-1} = q$$
$$\Rightarrow 2\sqrt{x-1} = q - p$$
$$\Rightarrow \sqrt{x-1} = \frac{q-p}{2}$$
$$\Rightarrow x - 1 = \frac{(q-p)^2}{4}.$$

SYSTEMS OF LINEAR EQUATIONS AND INEQUALITIES

You may be asked to solve a system of equations in two variables, for example:

$$2y + x = 22, \quad (1)$$
$$3y - 2x = -2. \quad (2)$$

Eliminate one of the variables. Rewrite equation (1) as $x = 22 - 2y$ and substitute in equation (2).

$$3y - 2(22 - 2y) = -2$$
$$\Rightarrow 3y - 44 + 4y = -2$$
$$\Rightarrow \qquad\qquad 7y = 42$$
$$\Rightarrow \qquad\qquad y = 6.$$

Substituting $y = 6$ in equation (1) or (2) gives $x = 10$.

Solution: $x = 10$ and $y = 6$

 An algebraic solution is not the quickest way of solving a system of equations on the SAT.

Example 10

The graphs of $y = 2x - 5$ and $x + 3y = -1$ intersect at

(A) $(-1, 2)$ (B) $(-2, -1)$ (C) $(2, -1)$ (D) $(-2, 1)$ (E) $(1, -2)$

Solution: The answer is **(C)**.

<u>Method I</u>: Plug-In Strategy

The ordered pair in the answer must satisfy both equations. Plug-in each answer choice until you find one that works. The numbers are easy, so you should be able to reject quickly those that don't pan out. Notice that choice (C) works:

$$-1 = 2(2)-5 \text{ and } 2+3(-1) = -1.$$

<u>Method II</u>: Graphing Calculator

 Plot $y = 2x - 5$ and $x + 3y = -1$ on the calculator. (Be sure to rewrite the second equation as $y = (-x - 1)/3$.) A quick look at the point of intersection on the graph tells you that choice (C) is the answer.

To solve a *system of linear inequalities* means to find the region on a graph that satisfies both inequalities. There are four steps to a correct solution:

1. Write each inequality in a standard form:

$$y < mx + b, \; y \le mx + b, \; y > mx + b, \text{ or } y \ge mx + b.$$

2. Sketch the line $y = mx + b$. This line is solid if the inequality is $\le$ or $\ge$, dotted for $<$ or $>$.

3. Shade the region above the line if the inequality is $>$ or $\ge$, below the line if the inequality is $<$ or $\le$.

4. The solution set for the system of inequalities is the intersection of the regions (i.e., where the shaded regions overlap).

For example, find the solution set for this system:

$4 - 2y \le x$ and $3y - 4x > 12$.

Step 1:
$$
\begin{aligned}
4 - 2y &\le x & 3y - 4x &> 12 \\
\Rightarrow -2y &\le x - 4 & \Rightarrow 3y &> 4x + 12 \\
\Rightarrow \quad y &\ge -\frac{1}{2}x + 2 & \Rightarrow y &> \frac{4}{3}x + 4
\end{aligned}
$$

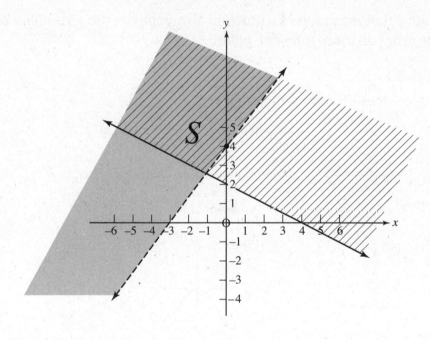

Step 2: Sketch $y = -\dfrac{1}{2}x + 2$ (solid line).

Sketch $y = \dfrac{4}{3}x + 4$ (dotted line).

Step 3: Shade above $y = -\dfrac{1}{2}x + 2$ and above $y = \dfrac{4}{3}x + 4$.

Step 4: Region S, where the two shaded regions overlap, is the solution set.

FUNCTIONS

Definition

A *function* is a relation in which each *x*-value corresponds to one and only one *y*-value. Here are some of the ways in which functions can be represented:

- A set of ordered pairs
- An equation in *x* and *y*
- A graph

From the definition you should see that a function cannot have two (or more) ordered pairs that start with the same *x*-value.

Here are three examples of functions:

(1) $y = x + 4$ (2)    (3) $\{(1, 1), (2, 1), (3, 1), ...\}$

Notice that the graph of a function always passes the *vertical line test*: No vertical line cuts the graph in more than one point.

Example 11

Which does *not* represent a function?

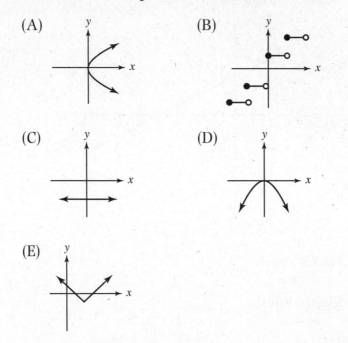

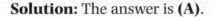

Solution: The answer is **(A)**.

Choice (A) is the only choice that fails the vertical line test. In the accompanying diagram, line ℓ, for example, cuts the graph in more than one place. In this diagram the given *x*-value corresponds to both a positive and a negative *y*-value, thereby violating the definition of a function.

Example 12

Which does *not* represent a function?

(A) $y = 4$ (B) $x + y = 4$ (C) $x^2 + y^2 = 16$ (D) $y + |x| = 1$ (E) $y = 10 - \sqrt{x}$

Solution: The answer is **(C)**.

The tip-off is the even power of y. If you solve for y, you get

$$x^2 + y^2 = 16 \Rightarrow y^2 = 16 - x^2$$
$$\Rightarrow y = \pm\sqrt{16 - x^2}$$

Take $x = 1$, for example. Both of the ordered pairs $(1, \sqrt{15})$ and $(1, -\sqrt{15})$ satisfy the equation. Two different y-values for the same x means that $x^2 + y^2 = 16$ does not represent a function. Each of the other choices gives no more than one value of y for any given x.

Function Notation

A function can be represented with $f(x)$ notation: $f(x) = (x - 3)^2$ is equivalent to $y = (x - 3)^2$. To evaluate $f(5)$, for example, means to find the value of $(x - 3)^2$ when $x = 5$:

$$f(5) = f(5 - 3)^2 = 4.$$

Similarly, $f(-1) = (-1 - 3)^2 = 16$, and $f(a) = (a - 3)^2$.

Example 13

If $f(x) = x^2 + 3$ and $g(x) = x - 5$, evaluate $f(g(9))$.

(A) 4   (B) 19   (C) 79   (D) 81   (E) 3,316

Solution: The answer is **(B)**.

To find $f(g(9))$, evaluate $g(9)$ first: $g(9) = 9 - 5 = 4$, so

$$f(g(9)) = f(4) = 4^2 + 3 = 19.$$

Example 14

If $f(x) = \dfrac{ax}{b}$ and $g(x) = \dfrac{cx^2}{a}$, then $g(f(a))$ equals

(A) ca (B) $\dfrac{a^2}{b}$ (C) $\dfrac{a^2c}{b}$ (D) $\dfrac{a^2c}{b^2}$ (E) $\dfrac{ca^3}{b^2}$

Solution: The answer is **(E)**.

This question is similar to Example 13. Just be careful with the algebraic substitution. To find $g(f(a))$, evaluate $f(a)$ first:

$$f(a) = \frac{a \cdot a}{b} = \frac{a^2}{b}$$

$$\Rightarrow g(f(a)) = g\left(\frac{a^2}{b}\right) = \frac{c}{a}\left(\frac{a^2}{b}\right)^2 = \frac{ca^4}{ab^2} = \frac{ca^3}{b^2}.$$

Domain and Range

The *domain* of a function is the set of all x-values for which the function is defined. The *range* of the function is the set of corresponding y-values produced by the function. Think of the domain as being the set of real numbers that are *allowable* x-values. Which values are *not* allowed? Any value that

- produces zero in a denominator (undefined expression) or
- produces negative values in a radical (imaginary number)

is not an allowable x-value.

Example 15

Which value is *not* in the domain of $f(x) = \sqrt{x - 5}$?

(A) 4   (B) 5   (C) 6   (D) 7   (E) 8.5

Solution: The answer is **(A)**.

Plug-in each choice for x until you find a value that gives a negative radicand. You will hit the jackpot with choice (A): $\sqrt{4 - 5} = \sqrt{-1}$. Since the radicand, $x - 5$, can't be negative, 4 cannot be in the domain of $f(x)$.

Example 16

What is the domain of $f(x) = \sqrt{81 - x^2}$?

(A) $-9 \le x \le 9$ (B) $-9 < x < 9$ (C) $0 \le x \le 9$ (D) $x \le -9$ or $x \ge 9$ (E) $x < -9$ or $x > 9$

Solution: The answer is **(A)**.

Method I: Algebra

Solve $81 - x^2 \ge 0$ (See quadratic inequalities.)

$$81 - x^2 \ge 0$$
$$\Rightarrow x^2 - 81 \le 0$$
$$\Rightarrow (x - 9)(x + 9) \le 0$$
$$\Rightarrow -9 \le x \le 9.$$

Method II: Graphing Calculator

Sketch $y = \sqrt{81 - x^2}$. Notice that you get a semicircle, where the x-values go from -9 to 9, inclusive.

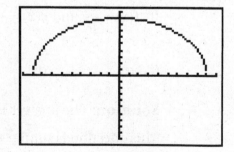

Example 17

What is the range of $f(x) = -(x - 2)^2 - 4$?

(A) All real numbers   (B) $y \ge -8$ (C) $y \le -8$ (D) $y \ge -4$ (E) $y \le -4$

Solution: The answer is **(E)**.

<u>Method I</u>: Graphing Calculator

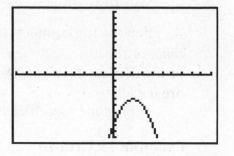

Graph $y = -(x - 2)^2 - 4$ on the graphing calculator. The graphing window shows that the
graph exists only where $y \leq -4$. Therefore, the
answer is choice (E).

<u>Method II</u>: Algebra

When a quadratic function is written in the form $f(x) = a(x - h)^2 + k$, the vertex is
(h, k). Therefore, in the given problem the vertex is $(2, -4)$. Also, since the coefficient of x^2
is negative, the curve is concave down and the function has a maximum. (Note that, if the
coefficient of x^2 is positive, the function has a minimum.) Since the maximum value of y
is -4, the range is all $y \leq -4$.

The Linear Function

A *linear function* is a function whose graph is a straight line. The *slope-intercept* form of the
equation is $y = mx + b$, where m represents the slope of the line and b the y-intercept.

If you know the coordinates of any two points on a line, you can find the slope using
the slope formula:

$$m = \frac{y_1 - y_2}{x_1 - x_2}, \ (1)$$

where (x_1, y_1) and (x_2, y_2) are the given points.

If you know the slope of the line and one point, (x_1, y_1), on the line, you can get the
point-slope form of the equation of the line:

$$y - y_1 = m(x - x_1), \ (2)$$

In particular, given two points on the line, you can get the slope first from equation
(1), and then the equation of the line, using either of the two points in equation (2).

A horizontal line has equation $y = k$, where k is a constant. The slope of a horizontal
line is zero.

A vertical line has equation $x = k$, and its slope is undefined. Note that a vertical line
does not represent a function, since there are infinitely many ordered pairs that have k as
the x-coordinate.

Here are two other facts about linear functions:

- Parallel lines have the same slope.
- Perpendicular lines have slopes that are negative reciprocals of each
  other.

Example 18

The slope of the line with equation $2x - 2y = 7$ is

(A) -1 (B) 1 (C) $\dfrac{7}{2}$ (D) $-\dfrac{7}{2}$ (E) 2

Solution: The answer is **(B)**.

Rewrite the equation in slope-intercept form:

$$2x - 2y = 7 \Rightarrow 2y = 2x - 7 \Rightarrow y = x - \frac{7}{2}.$$

Then slope = coefficient of x, which equals 1.

Example 19 Grid-In

What is the y-intercept of the line through points $(3, -2)$ and $(-1, 6)$?

Solution: The answer is 4.

The slope is

$$m = \frac{6 - (-2)}{(-1) - 3} = \frac{8}{-4} = -2.$$

The slope-intercept form of the equation is $y = -2x + b$, where b is the y-intercept. Plug in one of the points, $(-1, 6)$ say:

$$6 = -2(-1) + b \Rightarrow b = 4.$$

Grid-in 4.

Example 20

A line containing point $(2, 4)$ has slope 3. If point P lies on this line, which of the following could be point P?

(A) $(1, 7)$ (B) $(2, 6)$ (C) $(2, 7)$ (D) $(3, -1)$ (E) $(3, 7)$

Solution: The answer is **(E)**.

The slope of the line is 3. Use the slope formula with the given point $(2, 4)$ and each of the answer choices until you find a slope of 3 (plug-in strategy). Only one of the choices will work. The slope for $(3, 7)$, choice (E), and $(2, 4)$ is $\frac{7-4}{3-2} = 3$.

The numbers are easy. You should be able to zip through the choices, mentally applying the slope formula, until you find the answer. What you should *not* do is find the equation of the line containing (2, 4) with slope 3, and then plug in the coordinates of the given choices to see which satisfies the equation.

The 2400 Club is always on the lookout for shortcuts.

Example 21

What value of k will make the line containing points $(k, 3)$ and $(-2, 1)$ perpendicular to the line containing $(5, k)$ and $(1, 0)$?

(A) -4 (B) $-\frac{4}{3}$ (C) -1 (D) $-\frac{3}{4}$ (E) 4

Solution: The answer is **(B)**.

For the lines to be perpendicular, the product of the slopes must be −1:

$$\left(\frac{3-1}{k+2}\right)\left(\frac{k-0}{5-1}\right) = -1 \Rightarrow \left(\frac{2}{k+2}\right)\left(\frac{k}{4}\right) = -1 \Rightarrow k = -\frac{4}{3}.$$

Coaching:
On the SAT you will need to apply some judgment in choosing the best strategy.

The straight algebraic solution is quicker here. Plugging in requires you to deal with negative fractions and four different points, two of which contain k.

Example 22 Grid-In

The table of values shown is for some linear function $f(x)$. Find $f(10)$.

x	y
−2	−11
−1	−7
0	−3
1	1

Solution: The answer is 37.

Whichever method you choose to solve this problem, it will probably involve using the slope-intercept form of the linear equation: $y = mx + b$.

<u>Method I</u>: y-Intercept and Slope

Since $(0, -3)$ is a point on the graph, the y-intercept, b, is −3.
Since the y-values go up 4 units for every 1 unit that x goes up, the slope, m, is 4.
$\therefore$ Equation of $f(x)$ is $y = 4x - 3$
$\therefore f(10) = 4(10) - 3 = 37$.

<u>Method II</u>: y-Intercept and Plug-In

Since −3 is the y-intercept, the equation of $f(x)$ is $y = mx - 3$.
Now plug in any point from the table to find m. Plugging in $(1, 1)$ gives $1 = m - 3$ or $m = 4$. Therefore, the equation is $y = 4x - 3$, and

$$f(10) = 4(10) - 3 = 37.$$

Grid-in 37.

The Quadratic Function

A *quadratic function* is a function whose graph is a parabola. The standard form of the equation is

$$y = ax^2 + bx + c, \ a \neq 0.$$

The axis of symmetry of the graph is given by $x = -\dfrac{b}{2a}$. The constant term c represents the y-intercept. If the coefficient of x^2, a, is positive, the graph is concave up; otherwise it is concave down.

concave up, $a > 0$ concave down, $a < 0$

Also, a controls the "fatness" of the parabola: the bigger the magnitude of a, the narrower the parabola.

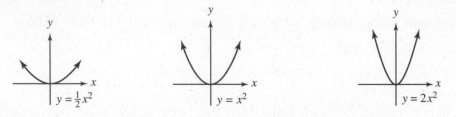

Here are some facts you should know about the quadratic function:

■ The x-intercepts (or roots) of the function can be obtained by solving $ax^2 + bx + c = 0$. Use factoring or the quadratic formula:

$$x = \frac{-b \pm \sqrt{b^2 - 4ac}}{2a}.$$

(**Note:** You will not be required to use the quadratic formula on the SAT.)

■ The sum of the roots is $-\dfrac{b}{a}$.

■ The product of the roots is $\dfrac{c}{a}$.

■ A quadratic function is often written in the form $y = (x - h)^2 + k$. The axis of symmetry is $x = h$, and the vertex is (h, k).

Example 23

Which could be the graph of $y = x^2 + 3x + k$, where k is an integer?

(A)   (B)   (C)

(D)   (E)

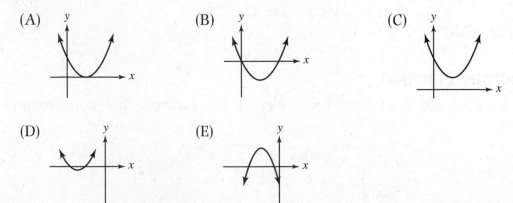

Solution: The answer is **(D)**.

Since the coefficient of x^2 is positive, the graph must be concave up, so eliminate choice (E). Also, the axis of symmetry is $x = -\dfrac{b}{2a} = -\dfrac{3}{2}$, which is to the left of the y-axis, so eliminate choices (A)–(C). The correct choice is (D).

Example 24

Which function has a double root?

(A) $y = x^2 + 4x - 4$ (B) $y = x^2 - 4$ (C) $y = x^2 + x + 1$ (D) $y = x^2 + 6x + 9$
(E) $y = x^2 - x - 6$

Solution: The answer is **(D)**.

Method I: Perfect Square
To have a double root, the quadratic expression must be a perfect square. Only choice (D), where $y = (x + 3)^2$, satisfies this requirement.

Method II: Graphing Calculator

For the function to have a double root, the parabola must be tangent to the x-axis. Graphing each answer choice will show choice (D) to be the only graph to satisfy this requirement. Using the graphing calculator on this problem, however, is a desperation measure: the method is unnecessarily time-consuming.

Example 25

If $f(x) = ax^2 + bx + c$, $a \neq 0$ and a, b, and c are all negative, which could be the graph of $f(x)$?

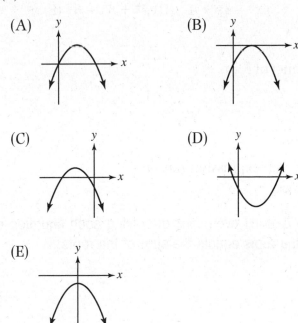

(A)

(B)

(C)

(D)

(E)

Solution: The answer is **(C)**.

Since $a < 0$, the graph must be concave down, so eliminate choice (D). Also since $c < 0$, the y-intercept must be negative, so eliminate choice (A). Finally, since $a < 0$ and $b < 0$, the axis of symmetry must be $x =$ (a negative number), since $x = -\dfrac{b}{2a}$. The only choice that satisfies this requirement is (C).

Example 26

The x-intercepts of a quadratic function are 2 and -4. Which could be the function?

$$\text{I.} \quad y = x^2 + 2x - 8$$
$$\text{II.} \quad y = -2x^2 - 4x + 16$$
$$\text{III.} \quad y = (x + 1)^2 - 9$$

(A) I only   (B) II only   (C) I and II only   (D) I and III only   (E) I, II, and III

Solution: The answer is **(E)**.

A quadratic function with roots 2 and -4 is $y = (x - 2)(x + 4) = x^2 + 2x - 8$, so function I works. Also, $y = a(x - 2)(x + 4)$ works. Function II is simply function I multiplied by -2, so Function II works also. Multiplying out Function III gives the same expression as in Function I. All three functions work.

Example 27

For the function $f(x) = ax^2 + bx + c$, $a \neq 0$, the sum of the roots is equal to the product of the roots. Which could be $f(x)$?

(A) $x^2 + x + 2$ (B) $x^2 - 2x + 1$ (C) $x^2 - 4x + 4$ (D) $x^2 + 3x - 6$ (E) $x^2 + x + 1$

Solution: The answer is **(C)**.

Notice that sum of roots $=$ product of roots

$$\Rightarrow -\frac{b}{a} = \frac{c}{a}$$
$$\Rightarrow -b = c.$$

Go through each choice to see which expression has $-b = c$.
Choice (C) is the only one that does.

 For problems such as Example 27, don't even *think* of solving each equation and then checking whether the product of the roots equals the sum of the roots.

Example 28

A stone projected vertically upward with initial velocity of 112 feet per second moves according to the equation

$$s = 112t - 16t^2,$$

where s is the distance, in feet, from the ground, and t is time, in seconds. What is the maximum height reached by the stone?

(A) 16 feet   (B) 96 feet   (C) 112 feet   (D) 196 feet   (E) 672 feet

Solution: The answer is **(D)**.

Method I: Graphing Calculator

 Graph $y = 112x - 16x^2$. Adjust the [WINDOW] to allow **Ymax** to be 200. The vertex of the parabola is close to **Ymax**. Therefore, the answer must be choice D, 196 feet. (You can check using [TRACE], but should not waste the time. None of the other answer choices is close!)

Method II: Axis of Symmetry

The maximum value is on the axis of symmetry, given by

$$t = \frac{-112}{2(-16)} = \frac{7}{2}.$$

$$\therefore s = 112\left(\frac{7}{2}\right) - 16\left(\frac{7}{2}\right)^2 = 196.$$

Notice that you have enough information to solve the problem without using the initial velocity (it is built into the equation).

> The 2400 Club is not sidetracked by extraneous tidbits of information.

Transformations

Here is a summary of different transformations and their effects on the graph of $f(x)$. Given the graph of $f(x)$, you should know which transformation produces a related graph. In the table, assume $k > 0$ is a constant.

Related Function	Transformation of $f(x)$ That Produces It
$f(x) + k$	Vertical shift, k units up
$f(x) - k$	Vertical shift, k units down
$f(x + k)$	Horizontal shift, k units to the left
$f(x - k)$	Horizontal shift, k units to the right
$-f(x)$	Reflection across the x-axis
$f(-x)$	Reflection across the y-axis
$kf(x)$	Vertical dilation from the x-axis by a factor of k
$f(kx)$	Horizontal dilation from the y-axis by a factor of $\frac{1}{k}$

For example, suppose that $f(x) = x^2$.

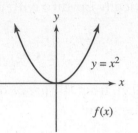

Shown below are the related graphs.

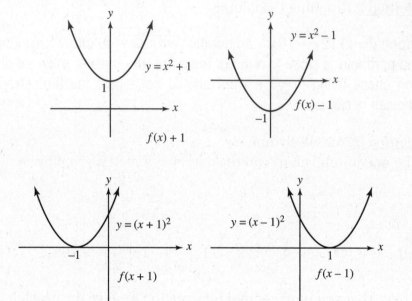

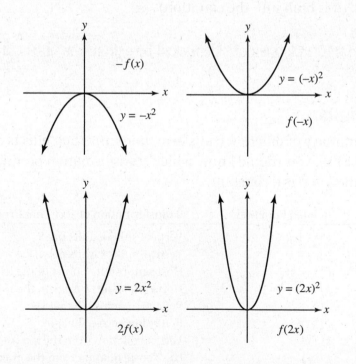

Example 29

If $f(x) = -x^2$, which represents the graph of $f(x) + 3$?

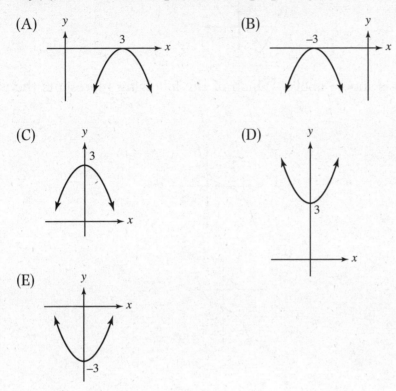

(A)

(B)

(C)

(D)

(E)

Solution: The answer is **(C)**.

Method I: Graphing Calculator

A calculator solution makes the problem trivial. Graph $y = -x^2 + 3$, and note that choice (C) matches the graph shown in the graphing window.

Method II: Transformation of $f(x) = -x^2$
The graph of $f(x) = -x^2$, shown below, is one you've memorized by now.

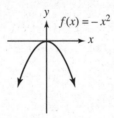

The required graph is the graph of $f(x)$ shifted vertically 3 units up—choice (C).

Example 30

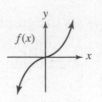

The graph of $f(x)$ is shown above. Which of the following represents the graph of $f(x-3)$?

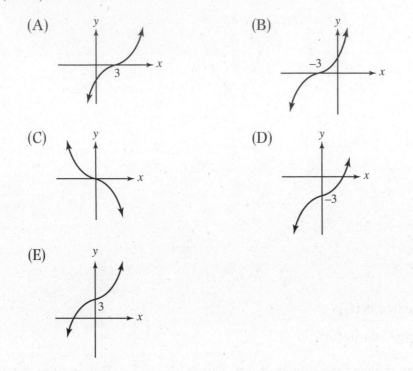

Solution: The answer is **(A)**.

The graph of $f(x-3)$ is produced when $f(x)$ is shifted horizontally 3 units to the right: choice (A).

Example 31

For the function $f(x) = x^2 + 2x - 6$, if the graph of $f(x)$ is reflected across the x-axis, the graph of a new function, $g(x)$, is produced. Find $g(3)$.

(A) –21   (B) –9   (C) –3   (D) 3   (E) 9

Solution: The answer is **(B)**.

When $f(x)$ is reflected across the x-axis, the graph of $-f(x)$ is obtained.

$$-f(x) = -x^2 - 2x + 6 = g(x)$$

Then $g(3) = -(3)^2 - 2(3) + 6 = -9$, choice (B).

Functions as Models

On the SAT you are often given a formula for a function and asked about the graph, or vice versa. But, as you know, real-world situations can be modeled using functions. Sometimes, therefore, you will be given the story behind the function and then be asked about the graph or the equation of the function.

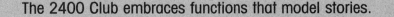

The 2400 Club embraces functions that model stories.

Example 32

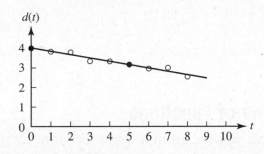

Joe bikes 4 kilometers to school. Because of the traffic and road conditions along the way, his speed varies. The dots on the graph above show his distance from the school at various times, starting at home at $t = 0$ (black dot). After 5 minutes Joe is 3.2 kilometers from the school (second black dot). The data show that his speed is almost constant, and his distance from the school can be approximated by a straight line. The graph of the function that models Joe's distance from school as a function of time, in minutes, is shown as a solid line. Which of the following equations best represents this function?

(A) $d(t) = -0.5t + 4$ (B) $d(t) = -6.25t + 4$ (C) $d(t) = -0.16t + 4$ (D) $d(t) = 0.16t + 4$
(E) $d(t) = 0.5t + 4$

Solution: The answer is **(C)**.

The given function is linear and has the form $d = mt + 4$. The slope m differs in each answer choice. The line shown has negative slope, so eliminate choices (D) and (E). Then eliminate choice (B): the slope in the given graph is small, close to 0, so a slope of -6.25 is too steep. You must now choose between choices (A) and (C).

 Even though you are given points (0, 4) and (5, 3.2) on the line, don't waste time with the slope formula. Get the answer quickly by noticing that $\dfrac{\text{rise}}{\text{run}} \approx -\dfrac{1}{5}$, which is closer to -0.16 than to -0.5.

Example 33

If you drive at x miles per hour and apply your brakes, your stopping distance, in feet, is approximately

$$f(x) = x + \frac{x^2}{20}.$$

By approximately what percent will your stopping distance increase if you increase your speed from 20 miles per hour to 30 miles per hour?

(A) 25%   (B) 35%   (C) 47%   (D) 75%   (E) 88%

Solution: The answer is **(E)**.

$$f(20) = 20 + \frac{400}{20} = 40 \text{ feet,}$$

$$f(30) = 30 + \frac{900}{20} = 75 \text{ feet,}$$

and increase = 75 − 40 = 35 feet.

Therefore, the percent increase is $\left(\dfrac{35}{40}\right) \times 100 = 87.5\% \approx 88\%$.

Unfamiliar Definitions of Functions

Sometimes on the SAT you are given a weird formula, with an unusual symbol, for producing a new value, for example, $a \triangle b = a - 2b^2$, where a and b are integers. You can say this formula in words: "a triangle b" equals the first number a minus two times the square of the second number b.

$$\therefore 12 \triangle 3 = 12 - 2(3)^2 = 12 - 18 = -6.$$

Example 34

Let $x_{(n)} \otimes y_{(n)} = $ the positive integer remainder when xy is divided by n, where x, y, and n are positive integers. What is the value of $4_{(4)} \otimes 8_{(4)}$?

(A) 0   (B) 1   (C) 2   (D) 3   (E) 4

Solution: The answer is **(A)**.

Put the formula into words: $4_{(4)} \otimes 8_{(4)}$ is the remainder when (4)(8) is divided by 4. The remainder is 0.

PRACTICE TEST QUESTIONS

1. The distance *d*, in miles, that an object travels at a uniform speed is directly proportional to the number of hours *t* it travels. If the object travels 6 miles in 2 hours, which could be the graph of the relationship between *d* and *t*?

(A)

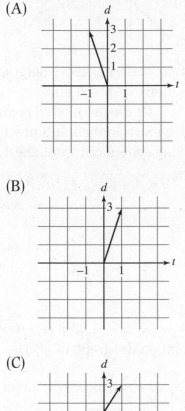

(B)

(C)

(D)

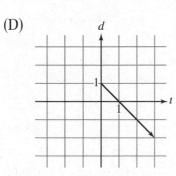

(E)

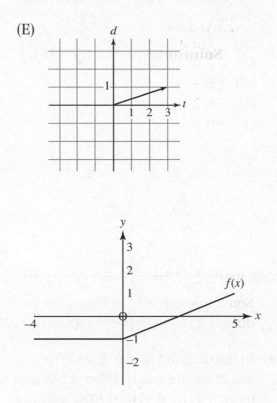

2. The graph of *f*(*x*), which is defined for all *x*-values from –4 to 5, inclusive, is shown above. What is the range of *f*(*x*)?

(A) $y \in \{-4, -3, -2, -1, 0, 1, 2, 3, 4, 5\}$
(B) $y \geq -1$
(C) $-4 \leq y \leq 5$
(D) $-1 \leq y \leq 1$
(E) All real numbers

3. A function *f*(*x*) is defined as follows:

$$f(x) = \begin{cases} \dfrac{3}{x-2}, & x < 0 \\ |x|, & x \geq 0 \end{cases}$$

What is the domain of *f*(*x*)?

(A) All real numbers
(B) All real numbers except *x* = 2
(C) All real numbers except *x* = 2 or –2
(D) $x \geq 0$
(E) $x \leq 0$

4. Let $[[x]]$ = the greatest integer that does not exceed x. If $f(x) = x + [[x]]$, then $f(-3.2) =$

(A) −7.2

(B) −7

(C) −6.4

(D) −6.2

(E) −6

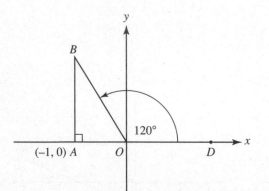

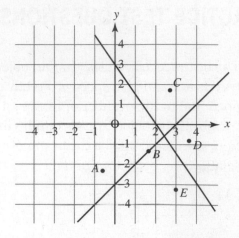

5. In the diagram above, A and D are points on the x-axis. Point A has coordinates $(-1, 0)$, and m < BOD measures $120°$. What is the slope of line $\overrightarrow{BO}$?

(A) $\sqrt{3}$

(B) $\dfrac{\sqrt{3}}{2}$

(C) $-\dfrac{1}{2}$

(D) $-\dfrac{\sqrt{3}}{2}$

(E) $-\sqrt{3}$

6. The lines shown in the above diagram have equations $x - y = 3$ and $3x + 2y = 6$. Of the five labeled points, A–E, which one is in the solution set of the following system of inequalities?

$$x - y < 3 \text{ and } 3x + 2y \leq 6$$

(A) A

(B) B

(C) C

(D) D

(E) E

7. Let $f(x) = -x^2 + 2x + 3$. If $g(x) = f(-x)$, then a point on the graph of $g(x)$ is

(A) $(-1, 6)$

(B) $(-1, 4)$

(C) $(-1, 3)$

(D) $(-1, 0)$

(E) $(-1, -1)$

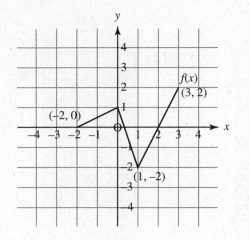

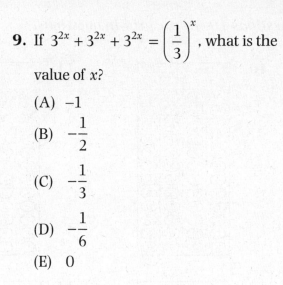

9. If $3^{2x} + 3^{2x} + 3^{2x} = \left(\dfrac{1}{3}\right)^x$, what is the value of x?

(A) -1

(B) $-\dfrac{1}{2}$

(C) $-\dfrac{1}{3}$

(D) $-\dfrac{1}{6}$

(E) 0

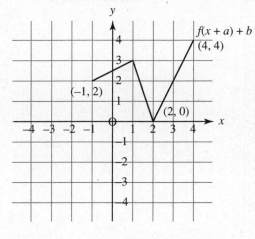

8. The graphs shown above represent $f(x)$ and $f(x + a) + b$, where a and b are constants. Which of the following is the ordered pair (a, b)?

(A) $(1, 2)$
(B) $(2, 1)$
(C) $(-1, 2)$
(D) $(2, -1)$
(E) $(-1, -2)$

Questions 10–14 are grid-in questions.

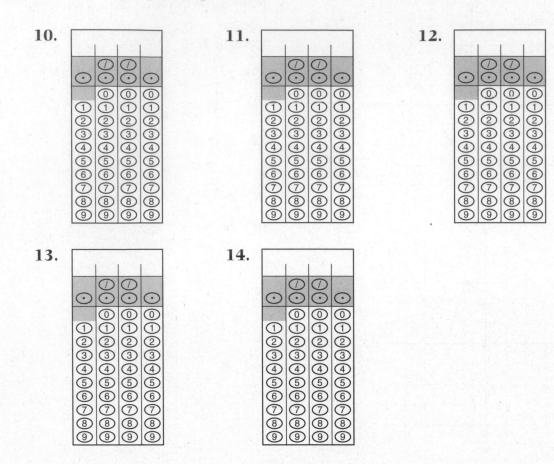

10. Find an integer value of x that satisfies both of the inequalities below:

$$|3x - 5| < 20 \text{ and } |x + 2| > 8.$$

11. Let $f(x) = x^2 - 5x + 2$ and $g(x) = f(x - 4)$. Find the positive root of the equation

$$f(x) = g(2).$$

12. A statistics class investigated the cost of cheesecakes at different bakeries around town. Given that $P(x)$ was the cost, in dollars, of a cheesecake with diameter x, the function that best fit the data collected by the class was

$$P(x) = \frac{1}{2}x^2 - 5x + 20.$$

According to this model, what was the *least* amount, in dollars, that a town resident could pay for a cheesecake?

13. If $f(x) = x^2 + x - 42$ and $f(p - 1) = 0$, what is a positive value of p?

14. If $\left(\dfrac{1}{3}\right)^x = \left(81\right)^{x-1}$, find the value of x.

ANSWERS AND EXPLANATIONS

The difficulty level for each question is specified in parentheses.

1. B (M)	**4.** A (H)	**7.** B (M)	**10.** 7 or 8 (M)	**13.** 7 (M)
2. D (M)	**5.** E (M)	**8.** C (H)	**11.** 7 (H)	**14.** 4/5 or .8 (M)
3. A (H)	**6.** A (M)	**9.** C (H)	**12.** 7.50 or 7.5 or 15/2 (M)	

10. 7 *or* 8   **11.** 7

12. 7.50 *or* 7.5 *or* 15/2

13. 7   **14.** 4/5 *or* .8

1. The answer is **(B)**.

   Since the object travels 6 miles in 2 hours, its speed, which is constant, is $\frac{6}{2} = 3$. The equation of the relationship is therefore $d = 3t$. The graph is a line passing through the origin with slope 3. Eliminate choices (C) and (D), which don't pass through the origin. Eliminate choices (A) and (again!) (D) since these have negative slopes. Choice (E) is wrong because the line has slope $\frac{1}{3}$ (rise of 1 over 3 horizontal units). The correct answer is therefore choice (B).

2. The answer is **(D)**.

   The range of $f(x)$ is the range of y-values produced by the function. In the graph, these y-values extend from -1 to 1, inclusive. Therefore, $-1 \le y \le 1$ is the required range.

3. The answer is **(A)**.

   You want all real values of x except those that give 0 in a denominator or a negative value in a radicand. Don't be fooled into thinking that choice B is the correct answer to this question. The function is defined as $f(x) = \frac{3}{x-2}$ for *negative x-values only*; the expression $\frac{3}{x-2}$ is defined for all $x < 0$. Similarly, $f(x) = |x|$ is defined for all x, and in particular for $x \ge 0$. Thus, $f(x)$ is defined for all x, and the domain is the set of all real numbers.

4. The answer is **(A)**.

   $f(x) = x + [[x]] \Rightarrow f(-3.2) = -3.2 + [[-3.2]]$.

   This is a straightforward question if you realize that the greatest integer not bigger than -3.2 is -4, not -3. High scorers know that you always go *left* on the number line to find the greatest integer that does not exceed x.

   $\therefore f(-3.2) = -3.2 - 4 = -7.2$.

5. The answer is **(E)**.

   From the given information you can conclude that $AO = 1$, m < $BOA = 60°$, and $\triangle BAO$ is a 30–60–90° triangle.

   $\therefore$ point B has coordinates $(-1, \sqrt{3})$.

   Use the slope formula or inspection to see that the slope of $\overleftrightarrow{BO}$ is $-\sqrt{3}$.

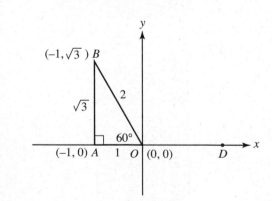

6. The answer is **(A)**.

Method I: Algebra (Your math teacher would be proud.)

Write the inequalities in standard form:

$y < mx + b$ and $y > mx + b$.

$x - y < 3 \Rightarrow -y < -x + 3 \Rightarrow y > x - 3$.

(Multiply both sides by -1.)

The points that satisfy this inequality are above the line $y = x - 3$, not including the line (dotted line in the graph).

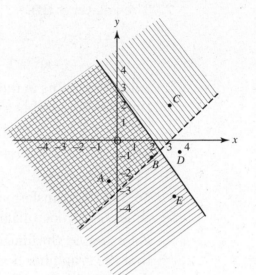

$$3x + 2y \leq 6 \Rightarrow 2y \leq -3x + 6 \Rightarrow y \leq -\frac{3}{2}x + 3$$

The points that satisfy this inequality are below the line $y = -\frac{3}{2}x + 3$, including the line (solid line in the graph).

The region that satisfies both inequalities is the double-hatched shaded region on the graph. Point A is the only point in the required region. Notice that point B is not correct because points on the dotted line are not included. If the given inequality had been $y \geq x - 3$, then B would have satisfied the system of inequalities.

Method II: Plug-In (Faster!)

Notice that the two intersecting lines divide the plane into four regions and that each point, with the exception of B, is in a different region. A fast way to solve this problem is to select an easy point with integer coordinates in each region. If your point satisfies both inequalities, then the given point in that region must be the answer. (Don't waste time with point B: it's on a line that must be dotted, indicating that the points on it are not part of the solution.)

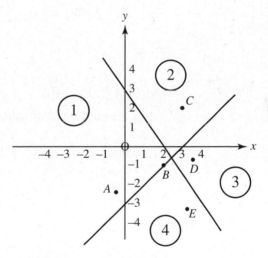

Choice (A): A good point to pick in A's region is $(0, 0)$.

$$x - y < 3 \qquad\qquad 3x + 2y \leq 6$$
$$\Rightarrow 0 - 0 < 3? \qquad \Rightarrow 0 + 0 \leq 6?$$
$$\text{Yes!} \qquad\qquad\qquad \text{Yes!}$$

Therefore point A is the required answer.

7. The answer is **(B)**.

$$f(x) = -x^2 + 2x + 3$$

$$\therefore f(-x) = -(-x)^2 + 2(-x) + 3 = -x^2 - 2x + 3 = g(x).$$

All of the points in the answer choices have $x = -1$. Find $g(-1)$ to locate the coordinates that satisfy the function:

$$g(-1) = -(-1)^2 - 2(-1) + 3 = -1 + 2 + 3 = 4$$

The required point is $(-1, 4)$.

8. The answer is **(C)**.

To find the transformation on $f(x)$, simplify the problem by following a single, easily identifiable point of $f(x)$.

For example, the image of $(-2, 0)$ is $(-1, 2)$. From this, you can work out that the graph has been shifted 1 unit to the right and 2 units up. Thus, $f(x + a) + b$ is $f(x - 1) + 2$, and (a, b) is $(-1, 2)$.

9. The answer is **(C)**.

Method I: Algebra

$$3^{2x} + 3^{2x} + 3^{2x} = \left(\frac{1}{3}\right)^x$$

$$\Rightarrow \quad 3\left(3^{2x}\right) = \left(3^{-1}\right)^x$$

$$\Rightarrow \quad 3^{2x+1} = 3^{-x}$$

$$\Rightarrow \quad 2x + 1 = -x$$

$$\Rightarrow \quad x = -\frac{1}{3}.$$

Method II: Plug-In

You can easily eliminate choices (A), (B), and (E).

Choice (A): $3^{-2} + 3^{-2} + 3^{-2} \stackrel{?}{=} \left(\frac{1}{3}\right)^{-2}$

$$\Rightarrow \frac{1}{9} + \frac{1}{9} + \frac{1}{9} \stackrel{?}{=} 3^2 \quad \text{No}$$

Choice (B): $3^{-1} + 3^{-1} + 3^{-1} \stackrel{?}{=} \left(\frac{1}{3}\right)^{-1}$

$$\Rightarrow \frac{1}{3} + \frac{1}{3} + \frac{1}{3} \stackrel{?}{=} 3 \quad \text{No}$$

Choice (E): $3^0 + 3^0 + 3^0 \stackrel{?}{=} \left(\frac{1}{3}\right)^0$

$$\Rightarrow 1 + 1 + 1 \stackrel{?}{=} 1 \quad \text{No}$$

Plugging in the negative fractions is somewhat harder, but the laws of exponents don't let you down, and you *can* come up with the answer.

Choice (C): $3^{-\frac{2}{3}} + 3^{-\frac{2}{3}} + 3^{-\frac{2}{3}} \overset{?}{=} \left(\frac{1}{3}\right)^{-\frac{1}{3}}$

$$\Rightarrow 3\left(3^{-\frac{2}{3}}\right) \overset{?}{=} 3^{\frac{1}{3}}$$

$$\Rightarrow 3^1 \cdot 3^{-\frac{2}{3}} \overset{?}{=} 3^{\frac{1}{3}} \quad \text{Yes!}$$

10. The answer is 7 or 8.

<u>Method I</u>: Algebra

$$|3x - 5| < 20 \qquad\qquad |x + 2| > 8$$
$$\Rightarrow -20 < 3x - 5 < 20 \qquad \Rightarrow x + 2 > 8 \text{ or } x + 2 < -8$$
$$\Rightarrow -15 < 3x < 25 \qquad \Rightarrow x > 6 \text{ or } x < -10$$
$$\Rightarrow -5 < x < 8\frac{1}{3}$$

The only integer values of x that satisfy both inequalities are 7 and 8. Pick either one of these and grid it in.

Your impeccable algebra in Method I just got you a gold star, but you didn't win any kudos on the SAT. You wasted a lot of time. The following time-saving method is far superior.

<u>Method II</u>: Plug-In

Notice that the smallest positive integer that satisfies $|x + 2| > 8$ is $x = 7$. Your plan should be to keep trying integers from 7 on until you find one that works in the other inequality. (**Note:** Since this is a grid-in question, the answer can't be negative.) When you plug in 7, it works: $|3(7) - 5| < 20$! End of story. Grid-in 7.

11. The answer is 7.

$$f(x) = x^2 - 5x + 2 \text{ and } g(x) = f(x - 4)$$

$$\therefore g(2) = f(2 - 4) = f(-2) = (-2)^2 - 5(-2) + 2 = 16.$$

Solve $f(x) = g(2)$:

$$x^2 - 5x + 2 = 16$$
$$\Rightarrow x^2 - 5x - 14 = 0$$
$$\Rightarrow (x - 7)(x + 2) = 0$$
$$\Rightarrow x = 7 \text{ or } -2.$$

The positive root is 7.

Grid-in 7.

12. The answer is 7.50 or 7.5 or 15/2.

Reduce the problem: Find the smallest possible value of

$$P(x) = \frac{1}{2}x^2 - 5x + 20.$$

<u>Method I</u>: Graphing Calculator

Graph $y = .5x^2 - 5x + 20$.
Use the **Minimum** function in the $\boxed{\text{CALC}}$ menu.
This shows $y = 7.5$ when $x = 4.9999996$.

Therefore, the least possible cost is $7.50.

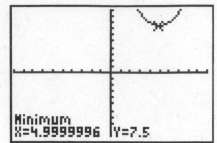

Minimum
X=4.9999996 Y=7.5

<u>Method II</u>: Algebra

The minimum value of a quadratic function occurs on the axis of symmetry.

Axis of symmetry is $x = \dfrac{-b}{2a} = \dfrac{-(-5)}{2\left(\dfrac{1}{2}\right)} = 5$.

$$P(5) = \frac{1}{2}(5)^2 - 5(5) + 20$$

$$= \frac{25}{2} - 25 + 20$$

$$= \frac{15}{2}.$$

Grid-in 7.5 or 7.50 or 15/2.

13. The answer is 7.

<u>Method I</u>: Algebraic Substitution

Let $k = p - 1$. Then:

$$f(p-1) = f(k) = k^2 + k - 42 = 0$$
$$\Rightarrow (k+7)(k-6) = 0$$
$$\Rightarrow k = -7 \text{ or } 6.$$
$$\therefore p - 1 = -7 \text{ or } p - 1 = 6.$$

A positive value for p is 7.

<u>Method II</u>: (Harder) Algebra

$$f(p-1) = 0 \Rightarrow (p-1)^2 + (p-1) - 42 = 0$$
$$\Rightarrow p^2 - 2p + 1 + p - 1 - 42 = 0$$
$$\Rightarrow p^2 - p - 42 = 0$$
$$\Rightarrow (p-7)(p+6) = 0.$$
$$\Rightarrow p = 7 \text{ is the positive root.}$$

Grid-in 7.

14. The answer is $\dfrac{4}{5}$ or .8.

Your goal is to write the left and right sides of the equation with the same base.

Remember: if $a^p = a^q$ then $p = q$. The numbers in the equation suggest base 3.

$$\left(\frac{1}{3}\right)^x = \left(81\right)^{x-1}$$
$$\Rightarrow \left(3^{-1}\right)^x = \left(3^4\right)^{x-1}$$
$$\Rightarrow \quad 3^{-x} = 3^{4x-4}$$
$$\Rightarrow \quad -x = 4x - 4$$
$$\Rightarrow \quad x = \frac{4}{5}.$$

Grid-in 4/5 or .8.

Chapter 15

TOPICS IN GEOMETRY

High scorers know the basic facts. Areas, angles, triangles, polygons, trig ratios, symmetries, solids, and coordinate geometry should be second nature to you. Other than knowing your facts, there is just one major strategy in solving problems in geometry: open your test booklet, pick up your active pencil, and **DRAW**!

2400 Club "Active Pencil" Strategy for Geometry . . .

Strategy 1: **D**raw a diagram if one is not provided.

Strategy 2: **R**ecord what's given on your diagram.

Strategy 3: **A**dd line segments to your diagram:

perpendicular lines,

parallel lines,

extended lines,

segments connecting points,

radii.

Strategy 4: **W**atch out for "Figure not drawn to scale." You may need to redraw to scale.

POINTS, LINES, ANGLES

The SAT distinguishes between geometric objects and their measures. You should be familiar with the following definitions and corresponding notations.

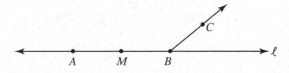

In the figure above:

- $\overleftrightarrow{AB}$, $\overleftrightarrow{MB}$, and $\overleftrightarrow{AM}$ all denote *line* ℓ, the line containing points A, M, and B.

- $\overline{AM}$ is the *line segment* with endpoints A and M. It does not contain point B.

- AM is the length of $\overline{AM}$.

- $\overrightarrow{BC}$ is the *ray* with endpoint B that contains C. Notice that ray $\overrightarrow{MA}$ does not contain B, but ray $\overrightarrow{AM}$ does.

- $\angle CBA$ is the *angle* formed by rays $\overrightarrow{BC}$ and $\overrightarrow{BA}$.

- m$\angle CBA$ is the measure of $\angle CBA$.

- M is the *midpoint* of $\overline{AB}$ if and only if $\overline{AM}$ is congruent to $\overline{BM}$, denoted as $\overline{AM} \cong \overline{BM}$. This implies that $AM = BM$.

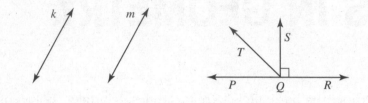

In the figure above:

- Line k is *parallel* to line m. Denote this as $k \parallel m$.

- Line $\overrightarrow{PR}$ is *perpendicular* to ray $\overrightarrow{QS}$, denoted as $\overrightarrow{PR} \perp \overrightarrow{QS}$. If $\overrightarrow{PR} \perp \overrightarrow{QS}$, then $\angle SQR$ and $\angle SQP$ are *right angles*, and m$\angle SQR$ = m$\angle SQP$ = 90°.

- $\angle TQP$ is an *acute angle* since m$\angle TQP$ is less than 90°.

- $\angle TQR$ is an *obtuse angle* since m$\angle TQR$ is between 90° and 180°.

- $\angle TQP$ and $\angle TQS$ are *complementary*, that is, the sum of their measures is 90°.

- Two angles are *supplementary* if the sum of their measures is 180°. Two adjacent angles on a line are supplementary. Thus the following pairs of angles are supplementary:

  $\angle PQT$ and $\angle TQR$, $\angle PQS$ and $\angle RQS$.

Parallel Lines

Here are some angle relationships that you should know when parallel lines are cut by a transversal and when two lines intersect.

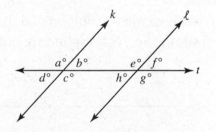

Given $k \parallel \ell$, cut by transversal t, in the figure above:
- *Corresponding angles* are congruent.
  $\therefore a = e$, $b = f$, $d = h$, and $c = g$.
- *Alternate interior angles* are congruent.
  $\therefore c = e$ and $b = h$.
- *Interior angles on the same side of a transversal* are supplementary.
  $\therefore b + e = 180°$ and $c + h = 180°$.

■ When two lines intersect, *vertical angles* are formed. Vertical angles are congruent.
∴ $a = c$, $b = d$, $e = g$, and $f = h$

Example 1

Let A, P, Q, and B be points on $\overline{AB}$, as shown above. If $AP : PQ = 1 : 4$, $PQ : QB = 8 : 3$, and AP, PQ, and QB are all integer lengths, which could be the length of $\overline{AB}$?

    (A) 61   (B) 62   (C) 63   (D) 64   (E) 65

Solution: The answer is **(E)**.

<u>Method I</u>: Logical Reasoning
Notice that $AP : PQ : QB = 1 : 4 : 1.5$. Since each length must be an integer, the lengths could be 2, 8, and 3. Total number of parts equals $2 + 8 + 3 = 13$. Of the choices given, only E, 65, is a multiple of 13. Note that $13 \times 5 = 65$, and multiplying each of the lengths 2, 8, and 3 by 5 gives 10, 40, and 15, which add up to 65. Note also that 2, 8, and 3 can be scaled so that their sum is any of answer choices (A)–(E), but only for a multiple of 13 do the lengths have integer values.

<u>Method II</u>: Algebra
The ratio $AP : PQ : QB = 2 : 8 : 3$.
If $AP = 2x$, then $PQ = 8x$, and $QB = 3x$.
∴ $AB = 13x$

If you set $13x$ equal to any of the answer choices, you notice that $13x = 65$ is the only case that gives integer values for each of the lengths.

Example 2 Grid-In

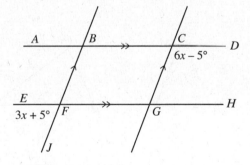

In the figure shown above, $\overleftrightarrow{BC} \parallel \overleftrightarrow{FG}$ and $\overleftrightarrow{BF} \parallel \overleftrightarrow{CG}$. If $m\angle EFJ = 3x + 5$, and $m \angle DCG = 6x - 5$, what is the measure, in degrees, of $\angle CBF$?

Solution: The answer is 115.

Label $\angle BFG$ and $\angle CBF$ as shown: $\angle 1$ and $\angle 2$, respectively.

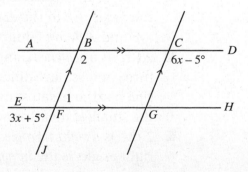

You are required to find $m \angle 2$.
$\angle 1$ and $\angle EFJ$ are vertical angles.
∴ $m \angle 1 = 3x + 5$ (vertical angles congruent).
$\angle 2$ and $\angle DCG$ are corresponding angles
($\overleftrightarrow{BF} \parallel \overleftrightarrow{CG}$ cut by $\overleftrightarrow{AD}$).

$\therefore \mathrm{m} \angle 2 = 6x - 5$ (corresponding $\angle$s' $\cong$).

$\angle 1$ and $\angle 2$ are interior angles on the same side as $\overrightarrow{BF}$.

$\therefore \mathrm{m} \angle 1 + \mathrm{m} \angle 2 = 180$ (since $\overleftrightarrow{BC} \parallel \overleftrightarrow{FG}$, interior angles supplementary).

$\therefore 3x + 5 + 6x - 5 = 180 \Rightarrow x = 20$.

Don't be careless— 20 is not the answer! You were asked for m$\angle 2$, not for x. You must plug 20 into $6x - 5$, getting 115 degrees.

Grid-in 115.

> The 2400 Club grids-in only after double checking what quantity is asked for.

✎ Your technique in solving this (and any other geometry) problem for which a diagram is given, should be to jot all the relevant quantities directly onto the diagram, as shown below.

With this information in front of you, you can quickly solve $3x + 5 + 6x - 5 = 180$.

Of course, it is assumed that high scorers are very much at home in the parallel line/ angle relationships universe.

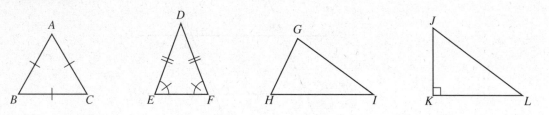

TRIANGLES

Types of Triangles

In the figures above:

- ■ $\triangle ABC$ is an *equilateral* triangle. All three sides are congruent, and each of the three angles measures $60°$.
- ■ $\triangle DEF$ is an *isosceles* triangle. Two sides, $\overline{DE}$ and $\overline{DF}$, are congruent. The third side, $\overline{EF}$ in the diagram above, is called the *base*. The *base angles*, $\angle E$ and $\angle F$, are congruent.
- ■ $\triangle GHI$ is a *scalene* triangle. All three sides have different lengths, and all three angles have different measures. The angle opposite the longest side has the greatest measure. The angle opposite the shortest side has the smallest measure.
- ■ $\triangle JKL$ is a *right triangle*. $\overline{JK}$ and $\overline{KL}$ are the *legs*. $\overline{JL}$, the side opposite the right angle, is the *hypotenuse*.

Some Triangle Facts

■ The triangle inequality theorem: The sum of the lengths of any two sides is greater than the length of the third side.

■ The sum of the measures of the three angles in a triangle is 180°.

■ The Pythagorean theorem: In any right triangle, the sum of the squares of the legs equals the square of the hypotenuse. In △ABC, $a^2 + b^2 = c^2$.

Special Right Triangles

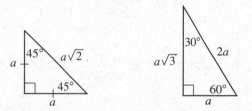

Know the lengths shown above! (But just in case, they are provided at the start of each math section.)

Trigonometric Ratios

Problems that require you to find missing lengths in right triangles can sometimes be solved using special right triangles or the Pythagorean theorem. The following trigonometric ratios are also helpful:

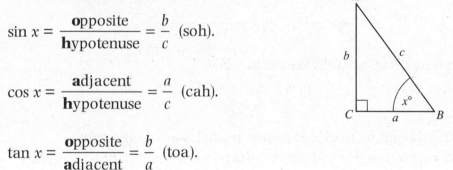

$$\sin x = \frac{\textbf{o}\text{pposite}}{\textbf{h}\text{ypotenuse}} = \frac{b}{c} \text{ (soh).}$$

$$\cos x = \frac{\textbf{a}\text{djacent}}{\textbf{h}\text{ypotenuse}} = \frac{a}{c} \text{ (cah).}$$

$$\tan x = \frac{\textbf{o}\text{pposite}}{\textbf{a}\text{djacent}} = \frac{b}{a} \text{ (toa).}$$

You are probably familiar with the words in parentheses, which provide a simple way of remembering which sides correspond to each ratio.

Example 3

The foot of a ladder leaning against the wall of a house is 4 feet from the base of the wall. If the ladder makes a 30° angle with the wall, what is the length, in feet, of the ladder?

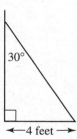

(A) $2\sqrt{3}$ (B) $4\sqrt{3}$ (C) $8\sqrt{3}$ (D) $\dfrac{8\sqrt{3}}{3}$ (E) 8

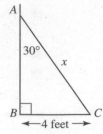

Solution: The answer is **(E)**.

<u>Method I</u>: Special Triangles
Let x be the length of the ladder shown at the right. Since $\triangle ABC$ is a 30–60–90° triangle, $x = 8$ (hypotenuse is double the length opposite the 30° angle).

<u>Method II</u>: Trigonometry

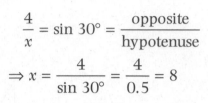

$$\frac{4}{x} = \sin 30° = \frac{\text{opposite}}{\text{hypotenuse}}$$

$$\Rightarrow x = \frac{4}{\sin 30°} = \frac{4}{0.5} = 8$$

 You can use your calculator to find $\dfrac{4}{\sin 30°}$, but be sure to check that the calculator is in **Degree** [MODE] !

Similar Triangles

- Two triangles are *similar* if their sides are proportional; that is, if the ratios of corresponding sides are equal.

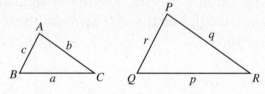

- Given that $\triangle ABC$ above is similar to $\triangle PQR$,

$$\frac{a}{p} = \frac{b}{q} = \frac{c}{r}.$$

- The corresponding angles in similar triangles are congruent.
- If two angles of a triangle are congruent to two angles of a second triangle, the triangles are similar.
- If two triangles are similar, and the ratio of a pair of corresponding sides is $\dfrac{x}{y}$, then, for these triangles, the ratio of their perimeters is $\dfrac{x}{y}$, the ratio of their altitudes is $\dfrac{x}{y}$, and the ratio of their areas is $\left(\dfrac{x}{y}\right)^2$.

For example:

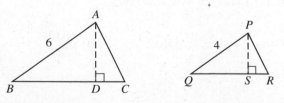

$\triangle ABC$ above is similar to $\triangle PQR$. Then:

$$\frac{AB}{PQ} = \frac{3}{2}, \ \frac{AD}{PS} = \frac{3}{2}$$

$$\frac{\text{Perimeter of } \triangle ABC}{\text{Perimeter of } \triangle PQR} = \frac{3}{2}$$

$$\frac{\text{Area of } \triangle ABC}{\text{Area of } \triangle PQR} = \left(\frac{3}{2}\right)^2 = \left(\frac{9}{4}\right)$$

Example 4 Grid-In

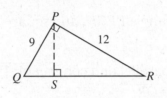

In the above figure, $\triangle PQR$ is a right triangle with the right angle at P. Line segment $\overline{PS}$ is an altitude, $PQ = 9$, and $PR = 12$. What is the area of $\triangle PQS$?

Solution: The answer is 19.4.

Here is what this problem boils down to: Find the area of a triangle that is similar to a triangle whose area you know. Each triangle, $\triangle PQR$ and $\triangle PQS$, contains a right angle, and both contain $\angle Q$. Therefore, the triangles are similar. Picture them side by side:

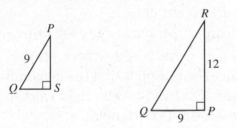

Once you realize that $\triangle PQS$ is similar to $\triangle RQP$, you can find ratio $\dfrac{PQ}{RQ}$.

By the Pythagorean theorem,

$$RQ = 15, \quad \therefore \ \frac{PQ}{RQ} = \frac{9}{15} = \frac{3}{5}.$$

$$\therefore \ \frac{\text{Area of } \triangle PQS}{\text{Area of } \triangle RQP} = \left(\frac{3}{5}\right)^2.$$

$$\therefore \ \frac{\text{Area of } \triangle PQS}{(\frac{1}{2})(12)(9)} = \left(\frac{9}{25}\right).$$

$$\therefore \ \text{Area of } \triangle PQS = \frac{(9)(54)}{25} \approx 19.4.$$

Grid-in 19.4.

Coaching:
Recognize this picture:

The three right triangles that you see are similar to each other.

QUADRILATERALS AND POLYGONS

Quadrilaterals

You need to know three types of *quadrilaterals*: squares, rectangles, and parallelograms:

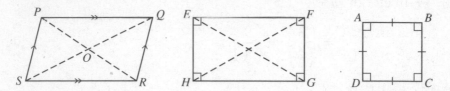

Parallelogram *PQRS*, rectangle *EFGH*, and square *ABCD* are shown above.

- In parallelogram *PQRS*:
  1. Opposite sides are parallel and congruent: $\overline{PQ} \parallel \overline{SR}$, $\overline{PS} \parallel \overline{QR}$, $\overline{PQ} \cong \overline{SR}$, and $\overline{PS} \cong \overline{QR}$.
  2. Opposite angles are congruent: $\angle P \cong \angle R$ and $\angle S \cong \angle Q$.
  3. The diagonals bisect each other: $\overline{PO} \cong \overline{RO}$ and $\overline{SO} \cong \overline{QO}$.
- Every rectangle is also a parallelogram. Thus, rectangle *EFGH* has all the properties of a parallelogram. Additionally:
  1. All four angles are right angles.
  2. The diagonals are congruent: $\overline{EG} \cong \overline{HF}$.
- Every square is also a rectangle. Therefore, square *ABCD* has all the properties of a rectangle (and a parallelogram!). Additionally:
  1. All four sides are congruent.
  2. The diagonals are perpendicular to each other.
  3. The length of a diagonal is $x\sqrt{2}$, where x is the length of a side. The reason is that the diagonal splits the square into two isosceles right triangles, each a special 45–45–90° triangle.

Angles in a Quadrilateral

The sum of the measures of the angles in a quadrilateral is 360°.

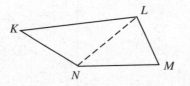

In quadrilateral *KLMN* above, diagonal $\overline{LN}$ divides the figure into two triangles, as shown:

Sum of the angles in $\triangle KLN = 180°$.
Sum of the angles in $\triangle MLN = 180°$.
Sum of the angles in $KLMN = 360°$.

Polygons

■ The sum of the measures of the angles in a polygon is $(n-2)\,180°$, where n is the number of sides in the polygon. You can see this if you pick any vertex and join it to each of the other vertices of the polygon.

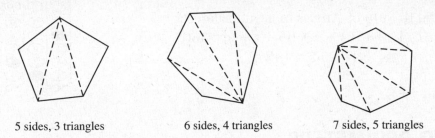

5 sides, 3 triangles   6 sides, 4 triangles   7 sides, 5 triangles

In each of the polygons shown above, the sum of the angle measures in the polygon is the number of triangles multiplied by $180°$, namely, $(n-2)\,180°$, where n is the number of sides of the polygon.

■ In a *regular polygon* all the sides are congruent and all the angles are congruent.

■ Another useful fact is that the sum of the exterior angles of any polygon is $360°$.

Example 5 Grid-In

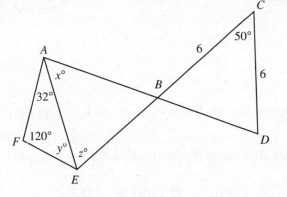

Note: Figure not drawn to scale.

In the above figure, what is the value of $x + y + z$?

Solution: The answer is 143.

On the diagram, fill in everything you can conclude from what's given.

$\triangle CBD$ is isosceles, $\therefore$ base angles are congruent.

Each base angle measures $65°$, since sum of angle measures in a triangle $= 180°$.

There are congruent vertical angles at B, so m $\angle ABE = 65°$.

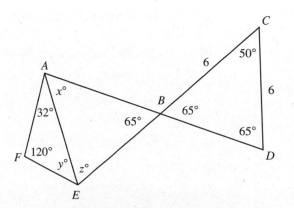

Note: Figure not drawn to scale.

Method I: Sum of Angles in a Triangle
In $\triangle ABE$, $x + z = 180 - 65 = 115°$.
In $\triangle AFE$, $y = 180 - 152 = 28°$.
$\therefore x + y + z = 115 + 28 = 143°$.

Method II: Sum of Angles in a Quadrilateral
In $FABE$, $120 + 32 + x + 65 + z + y = 360°$.
$\therefore x + y + z = 360 - 217 = 143°$.

Grid-in 143.

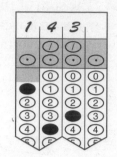

AREAS AND PERIMETERS

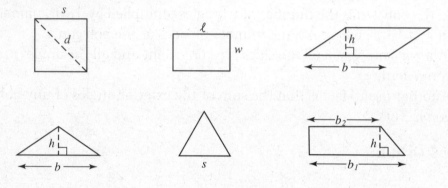

Area

You must know the formulas for the area A of each of the figures shown above:

- A square with side s and diagonal d: $A = s^2$ or $A = \dfrac{1}{2}d^2$

- A rectangle with length ℓ and width w: $A = \ell w$
- A parallelogram with base b and height h: $A = bh$
- A triangle (which is half a parallelogram) with base b and height h:

  $A = \dfrac{1}{2}bh$

- An equilateral triangle with side s: $A = \dfrac{s^2\sqrt{3}}{4}$

- A trapezoid with bases b_1 and b_2 and height h: $A = \dfrac{1}{2}h(b_1 + b_2)$

Perimeter

The *perimeter* of a polygon is the sum of the lengths of its sides.

Example 6

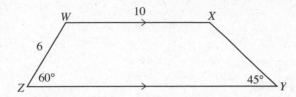

In the figure shown above, $\overline{WX} \parallel \overline{ZY}$. What is the perimeter of quadrilateral $WXYZ$?

(A) $29 + 3\sqrt{3} + 3\sqrt{6}$ (B) $29 + 3\sqrt{3} + 3\sqrt{2}$ (C) $29 + 6\sqrt{3} + 6\sqrt{6}$

(D) $35 + 3\sqrt{2}$ (E) $35 + 3\sqrt{6}$

Solution: The answer is **(A)**.

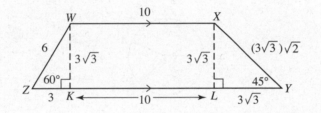

Fill in all the facts you can conclude on the diagram. The picture begs for altitudes; so draw $\overline{WK}$ and $\overline{XL}$. Angles of 60° and 45° are magic numbers on the SAT, and you should direct your energies toward creating special triangles that contain these angles.

$\triangle WZK$ is a 30–60–90° triangle, $\therefore$ leg $ZK = \dfrac{1}{2}$ hypotenuse $ZW = 3$.

Also, altitude $WK = 3\sqrt{3}$; $\therefore$ altitude $XL = 3\sqrt{3}$.

(Notice that quadrilateral $WXLK$ is a rectangle.)

$\triangle XLY$ is a 45–45–90° triangle, $\therefore$ leg $XL =$ leg $LY = 3\sqrt{3}$.

$\therefore$ Hypotenuse $XY = LY\sqrt{2} = 3\sqrt{3}\sqrt{2} = 3\sqrt{6}$.

$$\begin{aligned}
\text{Perimeter of } WXYZ &= WX + WZ + ZY + YX \\
&= WX + WZ + ZK + KL + LY + YX \\
&= 10 + 6 + 3 + 10 + 3\sqrt{3} + 3\sqrt{6} \\
&= 29 + 3\sqrt{3} + 3\sqrt{6}
\end{aligned}$$

CIRCLES

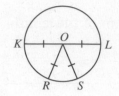

Circumference and Area

- All radii in a circle have the same length. Thus, if O is the center of the circle above, $OK = OL = OR = OS$.
- A radius is half the diameter. $\overline{KL}$ is a diameter, and $OR = \frac{1}{2}KL$.
- The *circumference* of a circle is πd or $2\pi r$, where d is the diameter and r is the radius.
- The *area* of a circle is πr^2.

Arc and Sector

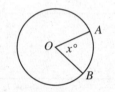

- An angle whose vertex is the center of a circle is a *central angle*.
- In the circle above, central angle AOB intercepts arc AB. The measure of arc AB is the measure of the central angle that intercepts it.
  $\therefore$ Measure arc $AB = \text{m}\angle AOB = x°$.
- High scorers distinguish between the measure of an arc (in degrees) and the *length* of an arc. Since there are 360° in a circle, an arc of $x°$ cuts off $\dfrac{x}{360}$ of the circumference. Let L be the length of an arc whose measure is x. Then $L = \dfrac{x}{360}2\pi r$. (**Note:** L has the same units as r.)
- A *sector* is a region in a circle bounded by a central angle and the arc it intercepts. The area of sector AOB is $\dfrac{x}{360}\pi r^2$.

Example 7

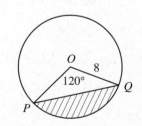

In the figure above, what is the area of the shaded region?

(A) $\dfrac{16\pi}{3} - 16\sqrt{3}$ (B) $\dfrac{16\pi}{3} - 16$ (C) $\dfrac{16\pi}{3} - 64\sqrt{3}$ (D) $\dfrac{64\pi}{3} - 32\sqrt{3}$ (E) $\dfrac{64\pi}{3} - 16\sqrt{3}$

Solution: The answer is **(E)**.

Finding shaded areas usually involves subtraction, and this problem is no exception.
Shaded area = area of sector OPQ – area of $\triangle OPQ$.

To find the area of $\triangle OPQ$, draw in an altitude and fill in the lengths for the 30–60–90° triangle.

Since $OP = OQ$, $\triangle OPK \cong \triangle OQK$ and $PQ = 8\sqrt{3}$.

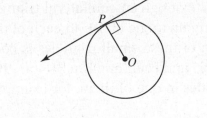

Area of $\triangle OPQ = \dfrac{1}{2}(8\sqrt{3})(4) = 16\sqrt{3}$.

Area of sector $OPQ = \dfrac{120}{360} \cdot \pi(8)^2 = \dfrac{64\pi}{3}$.

$\therefore$ Shaded area $= \dfrac{64\pi}{3} - 16\sqrt{3}$.

Tangents

> *Use subtraction for shaded areas.*

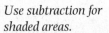

In the figure above, line ℓ is *tangent* to the circle with center O at point P, meaning that ℓ intersects the circle in exactly one point, namely, P. By the tangent–radius theorem, a tangent is perpendicular to a radius at the point of contact; therefore, $\ell \perp \overline{OP}$.

Inscribed Circles and Polygons

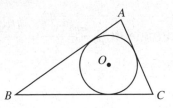

■ A circle is *inscribed* in a polygon if each side of the polygon is tangent to the circle. In the figure above, for example, circle O is inscribed in $\triangle ABC$.

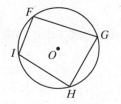

■ A polygon is *inscribed* in a circle if each vertex of the polygon is on the circle. In the figure above, for example, quadrilateral $FGHI$ is inscribed in circle O.

Example 8

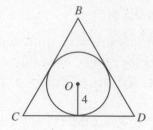

In the above diagram, the circle with center O is inscribed in equilateral triangle BCD. If the radius of the circle is 4, what is the ratio of the perimeter of $\triangle BCD$ to the area of $\triangle BCD$?

(A) $1 : 2\sqrt{3}$ (B) $1 : 2$ (C) $1 : \sqrt{3}$ (D) $1 : 4$ (E) $1 : 4\sqrt{3}$

Solution: The answer is **(B)**.

Draw in some line segments, as shown.

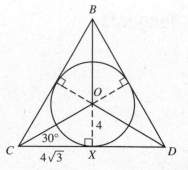

Each radius is perpendicular to a side of the triangle (tangent–radius theorem). Notice the symmetry of the picture. Each vertex of given equilateral triangle BCD is bisected, giving an angle of 30° in each of the small triangles. Each of these small triangles is congruent to every other, and each one is a 30–60–90° triangle. Label the sides in one of them, for example, $\triangle XOC$, as shown.

Perimeter of $\triangle BCD = 6(CX) = 24\sqrt{3}$.

Area of $\triangle BCD = 6(\text{area of } \triangle XOC) = 6 \left[\frac{1}{2} (4\sqrt{3})(4) \right] = 48\sqrt{3}$.

Alternatively:

Area of equilateral triangle $BCD = \dfrac{s^2\sqrt{3}}{2} = \dfrac{(8\sqrt{3})^2\sqrt{3}}{4} = \dfrac{(64)(3)\sqrt{3}}{4} = 48\sqrt{3}$.

∴ perimeter : area = 1 : 2.

SOLID GEOMETRY

Prisms and Cylinders

Recognize the solids shown below. Each is a right prism.

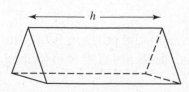

triangular prism

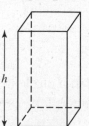

rectangular prism

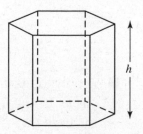

hexagonal prism

- A *right prism* has two congruent polygon bases connected by faces that are perpendicular to the bases. The name of the prism depends on the shape of the base. The height is the distance between the bases.
- The volume of a prism is (area of base) × (height)
- A *right circular cylinder* resembles a right prism: the bases are congruent circles, and the connecting curved surface is perpendicular to the bases. As with a prism, the height of a cylinder is the distance between bases.
- The volume of a cylinder is also (area of base) × (height) = $\pi r^2 h$.

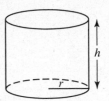

Cones and Pyramids

You should also recognize a sphere, a right circular cone, and a pyramid, shown below.

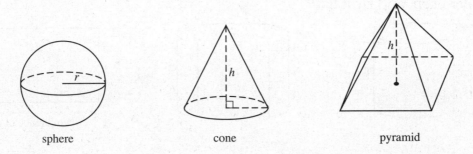

sphere   cone   pyramid

- A *sphere* is the set of points in space equidistant from the center. This distance from the center is r, the radius.
- A *right circular cone* has a circular base. The line connecting the vertex to the center of the base is perpendicular to the base.
- The base of a *pyramid* is a polygon. It is connected to the vertex by triangular faces. In a *regular pyramid*, the base is a regular polygon, and the triangular faces are congruent isosceles triangles.

You are not expected to learn complicated formulas for the SAT. You can, however, expect to see questions about the various solids.

Questions about the surface areas of solids can sometimes be solved using an "imaginary scissors" technique. Picture the solid as a hollow cardboard container. Now cut it open, and flatten it out to make a plane figure. For example, here is a rectangular solid, flattened out in the plane of the bottom of the box:

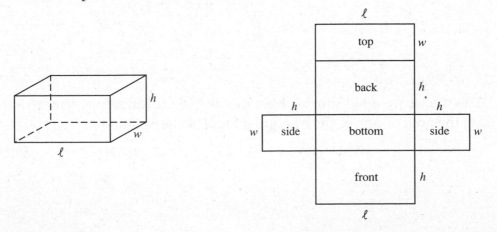

Example 9

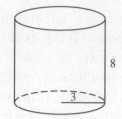

What is the total surface area of the cylindrical can shown above, including its lid?

(A) $18\pi + 64$ (B) $48\pi + 18$ (C) 57π (D) 66π (E) 90π

Solution: The answer is **(D)**.

Use the imaginary scissors technique. Cut off the lid and base; then cut the rest of the cylinder open, and lay it flat:

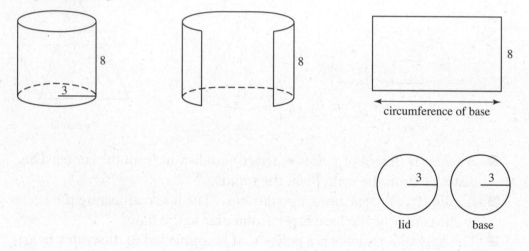

You can now see that the surface area *SA* is the area of two circles plus a rectangle whose length is the circumference of the base:

$$SA = 2\pi r^2 + 2\pi rh = 2\pi(9) + 2\pi(24) = 18\pi + 48\pi = 66\pi$$

Example 10

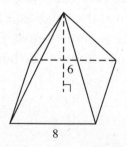

The square pyramid shown above has altitude 6 and side of square base equal to 8. What is the area of one of the triangular faces of the pyramid?

(A) $8\sqrt{13}$ (B) $16\sqrt{13}$ (C) 24   (D) 40   (E) 80

Solution: The answer is **(A)**.

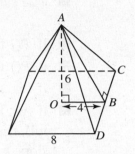

Draw in some line segments on the given diagram.

Visualizing the symmetry of the figure you should see that:

- $\overline{AB}$ is the height of $\triangle ADC$.
- O is the center of the square.
- OB = half the side of the square base, namely, 4.

Use Pythagoras in $\triangle AOB$:

$$AB^2 = 6^2 + 4^2$$

$$\therefore AB = \sqrt{52} = 2\sqrt{13}$$

$$\therefore \text{Area of } \triangle ADC = \left(\frac{1}{2}\right)(DC)(AB) = \left(\frac{1}{2}\right)(8)(2\sqrt{13}) = 8\sqrt{13}$$

COORDINATE GEOMETRY

High scorers have the following facts at their fingertips. Refer to the diagram below.

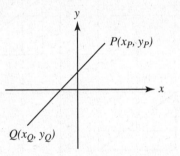

Distance

- The *distance* between two points in the plane is

$$PQ = \sqrt{(x_P - x_Q)^2 + (y_P - y_Q)^2}$$

- If P and Q are on the same horizontal line, you can subtract their x-coordinates to find PQ:

$$PQ = |x_P - x_Q| = |x_Q - x_P|$$

- Similarly, for P and Q on the same vertical line:

$$PQ = |y_P - y_Q| = |y_Q - y_P|$$

- The *midpoint* M of $\overline{PQ}$ is $\left(\dfrac{x_P + x_Q}{2}, \dfrac{y_P + y_Q}{2}\right)$ (the average of the x-coordinates and the average of the y-coordinates of the endpoints of the given segment).

Slope

- The *slope* of $\overleftrightarrow{PQ} = \dfrac{\text{change in } y}{\text{change in } x} = \dfrac{y_P - y_Q}{x_P - x_Q} = \dfrac{y_Q - y_P}{x_Q - x_P}$.

- If $\overleftrightarrow{PQ}$ is a horizontal line, its slope is zero.
- If $\overleftrightarrow{PQ}$ is a vertical line, it has no slope.
- If two nonvertical lines are parallel, they have the same slope.
- If two lines are perpendicular, and neither line is vertical (or horizontal), the product of their slopes is –1. (Therefore, if $\ell_1 \perp \ell_2$ and ℓ_1 has slope k, then ℓ_2 has slope $-1/k$.)

Geometric Transformations

You should be familiar with the following transformations in a plane:

- A *translation* shifts all points of a figure horizontally or vertically. There is no rotation, reflection, or distortion.

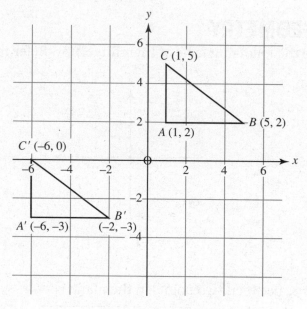

In the diagram, $\triangle ABC$ is translated 7 units to the left and 5 units down. The *image* after translation is $\triangle A'B'C'$.

- A *reflection* produces a mirror image across a line. Every point of the figure is the same distance from the line of reflection as its image.

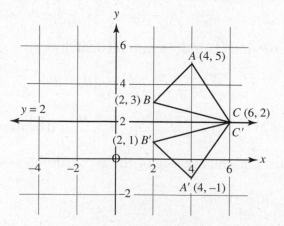

In the diagram, $\triangle A'B'C'$ is the *image* of $\triangle ABC$ reflected across the line $y = 2$.

■ A *rotation* rotates a figure about a point, called the center of rotation. After rotation, the image of the point is the same distance from the point of rotation as the original point.

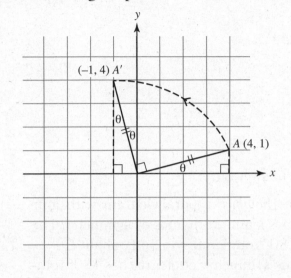

In the diagram, A' is the image of A rotated counterclockwise 90° about the origin.

Symmetry

There are two types of symmetry that you should know:

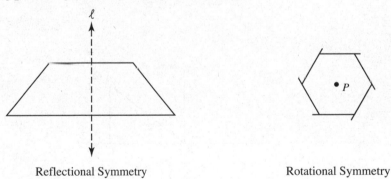

Reflectional Symmetry   Rotational Symmetry

A figure has *reflectional symmetry* or *symmetry about a line* if reflection across the line produces an identical figure. Line ℓ is a *line of symmetry* for the trapezoid shown above.

A figure has *rotational symmetry* or *symmetry about a point P* if a rotation of k degrees, $0 < k < 360$, clockwise or counterclockwise, about P produces an identical figure. The point P is a *point of symmetry* for the figure. The angle of rotation can be 60°, 120°, 180°, or 240° for the hexagon on the right above.

Note that the figure on the left does not have symmetry about a point, and the figure on the right does not have symmetry about a line. Many figures, however, have both types of symmetry.

Example 11

Which figure has both symmetry about a line (reflectional) and symmetry about a point (rotational)?

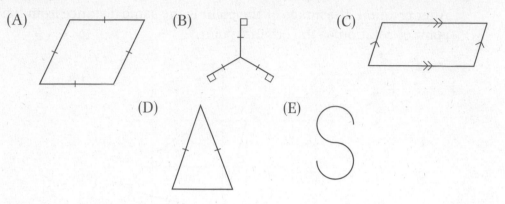

Solution: The answer is **(A)**.

The figure is a *rhombus*, a parallelogram with four congruent sides. Lines k and ℓ are lines of symmetry. The rhombus also has 180° rotational symmetry about P.

Choice (B) has no symmetry; choice (C) has 180° rotational symmetry but no line symmetry; choice (D) has line symmetry but no rotational symmetry; choice (E) has only 180° rotational symmetry.

Example 12

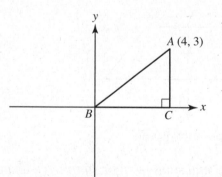

In the figure above, $\triangle ABC$ is rotated counterclockwise through 90° about the origin. Its image is $\triangle A'B'C'$. What is the slope of $\overline{A'B'}$?

(A) $\dfrac{3}{4}$ (B) $\dfrac{4}{3}$ (C) $-\dfrac{3}{4}$ (D) $-\dfrac{4}{3}$ (E) -3

Solution: The answer is **(D)**.

Reduce the problem. $\overline{A'B'}$ is the image of the hypotenuse. Therefore the rest of the triangle is irrelevant. You must rotate $\overline{AB}$ and find the slope of its image, $\overline{A'B'}$.

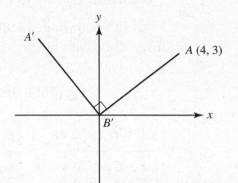

Since $\overline{A'B'} \perp \overline{AB}$, their slopes are negative reciprocals. The slope of $\overline{AB} = \dfrac{3}{4}$, so the slope of $\overline{A'B'} = -\dfrac{4}{3}$.

GEOMETRIC PROBABILITY

A typical SAT question chooses a point at random in a geometric figure, and asks you to find the probability that the point lies in a specified region.

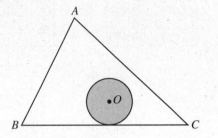

For example, a point is chosen at random in $\triangle ABC$, shown above. What is the probability that the point lands in circle O?

$$P(\text{point in circle}) = \frac{\text{area of circle } O}{\text{area of } \triangle ABC}.$$

Example 13 Grid-In

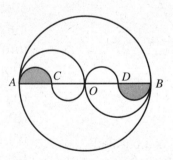

In the circle shown above, O is the center and $\overline{AB}$ is a diameter. There are two semicircles with diameters $\overline{AO}$ and $\overline{BO}$, and four smaller semicircles with congruent diameters $\overline{AC}$, $\overline{CO}$, $\overline{OD}$, and $\overline{DB}$. A point is picked at random in the large circle. What is the probability that it lands in a shaded region?

Solution: The answer is $\frac{1}{16}$.

Put the two shaded semicircles together to get one small circle whose radius is $\frac{1}{4}$ the radius of the given large circle. Then:

$$P(\text{point in small circle}) = \frac{\text{area of small circle}}{\text{area of large circle}} = \left(\frac{1}{4}\right)^2 = \frac{1}{16}.$$

Grid-in 1/16 or .062 or .063.

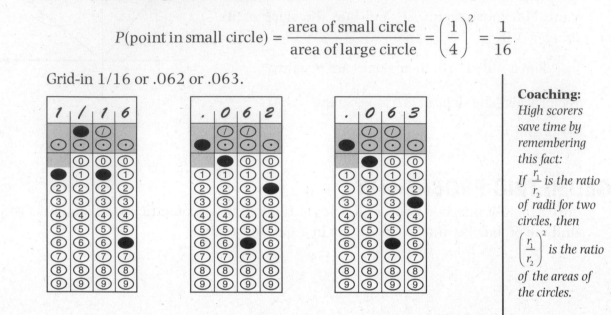

PRACTICE TEST QUESTIONS

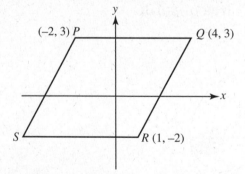

1. In the diagram above, *PQRS* is a parallelogram. What is the area of *PQRS*?

    (A) 15
    (B) 18
    (C) 30
    (D) $3\sqrt{34}$
    (E) $6\sqrt{34}$

2. A rectangular box with length 22 inches, width 5 inches, and height 5 inches is to be packed with steel balls of radius 2 inches in such a way that the centers of the balls are collinear. What is the maximum number of balls that can fit into the box, provided that no balls should protrude from the box?

    (A) 0
    (B) 5
    (C) 6
    (D) 10
    (E) 11

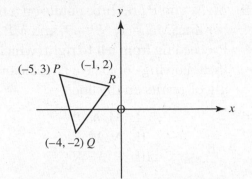

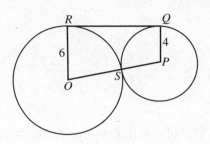

Note: Figure not drawn to scale.

3. Triangle *PQR*, shown in the diagram above, is translated 4 units to the right and 5 units down. The resulting triangle is then rotated 180° counterclockwise about the origin. What is the final image of point *P*?

(A) $(-1, -2)$
(B) $(1, 2)$
(C) $(2, 1)$
(D) $(-2, 1)$
(E) $(2, -1)$

5. In the figure above, the circle with center *O* has radius 6 and the circle with center *P* has radius 4. The circles are tangent to each other at point *S*. Line segment $\overline{OP}$ contains point *S*. If $\overline{RQ}$ is tangent to circle *O* at *R* and to circle *P* at *Q*, what is the length of $\overline{RQ}$?

(A) $2\sqrt{21}$
(B) $4\sqrt{6}$
(C) 8
(D) 9
(E) 10

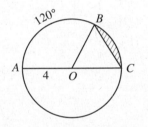

4. In the diagram above, the circle has center *O* and diameter $\overline{AC}$. The measure of arc *AB* is 120°, and $AO = 4$. What is the area of the shaded region?

(A) $\dfrac{16\pi}{3} - 8\sqrt{3}$

(B) $\dfrac{8\pi}{3} - 2\sqrt{3}$

(C) $\dfrac{8\pi}{3} - 4\sqrt{3}$

(D) $\dfrac{8\pi}{3} - 8\sqrt{3}$

(E) $\dfrac{4\pi}{3} - 4\sqrt{3}$

6. In the *xy*-plane, a circle with center $(6, 0)$ is tangent to the line $y = x$. What is the radius of the circle?

(A) $2\sqrt{6}$
(B) $2\sqrt{3}$
(C) $3\sqrt{2}$
(D) 3
(E) 6

7. In the *xy*-plane, points $A(2, 4)$ and $B(8, 4)$ are two vertices of $\triangle ABC$. If the sum of the sides of the triangle is less than 12, which of the following points could be point *C*?

        I. $(5, 4)$
        II. $(5, 5)$
        III. $(5, 8)$

(A) None
(B) II only
(C) III only
(D) II and III only
(E) I, II, and III

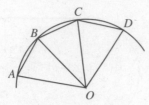

8. The above figure represents part of a regular polygon with n sides, inscribed in a circle with center O. In terms of n, what is the measure of $\angle OBC$?

(A) $\dfrac{360}{n}$

(B) $180 - n$

(C) $180n - 360$

(D) $180 - \dfrac{360}{n}$

(E) $90 - \dfrac{180}{n}$

9. M, N, and P are three points on a number line; $MN = 7$, $NP = 9$, and $MP = 2$. Proceeding from left to right, which of the following could be a possible ordering of points on the line?

I. M, N, P
II. N, M, P
III. P, M, N

(A) I only
(B) II only
(C) III only
(D) II and III only
(E) I, II, and III

10. A line intersects two parallel lines, forming eight angles. If one of the angles has measure $a°$, how many of the other seven angles are supplementary to it?

(A) 1
(B) 2
(C) 3
(D) 4
(E) 5

Questions 11–14 are grid-in questions.

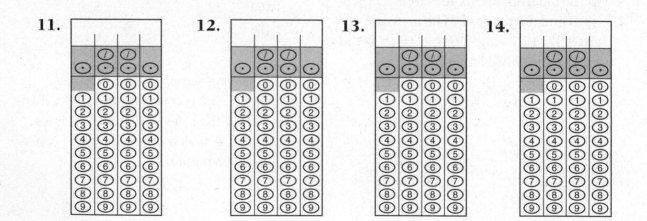

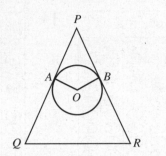

11. In the figure shown above, m∠Q measures 70°, $\overline{PQ} \cong \overline{PR}$, and $\overline{PQ}$ and $\overline{PR}$ are tangent to the circle with center O at points A and B. Find, in degrees, the measure of ∠AOB.

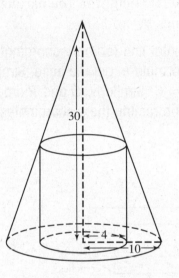

12. A cylinder is inscribed in a cone with height 30 and base radius 10, as shown in the above figure. If the radius of the base of the cylinder is 4, what is the height of the cylinder?

13. In the xy-plane, points P(1, 1), Q(2, 6), and R(6, 8) are three vertices of a parallelogram PQRS. What is the sum of the slopes of the sides of the parallelogram?

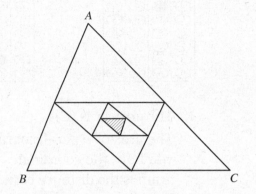

14. The triangles inside △ABC, shown above, are formed by joining the midpoints of the sides and then repeating the process. If a point is chosen at random inside △ABC, what is the probability that the point lies in the shaded region?

Note: Figure not drawn to scale.

ANSWERS AND EXPLANATIONS

The difficulty level for each question is specified in parentheses.

1. C (M)	**4.** C (M)	**7.** A (H)	**10.** D (H)	**13.** 11 (M)
2. B (H)	**5.** B (H)	**8.** E (H)	**11.** 140 (M)	**14.** 1/64 (H)
3. B (M)	**6.** C (H)	**9.** D (M)	**12.** 18 (H)	

11.

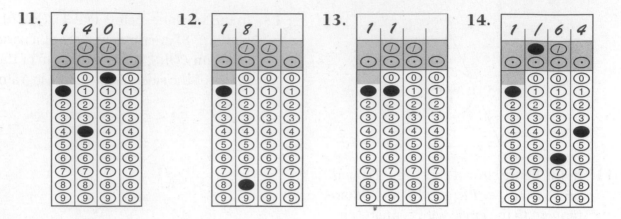

12.

13.

14.

1. The answer is **(C)**.

The area of a parallelogram equals base × height. Use $\overline{PQ}$ as base since you have the coordinates of both P and Q. The height of the parallelogram is the distance between horizontal lines $\overline{PQ}$ and $\overline{SR}$.

 Notice that *P* and *Q* are on the same horizontal line (same *y*-coordinate), so don't waste your time with the distance formula to get the base. Simply subtract the *x*-coordinates: *PQ* = 4 − (−2) = 6. Similarly, *Q* and *R* are on the same vertical line, so get the height by subtracting the *y*-coordinates of *Q* and *R*: 3 − (−2) = 5.

Area = bh = (6)(5) = 30

2. The answer is **(B)**.

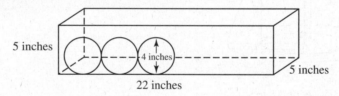

Some visualization is needed here. This is a long, skinny box, as shown above. The diameter of each ball is 4 inches, so the balls will need to be packed one by one, lengthwise, to fit into the box. Since this is a question about length, not volume, reduce the question to: How many 4-inch diameters will fit into the 22-inch length? The answer is $\frac{22}{4} = 5$, with a bit left over. Not enough room to squeeze another ball in, so the answer is 5.

3. The answer is **(B)**.

A careful reading of the problem tells you to reduce it to: Where does point *P* land? The rest of the figure is irrelevant, so don't waste time on it. *P′* (−1, −2) is the image of *P* after translating *P* 4 units right and 5 units down. *P″* (1, 2) is where *P′* lands, that is, it is the final image of *P* after rotating *P′* 180° through *O*.

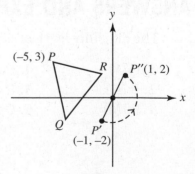

4. The answer is **(C)**.

Fill in on the diagram everything you know.

Measure of arc $AB = m\angle AOB = 120°$

$\therefore m\angle BOC = 60°$.

$OB = OC = AO = 4$ (radii).

$\triangle OBC$ is equilateral.

When asked to find a shaded area, think subtraction:

Shaded area = area of sector OBC – area $\triangle OBC$.

Area of sector $OBC = \dfrac{60}{360}\pi(4)^2 = \dfrac{8\pi}{3}$.

Area of $\triangle OPQ = \dfrac{s^2\sqrt{3}}{4} = 4\sqrt{3}$.

$\therefore$ Shaded area $= \dfrac{8\pi}{3} - 4\sqrt{3}$.

5. The answer is **(B)**.

Fill in on the diagram what you know so far: right angles at R and Q (tangent–radius theorem) and radii along $\overline{OP}$.

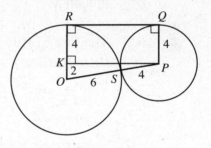

The secret here is to drop a perpendicular $\overline{PK}$ from P to $\overline{RO}$, which forms rectangle *QPKR*. Since *RQ = KP*, the problem reduces to: Find *KP*.

In right triangle PKO, $OP = 10$.

Also, $RK = 4$ (opposite side to $\overline{PQ}$).

$\therefore KO = 6 - 4 = 2$.

Now use Pythagoras in $\triangle PKO$:

$KP^2 = 10^2 - 2^2 = 96$.

$\therefore KP = \sqrt{96} = \sqrt{16 \cdot 6} = 4\sqrt{6} = RQ$

6. The answer is **(C)**.

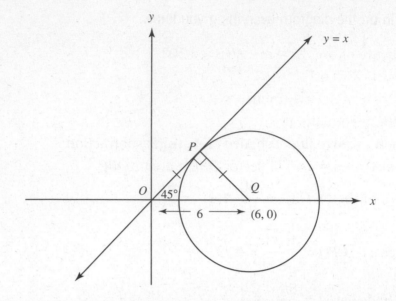

A diagram here is crucial, and be sure to include the radius to the point of tangency.

The key to this problem is seeing that $\triangle PQO$ is a 45–45–90° triangle, since the line $y = x$ makes a 45° angle with each axis.

$$\therefore PO = \frac{6}{\sqrt{2}} = 3\sqrt{2}$$

7. The answer is **(A)**.

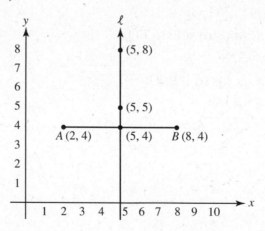

Clarify the situation by drawing a diagram of $\overline{AB}$, with each of the three given points, I, II, and III.

Notice that each of these points has x-coordinate 5, and therefore all lie on line ℓ, the perpendicular bisector of $\overline{AB}$.

I: $C = (5, 4)$: Reject it because it lies on $\overline{AB}$.

II: $C = (5, 5)$: Looks possible. Check the requirement that the sum of the sides is less than 12.

$CA = \sqrt{(5-2)^2 + (5-4)^2} = \sqrt{10} = CB$, since $(5, 5)$ is on the perpendicular bisector of $\overline{AB}$.

$CA + CB = 2\sqrt{10}$, which is slightly greater than 6.

$AB = 8 - 2 = 6$.

$\therefore AB + CA + CB > 12$.

Reject $(5, 5)$.

III: $C = (5, 8)$:

Reject this point without wasting time to check it! From your sketch you should be able to see that $AC + BC$ will be even larger than the value you got in choice II.

The 2400 Club understands the rewards that accompany a good sketch.

---

8. The answer is **(E)**.

The sum of the measures of all angles in a polygon with n sides is $(n-2)180°$. Since there are n congruent angles in a regular polygon, each

angle measures $\dfrac{(n-2)180}{n}$.

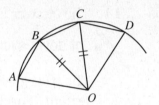

Notice that $\angle ABC$ is one of these angles.

From the symmetry,

$$m\angle OBC = \frac{1}{2}m\angle ABC$$

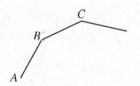

$$= \frac{(n-2)180}{2n} = \frac{(n-2)90}{n} = \frac{90n-180}{n} = 90 - \frac{180}{n}.$$

9. The answer is **(D)**.

Don't put down that active pencil—you need three little sketches here. Place the first two points in each Roman-numeral choice, and then try to place the third point so that the length requirements are satisfied.

I: Reject *M, N, P*, since it's not possible to place point P to the right of N and get $MP = 2$.

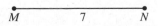

II is possible:

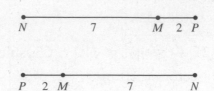

III is possible:

10. The answer is **(D)**.

A diagram always helps.

Two angles are supplementary if the sum of their measures is 180°. Either of the angles adjacent to the marked angle is supplementary to it. Mark these adjacent angles (each with an asterisk, say). Now, using the facts that corresponding angles are congruent, and alternate interior angles are congruent, mark all of the angles that are congruent to that "asterisk" angle, as shown. There are four such angles.

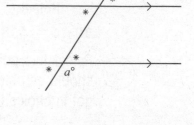

11. The answer is 140.

Jot down everything you know on the diagram.

The triangle is isosceles, so the base angles are congruent. Three angles in a triangle are supplementary, so m∠P = 40°. Radii are perpendicular to tangents, so there are right angles at A and B.

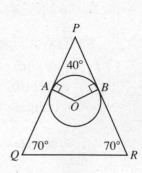

The problem is now easy to solve. $PAOB$ is a quadrilateral; therefore the sum of its angles is 360°.

∴ m∠AOB = 360 − (90 + 90 + 40) = 140°.

Grid-in 140.

12. The answer is 18.

You can reduce this three-dimensional setup to a question about similar triangles in a plane. If you draw in segment $\overline{AB}$, as shown below, you should see that △PAB is similar to △PQR (both contain a right angle and ∠P).

Let h be the height of the cylinder.

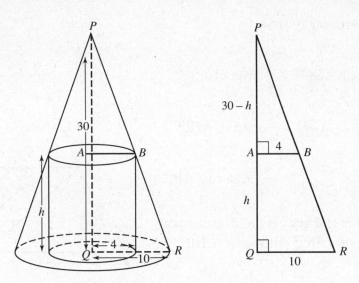

Then:

$$\frac{PA}{PQ} = \frac{AB}{QR} \Rightarrow \frac{30 - h}{30} = \frac{4}{10} = \frac{2}{5}.$$

Cross-multiply to solve for h:

$$5(30 - h) = 60 \Rightarrow h = 18.$$

Grid-in 18.

13. The answer is 11.

A quick sketch of parallelogram *PQRS* will help you visualize the sides and their slopes.

Slope of $\overline{RQ} = \dfrac{8 - 6}{6 - 2} = \dfrac{2}{4} = \dfrac{1}{2}$.

Slope of $\overline{QP} = \dfrac{6 - 1}{2 - 1} = 5$.

Since parallel lines have the same slope,

Sum of slopes $= 2\left(\dfrac{1}{2}\right) + 2(5) = 11.$

Grid-in 11.

14. The answer is 1/64.

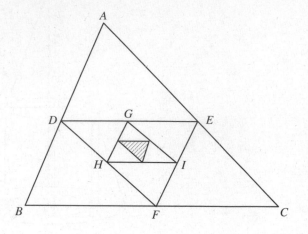

$$\text{area of } \triangle DEF = \frac{1}{4} \text{ area of } \triangle ABC$$

$$\text{area of } \triangle GHI = \frac{1}{4} \text{ area of } \triangle DEF$$

$$= \frac{1}{16} \text{ area of } \triangle ABC$$

Here is the sequence of areas you get, compared with area $\triangle ABC$:

$$1, \frac{1}{4}, \frac{1}{16}, \frac{1}{64}, \dots$$

This is a geometric sequence with common ratio $\frac{1}{4}$.

Since area of shaded region $= \frac{1}{64}$ area of $\triangle ABC$,

the probability of a random point landing there is $\frac{1}{64}$.

Grid-in 1/64.

Chapter 16

TOPICS IN STATISTICS

Previously mentioned strategies such as plug-in and pick-a-number apply also to problems in statistics. Bear these strategies in mind throughout the math section of the SAT. If, in addition, you follow the steps below in solving problems that display statistical graphs, you will be **HAPPY** with the outcome.

2400 Club Steps for Interpreting Graphs . . .

Step 1: The **H**eader. Read about the contents of the graph.

Step 2: The **A**xes. Study each one.

Step 3: One **P**iece. Internalize one piece of a pie chart; one bar in a bar graph; one picture in a pictograph.

Step 4: One **P**oint. State precisely what it means.

Step 5: **Y**ay! Celebrate your success. You followed steps 1–4 and solved the problem.

AVERAGES

Arithmetic Mean

$$\text{The } \textit{arithmetic mean} \text{ of } n \text{ values} = \frac{\text{sum of } n \text{ values}}{n}$$

For example, a student in the 2400 Club has the following test scores in math (so far): 98, 94, 98, 78, 82, 80, 92. Then:

$$\text{Arithmetic mean of her scores} = \frac{98 + 94 + 98 + 78 + 82 + 80 + 92}{7}$$

$$\approx 88.9$$

Median

To find the *median* of *n* values, *arrange the numbers in order.* If *n* is odd, the median is the middle number. If *n* is even, the median is the arithmetic mean of the two middle numbers. For example, to find the median of the test scores above, arrange them in order: 78, 80, 82, $\boxed{92}$, 94, 98, 98.

The median score is 92.

Now suppose that the same student takes another test and has a *really bad* day, scoring 70. Her scores, in order, are now 70, 78, 80, 82, 92 , 94, 98, 98. The number of scores is even, and the median equals $\dfrac{82 + 92}{2} = 87$.

Mode

The *mode* of a list of values is the value that occurs the most times. Look again at the student's test scores: 70, 78, 80, 82, 92, 94, 98, 98.

The mode is 98, since this is the only value that appears more than once.

It is possible for a list to have more than one mode. For example, the list 1, 1, 6, 6, 6, 9, 9, 10, 11, 11, 11, 14, 16, 20, 20, 20, has three modes: 6, 11, and 20.

It is also possible for a list to have no mode, as occurs if all the values appear only once.

Weighted Average

A *weighted average* is the average of two or more sets of values in which both or all of the sets do not all have the same size. For example, suppose that a class is divided into three groups:

Group A, with 10 students, has a test average of 65.
Group B, with 5 students, has a test average of 90.
Group C, with 7 students, has a test average of 80.

To find the class average, high scorers know that what you *can't* do is find $\dfrac{65 + 90 + 80}{3}$. What you must do is weight each score by multiplying by the number of students in that group. Then find the sum of the results and divide by 22, the total number of students.

$$\text{Arithmetic mean of scores} = \frac{(65)(10) + (90)(5) + (80)(7)}{22} \approx 75.5$$

Example 1

The Hadleys took a car trip to visit relatives. Mr. Hadley drove for 2 hours and covered 100 miles. For the last 60 miles, the teenage son, Hank, drove. He took 1 hour to complete this leg of the trip. What was the average speed (arithmetic mean), in miles per hour, for the trip?

(A) 50   (B) $53\dfrac{1}{3}$ (C) 55   (D) $56\dfrac{2}{3}$ (E) 60

Solution: The answer is **(B)**.

```
        2 hours           1 hour
  |----------------|----------------|
      100 miles         60 miles
```

Mr. Hadley drove 2 hours at $\dfrac{100}{2} = 50$ miles per hour.

Hank drove 1 hour at $\dfrac{60}{1} = 60$ miles per hour.

$$\text{Average speed} = \frac{(50)(2) + (60)(1)}{3} = \frac{160}{3} = 53\frac{1}{3} \text{ miles per hour.}$$

DATA INTERPRETATION

Tables (Matrices)

On the SAT you will be asked to interpret information that is presented in tables and graphs. Sometimes you will be given calculations based on that information. **Note:** A table that presents data is also called a *matrix*.

Example 2

In a certain school district, teachers are allowed to take three personal days, at full pay, during one school year. Here is a summary of the number of personal days taken by teachers in 2010–2011.

Number of Teachers Who Took Personal Days	Number of Personal Days Taken by Those Teachers
Fewer than 10	0
50	1
200	2
85	3

From this table you can accurately find

   I. the arithmetic mean of personal days taken
  II. the median number of personal days taken
 III. the mode of the number of personal days taken

(A) I only   (B) II only   (C) III only   (D) II and III only   (E) I, II, and III

Solution: The answer is **(D)**.

Think of the data as laid out, in order, as shown below:

$$\underbrace{0 \;\; 0 \;\cdots}_{< 10} \;\; \underbrace{1 \;\; 1 \;\; 1 \;\cdots}_{50} \;\; \underbrace{2 \;\; 2 \;\; 2 \;\cdots}_{200} \;\; \underbrace{3 \;\; 3 \;\; 3 \;\cdots}_{85}$$

It is not possible to find the arithmetic mean because you don't know how many items are in the list. (What will the denominator be?)

It is possible, however, to see that 2 is the middle number, whether 0 occurs zero or nine times. Therefore the median is 2.

You can also find the mode: 2 occurs more often than the other numbers.

GRAPHS

Circle Graphs

In a *circle graph* or *pie chart*, the size of a wedge is proportional to the size of the number it represents.

Example 3

Marital Status of U.S. Citizens over 15 in 2003

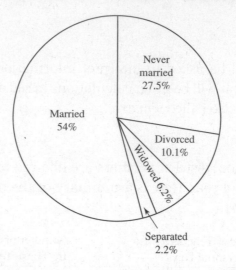

The graph shows the marital statuses of U.S. citizens ages 15 and over in 2003. If the total number of U.S. citizens over 15 was approximately 222 million in 2003, how many, to the nearest million, were divorced or separated?

(A) 2 million   (B) 3 million   (C) 10 million   (D) 22 million   (E) 27 million

Solution: The answer is **(E)**.

The pie chart shows that "Divorced" and "Separated" add up to 10.1 + 2.2 = 12.3%. 12.3% of 222 million ≈ 27 million.

Don't waste time using your calculator here. Since 10 percent of 222 ≈ 22, you should pick the only answer choice that is greater than 22.

Line Graphs

A *line graph* or *time plot* is a good way to examine trends over a given time period. Below is a double-line graph that shows the life expectancies at birth for males born in the United States between 1920 and 2000.

Life Expectancy of U.S. Males from 1920–2000

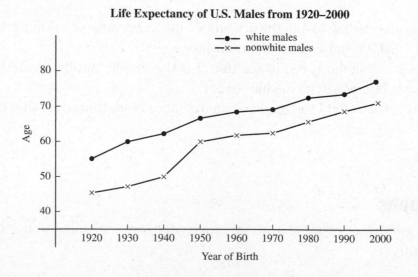

From this graph you can see many trends:

- The life expectancy of men in the United States has increased from 1920 to 2000.
- The life expectancy of white males has been greater than that of non-white males from 1920 to 2000.
- From 1920 to 2000, the greatest difference in the life expectancy of white and of nonwhite males occurred in 1930, a difference of about 13 years.

Bar Graphs

Another way to display data is in a *bar graph*. Each bar represents a different category, and the height of the bar represents a numerical value for that category. The bar graph shown below compares the percentages of several age groups who have completed 4 or more years of college.

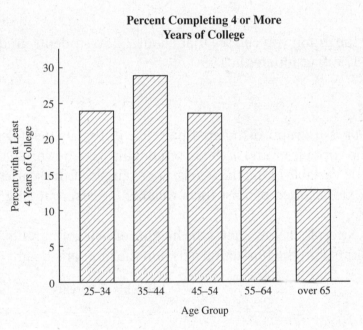

The graph shows that almost 30 percent of people aged 35–44 have completed at least 4 years of college. Also, at a glance you can see that older people are less likely to have achieved this level of education.

Pictographs

A *pictograph* presents data using pictorial symbols. Typically, one symbol represents a fixed number of items. The pictograph below shows the number of students who graduated each year from a small college.

Number of Students Graduating from a Small College

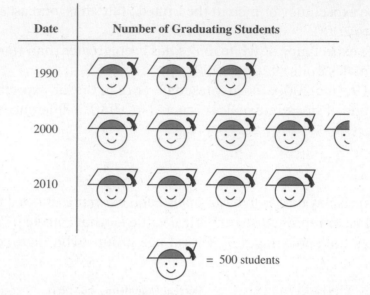

From the graph you can see that about 2,250 students graduated in 2000, but there were only 1,500 graduates in 1990.

Scatterplots

A *scatterplot* is a graph of ordered pairs (x, y) that is helpful in finding a relationship between the variables x and y. Often, but not always, the variable along the x-axis is a predictor for the variable along the y-axis. For example, if the scatterplot shows the heights of people (x-axis), plotted against their weights (y-axis), one might expect taller people to weigh more.

The scatterplot below shows the heights of pairs of parents. In each case, the father's height is plotted on the horizontal axis and the mother's height on the vertical axis.

Heights of Parents

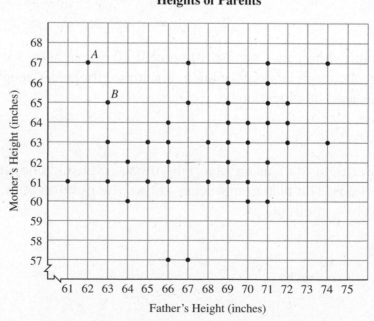

Here are some conclusions you can draw from the graph:

■ A point in this plot represents one pair of parents.

■ There are 40 such pairs, one per point.

■ There are only two pairs in which the mother is taller than the father: a 62-inch father with a 67-inch mother (point *A*), a 63-inch father with a 65-inch mother (point *B*).

■ There are six fathers who are 69 inches tall, and six others who are 71 inches tall. These numbers, 69 inches and 71 inches, are the two modes for fathers' heights.

■ There are eight mothers who are 63 inches tall. No other height occurs with a higher frequency for mothers; therefore, 63 inches is the mode for mothers' heights.

■ The median height of mothers is 63 inches. Imagine listing their heights in order. Start at the bottom of the graph, and move up: 57, 57, 60, 60, 60, ... The number 63 occurs in both the 20th and 21st (middle) slots.

■ The middle two heights for fathers are 68 and 69 inches. Therefore, the median height for fathers is 68.5 inches. Again, list the heights in order, starting at the left: 61, 62, 63, 63, 63, ... Just move right until you get to the middle. The 20th and 21st (middle) slots are 68 and 69.

Notice that the relationship between heights of fathers and heights of corresponding mothers seems to be weak, but it is not nonexistent: few tall women have short men as partners.

Line of Best Fit

On the SAT you may be asked to find the *line of best fit* for a scatterplot. This is a straight line that passes through the arithmetic means of the *x* and *y* variables. Typically, this line has the same number of points on either side of it. Sometimes called the "trend" line, the line of best fit indicates the correlation between the variables. If the slope is positive, there is a *positive correlation*; as one variable increases, so does the other. If the slope is negative, the correlation is negative; as one variable increases, the other decreases.

For example, a scatterplot of GPAs of high school students versus numbers of hours per day spent reading would be expected to show a positive correlation (see the diagram on the left below). On the other hand, a scatterplot of GPAs of high school students versus numbers of hours per day spent watching television would be expected to show a negative correlation, as in the diagram on the right.

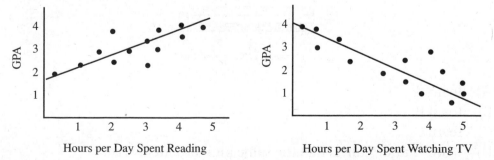

Tips for Solving Problems That Involve Statistical Graphs

The 2400 Club doesn't tackle a graph question until it knows precisely what the graph represents.

With that fact in mind, here are some pointers for approaching a graph question:

- Look at the **H**eader. It's a good clue about the contents of the graph.
- Study the **A**xes, and internalize what each one represents.
- For pie charts, bar graphs, and pictographs, make sure that you can verbalize what a single "**P**iece" represents:
    - For a pie chart: one piece of the pie.
    - For a pictograph: one picture.
    - For a bar graph: one bar.
- For graphs that involve points—line graphs, time plots, and scatterplots—you must be able to state precisely what a single **P**oint represents.

Coaching: *For graph questions, you will be a* **HAPPY** *student if you follow these steps:* **H**eader, **A**xes, **P**iece, **P**oint, **Y**ay— *you solved it!*

PRACTICE TEST QUESTIONS

1. Marie is an assembly-line supervisor at a plant that packages boxes of chocolates. Each week Marie reviews the production rates for the three teams that work on her assembly line. According to the following bar graph, which team had the highest overall production for week 20?

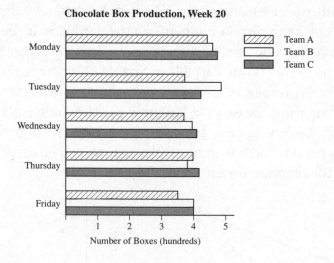

Chocolate Box Production, Week 20

(A) Team A
(B) Team B
(C) Team C
(D) Team A and Team B had the same high production rate
(E) Team B and Team C had the same high production rate

2. The Math Team and Debate Club at Jackson City High School buy their T-shirts from different stores. The tables below show the numbers of T-shirts ordered by the Math Team and Debate Club, and the costs of medium, large, and extra-large T-shirts.

Numbers of T-shirts Ordered

	Medium	Large	Extra-Large
Math Team	7	18	20
Debate Club	2	20	10

Costs of T-shirts

	Math Team	Debate Club
Medium	$11	$9
Large	$11	$10
Extra-large	$11	$14

Which statement about the costs of T-shirts, as shown in the tables, is true?

   I. The Math Team spent more on extra-large T-shirts than the Debate Club spent.

  II. On average, the Math Team paid more per T-shirt than the Debate Club paid.

 III. Of the three sizes, extra-large T-shirts had the highest median cost.

(A) I only

(B) II only

(C) III only

(D) I and III only

(E) I, II, and III

3. The toe shoes of professional ballerinas often wear out in less than a year. At a ballet school there are 20 students, all of whom bought new toe shoes of different brands and at varying prices. They kept track of how long their shoes lasted. Each point on the graph below shows the duration of a ballet student's toe shoes plotted against their price. Of the five labeled points, which one corresponds to the toe shoes that cost the greatest amount per month of use?

Duration of Toe-Shoes versus Cost

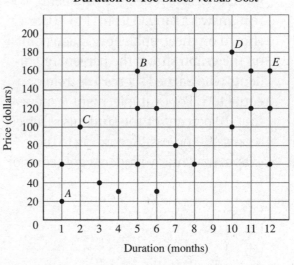

(A) A

(B) B

(C) C

(D) D

(E) E

Students and Test Scores

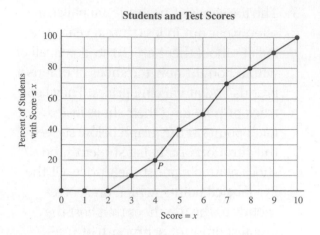

Score = x

4. When a 10-question true-false quiz was given to 50 students, the number of correct answers ranged from 3 to 10, as shown on the graph above. Each point on the graph shows the percent of students who earned scores less than or equal to x. For example, point P shows that 20 percent of the students received scores of 4 or less. According to the graph, how many students got scores of 6 ?

(A) 5
(B) 10
(C) 15
(D) 20
(E) 25

5. In the sequence $x, x + d, x + 2d, x + 3d$, assume that x and d are positive integers. What is the difference between the arithmetic mean and the median of the numbers in the sequence?

(A) $2x + 3d$

(B) $\dfrac{2x + 3d}{2}$

(C) $x + d$

(D) $\dfrac{x + d}{2}$

(E) 0

6. The table below gives the frequency with which various scores were obtained on a 20-question written section of a drivers' education test.

Score	12	13	14	15	16	17	18	19	20
Frequency	2	3	0	3	3	5	5	6	4

The mode of the data is

(A) 3
(B) 6
(C) 18
(D) 19
(E) 20

7. A psychologist's experiment involved timing 15 small children as they found the solution to a little puzzle. Each child received at least one similar puzzle to play with before being timed. The scatterplot below shows the time each child took to solve the puzzle, and the corresponding number of "practice" puzzles each child received. On the basis of these data, which of the following functions best models the relationship between t, the number of minutes taken to complete the puzzle, and p, the number of practice puzzles?

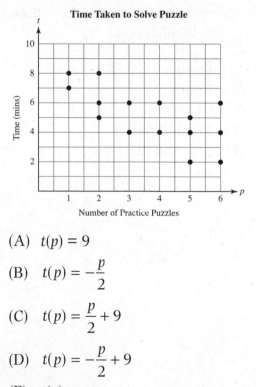

Time Taken to Solve Puzzle

Number of Practice Puzzles

(A) $t(p) = 9$

(B) $t(p) = -\dfrac{p}{2}$

(C) $t(p) = \dfrac{p}{2} + 9$

(D) $t(p) = -\dfrac{p}{2} + 9$

(E) $t(p) = -p$

Questions 8 and 9 are grid-in questions.

8. 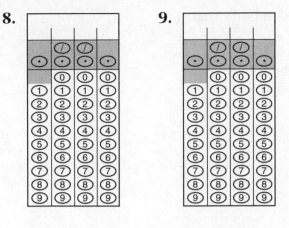   **9.**

9. A typing class in elementary school is divided into three groups. The Red Robins, with 6 students, has an average typing speed of 60 words per minute; the Blue Wax Bills, with 10 students, has an average typing speed of 45 words per minute; and the Gold Finches, with 16 students, has an average typing speed of 30 words per minute. What is the average (arithmetic mean) of the typing speeds, in words per minute, for the class?

Calories Burned for Exercise

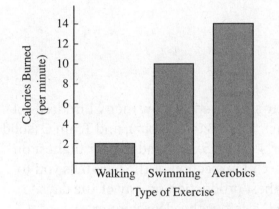

8. The above bar graph shows the number of calories burned per minute for three types of exercise, assuming that the exercise is performed vigorously. Jackie spent an hour exercising vigorously. She spent twice as much time doing aerobics as she did walking, and $1\frac{1}{2}$ times as much time swimming as she did aerobics. According to the graph, how many calories did Jackie expect to burn during that hour of exercise?

ANSWERS AND EXPLANATIONS

The difficulty level for each question is specified in parentheses.

1. C (H) **4.** A (H) **7.** D (M)
2. A (H) **5.** E (M) **8.** 600 (H)
3. C (H) **6.** D (M) **9.** 40.3 (M)

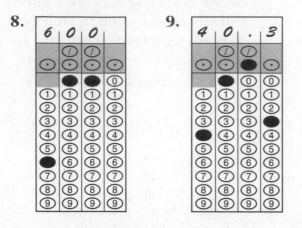

1. The answer is **(C)**.

Each set of three bars represents a single day's production: how many hundreds of boxes were packaged by Team A (striped bar), Team B (blank bar), and Team C (solid bar). Team C had the highest production for 3 of the 5 days and tied for highest on Friday. Don't waste time adding boxes. A careful inspection of the bars tells you to eliminate Team A: it did not achieve the highest production on any of the days. Team B was highest on Tuesday only. Team C is left as the clear winner.

2. The answer is **(A)**.

I: The Math Team spent $(20)(11) = \$220$ on extra-large T-shirts.
The Debate Club spent $(10)(14) = \$140$ on extra-large T-shirts.
$\therefore$ Statement I is true.

II: The average cost per T-shirt for the Math Team = $11.
The average cost per T-shirt for the Debate Club

$$= \frac{(2)(9) + (20)(10) + (10)(14)}{32} = \frac{356}{32} > 11$$

$\therefore$ Statement II is false.

 III: **To find each median cost, list data items in order:**

Medium: $\underbrace{9 \quad 9 \quad 11 \quad 11 \cdots 11}_{7}$ Middle term $=11$

Large: $\underbrace{10 \quad 10 \cdots 10}_{20} \quad \underbrace{11 \quad 11 \cdots 11}_{18}$ Middle term $=10$

Extra-large: $\underbrace{11 \quad 11 \cdots 11}_{20} \quad \underbrace{14 \quad 14 \cdots 14}_{10}$ Middle term $=11$

$\therefore$ Statement III is false; the median cost for extra-large was the same as for medium.

3. The answer is **(C)**.

Each point on the graph represents a single pair of toe shoes: how much it cost and how many months it lasted.

<u>Method I</u>: Arithmetic
Find the cost per month for each of the points given as choices.

A: $\dfrac{20}{1}$ = $20 per month.

B: $\dfrac{160}{5}$ = $32 per month.

C: $\dfrac{100}{2}$ = $50 per month.

D: $\dfrac{180}{10}$ = $18 per month.

E: $\dfrac{160}{12}$ ≈ $13 per month.

You can see that point C had the greatest cost per month.

<u>Method II</u>: Slope
For each pair of toe shoes, the cost per month equals the price of the shoes divided by its duration. For each point on the graph, this value corresponds to the slope of the line segment from point O to that point. For the five labeled points, look at the slopes of $\overline{OA}$, $\overline{OB}$, $\overline{OC}$, $\overline{OD}$, and $\overline{OE}$. Segment $\overline{OC}$ has the greatest slope, so point C is the answer.

4. The answer is **(A)**.

To answer this question correctly, you must take the time to study the axes and internalize the meaning of a single point: the percentage of students that got *at least* that score. According to the graph, 40 percent received scores of 5 or less, and 50 percent received scores of 6 or less. Therefore, exactly 10 percent received scores of 6, and 10 percent of 50 = 5.

5. The answer is **(E)**.

<u>Method I</u>: Pick-Convenient-Numbers Strategy
Take simple values for x and d. For example, $x = 2$ and $d = 3$ gives the sequence 2, 5, 8, 11.

Arithmetic mean = $\dfrac{26}{4} = 6\dfrac{1}{2}$.

Median = $\dfrac{5+8}{2} = 6\dfrac{1}{2}$.

∴ Difference = 0.

<u>Method II</u>: Logical Reasoning

$$\underset{\bullet}{x} \qquad \underset{\bullet}{x+d} \quad \underset{\bullet}{P} \quad \underset{\bullet}{x+2d} \qquad \underset{\bullet}{x+3d}$$

On the line, the numbers are equally spaced, so point P, the point right in the middle, must represent the arithmetic mean. The median is the average of the two middle numbers, which also is point P. Thus the difference between the two quantities is 0.

6. The answer is **(D)**.

The data items are the numbers of questions answered correctly. If you were to list them, they would look like this:

$$12, 12, 13, 13, 13, 15, 15, 15, \ldots$$

The number that would appear the most (six times) would be 19.

$\therefore$ mode = 19.

7. The answer is **(D)**.

The trend in the data shows that the time taken to complete the timed puzzle was lower if the child had more practice. If you placed a "best-fit" line through the points, namely, a line with roughly the same number of points on either side of it, the line would appear to start at roughly 9 on the t-axis and slope gently downward. This description represents a line with t-intercept around 9 and a negative slope.

Of the choices, $t(p) = -\dfrac{p}{2} + 9$ is the only equation that satisfies these requirements.

8. The answer is 600.

Say to yourself, "One bar on the graph represents the number of calories burned per minute for the given type of exercise." You need to find the ratio of swimming to aerobics to walking. Multiply walking by 2 to get aerobics, and aerobics by $\dfrac{3}{2}$ to get swimming. The ratio is

$$\text{swimming : aerobics : walking} = 3 : 2 : 1.$$

There are 3 + 2 + 1 = 6 parts altogether. Dividing the 60 minutes of exercise by 6 gives 10 minutes for each part. (You need to work in minutes, because the graph gives calories burned *per minute*. Did you study the axes and digest this fact?)

Time spent swimming = (3)(10) = 30 minutes.

Time spent on aerobics = (2)(10) = 20 minutes.

Time spent walking = (1)(10) = 10 minutes.

Now, consult the graph to find the number of calories burned for each exercise:

10 minutes of walking = (10)(2) = 20 calories burned.

20 minutes of aerobics = (20)(14) = 280 calories burned.

30 minutes of swimming = (30)(10) = 300 calories burned.

Total = 600 calories burned.

Grid-in 600.

9. The answer is 40.3.

Recognize this as a weighted average problem. Find the average of these typing speeds:

$$\underbrace{60 \quad 60 \cdot \cdot \; 60}_{6} \qquad \underbrace{45 \quad 45 \; \cdots \qquad 45}_{10} \qquad \underbrace{30 \quad 30 \quad \cdots \qquad\qquad 30}_{16}$$

$$\text{Average speed} = \frac{\text{sum of speeds}}{\text{number of students}} = \frac{(6)(60) + (10)(45) + (16)(30)}{32} \approx 40.3$$

Grid-in 40.3.

Chapter 17

WORD PROBLEMS

2400 Club Steps for Tackling a Word Problem

CARESS the problem. Yes, really!

Step 1: **C**oncentrate deeply during a first reading of the problem.

Step 2: **A**ctive pencil! Draw diagrams and charts. Assign variables.

Step 3: **R**educe the problem to a concise statement of what you need to find.

Step 4: **E**xpress the problem type so that you can apply a familiar technique.

Step 5: **S**olve the problem.

Step 6: **S**ensible answer? Ask yourself whether your answer makes sense.

WHY THE FUSS?

What, exactly, is a word problem? All of the SAT math problems have *words*, so why a special chapter?

The bugaboo about word problems exists because not only must you solve a math problem, but also you must first extricate that problem from statements embedded in a real-world scenario. You must extract the pertinent information from a web of details, some of which are extraneous. This can be a daunting task—but not for the 2400 Club. You are bringing years of math experience to the SAT, plus the ability and confidence to solve any question the test makers may devise.

HOW TO APPROACH A WORD PROBLEM

When you come to a word problem, especially one that looks tricky, don't flail about and panic. You need to be systematic and to force yourself to go through the following steps. If you need an acronym to help you remember, here's a thought: stay calm and CARESS the problem.

1. **C**oncentrate with 100 percent of your ability as you read the question carefully, beginning to end. This advice sounds trite, but it's important to absorb as much as possible on a first reading.

2. Use an **A**ctive pencil as you analyze the problem. Start writing things down as you think. Draw a diagram or a chart. Fill in pertinent values. Assign variables. Play with the problem on paper as you mull it over in your head.

3. **R**educe the problem to a concise statement of what must be calculated.

4. **E**xpress the question as a known problem type if at all possible. If you can identify the problem type, often you can apply a familiar technique or formula.

5. **S**olve the problem! By now you should have a pretty good idea how to do this.

6. **S**ensible answer? Ask yourself this question. If you came up with 62 as the average age of kindergartners, you need to reassess. Did you bubble in the quantity asked for? What a tragedy to correctly calculate Fran's current age, when the question actually asks how old she was 10 years ago!

Problem Types

Here are some of the problem types alluded to in Step 4:

- Rate problems, where p is proportional to q. Think: $\dfrac{p_1}{q_1} = \dfrac{p_2}{q_2}$.

- Inverse variation problems, where a is inversely proportional to b. Think: $a_1 b_1 = a_2 b_2$.

- Bacterial growth or population growth problems. Think: Geometric sequence.

- Percent increase problems. Think:

$$\text{Percent increase} = \frac{\text{new} - \text{original}}{\text{original}} \cdot 100.$$

- "Outfit" counting problems. Think: k hats, m shirts, and n slacks means $(k)(m)(n)$ possible outfits.

- "Committee" problems where order isn't important. How many different 3-person committees can be formed from 10 people?

  Think: Slots divided by arrangements of 3 people: $\dfrac{(10)(9)(8)}{(3)(2)(1)}$.

- "Committee" problems where order *is* important. How many different ways can you pick a secretary, treasurer, and president from 10 people? Think slots: $(10)(9)(8)$.

- Arithmetic mean of k values, $v_1, v_2, \ldots, v_k$: Think $\dfrac{v_1 + v_2 + v_3 + \cdots + v_k}{k}$.

- Median of data. Arrange data in order and find the middle value or average of the two middle values.

- Function modeling problems. For a linear function, find an equation of the form $y = mx + b$.

- Consecutive integers problems. Think: $n, n + 1, n + 2, \ldots$.
  For consecutive *even* integers, think: $n, n + 2, n + 4, \ldots$ (n even).
  For consecutive *odd* integers, think: $n, n + 2, n + 4, \ldots$ (n odd).

- Shaded areas problems. Think: Subtraction.

Translating English into Math

Translating English into math should be second nature to high scorers:

- 34 more than x: $x + 34$.
- 16 less than y: $y - 16$.
- The product of two numbers is: $xy =$.
- The cost of an opera ticket and dinner is: $t + d =$.
- Length ℓ is divided in the ratio 3 : 4: $\ell = 3x + 4x$, where x is one part.
- Marvin ate 5 candies for every 2 candies that Raymond ate: $\dfrac{m}{r} = \dfrac{5}{2}$.
- The difference between Sarah's salary and Jon's salary is $100: $|s - j| = 100$.
- The difference between Sarah's salary and Jon's salary is less than $100: $|s - j| < 100$.
- Peter is 4 years older than Lauren: $p = \ell + 4$.
- The discount is 25 percent off the price: $d = 0.25p$.

Some Additional Tips

In translating English into math, pick variable names that suggest what is represented to help you keep track. For example, Wendy's DVDs and Carol's videos should be represented as w and c, not x and y.

The verbiage in a problem that involves a graph can be extensive. Be systematic in examining the header, axes, and individual points.

Occasionally you will encounter a problem that you can't classify, a "no category" problem. Stay calm. High scorers are accustomed to using their brains. Gather your experience and wits, and focus in. Also, be aware that, if a problem is toward the end of a set, it will not be straightforward.

Here is a final thought that you should carry with you to the SAT:

> The 2400 Club has the talent to solve every math problem on the SAT.

Example 1

Mrs. Teukolsky gave a test that was so difficult that she decided to scale the grades upward. She raised the lowest score, 42, to 60, and the highest score, 77, to 90. A linear function that gives a fair way to convert any other test score x to the new score y is

(A) $y = -\dfrac{7}{6}x + 11$ (B) $y = -\dfrac{6}{7}x + 24$ (C) $y = -\dfrac{6}{7}x + 96$

(D) $y = \dfrac{7}{6}x + 11$ (E) $y = \dfrac{6}{7}x + 24$

Solution: The answer is **(E)**.

Active Pencil: Write $42 \to 60$ and $77 \to 90$, or $(42, 60)$ and $(77, 90)$.

Reduce the problem: Identify the linear function that contains $(42, 60)$ and $(77, 90)$.

Express the problem type: Find a linear function that contains two given points.

Solve: The quickest method is the plug-in strategy. Find the equation in the answer choices that works for each ordered pair.

Save time. Don't try the equations with negative slopes: as *x* increases, *y* increases, so the negative-slope choices can't be correct!

When you tried this problem, did you pick choice (D) because (42, 60) works?

$$60 = \frac{7}{6}(42) + 11 \Rightarrow 60 = 49 + 11, \text{ yes!}$$

If you did, you got the wrong answer, because *both* ordered pairs must work.
Sensible answer? Choice (E) seems reasonable.

Example 2

A solid white cube with an edge of 8 inches is painted red. The cube is then sliced into 512 1-inch cubes. How many of these cubes have exactly 2 red faces?

(A) 48   (B) 72   (C) 80   (D) 96   (E) 284

Solution: The answer is **(B)**.

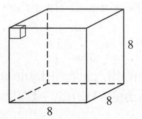

Concentrate! Picture that painted red cube in your mind's eye.

Active Pencil: Draw an 8-inch cube, and label the edges. Then draw in 1 or 2 little 1-inch cubes.

Reduce the problem: Find the number of "little" cubes that have exactly 2 red faces.

Express the problem type: Counting, and visualizing a three-dimensional solid.

Solve: Picture the little 1-inch cubes. Each corner cube will be red on 3 faces: top, side, and front. Now picture the non-corner cubes underneath the corner cube shown. These are the cubes you want. Can you see that there are 6 such cubes on each edge? Since there are 12 edges, there are (12)(6) = 72 cubes, each with exactly 2 red faces. The cubes in the "middle" of the faces have exactly 1 red face, and those on the "inside" of the big cube have no red faces, so 72 is the final answer.

Sensible answer? The total number of little cubes, 512, is the volume of the given cube. Most of the little cubes will *not* be red on 2 faces, so 72 is a reasonable answer.

Example 3

In January, Team *A* will play a tennis match against Team *B*. In February, Team *B* will play a tennis match against Team *C*. In March, Team *C* will play against Team *A*. Team *A* has a 75 percent chance of winning whenever it plays. Teams *B* and *C* are evenly matched, each with a 50 percent chance of winning when they play each other. What is the probability that Team *A* will lose both of its matches, and Team *B* will win both of its matches?

(A) $\frac{9}{16}$ (B) $\frac{1}{2}$ (C) $\frac{1}{16}$ (D) $\frac{1}{32}$ (E) $\frac{1}{128}$

Solution: The answer is **(D)**.

This problem is tricky and therefore likely to occur at the end of a set.

Active Pencil: Draw a diagram that summarizes the information in the problem. Write the probability of winning for each team.

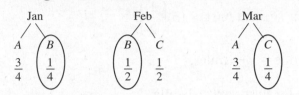

Reduce the problem: Find $P[(A \text{ loses to } B \text{ and } C) \text{ and } (B \text{ wins against } A \text{ and } C)]$.

Express the problem type: Probabilities of multiple events.

Solve: Circle the desired outcomes on your diagram; that is, circle the winners that give the desired results. Notice that you can rephrase the problem as follows: Find

$$P[(B \text{ wins in Jan.}) \text{ and } (B \text{ wins in Feb.}) \text{ and } (C \text{ wins in March})] = \left(\frac{1}{4}\right)\left(\frac{1}{2}\right)\left(\frac{1}{4}\right) = \frac{1}{32}.$$

Don't make the mistake of finding

$P[(A \text{ loses in Jan.}) \text{ and } (A \text{ loses in March}) \text{ and } (B \text{ wins in Jan.}) \text{ and } (B \text{ wins in Feb.})].$

These are not independent events: "A loses in Jan." is the same event as "B wins in Jan," so you mustn't count it twice.

Sensible answer? It's not very likely that the scenario whose probability you're calculating will happen, so choices (A), $\frac{9}{16}$, and (B), $\frac{1}{2}$, are poor picks. Also, given the probabilities in the question, choice (E), $\frac{1}{128}$, seems much too low. The answer is likely to be (C) or (D), so, $\frac{1}{32}$ makes sense.

Example 4 Grid-In

Lauren rode her bike from her house to a friend's house $3\frac{1}{2}$ miles away. On the first leg of her trip, she rode uphill at 3 miles per hour. The second part of the trip covered a larger distance but was downhill, and Lauren rode at 5 miles per hour. If the downhill part of the ride took half an hour, how many minutes did the uphill part take?

Solution: The answer is 20.

Concentrate. Both minutes and hours are mentioned, so units will be an issue.

Active Pencil: Draw a diagram showing the trip.

Reduce the problem: You are to find the time *in minutes* for the uphill part of the trip.

Express the problem type: Distance = speed × time.

Solve: Let x be the time for the uphill part of the trip. Work with x in hours, since the speeds are given in miles per *hour*. Write MINUTES in your test booklet to remind yourself to do the conversion at the end.

Distance for first part = $3x$.

Distance for second part = $(5)\left(\dfrac{1}{2}\right)$.

Total distance = $3\dfrac{1}{2}$ miles.

∴ Distance for first part = 1 mile.

∴ $3x = 1$

$\Rightarrow x = \dfrac{1}{3}$

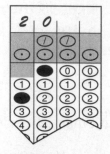

Sensible answer? Check! Don't blow it by gridding-in $\dfrac{1}{3}$. Your answer is in hours, but you are asked for time in minutes.

Grid-in 20.

Example 5

An ultramodern school building has weird, ultramodern clocks on the walls. In place of numerals from 1 to 12, a clock has 12 lights. The clock has no hour hand; instead, a flashing light signals the hour. The clock does, however, have a minute hand, which starts in a vertical position pointing up at 00, the start of the hour, and rotates clockwise through 360 degrees in 60 minutes. Here is how the clock shows various times:

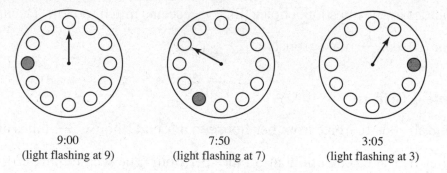

| 9:00 | 7:50 | 3:05 |
| (light flashing at 9) | (light flashing at 7) | (light flashing at 3) |

At 9:30 in the morning, while the teacher is out of the classroom, some mischievous students rotate the clock through 90 degrees counterclockwise, without touching the hand. In the next instant, before the clock display changes, the teacher reenters the room. She glances at the clock. What time does she see?

(A) 6:15　　　　(B) 3:00　　　　(C) 3:45　　　　(D) 12:15　　　　(E) 12:45

Solution: The answer is **(A)**.

Concentrate: You really need to make sure you understand how this crazy clock works.

Active Pencil: Draw the clock at 9:30, then rotate your figure through 90 degrees counterclockwise, and draw the new image.

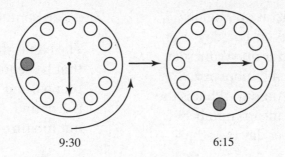

9:30   6:15

Reduce the problem: Find the time on the rotated clock.

Express the problem type: Find an image after rotation. This problem also requires you to understand a definition with strange symbols.

Solve: The actual solving is straightforward. Look at the new image of the clock, and note that it shows 6:15.

Sensible answer? Nothing is intuitive about this clock. Just make sure that you rotated in the right direction!

PRACTICE TEST QUESTIONS

1. Mika is doing an experiment with bacteria. She finds that, provided there is enough space and food, the population doubles every 2 hours. The population in hour $y + 10$ will be how many times the population in hour y?

   (A) 5
   (B) 10
   (C) 16
   (D) 32
   (E) 64

2. Ian has a job that pays him p dollars every day. From this amount he pays out $\dfrac{p}{5}$ dollars per day for supplies. He also spends an additional $\dfrac{1}{3}$ of what's left for lunch every day. He saves the rest of the money. In terms of p, how many days will it take Ian to save \$1,000?

   (A) $\dfrac{3,750}{p}$

   (B) $\dfrac{1,875}{p}$

   (C) $1,000p$

   (D) $\dfrac{800p}{3}$

   (E) $800p$

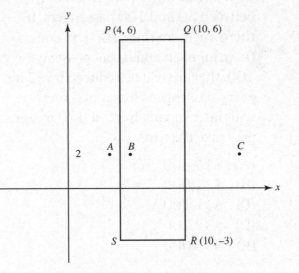

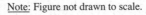
Note: Figure not drawn to scale.

3. In the figure above, $PQRS$ is a rectangle with $P(4, 6)$, $Q(10, 6)$, and $R(10, -3)$. Points A, B, and C all lie on the line $y = 2$. Points A and B are symmetric about line $\overleftrightarrow{PS}$, and points B and C are symmetric about line $\overleftrightarrow{QR}$. What is the length of $\overline{AC}$?

   (A) 10
   (B) 12
   (C) 14
   (D) 16
   (E) 18

4. Adam delivered n pizzas on Monday, 5 times as many pizzas on Tuesday as on Monday, 3 fewer pizzas on Wednesday than on Tuesday, and 7 more pizzas on Thursday than on Tuesday. What is the average (arithmetic mean) number of pizzas he delivered per day over the 4 days?

(A) $3n + 1$
(B) $3n + 4$
(C) $4n + 1$
(D) $\dfrac{3n + 5}{2}$
(E) $\dfrac{4n + 19}{4}$

5. A charter company will provide a plane for a fare of $300 per person if there are between 50 and 100 passengers. If there are more than 100 passengers, then, for each additional passenger over 100, the fare will be reduced by $2 for every passenger. How much revenue will the company make if 120 passengers take the trip?

(A) $16,400
(B) $24,000
(C) $31,200
(D) $35,200
(E) $36,000

6. The ratio of girls to boys at a certain school is 4 : 3. Which of the following could *not* be the number of students at the school?

(A) 1,430
(B) 1,477
(C) 1,547
(D) 2,107
(E) 2,450

7. A can contains $\dfrac{1}{4}$ pound of cashews.

The can is then filled with a mixture that has equal weights of cashews, pecans, and walnuts. If the final weight is 1 pound, what fraction of the final nut mixture is cashews?

(A) $\dfrac{1}{4}$
(B) $\dfrac{1}{3}$
(C) $\dfrac{1}{2}$
(D) $\dfrac{2}{3}$
(E) $\dfrac{3}{4}$

8. The Mayflower Diner has a rule that dessert pies must be sliced so that the angle at the tip of a piece of pie (where the tip is at the center of the pie) lies between 20 and 30 degrees. Which of the following inequalities can be used to determine whether an angle a at the tip of a pie slice satisfies the rule?

(A) $|a - 10| < 20$
(B) $|a - 25| < 30$
(C) $|a - 25| < 20$
(D) $|a| < 30$
(E) $|a - 25| < 5$

9. When an elastic object, such as a coil spring or rubber band, is subjected to a force *f*, an increase in length, called a *strain*, occurs. Hooke's law states that force *f* is directly proportional to strain *s*. Suppose that a coil spring has a natural length of 4 feet and that a force of 60 pounds stretches the length to 6 feet. What magnitude of force, in pounds, would stretch the spring to a length of 7 feet?

(A) 40

(B) $51\dfrac{3}{7}$

(C) 70

(D) 90

(E) 105

Questions 10 and 11 are grid-in questions.

10. Rachel is hanging posters in her new apartment, which includes a bedroom, a living room, and a den. She has 7 different posters. Assuming that she plans to place exactly 1 poster in each of the 3 rooms, how many choices does she have?

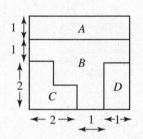

11. The figure above shows the top view of an open square box that is divided into four regions, *A*, *B*, *C*, and *D*, separated by very thin walls of equal height. Regions *A* and *D* are rectangular. Regions *B* and *C* have right angles at each corner. When a tiny pebble is dropped into the box at random, it falls into one of the regions. If it is equally likely that the pebble will land at any point in the box, what is the probability that it will *not* land in region *B*?

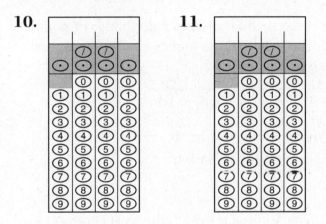

ANSWERS AND EXPLANATIONS
The difficulty level for each question is specified in parentheses.

1. D (H)	**4.** C (M)	**7.** C (M)	**10.** 210 (M)
2. B (H)	**5.** C (H)	**8.** E (M)	**11.** 9/16 or
3. B (H)	**6.** A (M)	**9.** D (H)	.562 (M)

10. **11.**

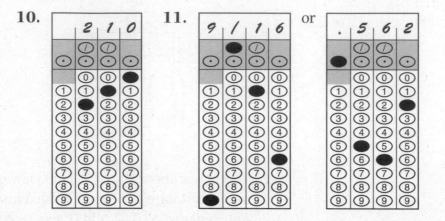

1. The answer is **(D)**.

From time y to time $y + 10$ there are 10 hours, and therefore 5 doublings of population. The bottom row of the table shows the geometric sequence for the population, assuming that the population at time y is p.

Time	y	$y + 2$	$y + 4$	$y + 6$	$y + 8$	$y + 10$
Population	p	$2p$	$4p$	$8p$	$16p$	$32p$

Thus, the final population is 32 times the original population.

2. The answer is **(B)**.

Use the pick-a-number strategy for fractions. Choose $p = \$15$, the least common denominator for $\frac{p}{5}$ and $\frac{1}{3}$.

After Ian pays $\frac{p}{5} = \$3$ for supplies, he has \$12 left.

An additional $\frac{1}{3}$ for lunch means \$4 for lunch, leaving \$8.

Number of days to save $\$1,000 = \frac{1,000}{8} = 125$.

Plug $p = 15$ into the answer choices to see which gives 125.

Choice (B)! $\frac{1,875}{15} = 125$.

3. The answer is **(B)**.

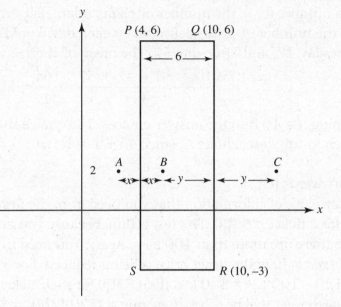

Note: Figure not drawn to scale.

Subtract the x-coordinates of P and Q to get $PQ = 6$. Since A and B are symmetric about $\overrightarrow{PS}$, they are equidistant from $\overrightarrow{PS}$.

Let the distance to $\overrightarrow{PS} = x$, and label it. Similarly, let y be the distance from B and C to $\overrightarrow{QR}$.

$AC = 2x + 2y = 2(x + y) = 2(6) = 12$.

Note: The information that points A, B, and C are all on line $y = 2$ tells you that these three points are collinear, and $\overrightarrow{AC} \| \overrightarrow{PQ}$. This fact allows you to simply add the lengths.

4. The answer is **(C)**.

<u>Method I</u>: Algebra

Make a chart showing the number of pizzas Adam delivered on each day:

Monday	n
Tuesday	$5n$
Wednesday	$5n - 3$
Thursday	$5n + 7$

$$\text{Arithmetic mean} = \frac{n + (5n) + (5n - 3) + (5n + 7)}{4} = \frac{16n + 4}{4} = 4n + 1$$

Method II: Pick-a-Number

Pick a number for n, the number of pizzas Adam delivered on Monday, such as 10. Then the number of pizzas delivered on each day would be Monday 10, Tuesday 50, Wednesday 47, and Thursday 57. The mean of these is

$$\frac{10 + 50 + 47 + 57}{4} = \frac{164}{4} = 41.$$

Now plug $n = 10$ into the answer choices. The choice that gives 41 is the correct answer, in this case, choice C, since $4n + 1 = 4(10) + 1 = 41$.

5. The answer is **(C)**.

The key piece of information that you need from the first sentence is that the base price for a ticket is $300. The rest is fluff, because you are dealing only with the case where there are more than 100 passengers. You need to make sure that you understand *exactly* how the ticket price is being reduced. For 120 passengers, all 120 will pay $(120 - 100)(2) = \$40$ less than $300 for their tickets: that is, the ticket price for each passenger will be $260. Revenue $= (120)(260) = \$31{,}200$.

6. The answer is **(A)**.

If $n =$ number of students, then $4x + 3x = n$, where x is some positive integer:

$$7x = n \Rightarrow x = \frac{n}{7}.$$

If n is not divisible by 7, you will end up with a fraction of a student. Realizing this possibility makes the problem go fast: choice (A), 1,430, is not divisible by 7.

7. The answer is **(C)**.

Amount of mixture added = final weight – original weight $= 1 - \frac{1}{4} = \frac{3}{4}$ pound.

Equal weights of cashews, pecans, and walnuts means that $\frac{1}{4}$ pound of each was

added. Since the can already contained $\frac{1}{4}$ pound of cashews,

$$\text{Final weight of cashews} = \frac{1}{4} + \frac{1}{4} = \frac{1}{2}, \text{ pound.}$$

This is $\frac{1}{2}$ of the final mixture.

8. The answer is **(E)**.

The problem boils down to this: Which of the given inequalities is equivalent to $20 < a < 30$?

Recall that $|x| < k \Rightarrow -k < x < k$.

Notice that choice (E) works:

$$|a - 25| < 5 \Rightarrow -5 < a - 25 < 5$$

$$\Rightarrow 20 < a < 30.$$

9. The answer is **(D)**.

Since f is directly proportional to s, $\dfrac{f_1}{s_1} = \dfrac{f_2}{s_2}$. Beware! Note that s is defined as an *increase* in length, so

$$s_1 = 6 - 4 = 2 \quad \text{and} \quad s_2 = 7 - 4 = 3.$$

The corresponding proportion is

$$\frac{60}{2} = \frac{f_2}{3} \Rightarrow f_2 = 90.$$

10. The answer is 210.

Method I: Slots.

A fast solution is to think of each room as a slot:

Bedroom	Living Room	Den

There are 7 poster choices for the bedroom, 6 choices for the living room, and 5 choices for the den: $(7)(6)(5) = 210$.

Method II: Combinations and Permutations

The problem asks for the number of ways Rachel can select 3 out of 7 posters, where order is important: Matisse in the bedroom, Picasso in the den, and Cezanne in the living room is not the same as Matisse in the den, Picasso in the living room, and Cezanne in the bedroom. Therefore, this is a permutation problem: find $_7P_3$.

$$_7P_3 = \frac{7!}{(7-3)!} = (7)(6)(5) = 210.$$

Grid-in 210.

11. The answer is $\dfrac{9}{16}$.

This is a geometric probability problem.

$P(\text{pebble does not land in } B) = P(\text{pebble lands in } A, C, \text{ or } D)$

$$= \frac{\text{area of } A + \text{area of } C + \text{area of } D}{\text{area of base of box}}$$

$$= \frac{4 + 3 + 2}{16}$$

$$= \frac{9}{16}.$$

Grid-in 9/16 or .562

Chapter 18

2400 CLUB GRAND MIXTURE

On the SAT, each math section is preceded by "Notes," which tell you that:

- You may use a calculator.
- The numbers in the problems are real numbers.
- Figures that accompany problems are in a plane unless stated otherwise. Also, the figures are drawn to scale unless otherwise noted.
- The domain of any function f is the set of all real numbers x for which $f(x)$ is a real number.

These notes are followed by "Reference Information" with formulas, like the section preceding the questions below.

Familiarize yourself with all the preamble ahead of time.

What follows is not a practice test. Rather, it is a mixture of the type of "medium" to "hard" problems discussed throughout the math section of this book. If you can solve these problems, you are headed for 800 on the SAT math. Go for it!

In this set of problems, questions 1–27 are multiple-choice, and questions 28–38 are grid-in.

PRACTICE TEST QUESTIONS

For the multiple-choice questions, select the best answer. For the grid-in questions, fill in your answer on the grid provided.

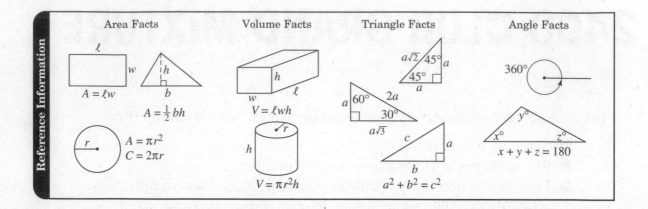

1. If x and y are real numbers, and $2\sqrt{x-4} - 2 = 1$, and $|y - 5| < 2$, what is the smallest possible integer value of $x + y$?

   (A) 9
   (B) 10
   (C) 11
   (D) 12
   (E) 13

2. The length of a rectangle is 4 less than double the width. If the area of the rectangle is 70, what is the perimeter of the rectangle?

   (A) 13
   (B) 17
   (C) 22
   (D) 30
   (E) 34

3. For all values of x and y, let $x * y$ be defined as $x * y = \dfrac{4xy}{3}$.
   If $6 * a = 2$, then $a =$

   (A) $\dfrac{1}{2}$

   (B) $\dfrac{1}{3}$

   (C) $\dfrac{1}{4}$

   (D) $\dfrac{1}{5}$

   (E) $\dfrac{1}{6}$

4. In a contest, each contestant could receive a score of 6, 7, 8, 9, or 10. The following bar graph shows how many contestants received each score.

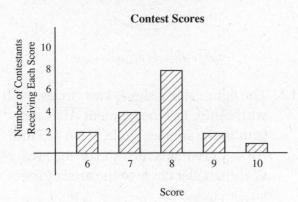

Contest Scores

The score of 8 is described by which of the following measures?

I. The average (arithmetic mean)
II. The median
III. The mode

(A) I only
(B) II only
(C) III only
(D) II and III only
(E) I, II, and III

5. Let $A = \{2, 3, 4, 7, 9, 10\}$ and $B = \{3, 6, 9, 12\}$.

If a number is chosen at random from set A, what is the probability that the number is in $A \cap B$?

(A) $\dfrac{1}{4}$

(B) $\dfrac{1}{3}$

(C) $\dfrac{1}{2}$

(D) $\dfrac{2}{3}$

(E) $\dfrac{3}{4}$

6. Let $f(x) = x^2 - x + 3$ and $g(x) = f(x + 3)$. What is the range of $g(x)$?

(A) All real numbers
(B) $y \geq 2.75$
(C) $y \leq 2.75$
(D) $y \geq 8.75$
(E) $y \geq 3$

7. The coordinates of the vertices of $\triangle ABC$ are $A(4, 5)$, $B(2, 1)$, and $C(6, 3)$. If P is a point such that $APBC$ is a parallelogram, what are the coordinates of P?

(A) $\left(\dfrac{9}{2}, 3\right)$

(B) $(1, 4)$
(C) $(8, 7)$
(D) $(1, 3)$
(E) $(0, 3)$

x	$f(x)$	$g(x)$
−1	−2	4
0	0	3
1	2	2
2	4	1
3	6	0
4	8	−1

8. According to the table above, for what value of x does $g(f(x)) = -1$?

(A) 8
(B) 4
(C) 3
(D) 2
(E) 1

9. If $\dfrac{a}{bc} = \dfrac{d}{ef}$, which of the following is *not* equivalent to each of the other expressions?

(A) $dbc = aef$

(B) $\dfrac{ae}{db} = \dfrac{c}{f}$

(C) $\dfrac{af}{d} = \dfrac{bc}{e}$

(D) $\dfrac{a}{d} = \dfrac{bc}{ef}$

(E) $\dfrac{ae}{f} = \dfrac{db}{c}$

10. If $12 + 6n$ is 20 percent larger than k, what is k?

(A) $\dfrac{12 + 6n}{5}$

(B) $10 + 5n$

(C) $2 + n$

(D) $\dfrac{6(12 + 6n)}{5}$

(E) $20 + 10n$

11. What is the domain of $f(x) = \dfrac{x}{\sqrt{1-x}}$?

(A) $x < 1$

(B) $x \le 1$

(C) $x > 1$

(D) $x \le 0$

(E) $x < 0$

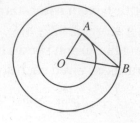

Note: Figure not drawn to scale.

12. The figure above shows two circles, each with center O. Line segment $\overline{AB}$ is tangent to the smaller circle. If $OA = 5$ and $AB = 12$, what is the ratio of the area of the smaller circle to the area of the larger circle?

(A) $5 : 13$

(B) $5 : 12$

(C) $25 : 169$

(D) $25 : 144$

(E) $144 : 169$

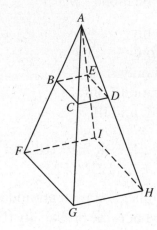

13. The pyramid in the figure above has square base $FGHI$, and all triangular faces are congruent. The base $BCDE$ of the small pyramid is also square, and is parallel to $FGHI$. If the ratio of the area of square $BCDE$ to the area of square $FGHI$ is $1 : 4$, what is the ratio of the volume of the small pyramid to the volume of the large pyramid?

(A) $1 : 2$

(B) $1 : 3$

(C) $1 : 4$

(D) $1 : 8$

(E) $1 : 32$

14. The original price of a shirt is x dollars. During a sale, the original price is marked down y percent. On the last day of the sale, an additional discount of z percent off the sale price is offered. Which of the following represents the price of the shirt, in dollars, after the additional discount?

(A) $\dfrac{xyz}{(100)(100)}$

(B) $\dfrac{x(1-y)(1-z)}{100}$

(C) $x\left(1-\dfrac{y}{100}\right)\left(1-\dfrac{z}{100}\right)$

(D) $x\left(1-\dfrac{y+z}{100}\right)$

(E) $x\left(1-\dfrac{yz}{100}\right)$

15. An electronics store charges \$24 for a set of stereo headphones and has been selling about 1,000 of them a week. The store manager estimates that for every \$1 price reduction, 100 more headphones can be sold per week. For example, he could sell 1,100 headphones at \$23 each and 1,200 headphones at \$22 each. Let $24 - x$ be the reduced price, in dollars, per set of headphones. Which function best represents the total expected revenue in a week for these headphones?

(A) $f(x) = (24 - x)(1{,}000 + 100x)$
(B) $f(x) = (x - 1)(1{,}000 + 24x)$
(C) $f(x) = 100(24 - x) + 1{,}000$
(D) $f(x) = (24)(1{,}000 + 100x) - x$
(E) $f(x) = (24 - x)(1{,}000 - 100x)$

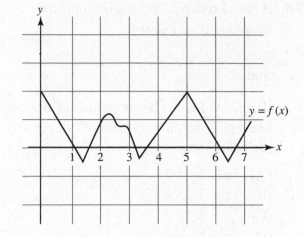

16. The above graph shows $f(x)$, which is defined for all real numbers. If $f(x + 5) = f(x)$ for all x, for how many x-values in the interval $0 \le x \le 17$ is $f(x) = 0$?

(A) 10
(B) 11
(C) 12
(D) 13
(E) 14

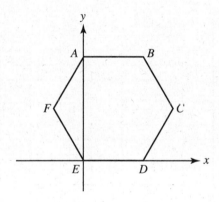

17. In the figure above, $ABCDEF$ is a regular hexagon. What is the slope of line $\overleftrightarrow{FE}$?

(A) $-\dfrac{1}{2}$

(B) $-\sqrt{3}$

(C) $-\sqrt{2}$

(D) $\sqrt{3}$

(E) $\dfrac{1}{2}$

18. A set of real numbers is represented graphically as follows:

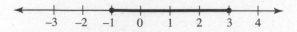

If x is a value in the set, which of the following inequalities represents all possible values of x?

(A) $|x - 3| \leq 4$
(B) $|x - 3| \geq 4$
(C) $|x - 1| \leq 2$
(D) $|x - 1| \geq 2$
(E) $|x - 3| \leq 1$

19. The management of a large sports-equipment store conducts a survey of its 15 treadmill salespeople. The average number of minutes spent with each potential customer and the number of treadmills sold in a week are recorded for each salesperson. The results are shown in the scatterplot below.

Treadmill Sales

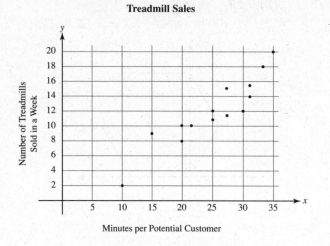

Minutes per Potential Customer

Which could be the line of best fit for these data?

(A) $y = 0.54x + 1.2$
(B) $y = 0.54x + 5$
(C) $y = -0.54x + 5$
(D) $y = -0.54x - 3.7$
(E) $y = 0.54x - 3.7$

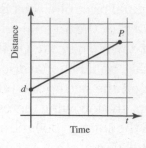

20. A particle moves at a constant speed. The graph above shows the distance traveled as a function of time, starting at distance d at time $= 0$. If the constant speed of the particle had been lower during the given time frame, which of the following could be the graph?

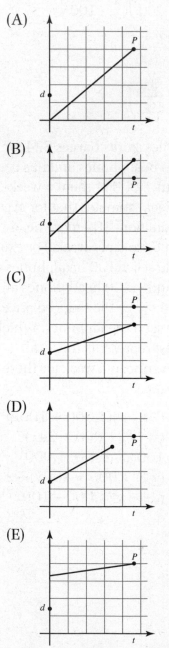

21. If $|x^2 + 4x - 21| > 0$, which must be true?

(A) $x < -7$ or $x > 3$
(B) $-7 < x < 3$
(C) $x \neq -7$ or $x \neq 3$
(D) $x \neq -3$ or $x \neq 7$
(E) x is any real number.

22. Which is equivalent to $x^{-\frac{2}{3}} = 4$?

(A) $x^{\frac{2}{3}} = \frac{1}{4}$

(B) $x^{\frac{2}{3}} = -4$

(C) $x^{-\frac{2}{3}} = -\frac{1}{4}$

(D) $x^{\frac{3}{2}} = \frac{1}{4}$

(E) $x^{-\frac{3}{2}} = \frac{1}{4}$

23. Consider this repeating decimal:

0.102003000400005 ... 800000000
900000000001020030004 ...

What will be the 118th digit of this number?

(A) 0
(B) 2
(C) 4
(D) 6
(E) 8

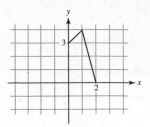

24. The graph shown above represents $f(x + 3)$. Which graph represents $f(x - 3)$?

(A)
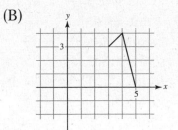

(B)
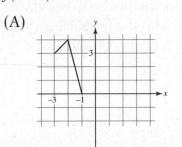

(C)
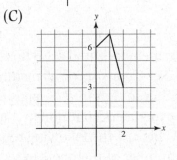

(D)
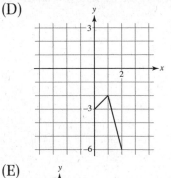

(E)
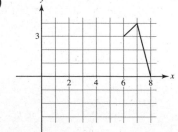

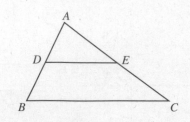

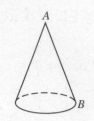

25. In the figure above, D is the midpoint of $\overline{AB}$ and E is the midpoint of $\overline{AC}$. A point is picked at random in $\triangle ABC$. If all points in $\triangle ABC$ are equally likely to be picked, what is the probability that the point lies in trapezoid $BDEC$?

(A) $\dfrac{1}{2}$

(B) $\dfrac{2}{3}$

(C) $\dfrac{3}{5}$

(D) $\dfrac{3}{4}$

(E) $\dfrac{4}{5}$

26. Set A has a members, and set B has b members. Set C consists of all members that are either in A or in B. Suppose that there are p members common to A and B, $p > 0$. Which of the following represents the number of members in set C?

(A) $a + b$
(B) $a + b - p$
(C) $a + b - 2p$
(D) $a + b + p$
(E) $a + b + 2p$

27. A hollow right circular cone made of cardboard is shown above. Point A is the vertex, and B is any point on the circular edge of the base. The cone is cut along line segment $\overline{AB}$, then opened up and flattened out. Which of the following could represent the plane figure obtained?

(A)

(B)

(C)

(D)

(E)

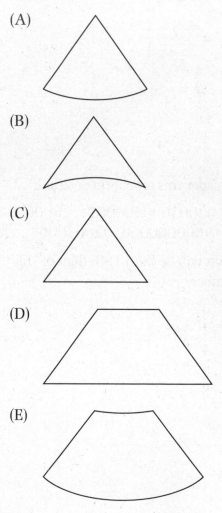

Questions 28–38 are grid-in questions.

28.

29.

30.

31.

32.

33.

34.

35.

36.

37.

38.

28. The consecutive multiples of 7 from −84 to 7k, k > 0, are added together. If the total is 189, what is k?

29. The following table shows the results of a survey of 40 high school students:

Favorite Subject

	Math	English	History
Girls	6	11	5
Boys	8	2	8

What percent of students surveyed preferred English or history to math?

A ———————————— B — C ——————— D ——————— E

Note: Figure not drawn to scale.

30. In the figure above, D is the midpoint of $\overline{CE}$, and the ratio AB : BC is 2 : 1. If the length of $\overline{BD}$ is 14 and the length of $\overline{AE}$ is 34, find the length of $\overline{AB}$.

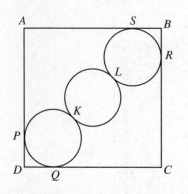

31. In the diagram above, ABCD is a square. The circles, whose centers lie on $\overline{BD}$, are congruent to each other. The sides of the square are tangent to the outer circles at P, Q, R, and S, and the circles are tangent to each other at K and L. If the radius of each circle is 1 inch, what is the area, to the nearest square inch, of the square?

32. The following table shows how the price of a certain computer has fallen since the year 2008:

Year	Price
2008	$2,020
2009	$1,500
2010	$1,250
2011	$1,100
2012	$1,000

According to this table, by what percent did the price decrease from 2008 to 2012?

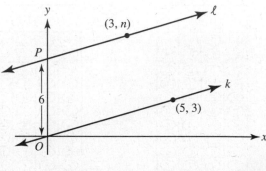

Note: Figure not drawn to scale.

33. In the xy-coordinate system shown above, the lines ℓ and k are parallel, and distance OP is 6. If point (5, 3) is on line k, and point (3, n) is on line ℓ, what is the value of n?

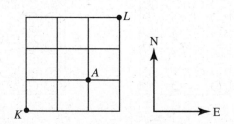

34. Suppose that, to get from point K to point L, shown in the figure above, a traveler must either go north or east (up or right). For example, one possible path is to go 3 steps east then 3 steps north. How many possible paths are there from K to L that *don't* include point A?

35. The weight of an object on or beneath the surface of the Moon varies directly as the distance of the object from the center of the Moon. The radius of the Moon is approximately 1,080 miles. If an object weighs 60 pounds on the surface of the Moon, how far beneath the surface, in miles, would it have to be to weigh 50 pounds?

36. One-third of the air in a tank is removed with each stroke of a pump. What percent of the original amount of air remains in the tank after five strokes?

37. In a theater, the front row has 30 seats. Each row behind the first row has 4 more seats than the row in front of it. If there are 26 rows, what is the total number of seats in the theater?

38. A hardware store owner finds that she can expect to sell n sets of wrenches per month if the price per set, in dollars, is

$$p(n) = \frac{3,000}{a+n}$$

where a is constant. If, according to this function, 25 sets of wrenches are sold in a month at $100 per set, how many sets can the owner expect to sell in a month if she raises the price to $200 per set?

ANSWERS AND EXPLANATIONS
The difficulty level for each question is specified in parentheses.

1. B (M)   9. E (M)   17. B (M)   25. D (M)   33. 39/5 or 7.8 or
2. E (M)   10. B (M)   18. C (M)   26. B (M)   7.80 (H)
3. C (M)   11. A (M)   19. E (M)   27. A (M)   34. 11 (H)
4. D (M)   12. C (M)   20. C (M)   28. 14 (H)   35. 180 (H)
5. B (M)   13. D (H)   21. C (H)   29. 65 (M)   36. 13.2 or 13.1 (H)
6. B (M)   14. C (H)   22. A (M)   30. 12 (H)   37. 2080 (H)
7. E (H)   15. A (H)   23. C (H)   31. 23 (H)   38. 10 (H)
8. D (H)   16. E (H)   24. E (H)   32. 50.5 or 50.4 (M)

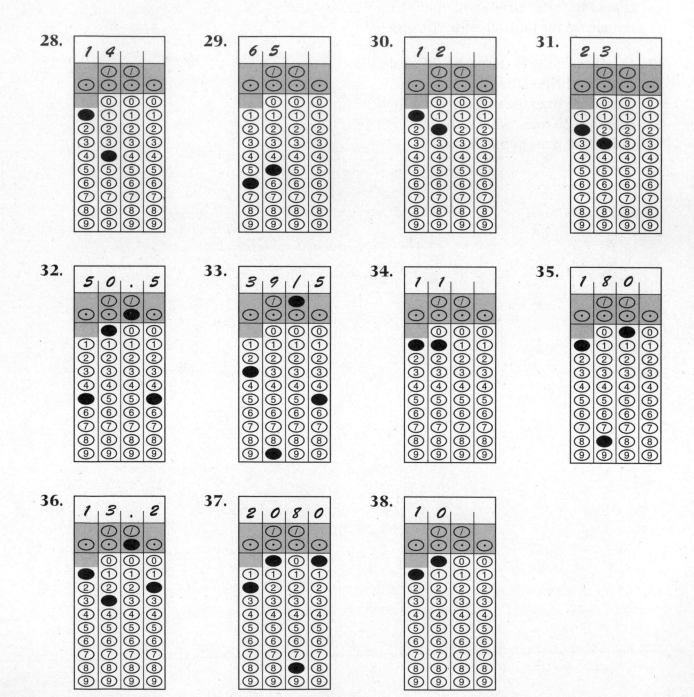

1. The answer is **(B)**.

$$2\sqrt{x-4}-2=1$$

$\Rightarrow 2\sqrt{x-4}=3$ (Isolate term with radical.)

$\Rightarrow 4(x-4)=9$ (Square both sides. Don't forget the 2!)

$\Rightarrow x=6\frac{1}{4}.$

$$|y-5|<2$$

$\Rightarrow -2<y-5<2$

$\Rightarrow 3<y<7.$

$\therefore$ Smallest integer value of $x+y=6\frac{1}{4}+3\frac{3}{4}=10.$

2. The answer is **(E)**.

Let the width be w. Then the length is $2w-4$. Since the area is 70:

$$w(2w-4)=70$$

$\Rightarrow \quad 2w^2-4w=70$

$\Rightarrow w^2-2w-35=0$

$\Rightarrow (w-7)(w+5)=0$

$\Rightarrow w=7.$ (Reject -5 since width cannot be negative.)

Dimensions are 7 and 10, so perimeter $= 2(7+10)=34.$

3. The answer is **(C)**.

$$x*y=\frac{4xy}{3}$$

$\therefore 6*a=2$

$\Rightarrow \dfrac{4(6)a}{3}=2$

$\Rightarrow \quad 8a=2$

$\Rightarrow \quad a=\dfrac{1}{4}$

4. The answer is **(D)**.

The arithmetic mean of the scores $= \dfrac{2(6)+4(7)+8(8)+2(9)+10}{17}.$

Since the numerator is not divisible by 17, the arithmetic mean is not equal to 8.

You don't need to do any calculation at all if you notice on the graph that the size of the bars on either side of 8 will weight the arithmetic mean to the left of 8.

If you were to list the data in order, you would see that the middle item is 8; therefore, the median is 8.

$$\underbrace{6 \quad 6}_{2} \quad \underbrace{7 \quad 7 \quad 7 \quad 7}_{4} \quad \underbrace{8 \quad 8 \quad \cdots \quad 8}_{8} \quad \underbrace{9 \quad 9}_{2} \quad \underbrace{10}_{1}$$

The item occurring the most times is 8; therefore, the mode is 8. Measures II and III only are correct.

5. The answer is **(B)**.
   $A = \{2, 3, 4, 7, 9, 10\}$, and $B = \{3, 6, 9, 12\}$.
   $\therefore A \cap B \{3, 9\}$, the common elements.
   Since there are 2 successful outcomes out of 6 possible outcomes,

$$P(\text{number in } A \cap B) = \frac{2}{6} = \frac{1}{3}$$

6. The answer is **(B)**.
   The graph of $f(x)$, shifted 3 units to the left, is $f(x + 3)$. This shift does not change the y-value of the minimum point. Therefore, the range of $g(x)$ will be the same as the range of $f(x)$. Don't waste time with $g(x)$! Work with $f(x)$.

   <u>Method I</u>: Graphing Calculator

   Graph $f(x)$ on the calculator, and notice that the minimum y-value is 2.75.

   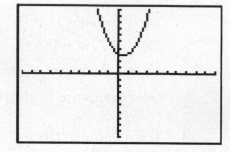

   <u>Method II</u>: Algebra
   $f(x) = x^2 - x + 3$
   $\quad\quad = (x - 0.5)^2 + 2.75$ (completing the square).
   The vertex of the parabola is $(0.5, 2.75)$. Since the graph is concave up, 2.75 is the minimum value of y.
   $\therefore$ Range is $y \geq 2.75$.

7. The answer is **(E)**.

   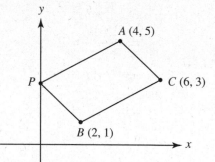

   Slope of $\overline{AC} = \dfrac{5 - 3}{4 - 6} = -1$. Slope of $\overline{AC}$ must equal slope of $\overline{PB}$. $P(0, 3)$ is the only point that works:

   $$\text{Slope of } \overline{PB} = \frac{3 - 1}{0 - 2} = -1$$

   Note that points A, P, B, and C must go in order, either clockwise or counterclockwise. Therefore, the placement of P as shown on the right, for example, is incorrect. It gives parallelogram $APCB$, which is not the parallelogram that was asked for, namely, $APBC$.

   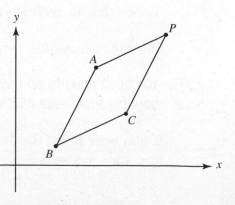

8. The answer is **(D)**.
   Since $g(4) = -1$ and $f(2) = 4$, $g(f(2)) = -1$.
   Since you're asked to find the x value for which $g(f(x)) = -1$,
   the correct x value is 2.

9. The answer is **(E)**.
   You are given $\dfrac{a}{bc} = \dfrac{d}{ef}$. Cross-multiplying gives $aef = bcd$. The easiest way to solve this
   problem is to cross-multiply each of the choices. Only one of these, choice E, does
   not give $aef = bcd$.

10. The answer is **(B)**.
    Method I: Algebra
    $12 + 6n$ is 20 percent larger than k.
    $$\Rightarrow 12 + 6n = \left(k + \frac{1}{5}k\right) = \frac{6}{5}k.$$
    $$\Rightarrow k = \frac{5(12 + 6n)}{6}$$
    $$= 10 + 5n$$

    Method II: Pick-a-Number
    Suppose $n = 10$. Then,
    $$12 + 6(10) = \frac{6}{5}k$$
    $$\Rightarrow \frac{6}{5}k = 72$$
    $$\Rightarrow k = 60$$

    Now plug $n - 10$ into each answer choice, and see which gives you 60. The answer
    is choice B, since $10 + 5(10) = 60$.

11. The answer is **(A)**.
    You are given $f(x) = \dfrac{x}{\sqrt{1-x}}$.
    All real numbers are in the domain except x values that give 0 in the denominator or
    negative values in the radical, so $1 - x$ must be positive.
    $$\therefore 1 - x > 0 \Rightarrow x < 1.$$

12. The answer is **(C)**.
    By the tangent-radius theorem, $\angle A$ is a right angle.
    Using Pythagoras in $\triangle ABC$ gives $OB = 13$.
    $$\frac{\text{Radius of small circle}}{\text{Radius of large circle}} = \frac{5}{13}$$
    $$\therefore \frac{\text{Area of small circle}}{\text{Area of large circle}} = \left(\frac{5}{13}\right)^2 = \frac{25}{169} = 25 : 169.$$

13. The answer is **(D)**.

$$\frac{\text{Area of small square}}{\text{Area of large square}} = \frac{1}{4}$$

$$\therefore \frac{\text{Side of small square}}{\text{Side of large square}} = \frac{1}{2}$$

$$\therefore \frac{\text{Volume of small pyramid}}{\text{Volume of large pyramid}} = \left(\frac{1}{2}\right)^3 = \frac{1}{8} = 1 : 8.$$

14. The answer is **(C)**.

Use the pick-a-number strategy. Start with $x = 100$ since this is a percent problem.
Now take easy numbers for y and z, for example, $y = 10$ and $z = 30$.
Original price = $100.
Mark down of 10 percent gives sale price of $90.
Additional 30 percent off leaves 70 percent of $90 = $63.
Now test each answer choice by plugging in $x = 100$, $y = 10$, $z = 30$ to see which gives an answer of 63.
Choice (C) works:

$$x\left(1 - \frac{y}{100}\right)\left(1 - \frac{z}{100}\right) = 100(1 - 0.1)(1 - 0.3)$$

$$= 100(0.9)(0.7) = 63.$$

15. The answer is **(A)**.

Method I: Pick-a-Number Strategy
Use the given example! If $x = 1$ (a $1 reduction), 1,100 headphones per week can be sold at $23 each. The revenue will be $(23)(1,100)$ or $(24-1)(1,000 + 100(1))$, which matches the function given in choice (A).

Method II: Logical Reasoning
Price per headphone $p = (24 - x)$
Number of headphones sold in a week, $n = (1,000 + 100x)$
Revenue for a week = pn
$\therefore f(x) = (24 - x)(1,000 + 100x)$

16. The answer is **(E)**.

Since $f(x + 5) = f(x)$ for all x, you know that the function is periodic and repeats itself every 5 units. Note that, in the interval $0 \le x \le 5$, $f(x) = 0$ four times. (You can see this because the graph cuts the x-axis four times.)
$\therefore$ In the interval $5 < x \le 10$, $f(x) = 0$ another four times, and so on.
$\therefore$ In the interval $0 \le x \le 15$, $f(x) = 0$ twelve times.
In the first two units of the next cycle, $f(x) = 0$ twice.
$\therefore$ In the interval $0 \le x \le 17$, $f(x) = 0$ fourteen times.

17. The answer is **(B)**.

Can you see that the slope of $\overline{FE}$ is independent of the length of the side of the hexagon? The angle at E will be the same, no matter what the length.

An interior angle of a regular hexagon

$$= \frac{(n-2)180}{n} = \frac{(6-2)180}{6} = 120°.$$

The adjacent angle at E measures 60°, so $\triangle FPE$ is a 30–60–90° triangle.

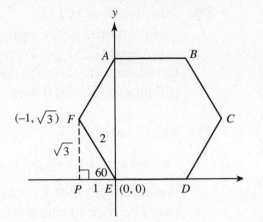

Suppose that $EF = 2$. Then $PE = 1$, and $PF = \sqrt{3}$, so F is point $(-1, \sqrt{3})$.

$\therefore$ Slope of $\overline{FE} = \dfrac{\sqrt{3}-0}{-1-0} = -\sqrt{3}$.

18. The answer is **(C)**.

The given set is $-1 \le x \le 3$. Notice that subtracting 1 from each expression of the inequality gives $-2 \le x - 1 \le 2$, which is equivalent to $|x-1| \le 2$.

If you don't see this solution, eliminate choices (B) and (D), since these inequalities give two disjoint (separate) regions. Then solve each of the remaining choices; (C) is the only choice whose solution gives $-1 \le x \le 3$, which is the set given on the number line.

19. The answer is **(E)**.

Treadmill Sales

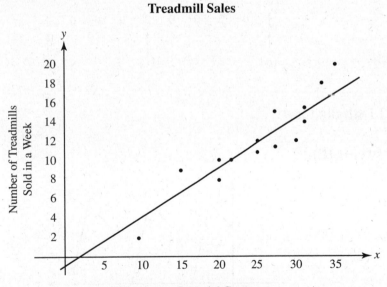

Minutes per Potential Customer

On your test booklet draw a line that roughly passes through the center of the points, as shown above. Notice that this line cuts the y-axis below the x-axis, giving a negative y-intercept, so you can eliminate choices (A), (B), and (C). Notice also that the line has a positive slope, so the correct answer is choice (E).

20. The answer is **(C)**.

The relationship between distance d, speed s, and time t is $d = st$. In the graph, s represents the slope. Therefore, a lower speed corresponds to a smaller slope. The initial starting distance does not change, so you can eliminate choices (A), (B), and (E). Since choice (D) does not change the slope, the correct answer is (C).

21. The answer is **(C)**.

$$| x^2 + 4x - 21 | > 0 \Rightarrow | (x + 7)(x - 3) | > 0.$$

It would seem that x could be any real number, since absolute value is always positive. The trick in this question is to realize that, when $x = -7$ or $x = 3$, the expression is zero. Therefore, you must eliminate these values.

22. The answer is **(A)**.

$$x^{-\frac{2}{3}} = 4 \Rightarrow \frac{1}{x^{\frac{2}{3}}} = 4$$

$$\Rightarrow \quad x^{\frac{2}{3}} = \frac{1}{4}$$

23. The answer is **(C)**.

Number of 0's in one cycle $= 1 + 2 + 3 + \cdots + 9 = \dfrac{(9)(10)}{2} = 45.$

$\therefore$ Number of digits in one cycle $= 45 + 9 = 54.$

$\therefore$ Number of digits in two cycles $= 108.$

$$
\begin{array}{ccccccccccc}
1 & 0 & 2 & 0 & 0 & 3 & 0 & 0 & 0 & 4 \\
\uparrow & & & & & \uparrow & & & & \uparrow \\
109 & & & & & 114 & & & & 118
\end{array}
$$

$\therefore$ The 118th digit is 4.

24. The answer is **(E)**.

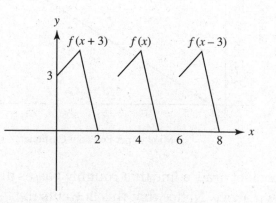

$f(x + 3)$ is the graph of $f(x)$ shifted 3 units to the left.

$f(x - 3)$ is the graph of $f(x)$ shifted 3 units to the right.

25. The answer is **(D)**.
△*ADE* is similar to △*ABC*.

$$\frac{AD}{AB} = \frac{1}{2}.$$

$$\frac{\text{Area of } \triangle ADE}{\text{Area of } \triangle ABC} = \left(\frac{1}{2}\right)^2 = \frac{1}{4}.$$

Then the area of △*ADE* is $\frac{1}{4}$ the area of △*ABC*.

∴ Area of trapezoid *BDEC* is $\frac{3}{4}$ area of △*ABC*.

∴ Probability that a randomly chosen point lies in trapezoid $BDEC = \frac{3}{4}$.

26. The answer is **(B)**.
Use the pick-the-numbers strategy.
For example, let $A = \{1, 2, 3\}$, and $B = \{2, 3, 4, 5\}$. Then $C = \{1, 2, 3, 4, 5\}$. In this case, $a = 3$, $b = 4$, and $p = 2$. The number of members in C is $3 + 4 - 2$. The point of this question is that you should not count the common members twice.

27. The answer is **(A)**.
As shown in the diagram, for a right circular cone, all points *B* on the circular edge of the base are equidistant from *A*, the vertex. Let this common distance be *r*. The plane figure obtained must therefore be a sector of a circle with radius *r*. Only choice (A) has this property.

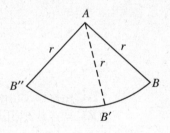

28. The answer is 14.
$(-84) + (-77) + (-70) + \cdots + 0 + 7 + 14 + \cdots + 77 + 84 = 0$.
Adding the next two multiples of 7 gives $91 + 98 = 189$.
Be careful that you answer the question asked. $7k = 98 \Rightarrow k = 14$.
Grid-in 14.

29. The answer is 65.
Of the 40 students surveyed, $11 + 2 + 5 + 8 = 26$ preferred English or history.

$$\frac{26}{40} = \frac{13}{20} = 65\%.$$

Grid-in 65.

30. The answer is 12.

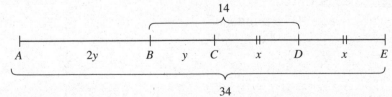

Label distances *x* and *y*, as shown on preceding page.

$x + y = 14 \Rightarrow x = (14 - y)$
and $2x + 3y = 34$
$\therefore 2(14 - y) + 3y = 34$ (substitution)
$\Rightarrow 28 - 2y + 3y = 34$
$\Rightarrow \qquad\qquad y = 6$

You are asked for *AB*, which is $2y$. Thus the answer is 12.

Don't waste time solving for *x*!

Grid-in 12.

31. The answer is 23.

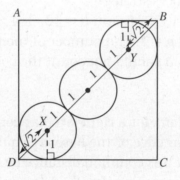

Length of diagonal $\overline{BD} = XY + XD + YB$
$XY = 4 \times \text{radius} = 4$.
Both $\overline{XD}$ and $\overline{YB}$ are in 45–45–90° triangles, and each has length $\sqrt{2}$.
$\therefore BD = 4 + 2\sqrt{2}$.
You are asked for the area of square *ABCD*.
<u>Method I</u>: One-Half Product of Diagonals

$$\begin{aligned}
\text{Area of } ABCD &= \left(\frac{1}{2}\right)(4 + 2\sqrt{2})(4 + 2\sqrt{2}) \\
&= (2 + \sqrt{2})(4 + 2\sqrt{2}) \\
&= 8 + 8\sqrt{2} + 4 \\
&= 12 + 8\sqrt{2} \\
&\approx 23
\end{aligned}$$

<u>Method II</u>: Side Squared
$\triangle DBC$ is a 45–45–90° triangle.

$\therefore$ If $BD = 4 + 2\sqrt{2}$, $DC = \dfrac{4 + 2\sqrt{2}}{\sqrt{2}} = \dfrac{4}{\sqrt{2}} + 2 = 2\sqrt{2} + 2$.

Area of square $= (2\sqrt{2} + 2)^2 = 8 + 4 + 8\sqrt{2} \approx 23$.
Grid-in 23.

32. The answer is 50.5 or 50.4.

$$\text{Percent decrease} = \frac{\text{amount of decrease}}{\text{original amount}} \cdot 100$$

$$\frac{2,020 - 1,000}{2,020} \cdot 100 \approx 50,4950495\%$$

Grid-in 50.5 or 50.4.

33. The answer is $\frac{39}{5}$ or 7.8 or 7.80.

Point P is $(0, 6)$.

Slope of $k = \dfrac{3-0}{5-0} = \dfrac{3}{5}$.

Since $\ell \parallel k$, slope of ℓ = slope of k.

$\therefore$ Slope of $\ell = \dfrac{3}{5} = \dfrac{n-6}{3-0} \Rightarrow 5n - 30 = 9 \Rightarrow n = \dfrac{39}{5}$.

Grid-in 39/5 or 7.8 or 7.80.

34. The answer is 11.

Method I: Combinations and Permutations

Number of paths from K to L, excluding those that contain A

$$= (\text{total number of paths from } K \text{ to } L) - (\text{number of paths that include } A).$$

To find the total number of paths from K to L, you need to go east (E) 3 times and north (N) 3 times. Here are 2 different ways you can do this: EEENNN, NENENE. Think of this problem as being the numbers of arrangements of 3 E's and 3 N's. There are 6 slots. The correct answer, however, is not $(6)(5)(4)(3)(2)(1)$, since the E's are indistinguishable from each other, as are the N's.

You must divide by the number of arrangements of these 3 E's and the 3 N's.

$\therefore$ Total number of paths from K to L $\dfrac{(6)(5)(4)(3)(2)(1)}{(3)(2)(3)(2)} = 20.$

Now find the number of paths that include A. There are 3 ways to get to A, before proceeding to L;

EEN_ _ _,   ENE_ _ _,   NEE_ _ _.

To get from A to L you must fill the other 3 slots with the remaining 1 E and 2 N's.

Number of arrangements of 1 E and 2 N's = $\dfrac{(3)(2)}{(2)} = 3.$

This result must be multiplied by those 3 ways to get to A.

$\therefore$ Number of paths from K to L that include $A = (3)(3) = 9$.

$\therefore$ Number of paths from K to L that exclude $A = 20 - 9 = 11$.

Grid-in 11.

<u>Method II</u>: Just Counting

Here is a neat, quick, intuitive way to solve this problem. Start at the end point, L, and count paths working backward, one cell at a time, until you reach the starting point A. When you get to A, you should have the total possible number of paths. Got it? Here's the basic strategy:

There is just one way to get to the end (point L) from the point just below it and also the point to the left of it. Label these with a 1, as shown:

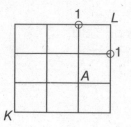

From the point directly below or left of any labeled point there is just one way to get to the labeled point. So for any point that has upper and right neighbors labeled, label that point with the sum of its upper and right neighbors. For any point that is outside the grid, pretend that it is labeled with a 0. Each label represents the total number of paths to point L from that grid point.

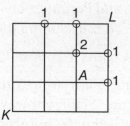

Continue with this labeling scheme, making sure to omit point A, which cannot be crossed. The final diagram, on the right below, shows that there are 11 paths starting at point K.

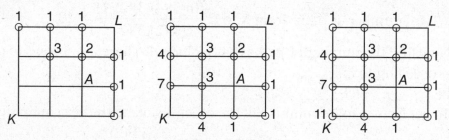

 In a path-counting problem, starting at the endpoint and working backward often leads to a fast and accurate solution.

35. The answer is 180.

Weight w varies directly as distance d from center of the Moon.

$$\therefore \frac{w_1}{d_1} = \frac{w_2}{d_2}.$$

$$\Rightarrow \frac{60}{1080} = \frac{50}{d_2} \Rightarrow d_2 = \frac{(50)(1,080)}{60} = 900 \text{ miles.}$$

$\therefore$ Distance beneath surface = 1,080 – 900 = 180 miles. (You didn't forget the last step, did you?)

Grid-in 180.

36. The answer is 13.2 or 13.1.

After 1 stroke, $\frac{2}{3}$ of the air is left.

After 2 strokes, $\left(\frac{2}{3}\right)^2$ of the air is left. Notice the pattern.

After 5 strokes, $\left(\frac{2}{3}\right)^5$ of the air is left.

$$\left(\frac{2}{3}\right)^5 = \frac{32}{243}.$$

As a percent, $\frac{32}{243} \cdot 100 \approx 13.1687\%$.

Grid-in 13.2 or 13.1.

37. The answer is 2080.

The 26th row has 30 + 25(4) = 130 seats.

The diagram shows a good way to find the total number of seats.

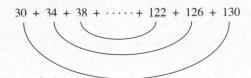

$$\text{Total number of seats} = \frac{26}{2}(30+130)$$
$$= 2,080.$$

Grid-in 2080.

38. The answer is 10.

25 sets sold at $100 $\Rightarrow 100 = \dfrac{3{,}000}{a+25}$

$$\Rightarrow \frac{30}{a+25} = 1$$
$$\Rightarrow a = 5$$

Since a is constant, the formula for $p(n)$ can be written as $p(n) = \dfrac{3{,}000}{5+n}$.

You can now reduce the problem to: Find n when $p(n) = 200$.

$$200 = \frac{3{,}000}{5+n} \Rightarrow \frac{15}{5+n} = 1 \text{ (Divide both sides by 200.)}$$
$$\Rightarrow n = 10$$

Grid-in 10.

Appendix

UPPER-LEVEL VOCABULARY BUILDING

2400 CLUB VOCABULARY IMMERSION

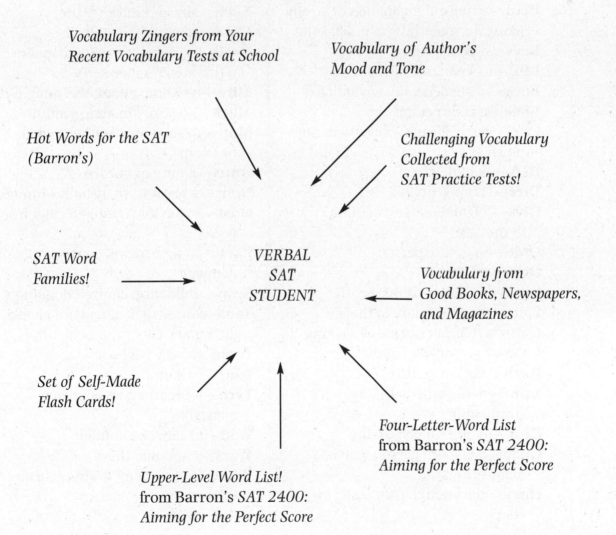

Vocabulary Zingers from Your Recent Vocabulary Tests at School

Vocabulary of Author's Mood and Tone

Hot Words for the SAT (Barron's)

Challenging Vocabulary Collected from SAT Practice Tests!

SAT Word Families!

VERBAL SAT STUDENT

Vocabulary from Good Books, Newspapers, and Magazines

Set of Self-Made Flash Cards!

Four-Letter-Word List from Barron's SAT 2400: Aiming for the Perfect Score

Upper-Level Word List! from Barron's SAT 2400: Aiming for the Perfect Score

FOUR-LETTER-WORD LIST FOR CLUB MEMBERS

These are not the four-letter words you may be thinking of—tsk, tsk.

This list could be the very first one of its kind. How exciting! Not all four-letter words are created equal, certainly, not all of them are "bad." In fact, if you're after an added edge, the little words that follow are worth knowing.

Some of these words can be considered part of "core and classic" SAT vocabulary. Others are a bit off the bell curve. Regardless, to a 2400 Club Member, all good words are worth knowing. Enjoy!

Acme—high point; zenith

Ajar—slightly open

Apex—high point; pinnacle; zenith

Avid—passionate; ardent

Bane—a cause for ruin

Bard—a poet

Bent—a natural inclination or strong liking for something; a predilection

Bevy—a large group

Bilk—to steal; to embezzle

Boon—a sudden gain; a windfall

Boor—a rude person

Curt—terse; abrupt; brief, bordering on rudeness

Deft—skillful; adept

Dire—serious, urgent

Diva—a female singer; a prima donna

Dolt—an obtuse person

Dupe—to trick

Fawn—to flatter subserviently

Foil—to baffle a plan; to thwart

Gait—a manner or rate of walking

Gale—a strong wind; gust

Garb—clothing; attire

Glib—easeful with speaking, storytelling

Glut—to oversupply; to stuff

Guru—a learned person who has followers

Hack—hackneyed, trite, stale; to chop

Hail—to praise

Hale—healthy

Heed—to listen to advice; to consider

Hone—to sharpen

Icon—a religious image or symbol

Iota—a very small amount

Keen—sharp-minded; acute

Laud—to praise; to adulate

Loom—to come into view, usually in a threatening manner

Mire—a swamp pit; mud; a quagmire

Mock—to poke fun at; to scoff at

Molt—to shed hair, feathers, shell, or horns

Onus—a duty or burden

Opus—a great work, usually of music

Oust—to forcibly remove a ruler from power

Pact—an agreement, contract; a compact

Sway—influence, control, dominion

Tact—finesse in dealing with people; diplomacy

Tome—a very big book

Tout—to flaunt

Tyro—a beginner; a neophyte; a fledgling

Void—to cancel; to nullify

Wary—cautious; chary

Whet—to sharpen; to stimulate an interest in

Wily—crafty, sly

UPPER-LEVEL WORD LISTS FOR CLUB MEMBERS

2400 Club members strive to learn more than the core words. You can find "core SAT words" in *Barron's Hot Words for the SAT* and in *Barron's How to Prepare for the SAT.* If you want the best shot at a 2400, it's foolish not to make every effort to learn these core, high-frequency words. You have a strong work ethic, and you're motivated to go beyond basic test prep, so the lists of hard words that follow have your name on them. You're up for the challenge!

Don't let hard words be stumbling blocks for you as you slog through the tough terrain of the hardest questions. Learn these upper-level words, and you'll move through the sentence-completion and critical reading questions with ease and celerity. Review these words and their definitions often to reinforce and solidify their meanings. The words were taken from *real* tests that the College Board has given over the past several years and from practice tests available through the College Board website. Words with an asterisk appeared in hard questions on the May 2011 SAT. Here's an idea—try using a few of these words in your essay!

2400 Club members do not shy away from big-league vocabulary words. Instead, they tackle them, determined to make these hard words part of their working lexicon. Don't be among the students who self-sabotage by crossing off answer choices just because they contain unfamiliar words. This is a self-defeating approach called "fear of the unknown." Be intrepid; learn these hard words!

One more maxim: A word list a day keeps average scores away!

Word List 1

A–B

Aesthete—one who appreciates and seeks beauty, art, or pleasure.

Alacrity—cheerful readiness

Anomalous—rare, unusual, abnormal

Aphorism—a wise saying; an adage; a maxim

Appropriate (v.)—to take another's property as one's own

Arable—able to be cultivated; farmable

Arboreal—relating to trees

Aspersion—misleading or false rumor; gossip

Asylum—a safe place to practice one's religion or follow one's convictions

Auspicious—foretelling well for the future

*Austerity—strict economy; relating to asceticism

Avant-garde—cutting-edge; new; experimental

Behemoth—a huge animal; something of great size or power

Bequest—a gift upon one's death

Breadth—a range or scope

Brook (v.)—to endure; to put up with

Bungle—to botch; to mess up

Byzantine—ornate, fancy

Word List 2

C–D

Calumny—slander, defamation

Celerity—cheerful speed

Cerebral—intellectual

Chagrin—embarrassment

Circumscribed—defined or limited; isolated

Cloying—oversweet; saccharine

Confound—to confuse; to perplex; to befuddle

Conjecture—a guess

Constituents—voters

Consummate—complete; perfect

Convoluted—complicated, complex

Crude—rude; lacking refinement

Curtail—to cut short; abridge

Debased—morally low; base

Decorous—having propriety

Denuded—made ineffective or infertile

Desultory—aimless; lacking a plan or purpose

Diaphanous—sheer, gauzy, see-through; transparent

Didactic—relating to instruction, lecturing

Dilatory—lacking goals or purpose; aimless

Din—noise

Dirge—a funeral song

Discomfited—embarrassed; disconcerted

Discretionary—based on personal choice; showing prudence

Disingenuous—dishonest; crafty

Disposed—behaviorally inclined

Divine—heavenly; godly

Word List 3

E–F

Edifice—a building

Effigy—a crude likeness of a loathed person

Egregious—blatantly wrong

Elusive—hard to grasp; escaping; evasive

Emollient—a soothing lotion

Empirical—based on data, evidence, and/or experiments

Enervate—to drain of energy; to weaken

Enfranchise—to free from slavery; to bestow the right to vote

Epitaph—words inscribed on a tomb

Espouse—to support

Expurgate—to delete obscene or other undesirable material from a text

Extant—existing

Fabrication—a lie

Facile—easy

Felicitous—suitable; pleasant

Feral—savage; wild

Flotilla—fleet of ships

Flotsam—wreckage, debris floating around

Word List 4

G–H

Galvanize—to incite; to arouse to action

Gaunt—thin; haggard

Gingerly—carefully

Grovel—to beg or plead; to crawl; to behave subordinately

Hapless—ill fated; unfortunate; unlucky

Harbinger—a messenger; an omen

Hermetic—sealed in an airtight manner

Histrionic—over theatrical; melodramatic

Hubris—excessive pride

Word List 5

I–J

Inanimate—not living

Incantation—a calling out for inspiration or guidance; an invocation

Inchoate—not fully formed

Incisive—harsh; cutting; vitriolic

Incumbent—one who holds political office

Indelible—unable to be erased; permanent

Ineffable—incapable of expression in words

Inexorable—steadfast; resolute

Inflammatory—likely to excite rage or disorder

Insular—isolated; remote

Intemperate—excessive; immoderate

Interlocutor—one who participates in conversation or dialogue

*Intractable—hard to manage or control

Jaded—bored from too much pleasure or overindulgence

Jingoism—aggressive touting of one's patriotism

Juggernaut—relentless force

Juxtapose—to place things side by side for the sake of comparing

Word List 6

K–L

Kinetic—relating to motion and energy

Legion—a very large number

Leviathon—a subaquatic, mythological sea creature; something huge

Licentious—morally lax

Word List 7

M–N

*Mawkishness**—overly sweet sentimentality

Melee—a hand-to-hand fight involving several participants

*Mendacity**—deceit, dishonesty, fabrication

Milieu—environment

Multifarious—numerous, varied, mixed, diverse, assorted

*Munificence**—generosity with money, time, compliments; kindness, forgiveness

Myopic—short-sighted

Naivete—lack of experience or sophistication

Nihilism—a philosophical belief involving the rejection of established values and morality

Nondescript—featureless; hard to describe

Nonplussed—confused to the point of being unable to act or speak

Word List 8

O–P

Obfuscate—to obscure the meaning of

Obliged—forced; made to do something because of conscience or obligation

Oblique—indirect; slanted

*Obstreperous**—unruly, clamorous, boisterous; bad-tempered, argumentative

Olfactory—relating to the sense of smell

Onerous—burdensome

Opprobrium—scorn, contempt

Ostensible—apparent

Panacea—a cure-all

Partisan—biased; opinionated

Pathos—empathy; sympathetic pity

Pedagogic—relating to education; instructive

Pedantic—narrowly or pretentiously learned

Perfidious—disloyal; traitorous

Petulant—irritable

Plaudits—applause; praise

Pontificate—to speak in a supercilious and self-important manner

Pragmatist—a practical person

Precept—a rule of behavior or action

Precipitate—to hurry up; to make happen before planned

Prescience—advance knowledge; foresight; anticipation

Probity—honesty; integrity

*Profligate**—extravagant to a fault; prodigal

Proliferate—to reproduce or multiply quickly

Promulgate—to make known, formally, a law or set of beliefs

Prose—language ordinarily used in speaking or writing; writing that is *not* poetry

Prototype—a model; an archetype; a first specimen

Prowess—valor, skill

Pundits—erudite (learned, scholarly) persons

Word List 9

Q–R

Qualm—doubt; hesitation; uneasiness

Quibble—to find fault with

Quixotic—romantic or dreamy

Raiment—clothing, apparel, attire

*Rectitude**—the quality of being right, moral, good

Refractory—stubborn

Relegate—to demote to an inferior position

Reprehensible—worthy of blame

Rescind—to take back; to withdraw

Retrograde—going backward and therefore not progressing

*Reverent**—respectful; showing deference

Word List 10

S–T

Sanctimonious—pretending to be religious

Sanction (v.)—to approve

Scrupulous—very conscientious

*Serendipity—occurring by chance, good fortune

Sophistry—deceptive thinking; invalid arguments

Spate—an outpouring

Specious—false, not authentic; spurious

Steadfastness—loyalty, resolve

Stupefy—to stun

Subterfuge—deception

Supplant—to replace; to substitute for

Surfeit (n.)—a surplus, an oversupply

Sybarite—a pleasure-loving person

Synergistic—working together and having a greater combined effect because of simultaneous operation

Table (v.)—to set aside an issue to be discussed at a later time

Tawdry—cheap-looking; gaudy

Temerity—reckless boldness

Temper (v.)—to lessen the severity of

Threadbare—very worn; shabby

Treachery—disloyalty, perfidy

Treacly or **Treacle**—overly sentimental

Truculent—belligerent

Turgid—swollen; pompous

Word List 11

U–V

Unctuous—inky, oily

Unheralded—unannounced

Unintelligible—unable to decipher, figure out, decode; garbled

Untenable—unable to be defended

Upstart—a rebel, an insurgent; a maverick

Utopian—relating to a perfect society; idealistic

Vaunt—to brag or boast

Venial—forgivable; pardonable

Verdant—green, lush

Verisimilitude—probability; something that has the appearance of truth

Vestigial—extremely small

Victuals—food

Vignette—a brief written description

Virile—manly, strong

Visceral—relating to the abdomen; instinctive rather than reasoned

Vitiate—to impair; to render ineffective

Vitriolic—harsh, biting, caustic

Vocation—a profession to which one feels called to carry out, especially a religious calling

Word List 12

W–Z

Watershed—a defining moment; a turning point

Waylay—to ambush

Wheedle—to cajole or coax

Wily—sly

Windfall—an unexpected gain or boon

Winsome—attractive

Witticism—a clever remark

Xenophobic—fearful of foreigners

Zephyr—a light breeze

EXERCISE: CHOOSE THE CORRECT SYNONYM

As you know, words can be defined in multifarious ways. *Opaque* for example, can mean dark, difficult, or even obscure. *Magnanimous* can mean generous, upright, or even noble. The challenge of this exercise is twofold: First, determine the definition that the group of synonyms shares. Then, select the word that best fits the given sentence completion and, therefore, has a distinct meaning from the others.

Directions: Each question in this exercise has two parts. For Part **A**, select the answer choice that best expresses the shared meaning among the group of synonyms—or fairly close synonyms—that are listed. For Part **B**, using the sentence (or sentences) provided as a guide, select the word from the list that best fits this particular context and, therefore, has an "exclusive" meaning that the other words do not share.

Practice Set A

1. circuitous, meandering, serpentine, sinuous

   PART A
   (A) joking, jesting
   (B) senseless, inane
   (C) electrical, dynamic
   (D) twisting, bending
   (E) strange, exotic

   PART B
   Which word (or word form) fits the exclusive meaning, as expressed in the sentence below?

   "Deceptive Dean speaks in a _____ manner."

2. conviction, credo, doctrine, dogma, tenet

   PART A
   (A) beliefs
   (B) guesses
   (C) predictions
   (D) rumors
   (E) fallacies

   PART B
   Which word (or word form) fits the exclusive meaning, as expressed in the sentences below?

   "After a lengthy trial, _____ was his fate."

   "The man on trial was eventually _____."

3. calculated, deliberate, intended, intentional, premeditated

PART A
(A) strong
(B) disgusted
(C) planned
(D) wily
(E) criminal

PART B
Which word (or word form) fits the exclusive meaning, as expressed in the sentence below?

"At first, the trial verdict seemed crystal clear, but then the jurors decided to _____ over the verdict a bit more."

"I must further _____ these weighty issues before I make my final decision."

4. acute, astute, keen, penetrating, perspicacious, sagacious, shrewd

PART A
(A) widely traveled
(B) scathingly critical
(C) infinitesimal
(D) mentally sharp; wise
(E) harsh in tone

PART B
Which word (or word form) fits the exclusive meaning, as expressed in the sentences below?

"To the fisherman's distress, the claws of the King Crab are _____ the dense, bulging fishing net."

"The steel arrow could easily _____ a wooden board."

Practice Set B

5. capricious, fickle, impulsive, volatile, whimsical

PART A
(A) relating to chemistry
(B) artistic
(C) lighthearted
(D) changeable
(E) stationary

PART B
Which word (or word form) fits the exclusive meaning, as expressed in the sentences below?

"An avid doodler, Justina loves to sketch _____ creatures like winged rabbits, ponies bedecked in jewels, and flying puppies!"

"Centaurs and unicorns are _____ creatures."

6. embroider, equivocate, fabricate, prevaricate

PART A
(A) fib, stretch the truth
(B) deal underhandedly
(C) create by hand
(D) express a strong bias
(E) rehearse

PART B
Which word (or word form) fits the exclusive meaning, as expressed in the sentences below?

"Talented with handicrafts, Nicole can _____ colorful and intricate butterflies and flowers onto any type of fabric, including linen and cotton."

"I will _____ this shirt from fine Chinese silk."

7. augur, divine, foresight, foretell, portend, predilection, premonition, prophesize

PART A
(A) associated with mythology
(B) belonging to members of the clergy
(C) pertaining to an early knowledge or prior knowing
(D) relating to Greek gods
(E) of or relating to personal virtue

PART B
Which word (or word form) fits the exclusive meaning, as expressed in the sentence below?

"Immortality and omniscience are traits of entities that are considered to be _____."

8. frugal, miserly, parsimonious, penurious, thrifty

PART A
(A) jaunty
(B) biased
(C) uninspired
(D) dishonest
(E) cheap

PART B
Which word (or word form) fits the exclusive meaning, as expressed in the sentence below?

"The _____ family lived in the impoverished side of town."

Practice Set C

9. dark, depraved, iniquitous, nefarious, sinister, wicked

PART A
(A) opaque
(B) abandoned
(C) evil
(D) ghost-like
(E) willful

PART B
Which word (or word form) fits the exclusive meaning, as expressed in the sentences below?

"Without streetlights, the long road was _____ and foreboding."

"It is quite _____ outside tonight."

10. embryonic, emerging, germinating, inchoate, incipient, nascent

PART A
(A) developing, at the early stages of
(B) inbred, developmentally impaired
(C) fertile, arable
(D) mentally prepared
(E) childlike, impulsive

PART B
Which word (or word form) fits the exclusive meaning, as expressed in the sentence below?

"The preschoolers are _____ small spider plants from the offshoots of their teacher's large and mature spider plant that she proudly displays on the classroom windowsill."

11. glacial, lethargic, phlegmatic, slothful, sluggish

PART A
(A) reserved
(B) animal-like
(C) jesting
(D) inquisitive
(E) slow-moving

PART B
Which word (or word form) fits the exclusive meaning, as expressed in the sentence below?

"Without an iota of warmth in her rock-hard expression, Clara gave us a _____ stare."

12. concrete, haptic, palpable, tactile, tangible

PART A
(A) subtly sensual
(B) jocular in spirit
(C) introverted
(D) able to be touched
(E) emotionally regressive

PART B
Which word (or word form) fits the exclusive meaning, as expressed in the sentences below?

"John calling Ted a 'jerk' was a _____ insult."

"Shaking like a leaf, Larry felt a _____ fear upon entering the Hall of Horrors!"

Practice Set D

13. affectionate, amorous, demonstrative, effusive, tender

PART A
(A) showing off
(B) overly sensitive in an insincere manner
(C) showing warmth of emotion
(D) heavy-hearted
(E) ridiculing

PART B
Which word (or word form) fits the exclusive meaning, as expressed in the sentence below?

"The gladiator's wound was very _____ after he was stabbed in the arm."

14. insurgence, mutiny, revolt, revolution, sedition, uprising

PART A
(A) allegiance
(B) rebellion
(C) war
(D) facade
(E) impasse

PART B
Which word (or word form) fits the exclusive meaning, as expressed in the sentence below?

"The _____ of the Earth along its orbit around the sun takes 365 days."

15. economical, financial, fiscal, monetary

PART A
(A) relating to charitable contributions
(B) pertaining to government
(C) pertaining to severe debt
(D) relating to the accumulation of property assets
(E) pertaining to money

PART B
Which word (or word form) fits the exclusive meaning, as expressed in the sentence below?

"Carmen is so _____ that she only shops at dollar stores."

16. annihilate, devastate, eradicate, raze, ruin

PART A
(A) burden
(B) destroy
(C) detach
(D) bungle
(E) decrease

PART B
Which word (or word form) fits the exclusive meaning, as expressed in the sentence below?

"The _____ of Ancient Rome are quite stunning."

Answer Key

Practice Set A

1. A. (D)
   B. *circuitous*; contextual meaning is deceptive

2. A. (A)
   B. *conviction*; contextual meaning is a guilty verdict, jail sentence; second sentence: *convicted*

3. A. (C)
   B. *deliberate*; contextual meaning is to contemplate, think over; second sentence: also *deliberate*

4. A. (D)
   B. *penetrating*; contextual meaning is piercing, breaking through in a literal sense; second sentence: *penetrate*

Practice Set B

5. A. (D)
   B. *whimsical*; contextual meaning is imaginative, fanciful; second sentence: also *whimsical*

6. A. (A)
   B. *embroider*; contextual meaning is to stitch, decoratively, on fabric; do needlework; second sentence: also *embroider*

7. A. (C)
   B. *divine*; contextual meaning is relating to gods or omnipotent powers

8. A. (E)
   B. *penurious*; contextual meaning is poor, penniless

Practice Set C

9. A. (C)
   B. *dark*; contextual meaning is, literally, without light; second sentence: also *dark*

10. A. (A)
   B. *germinating*; contextual meaning is growing

11. A. (E)
   B. *glacial*; contextual meaning is cold, lacking a warm spirit

12. A. (D)
   B. *palpable*; contextual meaning is blatant, overt, flagrant; second sentence: also *palpable*

Practice Set D

13. A. (C)
   B. *tender*; contextual meaning is tender to the touch, sore

14. A. (B)
   B. *revolution*; contextual meaning is one complete circling around

15. A. (E)
   B. *economical*; contextual meaning is careful with money, thrifty

16. A. (B)
   B. *ruins*; contextual meaning is wreckages, old buildings

USEFUL MATH FORMULAS

You can get a perfect score on the Math SAT without memorizing many formulas. Nevertheless, here are some formulas that may be helpful.

1. Area of a trapezoid with bases b_1 and b_2, and height h:

$$A = \frac{1}{2}h(b_1 + b_2)$$

2. Area of a rhombus with diagonals d_1 and d_2:

$$A = \frac{1}{2}(d_1 d_2)$$

3. Area of an equilateral triangle with side s:

$$A = \frac{s^2\sqrt{3}}{4}$$

4. Sum of angles in a polygon with n sides:

$$S = (n-2)180°$$

5. Sum of exterior angles in a polygon with n sides:

$$S = 360°$$

6. Area of a sector with radius r and central angle $m°$:

$$A = \frac{m}{360} \cdot \pi r^2$$

7. Arc length of a sector with radius r and central angle $m°$:

$$A = \frac{m}{360} \cdot 2\pi r$$

8. The nth term, a_n, of an arithmetic sequence with first term a and common difference d:

$$a_n = a + (n-1)d$$

9. The nth term, a_n, of a geometric sequence with first term a and common ratio r:

$$a_n = ar^{n-1}$$

10. The sum of n terms, S_n, of an arithmetic series with first term a and nth term a_n:

$$S_n = \frac{n}{2}(a + a_n)$$

11. The sum of n terms of an arithmetic series with first term a and common difference d:

$$S_n = \frac{n}{2}\left[2a + (n-1)d\right]$$

12. The sum of n terms of a geometric series with first term a and common ratio r:

$$S_n = a \cdot \frac{1-r^n}{1-r}$$

13. The sum of the first n positive integers:

$$S_n = \frac{n(n+1)}{2}$$

14. The number of permutations of n objects taken r at a time:

$$_nP_r = \frac{n!}{(n-r)!}$$

15. The number of combinations of n objects taken r at a time:

$$_nC_r = \frac{n!}{(n-r)!r!}$$

16. The surface area of a cube with edge e:

$$S = 6e^2$$

17. The surface area of a rectangular prism (box) with edges ℓ, w, and h:

$$S = 2(\ell w + \ell h + wh)$$

18. The surface area of a cylinder with base radius r and height h:

$$S = 2\pi r^2 + 2\pi rh$$

19. The volume of a cone with base radius r and height h:

$$V = \frac{1}{3}\pi r^2 h$$

20. The volume of a pyramid with base area B and height h:

$$V = \frac{1}{3}Bh$$

21. The surface area of a sphere with radius r:

$$S = 4\pi r^2$$

22. The volume of a sphere with radius r:

$$S = \frac{4}{3}\pi r^3$$

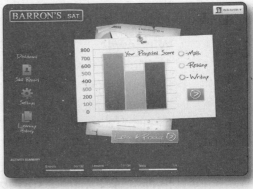

How to Use the CD-ROM

The software is not installed on your computer; it runs directly from the CD-ROM. Barron's CD-ROM includes an "autorun" feature that automatically launches the application when the CD is inserted into the CD-ROM drive. In the unlikely event that the autorun feature is disabled, follow the manual launching instructions below.

Windows®

1. Click on the Start button and choose "My Computer" or "Computer."
2. Double-click on the CD-ROM drive, which will be named **SAT_2400.exe**.
3. Double-click **SAT_2400.exe** to launch the program.

MAC®

1. Double-click the CD-ROM icon.
2. Double-click the **SAT_2400** icon to start the program.

SYSTEM REQUIREMENTS

(Flash Player 10.2 is recommended)

Microsoft® Windows®	MAC® OS X	Linux® and Solaris™
Processor: Intel Pentium 4 2.33GHz, Athlon 64 2800+ or faster processor (or equivalent).	Processor: Intel Core™ Duo 1.33GHz or faster processor.	Processor: Intel Pentium 4 2.33GHz, AMD Athlon 64 2800+ or faster processor (or equivalent).
Memory: 128MB of RAM.	Memory: 256MB of RAM.	Memory: 512MB of RAM.
Graphics Memory: 128MB.	Graphics Memory: 128MB.	Graphics Memory: 128MB.
Platforms:	Platforms:	Platforms:
Windows 7, Windows Vista®, Windows XP, Windows Server® 2008, Windows Server 2003.	Mac OS X 10.6, Mac OS X 10.5, Mac OS X 10.4 (Intel) and higher.	Red Hat® Enterprise Linux (RHEL) 5 or later, openSUSE® 11 or later, Ubuntu 9.10 or later. Solaris: Solaris™ 10.